BOURDIEU AND CHINESE EDUCATION

This book uses Bourdieu's sociological approach for research as a jumping-off point for framing our understandings and analyses of China and Chinese education. Three major themes – inequality, competition, and change – are explored across several theoretical and contextual bases. Bringing together top scholars in the field, the volume examines empirical studies that analyse social (im)mobility through education for students affected by the social divides of class, culture, and rural/urban locations; teacher identity and the field of schooling in the current Chinese environment and going forward; and the university as an institution for the production of knowledge about education in the globalising academy. Offering insights into the historical and cultural context for China's educational landscape, the contributions of this book revisit Bourdieusian concepts from a new empirical vantage point and bring together key studies that illuminate new pathways for the study of Chinese sociology of education.

Guanglun Michael Mu is Senior Research Fellow at Queensland University of Technology, Australia.

Karen Dooley is Associate Professor in the Faculty of Education at Queensland University of Technology, Australia.

Allan Luke is Emeritus Professor at Queensland University of Technology, Australia.

BOURDIEU AND CHINESE EDUCATION

Inequality, Competition, and Change

Edited by Guanglun Michael Mu, Karen Dooley, and Allan Luke

NEW YORK AND LONDON

First published 2019
by Routledge
711 Third Avenue, New York, NY 10017

and by Routledge
2 Park Square, Milton Park, Abingdon, Oxon, OX14 4RN

Routledge is an imprint of the Taylor & Francis Group, an informa business

© 2019 Taylor & Francis

The right of the Guanglun Michael Mu, Karen Dooley, and Allan Luke to be identified as the authors of the editorial material, and of the authors for their individual chapters, has been asserted in accordance with Sections 77 and 78 of the Copyright, Designs and Patents Act 1988.

All rights reserved. No part of this book may be reprinted or reproduced or utilised in any form or by any electronic, mechanical, or other means, now known or hereafter invented, including photocopying and recording, or in any information storage or retrieval system, without permission in writing from the publishers.

Trademark notice: Product or corporate names may be trademarks or registered trademarks, and are used only for identification and explanation without intent to infringe.

Library of Congress Cataloging-in-Publication Data
Names: Mu, Guanglun Michael, editor. | Dooley, Karen, editor. |
Luke, Allan, editor.
Title: Bourdieu and Chinese education : inequality, competition, and change / edited by Guanglun Michael Mu, Karen Dooley, and
Allan Luke.
Description: New York : Routledge, 2019. | Includes bibliographical references and index.
Identifiers: LCCN 2018031154 (print) | LCCN 2018045660 (ebook) |
ISBN 9781315104331 (ebook) | ISBN 9781351597784 (ebook) |
ISBN 9781351597791 (ebook) | ISBN 9781351597777 (ebook) |
ISBN 9781138098626 (hbk) | ISBN 9781138098671 (pbk) |
ISBN 9781315104331 (ebk)
Subjects: LCSH: Educational sociology--China. | Educational equalization--China. | Educational change--China. | Bourdieu,
Pierre, 1930-2002.
Classification: LCC LC191.8.C5 (ebook) | LCC LC191.8.C5 B68
2019 (print) | DDC 306.430951--dc23
LC record available at https://lccn.loc.gov/2018031154

ISBN: 978-1-138-09862-6 (hbk)
ISBN: 978-1-138-09867-1 (pbk)
ISBN: 978-1-315-10433-1 (ebk)

Typeset in Bembo
by Swales & Willis Ltd, Exeter, Devon, UK

CONTENTS

List of Figures	vii
List of Tables	viii
Preface	ix
Glossary of Chinese Terms	xiii

1 Introduction: China, Education, and Bourdieu   1
Karen Dooley, Guanglun Michael Mu, and Allan Luke

2 Market Economy, Social Change, and Educational
Inequality: Notes for a Critical Sociology of Chinese
Education   20
*Shibao Guo, Yan Guo, Allan Luke, Karen Dooley, and
Guanglun Michael Mu*

3 Bourdieu's Sociological Thinking and Educational
Research in Mainland China   45
Zhongying Shi and Chunying Li

4 "Make It Back"?: The Social Positioning of the New
Generation of Rural Teachers in China   62
Liang Du

Contents

5 Educational Practice in a Field of Mediation: Elite University Graduates' Participation Experience of an Alternative Program of Schoolteacher Recruitment for Rural China 81
Yue Melody Yin, Karen Dooley, and Guanglun Michael Mu

6 Rural Children's Academic Success, Transformative Habitus, and Social Mobility Cost 97
He Li

7 Resistance as a Sociological Process of Resilience: Stories of Under-resourced Migrant Families 120
Guanglun Michael Mu

8 Academic Competition and Parental Practice: A Study of Habitus and Change 144
Xu Zhao, Robert L. Selman, and Allan Luke

9 Capital Conversion and School Change: A Bourdieusian Analysis 175
Ning Jia and Guanglun Michael Mu

10 Using English at an International Doctoral Workshop: A Three-level Field Analysis 192
Guanglun Michael Mu, Liwei Livia Liu, Wangqian Fu, Dongfang Hao, Ning Jia, Yimei Qin, Hongmei Sziegat, Xiaodong Wang, and Xueqin Wu

11 Learning to Theorise from Bourdieu: Using *Zhōng wén* (中文) in English for Research Publication Purposes 214
Michael Singh

12 Re: Appropriating Bourdieu for a Sociology of Chinese Education 239
Guanglun Michael Mu, Allan Luke, and Karen Dooley

Notes on Contributors 264
Index 268

FIGURES

3.1	Quantity of Bourdieusian Chinese educational studies by year (1979–2017)	48
3.2	Network of Bourdieu's key concepts and Chinese educational studies (1979–2017)	50
5.1	Measurement model of self-benefiting reasons	87
5.2	Measurement model of altruistic reasons	88
5.3	Measurement model of role play based on EGRT values	89

TABLES

4.1	Participants of interviews and focus group discussions	68
5.1	Descriptive statistics and paired samples-T Test	89
5.2	Regression analysis results of predictors of EGRT value-based roleplays	90

PREFACE

This book is based on an ongoing dialogue that began in Beijing in 2015. We had embarked on a series of lectures and seminars with Chinese colleagues on Bourdieu's sociology, on the education of cultural and linguistic minorities, and on the education and experience of overseas Chinese communities at Beijing Normal University, Minzu University, Shaanxi Normal University, and North-east China Normal University. We were fascinated by the potential uses and applications of Bourdieu's sociology in Chinese education. Our discussions across China with Shibao Guo, Yan Guo, Du Liang, Yongbing Liu, and Benjamin Chang were part of an ongoing dialogue about the formation of the new China, the unprecedented emergence of new social fields, relations of exchange and, indeed, new Chinese dispositions and sensibilities.

We met in Beijing with several of the contributors to conceptualise this volume, to attempt to set its boundaries, fields, and topics. What emerged from those discussions was a shared view that, however well-outlined Bourdieu's sociology was in an English-language secondary literature, however clear in structure, parameters, and applications to fields like education, cultural studies, ethnology and, of course, sociology in the West – its applications to Chinese education were far from straightforward. While its focus on issues of class and reproduction were salient in relation to emergent issues of social, economic, and educational inequality in China – for us and for the Chinese scholars in the room, it was never a matter of the systematic application, transplantation, or deployment of a "universal" sociological model to a different social context, cultural history, and state formation. Given our own histories and the geo-location of these writings and the peoples about which they speak, taking the Bourdieu corpus as *doxa* was never an option. Taken together, the phenomenal and lived realities of the "new China" are an imperative to begin from a

x Preface

position that views Anglo/American and European social sciences as at best contingent and provisional, offering hypotheses and models to be applied and tested. Further, we were aware of the risk of yet another superimposition of a normative theoretical architecture created in a particular historical epoch, in particular cultural and political economic configurations (post-war France and, later, the neoliberal West) upon a very different time, place, and set of human and social phenomena – and, indeed, a place, culture, and nation state with a recent, and publicly recalled, history of colonisation and unique ongoing emergence on the world stage.

The result of those discussions is necessarily tentative, intercultural, multi-lingual, and inter-scholastic. This book is not a "correct" version of the canonical French-language or English-language versions of Bourdieu, tested for felicity to *his* original writings, statements, and claims. There are many such works in the sociological literature. Rather, the work here is partial, hypothetical and, by sheer historical necessity at this moment, speculative. It is an open text that sees and uses Bourdieu's works, his observations and analyses of his lifeworlds and historical milieux as an optics and a jumping-off point for framing our understandings and analyses of China and Chinese education. In this way, we wanted to continue to work towards a reflexive sociology: one that not only reflects upon the political, economic, and sociological conditions for its own construction as theory, but that is reflexive in a broader sense: as a set of hypothetical models, explanations, concepts, and namings that might apply, however partially and tentatively to the emergence of new social fields, new "markets", new forms of capital and systems of exchange, and, indeed, new human habituses.

The metaphor that has been constant from our first discussion, and that recurs through these chapters is that of *guān xì* (关系). While the traditional, and at times pejorative, definition refers broadly to social connection, exchange, and networking – *guān xì* is considered a form of social capital unique to pan-Chinese cultures, a defining element that deliberately bridges families, contexts, ideas, and linguistic and cultural resources. For each of the three editors, it defines not only the intercultural and scholarly exchange of putting this book together, but it also marks a common thread across our diverse standpoints and interests:

AL: I grew up in the Los Angeles Chinese-American community in the 1950s. My grandparents on both sides migrated to Hawaii and Seattle in the first decade of the twentieth century, part of the mass migration from the Pearl River delta following flood and famine. We were taught that we were part of something larger – an imaginary China, being Chinese, and all that that might have and could have and should have meant. Something that we were unable to see and touch, but that became mythic, grandiose, and mysterious, sometimes downright troubling and irritating – even as our parents and elders argued over Chinese and American politics, and did their very best to make their way through American culture and economy. It was part of pride, heritage, and all of that, later resisted, lost, and reclaimed by my generation and those that will follow. But it was also, my parents always reminded me, about surviving and contending with a world that could turn on you for your Chineseness at any time, whether you were wearing it or not, and without apparent rhyme or reason. As if they understood the habitus, which we all intuitively do, they would remind me that this Chineseness, and the extended family that came with it, would never go away, could not be washed away, overwritten, or ignored no matter what. Whatever the challenges *and* advantages of "being Chinese" in the US, Canada, and Australia – what surprised me half a century later was the degree to which there seemed to be some kind of solidarity, at once both imagined and real, but certainly durable and, as I now have begun to understand the term, embodied, between me and my Chinese friends and teachers, students and colleagues – whether in Beijing, Vancouver, Hong Kong, Singapore, or Brisbane. For me, this work with these colleagues and writers, coming at the end of my academic journey, is not about symbolic closure, but part of an intergenerational and intercultural act of *guān xì* – of exchange, connection, of gifting and riposte – that remains in progress.

KD: "I want to know how foreigners do things," she said, "Practise English."

"I want to know about China. School here. Learn Chinese."

"Here" was Shanghai, 1991. The middle-school student and the foreign English teacher felt their way into that first conversation, held out the first gift, read the first of countless notes written out carefully in the other's native script.

"If you make a friend," the English teacher's Canadian Chinese lecturer had advised during the pre-departure briefing in Brisbane, "It's for a long time."

Fifteen years later in Chinatown, Sydney. "What were you expecting me to be?" the ex-English teacher asked.

"Different," her former student said, "What did you learn?"

After nearly thirty years of gifts and greetings, friendship and favours, in a now wide circle of students, teachers, and colleagues in and of China, this foreign teacher-turned-sociologist grapples with *doxa* and *episteme*: 关系, *guān xì*, connections, social capital? There was something at work in the production of this volume other than the oftentimes fleeting coalitions of the self-interested agents of neoliberalism. 关系, so, this is what it feels like? And the gift of provocation to learn to see what I wasn't expecting?

MM: I was born into a middle-class family with a strong communist background. My maternal grandfather Li Hai (李海) was sent by the Party to the Soviet Union to study communism. He was then appointed by the former Premier Zhou Enlai (周恩来) to a senior position in Ningxia (an ethnic minority region in north-west China). My paternal grandfather Mu Keming (穆克明), also a Party member, worked as a professor at Dalian University of Technology. My grandparents' backgrounds, unfortunately, made the family victim of the Cultural Revolution – my parents were deprived of opportunities

xii Preface

for further education. To fulfil their lost dream, they supported my education by all means. I spent my childhood in different Chinese cities due to the mobile nature of my parents' work. Each time I moved, I had to painfully leave my friendship behind and establish new networks. But these early experiences, later I found, were enabling and rewarding. The very experience of my distance from the local culture and the traces of my non-standard local accent both complicated and enriched my horizon. Up to now, I have studied, worked, and lived in China, Canada, and Australia. Over the years, the subtle, inter-nested social identities and the nuanced, multi-tiered cultural tensions have repeatedly empowered me, constantly sparking my reflection on the social unease and gaffes that I have encountered: the diffidence when I corrected the academic writing of my white, English-speaking students; the obfuscation when I was overwhelmed by the bureaucracies, systems, and policies in powerful institutions exotic to me; the frustration when I failed to decode the cultural subtleties and politics made indiscernible to me. Yet I feel privileged for having encountered these gainful challenges. I feel privileged for having a Chinese heritage that has enculturated me into a disposition of practising *guān xì* to grapple with survivability and sustainability in dominant institutions. I feel privileged for having a strong *guān xì* with my Chinese colleagues, both in China and overseas. "You are truly a cosmopolitan literati," a senior staff at Queensland University of Technology once commented. "It's about networking," I responded. This very *guān xì* gave me a unique opportunity to work with the co-editors and the contributors of this volume to learn, understand, and analyse educational practices currently occurring in China.

★★★★★★

We wish to thank our colleagues in China, Canada, and Australia. Our initial meetings were supported by the Faculty of Education, Beijing Normal University and the Werklund School of Education, University of Calgary. The editorial compilation and additional research were supported by Queensland University of Technology and the Australian Research Council. We also wish to thank our colleagues Jiayong Li, Dennis Sumara, Yongbing Liu, Baohui Zhang, and Benjamin Chang for their generosity, hospitality, and encouragement. Naomi Silverman, our senior editor at Routledge, understood the reasons for this book, and Karen Adler and Emmalee Ortega have provided patient and expert editorial guidance. Yue Yin has assisted in editing the manuscript and preparing the glossary of Chinese terms.

GLOSSARY OF CHINESE TERMS

澳大利亚	*Ào dà lì yà*	Australia
百战不殆	*bǎi zhàn bù dài*	fight a hundred times with no failure
成语	*chéng yǔ*	idiom
代课教师	*dài kè jìao shī*	substitute teacher
叨叨	*dāo dāo*	nagging
读书	*dú shū*	reading/working hard in school
焚书坑儒	*fén shū kēng rú*	burning of the books and burying of the scholars
粉丝	*fěn sī*	fans
高考	*gāo kǎo*	University Entrance Examination
管	*guǎn*	training
管控	*guǎn kòng*	control
管理	*guǎn lǐ*	manage
惯习	*guàn xí*	habitus
关系	*guān xì*	networking
管制	*guǎn zhì*	control
海归	*hǎi guī*	overseas returnees
汉字	*hàn zì*	Chinese character
户口	*hù kǒu*	household registration
竞争机制	*jìng zhēng jī zhì*	competition mechanism
竞争意识	*jìng zhēng yì shí*	competition consciousness
科举制度	*kē jǔ zhì dù*	Imperial Examination System
粮票	*liáng piào*	grain ration coupon
笼中之鸟	*lóng zhōng zhī niǎo*	caged bird

(Continued)

xiv Glossary of Chinese Terms

(Cont.)

满汉一体	mǎn hàn yī tǐ	the integration of the Man and the Han
民族	mín zú	ethnicity
秦	qín	the first dynasty of imperial China (221–206 BC)
秦始皇	qín shǐ huáng	Emperor Qin
清	qīng	the last dynasty of imperial China (1636–1912)
人家的孩子	rén jiā de hái zi	other parents' kids
上进	shàng jìn	motivation to do better
少数民族	shǎo shù mín zú	ethnic minorities
师范	shī fàn	teacher education
师夷长技以制夷	shī yí cháng jì yǐ zhì yí	learn the advanced technologies of the West in order to resist the invasion of the Western powers
素质	sù zhì	quality
唐	táng	an imperial dynasty (618–907) regarded as a high point of Chinese civilisation
特岗计划	tè gǎng jì huà	Special Post Plan
网红	wǎng hóng	Internet celebrities
问心无愧	wèn xīn wú kuì	believe what I am doing is justifiable
戊戌变法	wù xū biàn fǎ	Wuxu Reform Movement
习惯	xí guàn	habit
习性	xí xìng	disposition
西学为体中学为用	xī xué wèi tǐ zhōng xué wèi yòng	Chinese learning as essence and Western learning for practice
严管	yán guǎn	strict monitoring
洋务运动	yáng wù yùn dòng	Self-Strengthening Movement
因材施教	yīn cái shī jiào	Teachers should conduct their teaching in accordance with student characteristics and capabilities
因地制宜	yīn dì zhì yí	appropriate plans or measures
元	yuán	an imperial dynasty established by Mongolians (1271–1368)
赵武灵王	zhào wǔ líng wáng	King Wuling
知己知彼	zhī jǐ zhī bǐ	know the characteristics of one's self as well as those of one's partners or opponents
重点学校	zhòng diǎn xué xiào	key school
中国	zhōng guó	China
中文	zhōng wén	Chinese language

1

INTRODUCTION

China, Education, and Bourdieu

Karen Dooley, Guanglun Michael Mu, and Allan Luke

Grounds for a Re-purposing

The late 1970s was an historically momentous period for China. The Cultural Revolution concluded in 1976; the *gāo kǎo* system (高考University Entrance Examination) resumed in 1977; at the National Science Conference in 1978, science and technology were defined as the primary productive forces of the nation; in the same year, family planning came to the fore of the government agenda and later was developed into the single-child policy; at the 3rd Plenary Session of the 11th Central Committee Conference of the Chinese Communist Party, Deng Xiaoping (邓小平) came to power and initiated the Reform and Opening-Up Policy; on 15 December 1978, the Joint Communique of the United States of America and the People's Republic of China was released in Washington and Beijing, indicating the official establishment of Sino-US diplomatic relations. Since then, China has made epochal advancements in economy, science and technology, and education. With the attendant social changes have come pressing issues of equity, stability, diversity, and cohesion. Given commitments both social and sociological, researchers have investigated the implication of education in new social realities – looking sometimes to the oeuvre of Pierre Bourdieu in doing so (e.g., Mu, 2018). The present volume has been assembled under the assumption that this endeavour requires attention to all the fields of education identified by Bourdieu – and more.

Bourdieu worked as an ethnologist and sociologist in mid-to-late twentieth-century Algeria and France. A philosophy graduate, Bourdieu made his initial foray into social science while serving in the French military during the Algerian war of independence. In the course of subsequent scholarly appointments in Algeria and France, he went on to produce numerous empirical studies. Education

2 Karen Dooley et al.

was integral – sometimes centrally – to those studies. Two decades into the twenty-first century, researchers of education in China are riffling through Bourdieu's oeuvre, taking what is useful for explaining new social realities.

In 2009, an analysis of journal articles published in CNKI[1] found that the use of Bourdieu's work by educational researchers in the thirty years since promulgation of the Reform and Opening-Up Policy seemed to have been second only to that of sociologists. This was attributed to the utility of the work for probing sociological problems associated with pressing social issues, in particular, "theory about education and cultural capital ... [for] the study of school outcomes and educational stratification" (Chen & Zang, 2009, p. 5). It was suggested, furthermore, that Chinese scholars might find the reflexive empirical practice of Bourdieu useful for building up the social sciences. Half a decade later, it was claimed that "Bourdieu's theoretical framework ha[d] been extensively used to explore social class, social classification and education in contemporary China" (Sheng, 2014, p. 31). However, it was noted that questions had been raised about the applicability of Bourdieu's conceptual tools to non-Western societies, including China. In the context of the transition from planned to market economy, it was observed, there was more flux and less stratification in Chinese society than there had been in the France of Bourdieu.

In his empirical studies, Bourdieu attended to what he dubbed in *Reproduction* education *familial, institutionalised* and *diffuse* (Bourdieu & Passeron, 1990). He focused variously on the pedagogic work of family members; those designated as educators within the school, museum, and other societal institutions; and educated participants in the everyday practices of groups such as social classes. The revolution in information and communication technology, further, has expanded the sociological parameters of pedagogic action. On Weibo and Wechat, QQ and Boke, the digitalisation of human existence continues apace. Pedagogic work is occurring amongst "friends" or gamers, 网红 (Internet celebrities) and 粉丝 (fans), online marketers and consumers. Half a century after Bourdieu's education-themed research, it is not only the case that pedagogic action has gone digital; nor is it only that the Internet has enabled education beyond the worlds of the domestic, the societal, and groups local and national. It is, rather, that the changes to education are in some degree qualitative. In its totality, the pedagogic action experienced by any one person may now be less coherent and more bespoke than might once have been the case, a development with ramifications both individual and societal. At the same time, the ontological changes afoot may be more than socio-historical: virtual reality and artificial intelligence challenge understandings of the very being of the human species that acts pedagogically. The remit of the sociology of education must be as broad, then, as the worlds of education in China (as indeed, elsewhere). But this is not enough.

Research on education in China demands new ways of thinking sociologically. The production of this volume has been impelled by the realisation that what is

China, Education, and Bourdieu **3**

going on in China – economically, culturally, and socially – is as significant, and will be as significant in defining and reshaping sociology, as the emergence of industrial capitalism in the mill towns of late seventeenth-century England, liberalism in the Europe of the eighteenth-century Enlightenment, and the Protestantism of the churches of twentieth-century America. Two decades into the twenty-first century, it is clear that a sociology of education is needed that accounts for a strong state which is able to reset, with notable effectiveness and, at times, centralised authority and control, parameters for agency and exchange in social fields – familial, societal, and other fields of education amongst these. The empirical reality here is something other than that of the "interventionism" of the neoliberal state of Western nations such as was investigated by Bourdieu in France. None the less, there are theoretical, conceptual, and methodological resources in the oeuvre of Bourdieu that researchers of education in China are re-purposing.

The aim of this volume is two-fold: To assemble studies of what education has become in China, and to show how educational researchers are taking from the work of Bourdieu to create sociology adequate to such research. An assumption is that the importation of Bourdieu's work into social science in China is not necessarily colonialist or imperialist. Rather, it might be understood as strategic reappropriation of the foreign, a Chinese tradition evident in the re-purposing of Deweyian progressivism, Russian didactics, and western learning theories in Chinese classrooms over a period of a century or so, and of dialectical materialism in Chinese philosophies of education (Luke, 2018).

The sociology produced and exported from China in this volume is of international salience. Given China's economic and political weight, the development of Chinese sociology would seem to be of interest for the discipline of sociology in national fields beyond China, and not only for scholars of China and of education in China. Furthermore, the re-purposing of Bourdieu's oeuvre by researchers of education in China offers insights for those who use that work in national settings other than China. Michel Foucault's analysis of the influence of the historian of science, Georges Canguilhem, in the French intellectual world points to the heart of the matter here.

By Foucault's (1991) analysis, a French translation of the 1929 lectures of the German phenomenologist, Edmund Husserl, marked the beginning of "contemporary" French philosophy (p. 8). Concerned with the philosophy of knowledge, rationality and the concept, the history of science developed by Canguilhem and Gaston Bachelard amongst others, represented one of two French readings of phenomenology; the other was a philosophy of the subject, evident in the work of Jean-Paul Sartre and Maurice Merleau-Ponty in particular, that was concerned with experience and sense. Canguilhem's philosophy of science, asserted Foucault, was a defining influence on many who were unable to cleave to the French intellectual establishment: "take away Canguilhem and ... you will no longer grasp what is specific to sociologists such as Bourdieu, Castel, Passeron and what marks them so strongly within

4   Karen Dooley et al.

sociology" (p. 8). The specific and distinctive characteristics noted by Foucault entailed:

> questionings which must be addressed to a rationality which makes universal claims while developing in contingency, which asserts its unity and yet proceeds only by means of partial modification when not by general recastings; which authenticates itself through its own sovereignty but which in its history is perhaps not dissociated from inertias, weights which coerce it, subjugate it.
>
> *(1991, pp. 11–12)*

Foucault's point was that scholars such as Bourdieu and himself were questioning the supposed universality and unity of the rationality of scientists and others, and the historical autonomy of such from external power. The modality of Foucault's assertions here is notable: the sovereignty of science and reason which had been won during the Enlightenment of the West "is perhaps not dissociated" from coercive and subjugating social inertias and weights. The stance in this volume is more definite.

Foucault (1991) proceeded to enumerate socio-historical conditions of the questioning of which he wrote. Amongst these was "the movement" at "the end of the colonial era" which had seen "people" ask whether the supposed universality of Western culture, science, social organisation, and rationality was a "mirage" generated by "economic domination" and "political hegemony" (p. 12). Nearly three decades on, this volume is part of another round of questioning. Only here, the questions are directed at the social science of Bourdieu, now one of the most internationally established of those who considered themselves to be separated from the establishment of their French intellectual world. While generally sympathetic, the volume is built on the assumption that Bourdieu's theory, conceptual tools, and empirical method might themselves be dissociated from a certain socio-historical inertia. The intent is to release potential for addressing urgent social issues and emergent sociological problems that researchers of education in China have glimpsed in the oeuvre of Bourdieu – and to plumb the limits of such.

We develop our case in three moves. First, we look at the materialist theory of knowledge by which the philosophy graduate turned ethnologist and sociologist sought to explain human existence, initially under the capitalism imposed by the colonising French in Algeria, and then under the neoliberalism which reached ever more widely and deeply into social life in France from the 1960s onwards. We write with an eye to adequacy for a China which has taken distinctive economic directions to transformative ends and with ramifications for cultural and social life. Second, we zoom in on an instance of Bourdieu's work in 1980s Japan, in which he speculated about Chinese education. We show that the French researcher's circulation of a model with claims to universality was socially contingent – conditional, in principle at least, on empirical similarities of societies.

Like many a liberal Westerner of the time and to this day, however, Bourdieu was mistaken in his understanding of educational phenomena in China, and thereby, in his assumptions about the adequacy of his sociology in addressing these. In contrast, the chapters assembled in this volume prod and probe the work of Bourdieu in order to see what can be taken from it so as to shape a discipline more adequate to empirical realities which differ somewhat from those in which sociology of education was grounded.

A Particular Materialism

In the course of extended self-analytic reflection at the end of his career, Bourdieu stated that education had been a "privileged object" of research in which he had been interested in "founding a materialist theory of knowledge" (2007, p. 18). Symbolic power, violence, and domination were at the core of this endeavour. In this section, we make a reading of three articles[2] that Bourdieu wrote on bachelorhood in Lesquire (pseudonym) in Béarn, the area of south-western France where he grew up. The articles provide a useful point of entry into the treatment of the material and the symbolic in Bourdieu's theory and attendant understandings of education.

Historically, the principle of primogeniture had meant that it was the younger sons of the peasantry who had been most likely to become bachelors; reproduction of the economic and social order sometimes required bachelorhood of sons who were not to inherit the means of production. By the time of Bourdieu's initial investigation in 1959 and 1960, however, bachelorhood had become the lot of elder sons; scandalously and perplexingly in an agricultural world, heirs to even large estates were deemed "unmarriageable" (Bourdieu, 2008, p. 3). Bourdieu's interest in this social problem was sparked by his pained observations of the self-conscious awkwardness of peasant men at a Christmas singles ball. For the next quarter of a century or so, Bourdieu was to grapple empirically and theoretically with the social enigma of "the new bachelors" (Bourdieu, 1962/2008, p. 39).

In articles written in 1962 and 1972, Bourdieu addressed traditional matrimonial exchanges (Bourdieu, 1972/2008). In the second of these, he developed his notions of practical logic and strategy. Marriage, Bourdieu noted, was one of the few occasions for monetary exchange in peasant society. Much turned on choices as to whether or not and who to marry: nothing less than the preservation, increase, or dissipation of the material, as well as symbolic capital (resources) of the family was at stake. In making these choices, families capitalised on their relative advantages, for instance, the extent of their land holdings or the birth order of a given child. Choice was strategic rather than intentional, generated by dispositions inculcated through material conditions of existence and familial education. Along with inter-related strategies of fertility and inheritance, strategies of (familial) education and marriage helped reproduce the peasant family and world.

6 Karen Dooley et al.

In the 1962 article and in the article he wrote in 1989, Bourdieu historicised the disruption of the traditional system of matrimonial exchange. In the first of these, he described economic and social changes which had undermined the system (Bourdieu, 1962/2008). Bound by honour to their inheritance even as the traditional world was dissolving, elder sons were especially vulnerable to a symbolic order which opposed all that was of the *hameaux*[3] (in which they lived) to all that was of the *bourg*[4] (from where hailed their relatively urbane rivals). When they took on the oafish image of the *paysanas empaysanit*,[5] these men were effectively excluded from marriage. As Bourdieu put it, the "economic and social condition influences the vocation to marriage mainly through the mediation of the consciousness that men attain of that situation" (1962/2008, p. 86).

To probe the possibility of generalisation, Bourdieu conducted a statistical study of marital status in 16 rural *cantons*[6] of the region of Brittany in north-western France. On finding patterns akin to those in Béarn, he proposed that the same sociological mechanism might be operative but that confirmatory research was needed: sameness of sociological mechanism cannot be read off phenomenal similarity. That type of comparative historical research, Bourdieu (2008) stated, demands a general and abstract model of symbolic exchange such as is to be found in the 1989 bachelorhood article. Interestingly, Bourdieu pointed to the genesis of that model in his learning (while reading up for a trip abroad) of the exclusion of Japanese peasants from matrimony.

Bourdieu argued in the 1989 article that the growing subordination of the peasant economy to the logic of the national economic market was not enough, in and of itself, to bring about the social dissolution epitomised by the new bachelors. Dissolution was produced, rather, by a relation of "circular causality" between the changes in the economic order and the emergence of a newly unified market in symbolic goods – marriageable persons amongst these (Bourdieu, 1989/2008, p. 177). Bourdieu invoked Karl Polanyi's re-working of Marx to argue that the problem was not the existence of a matrimonial market per se, but the absorption of the isolated, peasant-regulated market by a self-regulating symbolic market economy. In the "anarchy" of the latter, he argued after Friedrich Engels, persons were thrown back onto their own resources, abandoned as individuals to "the laws of the market". The elder sons were uncompetitive in this market because of the violence wrought on their self-image within the symbolic order.

In the 1989 article, Bourdieu stated that if his conclusions about the "decisive role" that symbolic domination on the unified matrimonial market had played in the reproduction crisis of the peasantry are accepted, then

> one must recognize that the attention given to the symbolic dimension of practices, far from representing an idealistic flight towards the ethereal spheres of the superstructure, constitutes the condition *sine qua non*, and

China, Education, and Bourdieu **7**

not only in this case, for a real understanding (which one may call, if one wishes, materialist) of the phenomena of domination.

(Bourdieu, 1989/2008, p. 191; original emphasis)

Bourdieu honed in here on what was required for the investigation of domination. If his analyses of bachelorhood are persuasive, he stated most forcefully, then it is apparent that domination can only be understood if the symbolic is analysed. Such an understanding (Bourdieu insisted) entails no idealist supposition of a super-structure; it is (he allowed) materialist. In other work, Bourdieu made it clear that his perspective was fundamentally realist-materialist; he considered "the realist representation of human action" to be "the first condition for scientific knowledge of the social world" (1998, pp. viii–ix); indeed, he argued that intellectuals' resistance to sociology stemmed from "a sort of ill-placed (spiritualist) point of honor" (1998, p. viii; original insertion). Bourdieu's is, however, a realism or materialism that engages with the symbolic and cultural.

Idealist and materialist perspectives had been in contention for much of the twentieth century. In general terms, idealists hold that there is a distinct realm of culture that is superior to that of politics and economy (an idea created by the European Romantics and central to anthropology and sociology from the time of Durkheim and Weber). Materialists, in contrast, do not make such a distinction; in the hardest variants there is no "culture" or "society", only the aggregation of individual action on a market or in compliance to the state (Milner, 1993).

Bourdieu grappled with what he called "the old debate between materialism and spiritualism" and the implication of education in this from the time of his earliest empirical studies of the transition of peasants into the capitalist economy in Algeria (Bourdieu, 1959/2013, pp. 50–51). An account of Bourdieu's position vis-à-vis the idealism of anthropological and sociological forebears, and the soft materialisms of contemporaneous marxisms, is beyond our purpose. What is relevant is that Bourdieu (1989/2008) explicitly rejected the idealism of the base-superstructure metaphor of Karl Marx. By that metaphor, the economic structure is viewed as the base of a legal and political superstructure, and thereby of social consciousness in religious, artistic, or philosophical form. Although secondary, a realm of cultural consciousness is admitted by this metaphor, a manifestation of an idealism that has been attributed to the young Marx's immersion in German Romanticism and the philosophy of G.W.F. Hegel (Milner, 1993).

For Bourdieu, the base–superstructure opposition was one of the oppositions which

> make it impossible to fully understand the infinitely subtle logic of the symbolic violence that is set up in the self-obscure relationship between socialized bodies and the social games in which they are engaged.
>
> *(Bourdieu, 1989/2008, p. 191)*

8 Karen Dooley et al.

In other words, Bourdieu argued that social reality could only be understood by a materialist perspective which entailed analysis of the symbolic. This point was reiterated in the prelude to *Masculine Domination*, a study of the sexual order as an exemplar of the logic of symbolic domination: "one has to seek in a materialist analysis of the economy of symbolic goods the means of escaping from the ruinous choice between the 'material' and the 'spiritual' or 'ideal' [*idéel*]" (Bourdieu, 2001, p. 3; original insertion). Bourdieu transcended the opposition of the material–real and the ideal–spiritual through his theory of symbolic exchange with its circular relations of causality between representation and the material. In this view, culture is constitutive of the social and of experience of the social, leading others to apply to it the label "cultural materialist" (Milner, 1993).

To clarify, Bourdieu's theoretical perspective resonated with that of self-professed cultural materialists in Britain in the 1960s–70s, who declared Bourdieu's work "resolutely materialist" (Garnham & Williams, 1980, p. 211). As developed in Britain, cultural materialism enabled analyses of the use of language (as practical consciousness made material) and of print and electronic technologies of writing as processes productive of the social (Milner, 1993) – a legacy of enduring utility for sociologists of education given the ongoing digital revolution. In his own work, it has been suggested, Bourdieu engaged with social and cultural ramifications of the development of mass culture. Specifically, the studies Bourdieu and co-investigators such as Jean-Claude Passeron conducted during the 1960s are seen to have:

> [t]acitly ... explored the impact of technology on traditional education and culture, whether in relation to the deployment of educational technology or in relation to the effect of photographic interventions on interpersonal relations, memory and identity.
>
> *(Robbins, 2009, p. 143)*

Bourdieu cited some of the "admirable" British work in the postscript of the bachelorhood volume (2008, p. 196). He pointed to the deleterious effect of representations that bourgeois social scientists and others brought to their writings on the peasantry from their own material conditions of existence.

The cultural materialist position Bourdieu developed enabled him to conduct delicate analyses of the implication of education in domination, in particular that of neoliberal capitalism – in all its hard materialism – from the 1960s onwards. The research on the bachelorhood of the elder sons is illustrative. As has been shown, Bourdieu presented a nuanced analysis of the circular and causal relations of changes in the economic and symbolic orders that produced the new bachelors. Along with the material conditions of existence of the elder sons as heirs to agricultural estates, familial education in the service of traditional matrimonial strategy helped render those sons uncompetitive on the new matrimonial market, thereby disrupting the reproduction of the peasant order. But families' strategies of formal education were implicated in this crisis, too.

Bourdieu observed that the peasantry had begun to see formal education as the means to the symbolic capabilities demanded by the unified economic market (e.g., mastery of standard French, skills in calculation). Accordingly, they were giving children – daughters in particular – more of the schooling they had long resisted. However, prolonged experience of the student condition had "de-realised" values inculcated by the family, re-directing "affective and economic investments away from reproduction of the lineage to reproduction by the singular individual of the position of the lineage in the social structure" (Bourdieu, 2008, p. 188). In other words, the most schooled were seeking individual advantage consonant with the social position of the family, rather than to reproduce the family in the biological sense.

In sum, Bourdieu's cultural materialist theory enables subtle analyses of the implication of education in social domination. The theory, Bourdieu claimed, is applicable to the logic of domination in the name of a multiplicity of symbolic principles including "language" (e.g., sociolects and dialects), "lifestyle" (the *bourg–hameaux* divide would be an example), and distinctive "properties" (e.g., sex, race). However, the purchase of the theory is limited to the normative habitus, to "the *paradox of doxa*", that is, to habitus that is inclined to respect rather than transgress or subvert the order of the world, and to perpetuate the established order despite sometimes intolerable conditions of existence (Bourdieu, 2001, p. 1; original emphasis). There is little in Bourdieu's analysis of elder sons who might have embraced bachelorhood by preference or so disported themselves that they were passed over in the line of inheritance (the position of heir was socially rather than strictly biologically distributed – the reigning patriarch could nominate another child as heir). In short, Bourdieu's is no theory of the divergent, bent, weird, pied, or odd habitus. Given Bourdieu's claim and acknowledgement that habitus cannot be overwritten, the focus on the normative would seem to limit its purchase on social reality, especially in conditions of change and heterogeneity. We turn now to limits to the international generalisation of Bourdieu's theory.

Bourdieu's International Circulation of His Ideas

Australian scholars have proposed that Bourdieu's work has drawn a more than usual amount of attention to questions about the "portability" of foreign social science (Bennett et al., 2013). Specifically, the international circulation of Bourdieu's work is perceived to have been accompanied by a singular preoccupation with national specificity. An essay by Wacquant (1993) is instructive. Wacquant tackled suppositions of French peculiarity while considering the transatlantic importation of Bourdieu's sociology from France to the US. He wrote of a US sociological field in which Bourdieu's work had been received for a decade, and through engagement with Bourdieu himself at workshops in Chicago in 1988 (Bourdieu & Wacquant, 1992) and a conference in 1989 (Calhoun, LiPuma, & Postone, 1993). After noting conflicting reactions to Bourdieu's theory, writing

10 Karen Dooley et al.

style, and conceptual tools, Wacquant addressed perceptions of the peculiarity of the French intellectual field.

Contra Bourdieu's critics, Wacquant (1993) maintained that the French sociologist was "uncommonly internationalist in intellectual background, outlook, and practice" (p. 244) and went on to speculate as to why this had not been apparent to scholars in the US. Amongst other things, he noted that American sociologists were unfamiliar by and large with the Continental traditions of French and German philosophy within which Bourdieu was located. Additionally, he pointed out that Bourdieu's theoretically grounded empirical sociology had been developed as an explicit alternative to the positivist social science ascendant in the American intellectual field and imported into France in the 1950s and 1960s by American-trained sociologists. Wacquant's point was that there was much in the field of American reception of Bourdieu's sociology that may have predisposed researchers to misconstrue that work as peculiarly French. It is notable that Wacquant emphasised the social relations amongst sociologists rather than the relation between sociologist and social reality.

Bourdieu construed the suppositions of French peculiarity as symptomatic of a more general problem of scientific nationalism and imperialism (e.g., Bourdieu, 1991; Bourdieu & Wacquant, 2005). To understand Bourdieu's alternative – his reflexive sociology of sociology – we here look more closely at the way that Bourdieu himself put his ideas into circulation between different national fields of sociology.

In a lecture in Tokyo in 1989, Bourdieu offered a Japanese reading of *The State Nobility*. That book reported Bourdieu's research on the elite schooling of the technocrats who were dominant in the neoliberalising field of power in France. The lecture was one of a series in which Bourdieu also offered Japanese and East German readings of *Distinction*. The lectures were published, with some integrative commentary by Bourdieu, in a themed 1991 issue of *Poetics Today* alongside articles from Estonia and Francophone Canada. Appearing under the title, National Literatures/Social Spaces, the issue was framed as an assembly of studies of social and cultural heterogeneity within the ostensibly homogeneous nation and its institutions (*Poetics Today*, 1991). Bourdieu's pieces were later published in *Practical Reason* (Bourdieu, 1998) with a different framing by Bourdieu himself. According to his preface, the volume was a collection of work produced in "situations where [he had] ... attempted to show foreign publics the universal validity of models constructed in relation to the specific case of France" (Bourdieu, 1998, p. vii). This statement flags the grounds on which Bourdieu not only rejected the charges of national peculiarity in his own work, but also envisioned a world field of sociology. In the late 1980s–early 1990s, Bourdieu imagined an alternative to the international situation of the sociology of his time: a field riven by scientific nationalisms and imperialisms with roots in local social *doxa*, in particular, those of the US (Bourdieu, 1991; Bourdieu & Wacquant, 2005).

China, Education, and Bourdieu   **11**

Consider Bourdieu's discussion of *The State Nobility* in Japan. Bourdieu developed the concept of the "field of power" central to that work as an alternative to the notion of "the ruling class". It is a field which consists of dominant agents from education, economy, and various other fields within a society; it is a field of struggle for primacy of the species of capital monopolised by those agents given their pre-eminence in the other fields – the embodied cultural capital of legitimate French culture in the educational field, for instance, or financial resources in the economic field. With his Japanese audience, Bourdieu spoke of ways that the school institution *contributes* to – without *determining* – the reproduction of the distribution of cultural capital and social position in "advanced countries". Bourdieu highlighted two "extremely intricate mechanisms" in this regard: familial strategies of social reproduction on the one hand, and the selective pedagogic logic of the school on the other (Bourdieu, Sapiro, & McHale, 1991c, p. 643).

With respect to familial strategy, Bourdieu stated that:

> Families invest all the more in school education (in transmission time, in help of all kinds, and in some cases, as today in Japan, in money, as witness the *juku*[7] and the *yobi-ko*) as their cultural capital is more important and as the relative weight of their cultural capital compared with their economic capital is greater – and also as the other reproduction strategies (especially succession strategies, which aim at the direct transmission of economic capital) are less effective or relatively less profitable ... This model ... allows us to understand the growing interest that families ... have in education in all advanced countries.
>
> *(Bourdieu et al., 1991c, p. 644)*

Bourdieu's focus here was on the increasingly important place of education in the strategies by which families sought to maintain or improve their social position in the "advanced countries" of late twentieth-century France and Japan. Bourdieu thereby suggested that France and Japan were similar and comparable. In such countries, he had hypothesised, education was most central to the reproduction strategies of those families which had more cultural than economic capital, especially as matrimonial, inheritance, and other strategies of social reproduction became less productive in the context of industrialisation, new inheritance laws, and so forth. Bourdieu took Japanese families' investment in shadow education as phenomenal evidence of his model of the reproductive mechanism. He went on to suggest that in Japan as in France, the cumulative effect of the investment strategies of individual families and the selective pedagogic logic of the school had created intense competition. The effect of this educational war of all against all, Bourdieu observed, was worn-out parents, exhausted children, and disappointed employers (Bourdieu et al., 1991c). On the basis of what he said he had read and been told, Bourdieu

12 Karen Dooley et al.

speculated about the similarity of the social mechanism in France, Germany, the USSR[8] – and China.

In short, Bourdieu extended to other countries the sociological model that he had created from his study of a particular French case. Commenting on this epistemological move, Bourdieu said that he had offered his audience in Japan "the means of corroborating, correcting, or refuting" his analyses (Bourdieu, Shapiro, & McHale, 1991b, p. 625), apparently by providing an exposition of his theoretical model. Twenty-seven years later, Bourdieu's "analyses" of tutoring as a component of Japanese families' educational strategies do not seem to have been tested (Aizawa & Iso, 2016), although they were exported back to France and tested with French families (Collas, 2013). The French research concluded that private tutoring was indeed part of a strategy of maintaining home advantage, but was unable to simply corroborate Bourdieu's assumptions about the causality of configurations of cultural and economic capital and of the pursuit of scholastic excellence; moreover, it was located in literature about the national peculiarity of social conditions of private tuition in Japan.

Our interest here is not in the actual corroboration, correction, or refutation of the analyses Bourdieu made in Japan, but in the epistemological acts illustrated by Bourdieu's "internationalist" practice in making those analyses. Offering his Japanese reading of *Distinction*, Bourdieu made an explicit statement in this regard:

> my entire scientific enterprise is based on the belief that the deepest logic of the social world can be grasped, providing only that one plunges into the particularity of an empirical reality, historically located and dated, but in order to build it up as a "special case of what is possible" as Bachelard puts it, that is, as an exemplary case in a world of finite possible configurations.
>
> *(Bourdieu, Shapiro, & McHale, 1991a, p. 628)*

With the French historians of science then, Bourdieu argued that the sociologist could grasp the general or universal by investigating empirical reality in all its historical particularity. Early in his career, Bourdieu seemed to pin his expectations in this regard on a method by which the sociologist: (1) wins the object of scientific knowledge from *doxa*; (2) constructs that object in coherent theoretical terms, and (3) confirms the object empirically (Bourdieu, Chamboredon, & Passeron, 1991). Later, Bourdieu drew the reflexivity involved in that method to the fore (e.g., Bourdieu & Wacquant, 1992; Bourdieu, 2004, 2007). Speaking and writing into international settings, he championed reflexive "scientific communication" as the alternative to sociological nationalisms and imperialism, advocating the pursuit of "propositions and procedures [which] conform to the rules of logical coherence and compatibilities with observational evidence" (Bourdieu, 1991, p. 376). In this vision, sociologists free themselves from social *doxa* by creating logically coherent objects and testing these empirically. Bourdieu grappled thereby with the social

China, Education, and Bourdieu **13**

inertia of knowledge, the socio-historical weights which coerce and subjugate the operation of scientific rationality (Foucault, 1991).

The position taken in this volume is that the use of Bourdieu's work in research on education in China needs to be subject to this same reflexivity. Consider what Bourdieu might have seen had he taken an educational tour of China just a few years after his speculations in Japan. We offer the following imaginary story.

> The visiting French man arrives at the trolleybus stop a few blocks from a key-point middle school in a coastal city in the east of China. As he alights, he sees a large billboard with an image of a smiling and fashionably dressed couple holding aloft a smiling baby girl, an artist's impression of a city agleam with glass towers behind them. From the street with its row of shabby shops, the French man turns into a wet market where he haggles over the price of an apple of superlative quality. As he approaches the school, none of the students seem extremely poor and few seem especially well off. A girl greets the foreigner in English. She tells him that she is self-studying radio English lessons at night because she is hoping to get into a famous American university.
>
> The whole school gathers in the quadrangle for exercises and to sing the national anthem before going off to class. At lunch time, the former Russian teacher, who is responsible for looking after foreigners, gives the French man some 粮票 (*liáng piào*, grain ration coupons) so that he can eat in the dining hall with the teachers and students. And then it is lessons for the rest of the day and an after-school class by the foreign English teacher. Before beginning work on the play they have been writing, the students are telling the English teacher about the Communist Youth League camp they will be attending later in the week. Outside, senior students are walking around the quadrangle reciting their textbooks in preparation for 高考(*gāo kǎo*, University Entrance Exams).
>
> As he is leaving the school, the French visitor notices that someone seems to be asleep on the verandah; the gatekeeper explains that the man is a peasant from a distant province who is labouring on the new classroom block. From the foreign language newspaper available in his hotel that evening, the French man learns about Deng Xiaoping's southern tour earlier in the year. Even more extraordinary changes are afoot.

The observational evidence from this school site is complex: the planned economy was being marketised by a state that retained its strong regulative hand; urban infrastructure was being redeveloped; tens of millions of peasants were pouring into distant cities where they were labouring and living without the benefits of local 户口 (*hù kǒu*, household registration); foreign expertise was being imported and deployed strategically in education and other fields; the size

14 Karen Dooley et al.

of the population was tightly controlled in the interest of quality, and competitively selected young people were being schooled up in privileged institutions as highly skilled cosmopolitans with powerful national loyalties. Bourdieu's materialist perspective, his concepts and theories, and his reflexive methodology would all seem to offer some purchase here. To tap that potential, the questions that might be asked of the empirical world include:

- What are the regulative rules of exchange in the fields of education?
- What kind of capital conversion is going on?
- What are the new Chinese habituses? Who is the new Chinese subject? How is this work of production of the subjective occurring in the field of education?
- How is the stuff of ethnicity, race, gender, sexuality, and other dimensions of human diversity embodied in habitus?
- How are habituses affiliated with stratified forms of distinction and social groups? How is class visibly playing itself out?
- Who is able to enter which fields and in which positions? How do they do so? On the basis of what exchanges of social capital is access enabled?
- With respect to the formation of class and distinction, how are the overlapping and coterminous fields of economy, of consumer culture and art, digital and face-to-face, situated in relation to the exchanges that occur in the educational field?
- Crucially, what is the state's role in all this? Is the state a meta-field? Is the concept of field of power adequate to understanding the work of the state?
- And finally, is Bourdieu's take on materialism adequate to the workings of policy within the strong Chinese state?

Attending to the Empirical Evidence in Chinese Education

Chapters 2 and 3 set the scene for much that follows. In Chapter 2, Shibao Guo, Yan Guo, Allan Luke, Karen Dooley, and Guanglun Michael Mu outline the parameters for a critical, reflexive sociology of Chinese education. They describe the transformations that have occurred in the material and symbolic conditions of existence of China's population as a result of the political economic settings that have accompanied the Reform and Opening-Up Policy under the regulatory hand of a strong state. The education field has seen devolution of policy, processes of marketisation and privatisation, and a shifting emphasis from ideological and moral to human capital production. With this have emerged stratification and differentiation of educational outcomes that are amenable to analysis in terms of classic sociological problematics. In Chapter 3, Zhongying Shi and Chunying Li survey the work that has already been undertaken with respect to these problematics in the national field of education research in China, in particular since questions of equity came to the fore in national policy and public debate. They provide an overview of Bourdieu's development in the French field of production, identify stages in the engagement of scholars with Bourdieu's work in the Chinese field of reception, and present bibliometric analysis of the use of Bourdieu in Chinese educational research. They conclude that researchers have yet to realise the potential of the Bourdieu's reflexive sociological methodology for addressing the distance between educational researcher and practitioner. Further, they advocate that researchers should develop habitus that would generate critique, challenges of, and modifications to, Bourdieu's sociology for educational research in China.

Much of the volume presents studies which investigate education for rural and migrant children, some of those least advantaged by economic and social reform. This would seem to reflect the concern of government and researchers alike in recent decades with educational inequalities.

In Chapter 4, Liang Du analyses the social positioning of the new generation of rural teachers, and in Chapter 5, Yue Melody Yin, Karen Dooley, and Guanglun Michael Mu investigate the experience of recruits to an alternative program of teacher preparation for rural China. The focus is on dispositions and capital exchanges that channel some young people to remote villages where they might teach for a lifetime (Du), and others, into rural placements for what might be a relatively brief sojourn in the course of a career of work and study in some of the most prestigious educational institutions in China and abroad (Yin et al.). Together, these chapters point to the complex realities of approaches to redressing educational inequity.

The volume turns then from the teachers of the less advantaged to the children themselves. In Chapter 6, He Li presents the findings of a study of the reproductive dynamics by which rural children most endowed with capital of all types were able to commit to and succeed in education. The analysis shows how discrepancy between position and disposition generated the transformative tendencies involved, but also imposed costs on young people who had made the journey from rural home to elite university. In Chapter 7, Guanglun Michael Mu presents findings from an ethnographic and quantitative study which investigated the sociological process of resilience on the part of both the "floating" children who migrate with their parents to cities, and the left-behind children who are typically raised by their grandparents after their parents' migration. Conclusions challenge deficit thinking – *doxic* and scientific alike – about the children, while insisting that resilience cannot shift the relations of power whereby under-resourced children such as these are marginalised.

The next two chapters address the work of families and principals as educational actors in the educational field of the reform era. In Chapter 8, Xu Zhao, Robert Selman, and Allan Luke study parental practice in the intensely competitive Chinese education system. They report an interview-focus group study of educational belief, practice, choice, and strategy conducted with parents and students living in different socio-economic conditions in Jinan and Shanghai.

16 Karen Dooley et al.

Findings highlight the capital exchanges by which families on low, middle, and high incomes acted strategically with respect to their children's education both within China and internationally. Conclusions are drawn about how the concept of habitus might be developed beyond Bourdieusian structuralism in order to describe educational phenomena in contemporary Chinese families adequately. In Chapter 9, Ning Jia and Guanglun Michael Mu likewise suggest a re-working of the Bourdieusian concept of *doxa*. They present a study of the conversion of the capitals of a principal in a Chinese school into a school *doxa* facilitative of organisational transformation. The chapter concludes with recommendations for enabling the conversions of capital required if individual institutions of education are to be transformed as envisioned by policymakers.

In the next two chapters, attention shifts from Chinese institutions of education per se to transnational contexts of research training for Chinese doctoral candidates. Chapter 10 was co-written by a group of Chinese scholars with diverse histories as students and academics in China, Australia, and Canada: Guanglun Michael Mu, Liwei Livia Liu, Wangqian Fu, Dongfang Hao, Ning Jia, Yimei Qin, Hongmei Sziegat, Xiaodong Wang, and Xueqin Wu. Together, these native Chinese-speaking scholars present a field analysis of a tri-nation doctoral workshop, highlighting the implication of English in relations of exchange, including those of publication and presentation. Much of the focus is on habituses in interactions in which English is both weapon and stake of struggle for legitimation. From a position of confidence which they trace to the cleft habitus of the cosmopolitan Chinese scholar, they draw conclusions for native speakers of Chinese and English alike, who are interested in creating transnational contexts in which more productive exchanges of knowledge might occur. In Chapter 11, Michael Singh describes a post-English-only intervention designed to build the intercultural self-confidence of Chinese doctoral candidates in an Australian university. The intervention challenged the privilege accorded English in scholarship, specifically through programs of English for research publication purposes. Inspiration is taken from Bourdieu's own efforts to insert the concepts he developed in French into scholarship in the Anglophone world, and the criticism by Kabyle scholars of Bourdieu's practice in Algeria during French colonisation. Chinese scholars (and non-Chinese colleagues) are challenged to work in the spirit of Bourdieu, and of the critique of Bourdieu, to invent concepts grounded in the diversity of linguistic and cultural experience of the entire world – not only that of the Anglophone or Francophone scholar.

In Chapter 12, the volume concludes with a reconsideration of Bourdieu's work in the light of reproduction and transformation in Chinese education. The three editors here call for a reflexive sociology that weaves between theory and context, the sociological imagination and the facticity of the social and material realities of the new China. Here we explore the grounds for expanding, critiquing, and reappropriating Bourdieu's ideas as part of the project of a new critical sociology of education in China.

The 21 authors here – from truly diverse generational and cultural trainings, histories, and standpoints – are engaging sympathetically but critically with the oeuvre of Bourdieu. In their investigations of education in China, they are re-purposing and recycling Bourdieu's work, re-forging tool and re-fashioning model, revoking assumption and relegating explanation. This is, inter alia, a collective attempt to release Bourdieu's work from some of its socio-historical inertia and its own accumulated *doxa* in order to understand educational realities that are not simply akin to those for which extant sociologies of education were created.

Acknowledgement

Dooley's work in this chapter was supported by Australian Research Council grant DP160100848 (*Private literacy tutoring: A sociology of shadow education*).

Notes

1 China National Knowledge Infrastructure (CNKI) – an e-publishing project providing access to the journal literature.
2 The articles were written in 1962, 1972, and 1989. Towards the end of Bourdieu's career, they were collected into a volume (2008) with integrative commentary by Bourdieu.
3 *Hameaux* ("hamlets") – small clusters of farmhouses around the *bourg*. The original French terms are retained in the English translation (and here) because the opposition between *hameaux* and *bourg* in the symbolic order is central to Bourdieu's analysis (translator's note: Bourdieu, 1962/2008, p. 11).
4 *Bourg* (market-village) – the main village in the *commune* (an administrative unit with a mayor).
5 The "empeasanted peasant" – a Béarnais term (Bourdieu, 2008, p. 198).
6 *Canton* – a district made up of several *communes*.
7 *Juku* are out-of-school educational institutions. *Yobikō* are *juku* that specialise in university entrance examination preparation and appeal to high achievers (Entrich, 2018).
8 USSR = Union of Soviet Socialist Republics (1922–91).

References

Aizawa, S. & Iso, N. (2016). The principle of differentiation in Japanese society and international knowledge transfer between Bourdieu and Japan. In D. Robbins (Ed.), *The Anthem companion to Pierre Bourdieu* (pp. 179–200). London: Anthem Press.

Bennett, T., Frow, J., Hage, G., & Noble, G., (2013). Antipodean fields: Working with Bourdieu. *Journal of Sociology, 49*(2–3), 129–150.

Bourdieu, P. (1959/2013). The clash of civilizations. In P. Bourdieu (Ed.), *Algerian sketches* (T. Yacine, trans. D. Fembach) (pp. 39–51). Cambridge: Polity.

Bourdieu, P. (1962/2008). Bachelorhood and the peasant condition. In P. Bourdieu (Ed.), *The Bachelors' Ball: The crisis of peasant society in Béarn* (Trans. R. Nice) (pp. 7–129). Cambridge: Polity Press.

Bourdieu, P. (1972/2008). Matrimonial strategies in the system of reproduction strategies. In P. Bourdieu (Ed.), *The Bachelors' Ball: The crisis of peasant society in Béarn* (Trans. R. Nice) (pp. 131–163). Cambridge: Polity Press.

Bourdieu, P. (1989/2008). Reproduction forbidden: The symbolic dimension of economic domination. In P. Bourdieu (Ed.), *The Bachelors' Ball: The crisis of peasant society in Béarn* (Trans. R. Nice) (pp. 165–200). Cambridge: Polity Press.

Bourdieu, P. (1991). Epilogue: On the possibility of a field of world sociology (Trans. L.J. D. Wacquant). In P. Bourdieu & J.S. Coleman (Eds.), *Social theory for a changing society* (pp. 373–387). Boulder: Westview Press.

Bourdieu, P. (1998). *Practical reason: On a theory of action.* Stanford: Stanford University Press.

Bourdieu, P. (2001). *Masculine domination.* Cambridge: Polity.

Bourdieu, P. (2004). *Science of science and reflexivity.* Cambridge: Polity.

Bourdieu, P. (2007). *Sketch for a self-analysis* (Trans. R. Nice). Cambridge, UK: Polity Press.

Bourdieu, P. (2008). *The Bachelors' Ball: The crisis of peasant society in Béarn* (Trans. R. Nice). Cambridge: Polity Press.

Bourdieu, P., Chamboredon, J.C., & Passeron, J.C. (1991). *The craft of sociology: Epistemological preliminaries* (Ed. B. Krais, Trans. R. Nice). Berlin & New York: Walter de Gruyter.

Bourdieu, P. & Passeron, J.C. (1990). *Reproduction in education, society and culture* (2nd Ed.). (Trans. R. Nice). London: Sage.

Bourdieu, P., Sapiro, G., & McHale, B. (1991a). First lecture. Social space and symbolic space: Introduction to a Japanese reading of *Distinction. Poetics Today, 12*(4), 627–638.

Bourdieu, P., Sapiro, G., & McHale, B. (1991b). Proofreading. *Poetics Today, 12*(4), 625–626.

Bourdieu, P., Sapiro, G., & McHale, B. (1991c). Second lecture. The new capital: Introduction to a Japanese reading of *State Nobility. Poetics Today, 12*(4), 643–653. Polity.

Bourdieu, P. & Wacquant, L.J.D. (1992). *An introduction to reflexive sociology.* Cambridge: Polity Press.

Bourdieu, P. & Wacquant, L.J.D. (2005). The cunning of imperial reason. In L. Wacquant (Ed.), *Bourdieu and democratic politics* (pp. 178–198). Cambridge: Polity.

Calhoun, C., LiPuma, E., & Postone, M. (1993). *Bourdieu: Critical perspectives.* Cambridge: Polity.

Chen, N. & Zang, X. (2009). Bourdieu and Chinese sociology. *Sociologica, 1*, 1–16.

Collas, T. (2013). Users of private tutoring in France: Varieties of scholastic support and family shaping of education (Trans. A. Jacobs). *Revue française de sociologie (English Edition), 54*(3), 463–502.

Entrich, S.R. (2018). *Shadow education and social inequalities in Japan: Evolving patterns and conceptual implications.* New York: Springer.

Foucault, M. (1991). Introduction. In G. Canguilhem (Ed.), *The normal and the pathological* (pp. 7–24). New York: Zone Books.

Garnham, N. & Williams, R. (1980). Pierre Bourdieu and the sociology of culture: An introduction. *Media, Culture and Society, 2*, 209–223.

Luke, A. (2018). On new critical East Asian educational studies. *Curriculum Inquiry, 48*(2), 253–259.

Milner, A. (1993). *Cultural materialism.* Carlton, Vic.: Melbourne University Press.

Mu, G.M. (2018). *Building resilience of floating children and left-behind children in China: Power, politics, participation, and education.* London: Routledge.

Poetics Today. (1991). Editors' note. National literatures/social spaces. *Poetics Today*, *12*(4), 623–624.

Robbins, D. (2009). After the ball is over: Bourdieu and the crisis of peasant society. *Theory, Culture & Society*, *26*(5), 141–150.

Sheng, X.M. (2014). *Higher education choice in China: Social stratification, gender and educational inequality*. London: Routledge.

Wacquant, L. (1993). Bourdieu in America: Notes on the transatlantic importation of social theory. In C. Calhoun, E. LiPuma & M. Postone (Eds.), *Bourdieu: Critical perspectives* (pp. 234–262). Chicago: University of Chicago Press.

2

MARKET ECONOMY, SOCIAL CHANGE, AND EDUCATIONAL INEQUALITY

Notes for a Critical Sociology of Chinese Education

Shibao Guo, Yan Guo, Allan Luke, Karen Dooley, and Guanglun Michael Mu

Introduction

With the policy of Reform and Opening-Up of 1978, China began the transition from a centrally planned to market economy. Forty years later this transition is still without precedent and in progress. But even as economists and other social scientists debate its regulatory and ideological parameters, longitudinal consequences of the economic shift are clear. In 2013, a joint report of the World Bank and the Development Research Center of the State Council (hereafter, TWB-DRCSC, 2013) predicted that China, once a low-income country, would attain high-income status by about 2030. China is on track to reclaim the position of the world's largest economy, a position it enjoyed from the early sixteenth to nineteenth centuries. Shortly after the TWB-DRCSC report, China was placed ahead of the United States by the International Monetary Fund (IMF) in its ranking of world gross domestic product (GDP) purchasing power parity (PPP), although the positions of the two countries were reversed for the world GDP (nominal) ranking.[1] With respect to GDP per capita, however, neither country topped the rankings; China and the US were ranked respectively 90th and 11th in the world for GDP (PPP) and 80th and 10th for GDP (nominal) (Statistics Times, 2015a, 2015b, 2015c, 2015d). According to the World Bank, China's annual average growth rate of nearly 10 per cent over a period of forty years has achieved "the fastest sustained expansion by a major economy in history – and has lifted more than 800 million people out of poverty" (The World Bank, 2018a). At the same time, the absolute number of people living in poverty remains large (The World Bank, 2018a, 2018b), and there are persistent and growing disparities in wealth between a high-profile entrepreneurial and cosmopolitan elite, an emergent urban middle class, and the rural and urban poor – many of whom remain displaced without access to services and, indeed, education. The Reform and Opening-Up have set the terms for these changes to the material conditions, and social and economic relations. Given China's economic, military, and geopolitical ascendancy, there is a growing interest in understanding the parameters, structures, and, indeed, the future prospects of this blend of market economics with centralised state planning and control.

Education is viewed as a key pillar of China's economic reform and social development. Substantial efforts have been made to increase the quantity and quality of education following the rationale of a human capital model.[2] The intent is to enable the national economy to ascend the value chain from labour-intensive, to skill-intensive production (TWB-DRCSC, 2013) and, currently, from established energy-intensive manufacturing sectors to service and information-based work. Educational policy, therefore, is a very deliberate attempt to engineer and enhance structural economic change and, with this, to remake the workforce. This is nothing less than a state intervention aiming to reshape and redistribute the aggregate cultural capital – the skills, knowledge, capacity, and credential-base – of an educated Chinese population.

Across this half-century period, the formal institutions of education themselves have been subject to successive waves of reform and restructuring. These have been complicated further by shifts in the adjacent fields of employment, housing, healthcare, consumption, and popular culture, and of the core structure of the nuclear family. During this period, there have been some significant educational achievements. These include Shanghai's widely-cited performance on the 2009 PISA and other comparative international studies; high-profile scientific and technological achievements and patents; and the expansion, modernisation, and internationalisation of China's top tier of universities. Despite current tensions over trade and intellectual property, academic and scientific exchange between China's research institutions, graduate students and their Western counterparts continues to expand. Further, leading Chinese research institutions, corporations, and businesses have begun to attract high-calibre domestic and international academic and professional expertise. There is evidence, then, that the policy shift towards a marketised model of education described in this chapter has succeeded at fulfilling an "attraction function" (Luke, 2018) of generating and expanding the bases of cultural and economic capital. Whether and how it has maintained a parallel "ameliorative function" (p. 149) of addressing the affiliated patterns of stratified and unequal distribution of capital is the focal issue in this chapter.

This has been the focus of concern expressed at various levels of government in China, and amongst educators, students, and families: the social and economic disparities associated with formal education – especially amongst rural, regional, and cultural minority communities – and the burden of a highly competitive system borne by young people and their families (Zhang & Bray, 2017). Questions of educational access, participation, and equity are focal in contemporary

22 Shibao Guo et al.

policy analyses of Chinese education (e.g., Guo & Guo, 2016). This chapter sets out to provide a broad descriptive overview of the field of Chinese education as a context for the studies in this volume. Our aim is to describe changes in the social fields of education in the larger historical context of the transition from a centrally planned to a market economy. What are the major changes in the fields of education under China's market economy? How might we bring a reflexive sociology to bear on analysing and understanding these changes?

We begin with an overview of complex processes that have played out in the course of economic growth and modernisation: industrialisation, privatisation, economic liberalisation, mass migration, and urbanisation. We then examine how these processes have produced fundamental changes in the material and symbolic conditions of everyday life, raising significant problems of social and economic inequality. This is followed with a critical review of how social scientists have defined this new political economy in China as a yet unresolved amalgam of neoliberal marketisation and socialist egalitarianism. Our focus here is on how these broader changes in economic and social policy have been reflected in a reshaping of the educational field, where the state's policies have enabled the devolution of governance and funding of schools and universities, the marketisation of these institutions, and the emergence of private and shadow education sectors. Appraising the effects of these reforms, we move towards an outline of the parameters for a critical, reflexive sociology of Chinese education.

Transition to a Market Economy

The economic ascent of China rests on a series of economic and social reforms and transitions. A first step involved *economic liberalisation* of the agricultural sector through introduction of the household responsibility system in place of the collective commune. Complementary measures were taken to reform industry, initially through the encouragement of joint ventures with foreign companies. None the less, foreign direct investment (FDI) was constrained until after the famous 1992 southern tour, when Deng Xiaoping committed the nation to the pursuit of a market economy (Han, Liu, & Zhang, 2012). A decade later, another major round of liberalisation occurred with China's accession to the World Trade Organisation (WTO). After fulfilling its pledge to open its markets in 2006, China formally entered into an era of market economy. During this period of economic liberalisation, China has also undergone interrelated processes of industrialisation, privatisation, mass migration, and urbanisation. These longitudinal transitions to a market economy have enabled the emergence of a private sector and a culture of individual aspiration and entrepreneurship, while maintaining both centralised state regulatory control over that market and the coexistence of state-controlled enterprises.

Industrialisation has been key to China's economic reforms: expansion of China's industrial capability, scale, and output in both traditional manufacturing

Economy, Social Change, Education **23**

and, most recently, a progressive emphasis and shift towards digital and information technologies. When reform began at the end of the 1970s, Chinese industry was primarily owned by the state and located in urban areas; at the time, state-owned enterprises (SOEs) delivered 78 per cent of the nation's industrial output (Brandt, Rawski, & Sutton, 2008). Incentives were introduced in the initial stages of industrial reform to encourage the growth of township and village enterprises (TVEs). These new drivers of the economy were able to take advantage of labour that had been released from farming with the introduction of the household responsibility system – a factor in rising agricultural productivity (Fan & Pardey, 1997). During the 1980s, industrial firms which employed almost 50 million workers proliferated; the number of firms jumped from 377,000 in 1980 to 1.33 million in 2004. In the construction sector alone, the number of firms soared from 6,604 in 1980 to 58,750 in 2005 (Brandt & Rawski, 2008). From the mid-1990s, a range of market measures was introduced with the intent of industrial restructuring, including privatisation of TVEs and large-scale layoffs in the SOE sectors. Marketisation and privatisation, then, became the key underpinnings of China's industrial transformation, torqueing it towards traditional factory-based manufacturing. China is the world's leading supplier of manufactured goods, surpassing that of the United States in 2011 (Sutter, 2012).

After the liberalisation of trade and investment structures internationally during the 1980s and 1990s, the volume of cross-border trade soared from $21 billion in 1978 to over $1.1 trillion in 2004 (Branstetter & Lardy, 2008). By 2010, China had become the second largest trading economy in the world and the largest exporting nation (Sutter, 2012). China's commitment to economic liberalisation in the form of the reciprocal opening of global markets has exceeded that of many OECD countries – this is, indeed, a central point of contention in current trade disputes with the US. The openness of the trade and FDI regime that China has put in place has been described as "one of the most significant accomplishments of the reform era" (Bransletter & Lardy, 2008, p. 676). During the 1990s, the nation undertook tariff reduction and other trade liberalisation measures in the course of its accession to the WTO (Branstetter & Lardy, 2008). China's admission to the WTO in 2001 was a watershed moment that opened up its service-sector exports. There has also been a shift in the composition of the manufactured goods China exports to the world: labour-intensive products (e.g., textiles, clothing, and toys) have given way to sophisticated machinery, and now, electronic and information technology products (Brandt et al., 2008). Ambitious targets are now set for increased exports of service and information-based products ranging from software, data analysis, design, development, and marketing. There are also major state-sponsored interventions to take global leadership in the development and export of green and clean energy production. This latest shift coincides with crises in urban pollution and, more generally, the effects of a continued dependency on fossil fuels, and energy-intensive, industrial manufacturing, on climate change and environmental degradation.

This economic growth has triggered and been enabled by massive *internal migration*, a movement of people from rural to urban China that has been described as the largest in human history (Fishman, 2005). In 1958, the *hù kŏu* (户口, household registration) system was introduced with the explicit intent of restricting rural-to-urban migration. At the time, urban wages were suppressed but cities were provided with benefits that included housing, education, healthcare, pensions, and urban amenities. As a result, urban residents enjoyed much higher real incomes than those in rural areas. Established with the aim of full employment, the *hù kŏu* system constrained migration during the early years of Reform and Opening-Up. Given the rationing of oil and grain that remained in place until the early 1990s, urban life was difficult for migrants who did not have the *liáng piào* (粮票, grain coupons) used by urban residents. With the discontinuation of *liáng piào*, a major impediment to rural–urban migration was removed. From a base of 6.57 million in 1982, the number of migrants soared, in particular, between 1990 and 1995 when the migrant population jumped from 21.35 million to 70.73 million. By 2013, the migrant population had topped 236 million (Lu & Xia, 2016). Of particular interest here is that the *hù kŏu* system set the conditions both for the lack of access to state schooling for an estimated 30 million children of urban migrants – the "floating" children – and the 60 million[3] "left-behind" children in rural communities (Mu, 2018).

Beginning in 1995, tertiary-sector (service) employment in China outstripped that of the secondary sector (manufacturing). However, the largest groups of migrants were employed in manufacturing and construction up until about 2013, when the group in services became the largest, although still smaller than the total manufacturing workforce (Lu & Xia, 2016). For decades, then, migrants have provided an abundant source of cheap, mobile, and exploitable labour. Even though they have been an essential component of economic growth, the social and political position of these workers is perilous. Working conditions are poor: hours are long and the jobs are amongst the dirtiest and most dangerous. Moreover, migrants are confronted by regulatory and practical barriers to full participation in social life in urban areas (Guo & Zhang, 2010; Lu & Xia, 2016). Given institutional and economic barriers to affordable housing, many reside in "migrant enclaves" – effectively, "slums or shantytowns characterised by chaotic land use, dilapidated housing, severe infrastructure deficiency, intensified social disorder, and unsightly urban eyesore" (Zhang, 2005, p. 250). An urban "underclass"[4] is now present in all of the China's major cities (Solinger, 2008).

Internal migration has been a driving factor in the rapid *urbanisation* of China over the last 40 years. In 1980, a few years into the era of Reform and Opening-Up, the urban population accounted for only 19.6 per cent of China's population; in 2005, 25 years later, that figure had increased by 23 per cent to 43 per cent (Yusuf & Nabeshima, 2008). In 2017, only twelve years later, the figure had increased to 58.52 per cent (*Business Times*, 2017). Zhang (2008) argues that China's fast-track urbanisation has entailed extensive restructuring and multi-scalar spatial reorganisation of the urban system. At the highest scalar level, the eastern coastal cities are urbanising most rapidly. Below that, city-regions with aspirations of becoming global trade hubs have been in the making since the 1990s. At the city scale, the most significant development would seem to be the redrawing of municipal boundaries to bring rural areas into the ambit of the urban by converting counties into cities. Once wholly controlled by the central state and subordinated to "forging-ahead" industrialisation, urbanisation is now a contentious process by which local authorities consolidate their accumulation regimes, political capital, and local power. That is, China's urbanisation is not a predictable outcome of industrialisation, but a process that has been shaped by the ownership arrangements and multi-tiered governance of the economic system.

Ong (2014) also is sceptical of the axiomatic view that urbanisation is a logical historical consequence of economic development and industrialisation. For Ong, urbanisation has been a state-engineered process, stemming from the fiscal imperatives of government. Land transactions and real estate development have become indispensable sources of fiscal revenue for municipal and regional government. Ma (2002) makes the case that it is this political economy of private property ownership and investment that is at the core of the economic and urban transformation of China. The state's overall approach to modernisation through marketisation has created a system of exchange where urbanisation has been tied closely to private ownership of land and real estate, and the rapid expansion of urban service and commodity-based lifestyles amongst the middle and upper classes. This includes the development of mixed public/private urban markets in education. In effect, the meta-field of the state regulated, marketised economy has set the terms for aspirational working and middle classes, and strategic elite classes – which are now comprised of active participants in a competitive educational field.

The economic transition from planned to market economy has entailed and enabled unprecedented processes of industrialisation, privatisation, economic liberalisation, mass, and urbanisation. The balance has shifted from a politicised economic state to a broader *economicisation and commercialisation* that has left few dimensions of Chinese society untouched (Chen, 2002). Prior to 1978, Chinese society was explicitly politicised; that is, before Reform and Opening-Up, economics ceded to national political ideology as both means and ends of state policy. At that time, the concepts of class struggle and anti-imperialism remained a key conceptual and ideological links in political and social life. Accordingly, the ideological principle of egalitarianism acted as a public brake on economic and social inequality, but equally appeared to constrain the emergence of aspirational working classes and entrepreneurial middle classes. The policy changes of 1978, then, were a watershed for the Chinese nation as it marked out a first de facto depoliticisation and economicisation of the Chinese state. As a result, government at all levels began to focus sharply, first on economic productivity and growth, and subsequently on efficiency and diversification. The imperative has been to boost national productivity, the efficient

26 Shibao Guo et al.

production of goods and services, and thereby, global competitiveness. With this new policy orientation of "letting a portion of the population get rich first", social issues and problems affiliated with inequality were subordinated. It is to the social consequences of the transformation that we now turn.

Social Change, Reform, and Equity

China has undergone far-reaching social change and transformation as a result of the market economy. With decentralisation, a large measure of authority and responsibility for decisions was transferred hierarchically from central government planning to local government and state-owned enterprises. The urban reform of 1984 was directed towards the creation of a mixed market of private and state-owned businesses. This reform effected radical changes in the distribution of power. Substantial control of economic decision-making was ceded to urban industries, thereby generating more local initiatives and control of resources. The reform also entailed partial devolution of power from public administration to the private sector (Painter & Mok, 2008). Decentralisation thereby diversified ownership, challenging the *doxa* of state ownership. The gradual change in ownership structures, along with mechanisms of resource allocation and capital accumulation, effected by the government was seen to mark the transformative capacity of the socialist system (Zhang, 2008). But this transition was not limited to the economic field. Substantial elements of educational decision-making were transferred from central to provincial and municipal governments, which in turn established systems of regional and school-based administration.

With China's shift to a market economy, the labour system has also undergone significant changes. In the interest of economic growth, lifetime employment was scrapped and replaced with a contract system. Known as "the iron rice bowl", lifetime employment with guaranteed income and social benefits was a signature achievement of the Chinese nation after 1949. In 1986, employers were given the power to lay off surplus labour in order to slash production costs and improve productivity. The abolition of permanent lifetime employment had a direct and powerful impact on material conditions. Under the old system, the enterprise-based work unit was responsible for worker welfare. In addition to guaranteed income, it provided statutory welfare entitlements, including housing, health care, pensions, and education. Workers' welfare was thereby integrated with the workplace. Serious issues of social security arose with the economic reform (Chen, 2002). With respect to housing, marketisation and privatisation required workers to purchase the public housing apartments in which they had lived at little or no cost. Skyrocketing real estate prices in many urban areas meant that employees were sometimes unable to do so. Responsibility for primary health care was likewise transferred from the work unit to the individual. A study of health status, health equity, and economic reform in China (Gao et al., 2002) found that economic reform was precipitating increased inequities in health care. As government subsidies were cut, user-pays market mechanisms were introduced, creating a major financial burden, especially for low-income earners in both urban and rural areas. In addition to housing and health care, other social services once provided by work units have been either reduced or shifted onto the local community. Finally, pensions have become precarious under the new labour system. Previously, pensions financed by the work units were available on retirement from a lifetime of secure employment. Now many accumulated pension benefits are often lost with one's job (Cai & Cheng, 2014).

Until reforms began in the 1980s, assets were usually collectively or publicly owned; little wealth was in private hands. With economic restructuring, privatisation,ownership reforms, and changes in the labour system, the income gap among households and individuals has opened up considerably. Income inequality has risen from a relatively low level in the early 1980s to a level that is high by international standards (Benjamin et al., 2008; Gustafsson, Li, & Sicular, 2008; Sutherland & Yao, 2011). New phenomena of large-scale urban unemployment and underemployment have emerged, while rural poverty persists. As private ownership of enterprises and urban housing has expanded, many middle-class households have accumulated wealth in the form of business assets, real estate, shares, and investments. For those with access to social networks and financial means, the privatisation of housing has presented opportunities for the accumulation of new forms of financial assets (Gustafsson et al., 2008). These include domestic and offshore real estate and investments, shares, foreign currency, and other forms of capital. The unequal distribution of wealth and widening income gap have become serious national social and economic issues.

The social and economic reforms enacted in China thus have transformed the structure and functioning of the Chinese state and society, bringing about serious tensions between economic growth and the maintenance of the socio-political order, and ushering in significant social problems and inequality (Chen, 2002). As described above, China's transformations under the market economy have involved fundamental shifts from a centrally planned to a market economy, from centralised to decentralised government, from state ownership to privatisation. This is a transition from a state that centrally managed exchange within all economic and institutional fields to one that coordinates the allocation of resources and the regulatory system that governs these processes (Zhang, 2008). Yet the state has not simply relinquished control over flows and exchanges of capital, labour, goods, and services to a self-regulating market. In effect, the state operates as a meta-field of power, regularly intervening to redirect or alter the relations and exchanges in specific overlapping social and institutional fields, including the banking sector, the stock market, the military-industrial complex, education systems, and remaining state-managed and run enterprises and corporations. In this way, the logic of practice of these specific fields tends to be continuously realigned and re-examined in relationship to the rules of exchange set centrally by the state.

28 Shibao Guo et al.

Not all have benefited equally from the reforms. Many have lost out, amongst these, those with rural *hù kǒu* (whether residing in the countryside or in cities); low-income earners; those with little formal education; the unemployed; those working in factories, primary resource extraction and in financially troubled state-owned enterprises; non-Party members; many cultural minority communities and residents in the interior and western provinces; women, and those who are middle-aged or older (Han & Whyte, 2009).

Describing the New Political Economy

There is no consensus on the description of this model of political economy. Quite the contrary, China's model is viewed and explained as everything from "socialist-developmental" to "predatory", "corporatist" to "rent-seeking", and "market-Leninist" to "entrepreneurial" (Peck & Zhang, 2013). Policy analysts in China primarily describe the development model as "socialism with Chinese characteristics" (Yang, 2007; Zhuang, 2007). Other social scientists have used such terms as "postsocialist market economy" (Dirlik, 1989), "neoliberalism with Chinese characteristics" (Harvey, 2005), and "capitalism with Chinese characteristics" (Huang, 2008).

From within China, Zhuang (2007) described the nation's market economy as socialist with "the bright and sound nature of socialism" (p. 355). Zhuang posits that the essence of China's socialist market economy is not a capitalist market economy, nor will it be made to move, in any way, in that direction. For Zhuang, the socialist market economy is the result of China's unique political, economic, and cultural system. Another Chinese commentator, Yang (2007), has contended that after thirty years of pioneering work, China is combining the market economy with socialism in order to develop "socialism with Chinese characteristics" (Yang, 2007). This form of socialism is different not only from socialism as it was historically defined, but also from Western democratic capitalism. Socialism with Chinese characteristics emphasises the function of the social system in emancipating and developing productive forces, eliminating exploitation and class conflict, and ushering in common prosperity. Yang argues that past experience in China has demonstrated that combining socialism with a market economy promotes rapid, stable socio-economic development. Further, he makes the case that this model is the only one that can make China a wealthy, democratic, and civilised society. Both Yang and Zhuang begin from acknowledgement of the differential effects of uneven development on urban and rural areas, among regions, and across different groups in the population. Furthermore, they acknowledge issues of social inequality associated with differential access to education, environmental degradation, the shortcomings of the social security system, and polarisation of rich and poor. But they are confident, none the less, that by adhering to socialism's core values, China will be able to manage the market economy to optimise social justice as well as economic prosperity. They insist that abandoning socialism is not a realistic option for China and that fear of such is unfounded.

In contrast, Dirlik (1989) deploys the term "postsocialism" to theorise the changes in post-Mao China. Crucially, postsocialism is also postcapitalist, in the sense of a socialism representing "a response to the experience of capitalism and an attempt to overcome the deficiencies of capitalist development" (p. 364). For Dirlik, postsocialism seeks to avoid a return to capitalism but takes up capitalist methods of development so as to redress its own deficiencies. Dirlik argues further that postsocialism works to keep alive a vague vision of socialism as the common goal of humankind while denying it an immanent role in the formulation of contemporary policies of the state. In contrast, Harvey (2005) is of the view that China is a case of the neoliberalisation of both economic and domestic domains. He contends that China's market economy has been constructed to interlink neoliberal elements with the centralised control of an authoritarian state. His position is that the emergence of China as a global economic power after 1980 should be understood as an unintended consequence of the neoliberal turn in the advanced capitalist world. He describes the changes in China as a wholesale process of proletarianisation. This process is marked by the various stages of privatisation in the economy, including the measures taken to bring about greater flexibility in the labour market. In light of this, Harvey argues, "China certainly qualifies as a neoliberal economy, albeit 'with Chinese characteristics'" (p. 144). In this view, neoliberalism with Chinese characteristics has set the terms for "a social system where capitalist enterprises can both form and function freely" (p. 150).

Clarifying the notion of "capitalism with Chinese characteristics", Huang (2008) argues that this model is a function of "a political balance between two Chinas – the entrepreneurial, market-driven rural China vis-à-vis the state-led urban China" (p. xvi). This argument draws attention to two different moments in China's recent economic history. The first was the 1980s when rural China had the upper hand under a Chinese form of capitalism that was independent politically and entrepreneurial, a capitalism that was competitive in conduct and virtuous in effect. The second moment began in the 1990s when policy prioritised investment and credit allocations for cities, imposing heavy taxes on the rural sector so as to finance a state-led boom in the urban economy. Huang argues that "entrepreneurial capitalism thrives and produces many of its associated virtuous effects" (p. 9) when policy supports and affords greater operational freedom to rural enterprises that are small in scale, oriented to the market, broad in base and politically independent. That model of capitalism was superseded, however, with the move towards political dependency on the Chinese state in the 1990s and a form of capitalism rooted in a technocratic industrial policy blueprint with an urban bias. Huang notes that the role and magnitude of the private sector is one of the most important hallmarks of a market economy.

30 Shibao Guo et al.

During the 1990s, however, policy weakened the position of an indigenous private sector. In this account of capitalism with Chinese characteristics, Huang contends that China's commanding-heights economy is fundamentally different from those of capitalism with East Asian characteristics (e.g., Japan, Korea, Singapore). The differences relate to the role and the size of the private sector, along with the degree to which the state intervenes and shifts resources and support to and from different industries, and fields – establishing a regulatory and interventionist meta-field of exchange. The degree to which any economic or institutional field acts as a "free market", then, is contingent upon the master economic templates and political agendas of the strong state.

At this historical juncture, then, China's economic development entails ambiguity and contradiction. Peck and Zhang (2013) propose that if indeed there is a model in play, then that model is "complex and heterogeneous" (p. 386). They point to the simultaneous contradiction and complementarity of socialist ideology and capitalist practice. A pattern of oscillations between market-led and state-led development make attempts at conceptualisation and categorisation partial and contingent. Accordingly, Peck and Zhang (2013) maintain, Chinese capitalism might be defined more appropriately in terms of its durable contradictions and tensions. It is, clearly, an emergent political economic reality which is unprecedented in its scope and rapidity of development. The hybridity of the model and its points of disequilibria suggest that this is something more than a simple, linear development or transition from one system to another. In a recent study of a new system of urban elite "public" schools, Liu (2018) refers to the overall composite model as a form of "neoliberal global assemblage", with a host of unplanned, collateral effects at the local level. To simply "add" China to the existing developmental typologies of capitalisms (e.g., postindustrial, late, transnational, fast, or hyper-capitalism) does not suffice. The point here is that China is not proceeding by following an orderly defined model or historical precedent; rather, by definition, "China *combines* contradictory forms" (Peck & Zhang, 2013, p. 380).

Our view of these commentaries is twofold. First, the formation, reformation, and alignment of this meta-field of power is not undertaken by China per se – as a reified, nominalised entity. These alignments, adjustments, and redirections are the means and ends of a specific "strong state" (Lim & Apple, 2016), which continues to assert degrees of centralised monitoring and surveillance, control, and regulatory intervention across all of the aforementioned social and institutional fields – despite and in relation to the marketised economy, without the requirement for broad public debate, consensus, or agreement with businesses and workers. The state is *not*, as in Bourdieu's (1998) and others' early analyses of neoliberalism in the West, a *contender* amongst many for power to mediate and influence markets, transnational corporations, or a labouring and consuming public. As we have argued here, it is actively and definitively shaping and aligning relationships of exchange within and between overlapping fields – modifying these relationships as it goes. There should be no illusions amongst these commentators about the ideal types of a liberal free market or a rampant corporate, transnational neoliberalism at work on the ground, untethered from state oversight and control. Where they are allowed to operate in China, Silicon Valley tech corporations or Western multinational manufacturers alike are allowed entry into the market at the state's forbearance and according to its terms. There may be moments where the deliberate alignment and shaping of fields appears less than seamless, as in the implementation of the stock market, the management of urban poverty, current attempts to stem flows of capital to offshore markets, or the over-proliferation of private schooling in urban enclaves. But it is not a case of market forces in and of themselves driving the agenda. Unlike in versions of Western capitalism, where the onus is on government to justify its intervention in the market, these are *de facto* and *de jure* state-established and governed marketplaces.

Second, the ongoing state official re-engagement with Marxism is continuing, as this book goes to press. Indeed, historical contradiction as a negation of existing material and social relations is a central concept of dialectical materialism – and can be enlisted to provide an explanatory template both for this historical moment, and the necessity for further centrally guided reform and alignment across fields. This provides ample space, for example, for the reassertion of an ideology of nationalism as part of such combined and complex geopolitical, economic, and military strategies as the China Dream, the New Silk Road and expansion into the South China Sea, and the anti-corruption campaign. In this regard, and even in a transitional and empirically complex situation, the state remains as a meta-field – an arbiter and mediator whose policies, laws, regulations, and authorities are omnipresent in the shaping and alteration of systems of exchange within specific fields. With this in mind, we turn to developments in the field of education.

Marketisation of the Educational Field

As state ideology and institutional practice shifted away from that of a centrally planned to a market-driven economy, educational policy reshaped the field (Guo et al., 2013; Guo & Guo, 2016). The paradigm shift was the devolution from centralised to multi-tiered local governance. Marketisation and privatisation led to whole-scale changes in provision and access, student enrolment, curriculum, and financing. The field of education was realigned with the field of economy. Its function shifted from its historical focus on national ideology and moral formation, to an explicit focus on the production of human capital: professional credentials, job-specific skills and capacities, bilingualism and biliteracies, STEM, and, most recently, preparation for transnational, digital economies and culture industries.

In 1985, the Chinese government devolved responsibilities for the administration of school affairs and all attendant decision-making authority to the local level (Chan & Mok, 2001; Hawkins, 2000). In 1993, policies for reform and development through decentralisation were outlined in the landmark policy, *Compendium of Educational Reform and Development in China* (cf. Zhang, Dai, & Yu, 2016). In 1995, further emphasis was put on the decentralisation of management and financing: educational institutions were granted greater autonomy in decisions relating to student enrolment, academic credentials, and staff recruitment. Under the planned economy, the state previously had a placement system that guaranteed every graduate a job (Niu, 2009). With the shift to the contract labour system, education has become one of the nation's largest markets. Schools and universities are now able to hire and dismiss teachers, lecturers, and professors on the basis of credentials, experience, and performance. Lifelong job security in the education sector, then, was replaced by individual competition. Indeed, a whole category of the precariously employed has emerged: "temporary teachers" (Niu, 2009). Moreover, Niu argues, the new system has precipitated a domestic brain-drain as teachers move from poor rural to more affluent urban centres. This has had flow-on effects that include a widening of the rural/urban gap in teacher quality.

In higher education, the administration of institutions spread across all three levels of government. The central government transferred the administrative control of upwards of 90 per cent of the nation's institutions of higher education to local authorities, retaining control of a top tier of research and postgraduate training institutions (Wu & Zheng, 2008). By 2016, the ratio of provincial to centrally funded higher education institutions had risen to 93 per cent (Yan, Mao, & Zha, 2016). More autonomy was granted to universities to set enrolment targets for their context. As in the West, higher education funding was diversified to include a blend of annualised government funding, plus public donations, teaching income, competitive research funding, and student tuition fees. In this context, space opened up for de facto privatisation of higher education institutions and the introduction of domestic joint degrees and ventures with overseas institutions. The result has been a proliferation of institutions and spiralling enrolment numbers that positioned China as the largest global marketplace and provider of higher education (Shan & Guo, 2016). This "massification" of higher education raises issues of course quality, credential inflation, oversupply of graduates, and the regulation of private and commercial service providers.

There are distinctive features of the push to marketisation: (1) The emergence of private or non-government schools; (2) the rise of non-state, private-sector funding sources; (3) the phenomenon of self-funded students, and (4) the creation of market-driven curricula (Chan & Mok, 2001). With reductions in state funding and the introduction of variable student tuition, institutions have focused on revenue-generating programs. Education, then, has transitioned from a state entitlement to a commodity for purchase, and schools and universities have moved towards business models of administration, staffing, and budgeting. This commodification includes continuing expansion of the flow of middle- and upper-class students to overseas secondary schools and universities, supported both through

Economy, Social Change, Education **33**

government scholarships and family economic capital. Moreover, curricular content has shifted to emphasise practical and applied knowledge for the labour market. In this way, the higher education and schooling sectors have undertaken a parallel shift towards marketisation and privatisation, and the commodification of knowledge under the auspices of a human capital model – the latter aligned with the larger shift in state political economy.

In the school sector, the financial burden on families has grown. National education law stipulates nine years of free compulsory education for all children 6–14 years of age. However, at the local level, schools are charging students a wide range of fees. Two other developments epitomise this moment in Chinese education: the emergence of private schools and of a growing shadow education market. Private schools depart from the socialist principle that education should be provided by the state in the collective interest. Although some are run by community associations, many private schools are for-profit businesses that market credentials, knowledge, and skill sets in response to demand (Kwong, 1997), specifically that of an emergent urban middle class.

Shadow education or private supplementary academic tutoring sits at the confluence of the public and private sectors in China (Zhang & Bray, 2017). This form of private education "shadows" the regular school curriculum: it is a grassroots edu-business where teachers and entrepreneurs supply fee-for-service private tuition to students whose families seek competitive advantage, distinction, and success in an examination-driven system. As such, shadow education is a form of micro-level neoliberalism, an informal service-based market ranging from individual teachers to storefront institutions. While the growth of this sub-field of educational exchange was initially unplanned and unregulated, its scale is huge: research with grade 3–9 Shanghai students documented participation rates of 81.5 per cent for mathematics and 76.8 per cent for English. There are several concerns about this system: that it will increase social disparities, in so far as participation requires surplus economic capital; that it amplifies obsessive study pressure on young people and their families, and that it creates the conditions for corruption and conflict of interest amongst teachers and schools.

The foregoing is but a brief overview of fundamental changes in the field of Chinese education. These changes in the field of education – their unplanned effects and idiosyncratic local variations notwithstanding – are enabled by and supportive of the larger shift in political economy. The educational field is now informed by models of state-regulated capitalism, individuated action, entrepreneurship, and economic self-interest, a private sector testing the limits of regulation in a dual economy, and fields of visible class differentiation and distinction (Kwong, 1997). On one level, the Chinese state has relinquished its long-standing model of centralised control and standardisation of schools and universities, delegating this across three levels of government and enabling a semi-autonomous private system and encouraging a variegated government system. In so doing, it has moved away from its socialist guarantee of free

34 Shibao Guo et al.

public education for all on the basis of merit, without consideration of cultural background, geographic location, or class position. This said, the state has maintained regulatory and ideological control oversight of these systems – through examination and credentialing systems, sponsorship of national and international comparative rankings, high-profile interventions in curriculum and textbook debates, regulation of the private and shadow sectors, and through publicised cases of the restriction of critique and dissent amongst academics. As elsewhere, this reconceptualisation of educational field as a market with competing and complementary institutions raises important questions about the nature of education as a public good and about the consequences of these reforms. While often lauded for successful production of human and economic capital, these "new neoliberal assemblages" (Liu, 2018) have set new grounds for material conditions of social and economic inequality.

Educational Inequality in China

The growing disparities in educational access and quality are significant contributors and indicators of social inequality and poverty in China (Davis & Wang, 2009; Hannum & Adams, 2009). Enrolment is lowest and drop-outs highest amongst the rural poor, ethnic minorities, girls, and migrants, while the urban middle class reaps disproportionate benefits from schooling (Postiglione, 2006). These patterns also reflect the geographic concentration of wealth and power in China's eastern cities. We here turn our attention from the overall formation of the field, to the differential and relative capital positions occupied by agents or institutions.

A major study of census data provides a useful longitudinal overview of inequalities in compulsory education. Parkhouse and Rong (2016) investigated variations in educational attainment based on gender, rural or urban residence, and ethnic minority status over a twenty-year period. From 2006 to 2016, unequal economic development has generated regional differences in attainment: while education attainment levels have increased overall, ethnic/linguistic minorities, females, and rural residents are disproportionately represented amongst those who are accruing less benefit from schooling. Studying the rural/urban achievement gap, Wang (2016) concluded that benefits of the market economy have flowed unequally to rural and urban students. There are identifiable differences in the development of skill and capability (i.e., cultural capital), funding and resources (i.e., economic capital), and basic educational access (i.e., social capital). High dropout and low graduation rates occur at both elementary and high school levels (Wang & Li, 2009), with notable gaps in mathematics, English, and Chinese language arts. The struggle of rural elementary schools in rural areas to provide more than basic curriculum content remains a significant national problem. The strategy of marketisation and privatisation, then, has not bridged the divide between education in rural and urban areas – nor between the

Economy, Social Change, Education **35**

Western/Northern China and the major population centres in the centre and on the coast, nor between ethnic cultural and linguistic minorities and the majority Han Chinese population.

The educational plight of the children who accompany their migrant worker parents to cities has also been of widespread concern. These children are sometimes known as "floating children" because of their precarious life conditions, especially with respect to schooling (Mu, 2018). China's education law stipulates nine years of compulsory education for all school-aged children. In practice, however, migrant children are often deprived of such opportunities (Chen et al., 2013; Lu, 2007; Zhu, 2001). Migrant children are much less likely to be enrolled in school compared to local children, and a significant proportion of these children experience delays due to migration. According to Liang and Chen (2007), the disruption is sharpest during the first year of relocation, with an enrolment rate of about 60 per cent. It takes five years for parity of enrolment to be attained. In earlier years, fees totalling up to thousands of *yuan* were a barrier to migrant children's entry into local public schools. Those fees have since been prohibited, but many of the children are still excluded because they are unable to furnish the required documents. Further, migrants often lack the requisite social and cultural capital to engage with public (state) schools (Mu & Hu, 2016), and public schools may be reluctant to accept migrant students on the grounds of concern that their performance will lower overall academic standards and ranking (Mu, 2018). Those migrant children who are "lucky" enough to navigate the entrance requirements, still often find themselves confronted by cultural and social stigmatisation and discrimination because of their migrant status, outdated clothing, and regional accents (Li et al., 2010; Mu & Jia, 2016). As a result, many of these children suffer from social isolation, low self-esteem, and social withdrawal.

For those migrant children for whom public schools are neither accessible nor affordable, the option has been entry into unlicensed, under-funded, and inadequately staffed schools specifically created for migrant students (Goodburn, 2016; Lai et al., 2012; Woronov, 2004). In 2013, a study by Lai and colleagues indicated that there were 230 of these migrant schools in Beijing. Some of the proprietors of these schools were altruistically driven to provide migrant children with affordable education, but others were motivated either fully or partially by profit. Many are shanty schools located in makeshift sheds; most are unsafe and overcrowded, with poor lighting and air quality (Kwong, 2004; Zhu, 2001). Pedagogical standards are typically low and the quality of teaching poor due to a lack of qualified teachers, adequate equipment and books, and other essential teaching materials. Teachers in migrant schools are paid less, live in inferior housing, and face intensive workloads (Guo, 2012). To survive economically, some of these teachers are driven to tutor outside of school hours or to take on a second job. Crucially, migrant schools do not enjoy government recognition or support; the problem is that these schools are seen to encroach on government jurisdiction (Li et al., 2010). The 2010 EFA *Global*

Monitoring Report recognises the seriousness of the educational situation of migrant children; it claims that "migrant children are among the most educationally marginalised in China" (UNESCO, 2010, p. 177).

The transition from higher education to work is a key juncture for the analysis of inequitable outcomes. Lu and Zong (2016) used Bourdieusian concepts to look at the implications of socio-economic status (SES) in university graduates' education–work transitions. The researchers compared the experiences of low SES students with those of middle- and upper-class students. Their findings indicate that a university degree may now be important, if not necessary, but is not sufficient in and of itself for securing a job. Family background, in the form of social and cultural capital, indirectly influences students' employment outcomes. Moreover, there is a persistent employment gap in this regard between female and male students. Female students of poor rural backgrounds may confront a double-disadvantage. They have fewer educational and employment opportunities than men. This disadvantage is compounded because their family background does not facilitate acquisition of the social and cultural capital required for upward mobility. Other recent empirical research addresses the effects of family backgrounds on educational attainment, career placement at job entry, and career mobility outcomes. Family backgrounds, especially paternal educational status, strongly affected the educational attainment of a child. The higher the father's education level, the greater the child's opportunity to attain a higher level of education. Furthermore, father's political status (e.g., Communist Party membership, status in the managerial elite) also strongly affects a child's educational attainment, especially in the most recent period of the reform era.

There is, then, an extensive body of empirical work on stratified and differentiated educational outcomes in Chinese education. These are a baseline from which sociological inquiry can proceed. Whether these are the effects of marketisation per se, or any specific reform, is, of course, difficult to demonstrate empirically – particularly given the complex picture of interlocking reforms and local implementation, planned and unplanned. Based on an aggregate view of the current system, many of the classical patterns and effects of "cultural and economic reproduction in education" described by Bourdieu and Passeron (1990) are relevant templates for assembling a larger sociological picture of an overall logic of practice. Chinese educational inequality is reflective of the acknowledged patterns across China since Reform and Opening-Up: that is, along classical dividing lines of social class, gender, urban/rural location, minority/majority culture and language, and, unique to this situation, migrant/resident status communities in urban settings. This would entail an analysis of cultural capital as an intersectional phenomenon, and the documentation of who succeeds and fails; how; through what educational logic, practices, and capital exchanges; with what longitudinal social, economic, and cultural consequences, as they proceed across other social fields of work and consumption, popular culture, family and community life, in China and globally.

Economy, Social Change, Education **37**

Towards a Critical Sociology of Chinese Education

Since the Reform and Opening-up Policy in 1978, China has focused on economic development. The logic of practice of the field of education has also been reframed and redefined in relation to a new economic rationalism which oscillates between the normative logic of market capitalism and a public discourse of socialist egalitarianism. This is part of the reshaping of political economy through marketisation, privatisation, and local devolution of governance – within the regulatory field of the strong state. This decentralisation process, further, highlights the highly variable local and regional uptakes of policy, where locally constituted relations mediate and shape what is made to count as capital, as field and, indeed, as policy – often in unplanned, unpredictable, and idiosyncratic ways. The question for a sociology of education is how we might analyse these locally grounded changes in the dynamics of field and their social, cultural, and economic consequences. To do so, Bourdieu draws attention to: "three necessary and internally connected moments" (Bourdieu & Wacquant, 1992, p.104): First, the position of the field under examination vis-à-vis the field of power; second, the objective structure of relations and positions between competing agents and institutions within the field, and third, the systems of dispositions acquired by internalising the objective social and economic positions.

To apply the model to the educational field in China, then, would require: first, an analysis of the actions of the state as shaping and disciplining relations of a meta-field of power that informs education and other adjacent and overlapping institutional fields; second, an analysis of the quotidian social and material relations of exchange between human subjects in schools, universities, and other educational institutions, and third, the study of the new Chinese habitus – of its educational formation and social, cultural, and economic realisation. These could be realised variously through an amalgam of conventional approaches and methodologies, including: Policy studies, discourse, documentary and historical analysis; case studies of institutions, communities, and individuals, and quantitative studies of specific populations and cohorts.

In terms of the meta-field of the state, this would entail an analysis of the incremental policy changes by central, provincial, and municipal governments, and how these are interpreted and translated in specific institutional sites, with what larger-scale patterns of demographic, cultural, and social effects and outcomes. A contrastive analysis of normative logic and narratives of policy would view such policies as attempts to form and shape, constrain and direct the fields of education. Educational policies are never stand-alone phenomena, but typically sit in complementary and contradictory relationships with adjacent social and economic policies that attempt to establish and regulate flows of capital (Luke, 2018). In the case of China, educational provision is influenced by and interacts with material conditions in housing and urban migration, health and welfare, policies governing

38 Shibao Guo et al.

the status and entitlements of cultural and linguistic minorities, and, to take a current example, family planning and the aftermath of the one-child policy (changed to a two-children policy in 2016). Finally, urban environmental pollution now forms a major challenge and practical issues for families, children, and schools. Taken together, the composite of educational and affiliated policies are attempts by the state to shape the institutional sub-fields of education: ranging from families and childcare, to schooling and to higher education. This work, especially at the policy analytic level, is well underway.

The analysis of capital exchange and the formation of the habitus in institutional fields of education necessarily varies by scale: these range from population/census studies of educational outcomes cited here, to local ethnographies, case studies, and micro-sociological studies of school reform and classroom interaction. The aim of these studies would be to analyse the relations of exchange between families, communities, and schools, and, significantly, between students and teachers in face-to-face classroom exchange. There is a strong emergent corpus of work that focuses on school and system reform at the local level, describing administrators and teachers, students and families' responses to local reform as they engage with both long-standing, residual practices and beliefs, and participate in new systems of exchange in marketised schools and universities.

However, documentation of (mis)recognition, exchange, and conversion of capital, will require the close examination of everyday life in schools and classrooms, where students and teachers shape and experience an enacted curriculum. It is through "pedagogic action" (Bourdieu & Passeron, 1990) that the system is bidding to shape, position, and define a particular kind of knowing, working, consuming, and acting human subject: a normative version of the educated Chinese, with specific knowledges, skills, and competences for globalised, competitive economies and, indeed, for orderly and rule-governed civic and social participation. Studies of schooling, further, would need to be augmented by studies of youth digital culture, gaming, and online exchanges, which increasingly are influencing and shaping middle-class childhood. Taken together, this is the third step in such a critical sociological agenda, policy intents and grand models aside: to document and describe the emergence of a new Chinese *Homo economicus/educatus*, and, indeed, the dispositions of its *Others* who remain at the margins of the system.

Part of the question here is the relationship of education as a field of cultural production and a system of representation – and the degrees and ways in which that field overlaps, reproduces, or reflects the *doxa* of the broader market economy. The first task at hand is well represented in this volume: case studies of cultural and economic reproduction in Chinese education. The combination of a traditional meritocratic ethos, a centralised examination system, and recent curriculum reforms frame up the dual policy challenges facing Chinese education: an "attraction function" that attempts to shape and mobilise human capital to support the continued economic growth and expansion, and an "ameliorative

Economy, Social Change, Education **39**

function" (Luke, 2018, p. 149) whereby the system attempts to compensate for the effects of the unequal spread and distribution of cultural, social, and economic capital. Sociological analysis then, necessarily, would document the education of those children and youth from poor, rural, and minority communities, including a specific focus on left-behind and floating children and on those from ethnic minority communities. This said, a parallel focus on the emergent educated middle class (Yochim, 2016) and the transnationally educated elite is also of value in terms of identifying the kinds of habitus and capital exchange that are made to count in the new Chinese and global economic and political order.

This chapter has outlined China's journey from a centrally planned to a market economy, from centralised to decentralised decision making, from state ownership to privatisation. This is a shift from politicisation of the economic state to full economicisation or commercialisation of Chinese society. Initially, the depoliticised Chinese state focused almost exclusively on the economy, with a stated mission to boost productivity, efficiency, and global competitiveness. Priority was thereby accorded to efficiency, effectiveness, and economy over fairness, justice, and equality. Hence, the market economy has produced not only economic growth but also glaring inequality. China is converging toward a pattern of inequality in which "the returns to capital exceed those to labour" (Davis & Wang, 2009, p.16), with the practices and institutions of socialism in recession.

Many Western political observers and economists prognosticated an incremental movement towards liberal governance affiliated with market capitalism. The assumption was that the economic base of a version of market capitalism would generate concomitant effects in adjacent and overlapping social fields of education, cultural production, and, ultimately, have a reflexive effect on state formation and governance. Such a linear, causal narrative has not transpired. China has achieved levels of economic growth and modernisation at an unprecedented rate and scale. However, the country faces many challenges, including rising social inequality, cultural divide and conflict, the rural–urban divide, regional disparity, environmental degradation, declining health and education conditions for many, and polarisation between rich and poor. China is asserting its economic and technological, political and cultural power globally, but it has also become one of the world's most unequal societies. It is this inequality in the context of growth and modernisation that is the core challenge of a critical, reflexive sociology of Chinese education.

Notes

1 GDP can be compared by using market rates (nominal) or adjusting for national differences in prices (purchasing power parity or PPP) (*Statistics Times*, 2015a, 2015b).

2 "Human capital" denotes resources for productivity such as knowledge and worker health (Becker, 2002); "cultural capital" was developed in explicit opposition to the orthodox economic assumptions of that concept (see Bourdieu, 2005, p. 9).

3 In 2016, the State Council redefined left-behind children as those below the age of 16 who have both parents working in a city or one parent working in a city while the other parent has no caregiving/guardianship competence. This new definition *expectedly* drops the population of left-behind children down to 9 million.

4 For Bourdieu, the notion of "underclass" was part of the *doxa* of neoliberal poverty management by which the particularities of US society were being exported and imposed, or imported and assumed, from "Berlin to Beijing and from Milan to Mexico" (Bourdieu & Wacquant, 2005, p. 178).

References

Becker, G.S. (2002). The age of human capital. In H. Lauder, P. Brown, J. Dillabough & A.H. Halsey (Eds.), *Education, globalization and social change* (pp. 292–294). Oxford: Oxford University Press.

Benjamin, D., Brandt, L., Giles, J., & Wang, S. (2008). Income inequality during China's economic transition. In L. Brandt & T.G. Rawski (Eds.), *China's great economic transformation* (pp. 729–775). New York: Cambridge University Press.

Bourdieu, P. (1998). *Acts of resistance*. (R. Nice, Trans.). New York: New Press.

Bourdieu, P. (2005). *The social structures of the economy* (C. Turner, Trans.). Cambridge: Polity.

Bourdieu, P., & Passeron, J. C. (1990). *Reproduction in education, culture and society*, 2nd Ed. (R. Nice, Trans.). London: Sage.

Bourdieu, P., & Wacquant, L.J.D. (1992). *An invitation to reflexive sociology*. Cambridge: Polity Press.

Bourdieu, P., & Wacquant, L.J.D. (2005). The cunning of imperial reason. In L. Wacquant (Ed.), *Bourdieu and democratic politics* (pp. 178–198). Cambridge: Polity.

Brandt, L., & Rawski, T.G. (2008). China's great economic transformation. In L. Brandt & T.G. Rawski (Eds.), *China's great economic transformation* (pp. 1–26). New York: Cambridge University Press.

Brandt, L., Rawski, T.G., & Sutton, J. (2008). China's industrial development. In L. Brandt & T.G. Rawski (Eds.), *China's great economic transformation* (pp. 569–632). New York: Cambridge University Press.

Branstetter, L., & Lardy, N. (2008). China's embrace of globalization. In L. Brandt & T.G. Rawski (Eds.), *China's great economic transformation* (pp. 633–682). New York: Cambridge University Press.

Business Times (2017). China's urbanization rate reaches 58.5% by end of 2017: Xinhua (February 5). Accessed 12 May 2018, www.businesstimes.com.sg/government-economy/chinas-urbanisation-rate-reaches-585-by-end-of-2017-xinhua

Cai, Y., & Cheng, Y. (2014). Pension reform in China: Challenges and opportunities. *Journal of Economic Surveys*, 28(4), 636–651.

Chan, D., & Mok, K.H. (2001). Educational reforms and coping strategies under the tidal wave of marketization: A comparative study of Hong Kong and the mainland. *Comparative Education*, 37(1), 21–41.

Chen, S. (2002). Economic reform and social change in China: Past, present, and future of the economic state. *International Journal of Politics, Culture, and Society*, 15(4), 569–589.

Economy, Social Change, Education **41**

Chen, S., Adams, J., Qu, Z., Wang, X., & Chen, L. (2013). Parental migration and children's academic engagement: The case of China. *International Review of Education, 59*(6), 693–722.

Davis, D., & Wang, F. (2009). Poverty and wealth in postsocialist China: An overview. In D. Davis & W. Feng (Eds.), *Creating wealth and poverty in postsocialist China* (pp. 3–19). Stanford, CA: Stanford University Press.

Dirlik, A. (1989). Postsocialism? Reflections on socialism with Chinese characteristics. In A. Dirlik & M. Meisner (Eds.), *Marxism and the Chinese experience: Issues in contemporary Chinese socialism* (pp. 361–384). New York: M. E. Sharpe.

Fan, S., & Pardey, P.G. (1997). Research, productivity, and output growth in Chinese agriculture. *Journal of Development Economics, 53*, 115–137.

Fishman, T. (2005). *China, Inc: How the rise of the next superpower challenges America and the world*. New York: Scribner.

Gao, J., Qian, J., Tang, S., Eriksson, B., & Blas, E. (2002). Health equity in transition from planned to market economy in China. *Health Policy and Planning, 17*(1), 20–29.

Goodburn, C. (2016). Educating migrant children: The effects of rural-urban migration on access to primary education. In S. Guo & Y. Guo (Eds.), *Spotlight on China: Changes in education under China's market economy* (pp. 365–380). Rotterdam, The Netherlands: Sense.

Guo, S. (2012). Globalization, market economy and social inequality in China: Exploring the experience of migrant teachers. *Canadian and International Education, 41*(2), 8–27.

Guo, S., & Guo, Y. (Eds.) (2016). *Spotlight on China: Changes in education under China's market economy*. Rotterdam, The Netherlands: Sense.

Guo, S., Guo, Y., Beckett, G., Li, Q., & Guo, L. (2013). Changes in Chinese education under globalisation and market economy: Emerging issues and debates. *COMPARE: A Journal of Comparative and International Education, 43*(2), 144–164.

Guo, S., & Zhang, J. (2010). Language, work and learning: Exploring the urban experience of ethnic migrant workers in China. *Diaspora, Indigenous, and Minority Education, 3*(4), 47–63.

Gustafsson, B., Li, S., & Sicular, T. (2008). Inequality and public policy in China: Issues and trends. In B. Gustafsson, L. Shi, & T. Sicular (Eds.), *Inequality and public policy in China* (pp. 1–34). Cambridge: Cambridge University Press.

Han, C., & Whyte, M.K. (2009). The social contours of distributive justice feelings in contemporary China. In D. Davis & W. Feng (Eds.), *Creating wealth and poverty in postsocialist China* (pp. 193–212). Stanford, CA: Stanford University Press.

Han, J., Liu, R., & Zhang, J. (2012). Globalization and wage inequality: Evidence from urban China. *Journal of International Economics, 87*(2), 288–297.

Hannum, E., & Adams, J. (2009). Beyond cost: Rural perspectives on barriers to education. In D. Davis & W. Feng (Eds.), *Creating wealth and poverty in postsocialist China* (pp. 156–171). Stanford, CA: Stanford University Press.

Harvey, D. (2005). *A brief history of neoliberalism*. Oxford, UK: Oxford University Press.

Hawkins, J.N. (2000). Centralization, decentralization, recentralization: Educational reform in China. *Journal of Educational Administration, 38*(5), 442–454.

Huang, Y. (2008). *Capitalism with Chinese characteristics: Entrepreneurship and the state*. Cambridge: Cambridge University Press.

Kwong, J. (1997). The reemergence of private schools in socialist China. *Comparative Education Review, 41*(3), 244–259.

Kwong, J. (2004). Educating migrant children: Negotiations between the state and civil society. *The China Quarterly, 180*, 1073–1088.

Lai, F., Liu, C., Luo, R., Zhang, L., Ma, X., Bai, Y., Sharbono, B., & Rozelle, S. (2012). *Private migrant schools or rural/urban public schools: Where should China educate its migrant children?* Stanford REAP Working Paper #224. Stanford, CA: Stanford University.

Li, X., Zhang, L., Fang, X., Stanton, S., Xiong, Q, Lin, D., & Mathur, A. (2010). Schooling of migrant children in China: Perspectives of school teachers. *Vulnerable Children and Youth Studies, 5*(1), 79–87.

Liang, Z., & Chen, Y.P. (2007). The educational consequences of migration for children in China. *Social Science Research, 36*(1), 28–47.

Lim, L., & Apple, M.W. (Eds.) (2016). *The strong state and curriculum reform in Asia*. New York: Routledge.

Liu, S. (2018). Neoliberal global assemblages: The emergence of "public" international high-school curriculum programs in China. *Curriculum Inquiry, 48*, 203–219.

Lu, M. & Xia, Y. (2016). *Migration in the People's Republic of China*. ADBI Working Paper Series, No. 593. Tokyo: Asian Development Bank Institute. Accessed 13 May 2018 www.adb.org/sites/default/files/publication/191876/adbi-wp593.pdf.

Lu, Y. (2007). Educational status of temporary migrant children in China: Determinants and regional variations. *Asian and Pacific Migration Journal, 16*(1), 29–55.

Lu, Y., & Zong, L. (2016). Social inequality in postgraduate transition: A case study of university students in western China. In S. Guo & Y. Guo (Eds.), *Spotlight on China: Changes in education under China's market economy* (pp. 267–289). Rotterdam, The Netherlands: Sense.

Luke, A. (2018). *Educational policy, narrative and discourse*. London: Routledge.

Ma, L. (2002). Urban transformation in China, 1949–2000: A review and research agenda. *Environment and Planning A, 34*, 1545–1569.

Mu, G.M. (2018). *Building resilience of floating children and left-behind children in China: Power, politics, participation, and education*. London: Routledge.

Mu, G.M., & Hu, Y. (2016). *Living with vulnerabilities and opportunities in a migration context: Floating children and left-behind children in China*. Rotterdam, The Netherlands: Sense.

Mu, G.M., & Jia, N. (2016). Rural dispositions of floating children within the field of Beijing schools: Can disadvantaged rural habitus turn into recognised cultural capital? *British Journal of Sociology of Education, 37*(3), 408–426.

Niu, Z. (2009). Reforms on teachers' employment system and children's rights to education in China. *International Journal of Educational Management, 23*(1), 7–18.

Ong, L. H. (2014). State-led urbanization in China: Skyscrapers, land revenue and "concentrated villages". *The China Quarterly, 217*, 162–179.

Painter, M., & Mok, K.H. (2008). Reasserting the public in public service delivery: The de-privatization and de-marketization of education in China. *Policy and Society, 27*(2), 137–150.

Parkhouse, H., & Rong, X.L. (2016). Inequalities in China's compulsory education: Progress, inadequacies, and recommendations. In S. Guo & Y. Guo (Eds.), *Spotlight on China: Changes in education under China's market economy* (pp. 311–327). Rotterdam, The Netherlands: Sense.

Peck, J., & Zhang, J. (2013). A variety of capitalism with Chinese characteristics. *Journal of Economic Geography, 13*(3), 357–396.

Postiglione, G.A. (Ed.) (2006). *Education and social change in China: Inequality in a market economy*. Armonk, NY: M.E. Sharpe.

Shan, H., & Guo, S. (2016). Massification of Chinese higher education: Opportunities and challenges in a globalizing context. In S. Guo & Y. Guo (Eds.), *Spotlight on China: Changes in education under China's market economy* (pp. 215–229). Rotterdam, The Netherlands: Sense.

Solinger, D. (2008). The political implications of China's social future: Complacency, scorn, and the forlorn. In L. Cheng (Ed.), *China's changing political landscape: Prospects for democracy* (pp. 251–266). Washington, DC: Brookings Institution.

Statistics Times (2015a). List of countries by GDP (PPP) per capita. Accessed 10 May 2018 http://statisticstimes.com/economy/countries-by-gdp-capita-ppp.php

Statistics Times (2015b). World GDP (nominal) ranking. Accessed 10 May 2018 http://statisticstimes.com/economy/world-gdp-ranking-ppp.php

Statistics Times (2015c). World GDP (nominal) per capital ranking. Accessed 10 May 2018 http://statisticstimes.com/economy/world-gdp-capita-ranking.php

Statistics Times (2015d). World GDP (PPP) ranking. Accessed 10 May 2018 http://statisticstimes.com/economy/world-gdp-ranking-ppp.php

Sutherland, D., & Yao, S. (2011). Income inequality in China over 30 years of reforms. *Cambridge Journal of Regions, Economy and Society, 4*(1), 91–105.

Sutter, R. G. (2012). *Chinese foreign relations: Power and policy since the cold war.* Lanham, MD: Rowman & Littlefield.

The World Bank (2018a). The World Bank in China. China-at-a-glance (Overview). Accessed 10 May 2018 www.worldbank.org/en/country/china.

The World Bank. (2018b). Promoting a more inclusive and sustainable development in China. Accessed 10 May 2018 www.worldbank.org/en/news/press-release/2018/02/22/promoting-a-more-inclusive-and-sustainable-development-for-china).

The World Bank and the Development Research Center of the State Council, P.R. China. (2013). *China 2030: Building a modern, harmonious, and creative society.* Washington, DC: The World Bank and the Development Research Center of the State Council, P.R. China. Accessed 10 May 2018 www.worldbank.org/content/dam/Worldbank/document/China-2030-complete.pdf.

UNESCO. (2010). *EFA global monitoring report 2010: Reaching the marginalized.* Paris: UNESCO.

Wang, J., & Li, Y. (2009). Research on the teaching quality of compulsory education in China's west rural schools. *Frontiers of Education in China, 4*(1), 66–93.

Wang, L. (2016). Widening urban rural divides: Examining social exclusion and education inequality in Chinese schools. In S. Guo & Y. Guo (Eds.), *Spotlight on China: Changes in education under China's market economy* (pp. 329–243). Rotterdam, The Netherlands: Sense.

Woronov, T.E. (2004). In the eye of the chicken: Hierarchy and marginality among Beijing's migrant schoolchildren. *Ethnography, 5*(3), 289–313.

Wu, B., & Zheng, Y. (2008). *Expansion of higher education in China: Challenges and implications.* (Briefing Series – Issue 36). Nottingham: China Policy Institute, University of Nottingham.

Yan, F., Mao, D., & Zha, Q. (2016). Institutional transformation and aggregate expansion of Chinese higher education system. In S. Guo & Y. Guo (Eds.), *Spotlight on China: Changes in education under China's market economy* (pp. 91–213). Rotterdam, The Netherlands: Sense.

Yang, J. (2007). The future of China's socialist market economy. *Nature, Society, and Thought, 20*(1), 61–79.

Yochim, L. (2016). Navigating the aspirational city: Processes of accumulation in China's socialist market economy. In S. Guo & Y. Guo (Eds.), *Spotlight on China: Changes in education under China's market economy* (pp. 329–347). Rotterdam, The Netherlands: Sense.

Yusuf, S., & Nabeshima, K. (2008). Optimizing urban development. In S. Yusuf & T. Saich (Eds.), *China urbanizes: Consequences, strategies, and policies* (pp. 1–40). Washington, DC: The World Bank.

Zhang, L. (2005). Migrant enclaves and impacts of redevelopment policy in Chinese cities. In L. Ma & F. Wu (Eds.), *Restructuring the Chinese city: Changing society, economy and space* (pp. 243–259). London: Routledge.

Zhang, L. (2008). Conceptualizing China's urbanization under reforms. *Habitat International, 32*(4), 452–470.

Zhang, L., Dai, R., & Yu, K. (2016). Chinese higher education since 1977: Possibilities, challenges and tensions. In S. Guo & Y. Guo (Eds.), *Spotlight on China: Changes in education under China's market economy* (pp. 173–189). Rotterdam, The Netherlands: Sense.

Zhang, W., & Bray, M. (2017). Micro-neoliberalism in China: Public-private interactions at the confluence of mainstream and shadow education. *Journal of Education Policy, 32* (1), 63–81. 10.1080/02680939.2016.1219769.

Zhu, M. (2001). The education problems of migrant children in Shanghai. *Child Welfare League of America, 80*(5), 563–569.

Zhuang, J. (2007). China's socialist market economy and its difference from neoliberalism. *Nature, Society, and Thought, 20*(1), 355–361.

3

BOURDIEU'S SOCIOLOGICAL THINKING AND EDUCATIONAL RESEARCH IN MAINLAND CHINA

Zhongying Shi and Chunying Li

When Bourdieu's sociology was introduced to mainland China in the late 1970s, it sparked extensive interest and discussion in the Chinese literary world. Chinese literary researchers were most interested in Bourdieu's exposition of the relationship between literary taste and social class (Xu, 2003). Two decades later, when the issue of equity became the priority of national policy and public debate, Bourdieu's writings and theories began to have increasing impact on Chinese education. His analytical framework and sociological perspective on education have been widely used in the discussion of numerous educational issues. There is no doubt that Bourdieu's sociology has become one of the most important Western influences on Chinese educational research in the twenty-first century. The review and analysis undertaken here documents the spread of Bourdieu's sociology in mainland China, examines the development of Chinese educational theory and practice in the past twenty years, and analyses Chinese educational responses to Bourdieu's sociological theories.

An Overview of Bourdieu's Sociological Theories and Educational Arguments

Pierre Bourdieu (1930–2002) is a contemporary French thinker with an international influence. He was a prolific author whose publications straddled many research areas including anthropology, sociology, education, history, politics, philosophy, aesthetics, literature, and linguistics. Chinese scholars commonly regard Bourdieu as one of the three most distinguished contemporary European sociologists, together with Anthony Giddens in England and Jürgen Habermas in Germany.

In Bourdieu's early studies and research, the structuralism represented by Claude Levi-Strauss stood against the existentialism represented by Jean-Paul Sartre in French academia. The former emphasised the power of structure, while the latter stressed individual uniqueness. To grapple with the either/or dilemma, Bourdieu used Marxism and phenomenology as tools and proposed a series of unique concepts and propositions, hoping to break the binary thinking brought about by the opposition of structuralism and existentialism (Li, 2003). From an academic historical point of view, Bourdieu's career developed through three stages. The first is structuralism-informed anthropology. In this stage, Bourdieu engaged in anthropological studies of Algerian peasants' lives using a quasi-structuralist approach. The second is the development of a theory of practice. In this stage, Bourdieu went beyond structuralism and emphasised the logic of practice. The last is a theory of symbolic power and reflexive sociology. In this stage, Bourdieu mainly focused on the relationship between language and power, and the connection between theory of practice and reflexive sociology. The last is also the stage through which Bourdieu turned reflexive and empirical research on the academic fields where he was situated (Pang & Ding, 2001). In the second and third stages, Bourdieu tried to revise the structuralist tendency in his early thought and responded to the alleged determinism of his theory. He did this through sociological concepts such as field, habitus, and practice, especially the concept of habitus. He replied to the query of whether habitus has the decisive effect on individual agents,

> habitus is not the fate that people read into it. Being the product of history, it is an open system of dispositions that is constantly subjected to experiences, and therefore constantly affected by them in a way that either reinforces or modifies its structure. It is durable but not eternal!
>
> *(Bourdieu & Wacquant, 1992, p. 133)*

Like other French thinkers, such as Émile Durkheim and Michel Foucault, while studying a wide range of social issues, Bourdieu was also concerned with education. This might be attributed to his early educational experience. Upon his admission to the *École Normale Superieure*, Bourdieu recognised the structural gap between his habitus and the habitus demanded in the French academic field in the 1950s. The ensuing Algerian War of Liberation prompted him to question the privileges of the scholars who felt superior to, and detached from, research subjects. These early experiences of education and research led him to shift from philosophical speculation to detailed fieldwork and empirical research. He thus conducted a comprehensive study of the French school system and authored numerous books and articles to debate the role of education in both social and cultural reproduction.

Bourdieu's masterpieces include *Les Héritiers: Les Etudiants et la Culture* (1964), *La Reproduction: Éléments pour une théorie du système d'enseignemen* (1970), *and*

La Noblesse d'État: Grandes écoles et esprit de corps (1989). *Les Héritiers: Les Etudiants et la Culture* was translated into Chinese by Xing Kechao in 2002. The book was built on the empirical work of Bourdieu and the research team at the *Centre de Sociologie Européenne*. It unveiled the social inequity resulting from the intersectionality of class and education. It criticised using traditional talent theory to explain educational and social inequity. *Éléments pour une théorie du système d'enseignemen* was translated and published in the same year (2002). In this book, Bourdieu argued that the school system was only a seemingly fair institution, purporting to remove the privileged class. In fact, school has succeeded more than ever in covering up its functions to preserve class relations. Compared with *Les Héritiers, La Reproduction* more systematically explained the secret of cultural reproduction based on the theory of cultural capital. *La Noblesse d'État. Grandes écoles et esprit de corps* was translated by Yang Yaping in 2004. In this book, Bourdieu elaborated on the specific tactics of cultural reproduction and matured his theoretical system of cultural capital. Research reported in this book was concerned with the fields of prestigious university and power, as well as the changes in these two fields. The three books mentioned above have made dramatic contributions to educational research. On the one hand, they indicate that educational research is the starting point and core of Bourdieu's sociological thoughts to reveal the mechanism of social practice. On the other hand, they provide a powerful theoretical tool and research paradigm to reflect on modern educational problems.

Bibliometric Analysis of Bourdieu's Influence on Chinese Educational Research

To provide an overview of the spread of Bourdieu's sociological theories in Chinese educational research over the past four decades, we searched the keyword "Bourdieu" in the published educational studies using China's largest academic database – the China National Knowledge Infrastructure (CNKI). By 2017, the keyword "Bourdieu" had appeared in 304 articles about Chinese education. A preliminary analysis indicates that "field" and "cultural capital" are two keywords appearing most frequently within the obtained literature. This suggests that Bourdieu's cultural capital theory is widely discussed by Chinese scholars. We then searched keywords "cultural capital" and "field" in Chinese educational studies included in the CNKI. We found 1,027 studies published between 1979 and 2017. The quantity of publications by year is shown in Figure 3.1.

Preliminary review of the published studies over the decades suggests that the translation and use of Bourdieu in Chinese educational research can be divided into three stages: initial introduction (1979–2001), broad exploration (2002–09), and in-depth discussion (2010–17). In 1979, Xia Xiaochuan translated the article "Pierre Bourdieu: The Cultural Transmission of Social

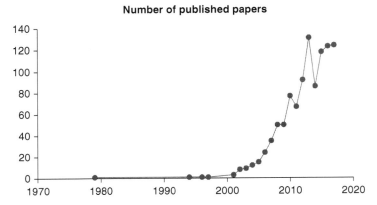

FIGURE 3.1 Quantity of Bourdieusian Chinese educational studies by year (1979–2017)

Inequality" written by David Swartz in the *Harvard Educational Review* (1977, 47(4), pp. 545–555), and published the translated piece in the Chinese journal of 外国教育资料. The article briefly introduced Bourdieu's *La Reproduction*, and elaborated and evaluated Bourdieu's definition of cultural capital and the relationship of reproduction between higher education system and social class structure (Swartz, 1977). To the best of our knowledge and belief, this translated work is the first time that Bourdieu's sociology was introduced to educational academia in mainland China. The next 20 years, however, saw little introduction of Bourdieu to Chinese educational academia, with only a handful of exceptions. For example, in 1991, Fan Guorui translated "Movements of Thought in Modern Education" written by the American educational philosopher, George Kneller. The article introduced Bourdieu's sociological thinking and discussed the relations between cultural capital/linguistic capital and student academic performance (Kneller, 1984). In general, Chinese educational scholars began to read Bourdieu between 1979 and 1991. Yet few articles were published, with none in most years. The dearth of Chinese publications on Bourdieu during these years may be attributed to the exclusive priority given to economic growth, rather than inequality or inequity. At that time, the primary goal of national policy was to stimulate and promote economic growth rather than address the problems of inequality brought about by this economic growth.

The above situation has changed since 2002, the year of Bourdieu's death. Since then, Chinese academia started to pay increasing attention to Bourdieu's works that have been translated and publications on Bourdieusian educational studies began to appear more frequently. The years that follow saw an exponential increase. The reason for this is that Chinese policies started to pay close attention to equity. Since 1978, the Reform and Opening-Up Policy implemented in mainland China has achieved remarkable and consistent economic outcomes. By 2000, China had attained sixth place in the world in terms of

Bourdieu in Chinese Educational Research **49**

gross domestic product. However, the post-Reform and Opening-Up era has also witnessed a widening income gap. According to data released by the National Bureau of Statistics of China, the Gini coefficient of China in 2000 crossed the cordon line of 0.4 and has remained at a high level ever since. Against this backdrop, the Chinese government, on the one hand, insistently placed economic development as its priority; on the other hand, it began to respond to social inequality, educational inequality included. Accordingly, studies on educational equality issues began to multiply. Bourdieu's sociological theories came to the fore due to its analytical power in grappling with the roots and mechanisms of educational inequity in particular, and social inequity in general.

In 2010, the Chinese government released the *"Outline of the National Medium and Long-term Education Reform and Development Plan (2010–20)"* to guide the reform and development of education. The Outline proposed that educational equity is the important foundation of social equity and defined it as the basis for national policy making in education. The Outline also points out that the basic requirement of educational equity is to ensure equal rights to education of all citizens. Of equivalent importance is the requirement to promote the balanced development of compulsory education and to support disadvantaged groups. The fundamental approach to closing educational gaps is allocation of educational resources, with priority given to rural, remote, impoverished areas and ethnic minority regions. The Outline further sparked research interest in educational equity. Relatedly, the use of Bourdieu became more visible than ever in Chinese educational research. Compared with the first stage where Bourdieu was only sporadically introduced and translated, and the second stage where the use of Bourdieu was still superficial, the third stage has seen numerous articles published to elaborate on Bourdieu's sociological thoughts and employ them in educational practice. In this stage, Chinese researchers have widely drawn on field, cultural capital, and the logic of practice to grapple with educational problems. Core topics under discussion include conflictive roles and interests in education, urban-rural educational disparity, the schooling of "floating" children, just to name a few – all of which are consistent with the national education policy foci.

It is noticeable that some scholars started to reflect on the limitations of Bourdieu's sociological theories. For example, Liu Luhu argued, "Although the theory of cultural capital constructs a detailed pathway to reproduction through education and guides a large amount of empirical research, cultural capital theory, at both logic and empirical levels, faces insurmountable challenges" (Liu, 2014, pp. 16–18). In Liu Luhu's opinion, the challenges and dilemmas encountered by Bourdieu's cultural capital theory result from not only the shortcomings of the concept of habitus, but also the propositions which involve intergenerational transmission of family cultural capital, cultural dominance of the middle class in schooling, and the facilitation of cultural reproduction through schooling. These propositions have strong analytical power in explaining reproduction through education, but less so when explaining social mobility achieved through education. From Liu's viewpoint, Chinese educational researchers have not yet critically engaged in Bourdieu's cultural capital theory and largely overlooked the explanation of social mobility. In an era when China is undertaking social changes, sometimes quite controversial ones, much scholarly attention is drawn to political and economic factors, rather than education. Liu's critique shows that education researchers in mainland China began to take a more serious approach to Bourdieu's sociological thinking and a more critical perspective of Bourdieu's analytical power in the face of Chinese educational problems.

In addition to the three stages of using Bourdieu in Chinese educational research, bibliometric analysis nets the keywords and their connections within Bourdieusian Chinese educational studies (see Figure 3.2). Such analysis helps to understand the foci of using Bourdieu in Chinese educational research.

Among the 1,027 retrieved studies, "cultural capital" appears 292 times and is the most frequently used of Bourdieu's concepts in Chinese educational research. "Field" appears 275 times, and "habitus" appears 66 times. These three concepts are not only the core concepts of Bourdieu's sociology, but also the three concepts that have the greatest impact on the study of education. They are also used in connection with other key terms in Chinese education, such as "social capital", "college students", "educational equity", "higher education", "cultural reproduction", "teachers", and "social stratification". The

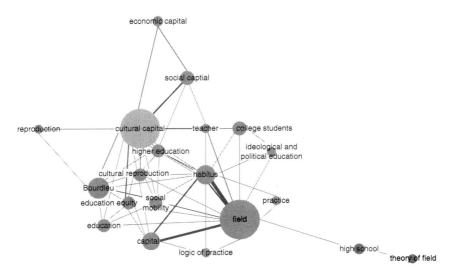

FIGURE 3.2 Network of Bourdieu's key concepts and Chinese educational studies (1979–2017)

Bourdieu in Chinese Educational Research **51**

connections between Bourdieu and Chinese educational key terms constitute a complex network of the use of Bourdieu in Chinese education.

Bourdieu's Core Concepts and Chinese Educational Research

The above bibliometric analysis suggests that "cultural capital", "field", and "habitus" are the three most widely used core concepts of Bourdieu. In addition, the concept of "logic of practice" is receiving increasing attention in recent years. We now turn to a discussion of how these core concepts are understood and used in Chinese educational research.

Field

"Field" is the arena where Bourdieu's sociological theories unfold, and it takes a critical place in the system of Bourdieu's sociological thought. A field is "a network, or a configuration, of objective relations between positions" (Bourdieu & Wacquant, 1992, p. 97). It represents the objective relationships of agents in different positions objectively defined by various forms of capitals and power in different social spaces. Bourdieu replaced the notion of "society" with the concept of "field". Society is composed of various fields and social sciences research needs to focus on highly differentiated fields rather than a monolithic society (He, 2011). The concept of field distinguishes Bourdieu's reflexive sociology from the empirical sociology of Comte and Durkheim in terms of the researched and the relationships between the researcher and the researched. In this respect, field is fundamental to Bourdieu's sociology in that it intends to transcend the dualism between objectivism and subjectivism.

Since the concept of field was introduced to Chinese educational research, many scholars, when analysing the institutional nature of school, have not only employed Bourdieu in their research but also extended Bourdieu's original conceptualisation. For example, Ma Weina (2002) argued that the field contains such aspects as the network of relationships, the concomitant synchronic and diachronic features, the intermediary of formation, the difference-based dynamic mechanism, and the interconnections of field, capital, and relations. Guo Kai (2005) understands field from four points. First, field is a working space. Any analysis of any object in any field cannot merely focus on the internal nature of the object. In other words, the analysis cannot be independent of the relations within the field. Second, field is a social space of competition. Third, field is the space of objective relationships with its own logic, relative autonomy, and necessity. Fourth, field is diachronically formed, i.e. it is historically formed through the interactions between human subjects and social structures. Thus it can be seen that since Bourdieu was introduced to Chinese educational research, scholars have not only clearly grasped the nature of the concept of field – relationship, mediation, and competition – but also recognised its crucial position in Bourdieu's theoretical system.

Based on Bourdieu's notion of field, many Chinese scholars redefined schooling in different ways. Ma Weina (2003a) defined the school field as a network of multiple relationships of multiple positions, complexities, and contradictories in school. It integrates tangibles and intangibles, as well as constant reconfigurations of various forces. Here, the school field is considered to be more symbolic, or the intermingling of the symbolic and the physical. Zhuang Xizhen (2004) defined the school field from the perspective of school organisational culture. The school field is a social space composed of school administrators, teachers, and students who occupy different positions and vie with each other to obtain, accumulate, and monopolise different forms of capital, so as to maintain and improve their positions in this field. Liu Shengquan (2006) defined the educational field as a network of objective relationships among educators, education recipients, and education stakeholders that aim to produce, inherit, transmit, and consume knowledge, with the ultimate goal of developing, shaping, and promoting human beings. In his view, the educational field is not only a sub-concept of field, but also an expansion of the concept of field. It has its own uniqueness and autonomy. To move beyond superficial analysis, analysis of agents and practices within the educational field needs to take into account the relationship framework of this field. Wei Hongju (2008) considered teaching to be space-time that is both tangible and intangible. The tangible refers to various visible educational layouts, while the intangible is the field that has a management effect on students on the basis of tangible space-time. Wei's opinion is similar to Ma's in that the school field is both symbolic and physical. Here, we consider Bourdieu's concept of field to be categorically different from static concepts, such as place, domain, and scope. Field is a dynamic, diachronic concept. Therefore, it remains to be discussed whether there is a dichotomy between symbolic field and physical field, tangible field and intangible field.

Cultural Capital

Bourdieu's development and interpretation of cultural capital is inspired by the concept of capital by Karl Marx. In Marx's *Capitalism*, capital is the value that can bring surplus value. While workers are treated as labour capital, capitalists become personalised capital too. Bourdieu expanded Marx's capitalism, arguing that capital includes not only tangible goods in the production process and labour force transformed into tangible goods (economic capital), but also intangible cultural habitus and social relationships, namely cultural capital and social capital. Cultural capital is an exclusive possession of certain forms and quantities of cultural resources. It has three states: the embodied state (cultural competence), the objectified state (cultural product), and the institutionalised state (cultural institution). The amount of cultural capital is constrained by multiple cultural factors, such as social class and family background. It comes to define (un)favourable positions in a specific field.

Bourdieu's development of cultural capital provides a new perspective for studying social inequity, including educational inequity. Yu Xiulan (2004) asked first grade students in two schools to write stories about the pictures they saw, and compared the writing literacy of students from these two schools. It was found that students in the urban primary school exceeded those in the rural primary school in accuracy and consistency of their understanding of the meaning embedded in the pictures, the completeness and vividness of their writing, and the richness of their vocabulary. Using Bourdieu's theory of cultural capital, Yu explained that as a cultural capital, language has a significant influence on children's academic achievement. The language used by urban families is closer to the language used in school, while the language used by rural families consists mainly of dialects. Zhou Hailing (2008) studied the cultural capital of floating children who came to cities with their migrant parents. It was found that floating children were disadvantaged due to less quantity of cultural capital in all three states, which became structural barriers for realising equal educational rights and opportunities for floating children. Similarly, Gao Guizhong and Lv Guoguang (2011) drew on cultural capital and analysed the impact of family cultural capital on academic performance of Tibetan students. They concluded that different forms of cultural capitals influence the academic performance of Tibetan students in different ways. In general, Tibetan children who obtained higher academic achievement were those with higher parental educational qualifications (institutionalised cultural capital), more collections of books at home (objectified cultural capital), and higher aspiration for school language, academic aspiration, and career aspiration (embodied cultural capital). The abovementioned studies indicate that Bourdieu's notion of cultural capital not only provides a powerful conceptual tool to analyse academic performance among students from different social classes, but also challenges traditional trait theory for attributing school success to intelligence and effort.

Habitus

"Habitus" (惯习) is another important but nebulous concept in Bourdieu's sociology. It is important because it is a powerful weapon to refute the criticism of Bourdieu's determinism, but it is nebulous because it is often confused with "habit" (习惯). Habitus was once translated as "习性" (learned dispositions). After *An Invitation to Reflexive Sociology* was translated and published in Chinese, scholars began to use the translation "惯习" (habitus). While translating *La Noblesse D'état*, Yang Yaping believes that "惯习" better captures the linguistic and conceptual meaning of habitus, and "习性" is the disposition to which Bourdieu refers. Accordingly, 惯习 (habitus) is the assemblage of a set of 习性 (dispositions) (Bourdieu, 1989/2004). We understand "习性" as "learned propensities" accumulated and shaped through prolonged practice in natural conditions and social conditions. Since "习性" focuses more on "structured structures", it is less useful to denote "structuring structures". Therefore, we appreciate the translation of "惯习", although this translation is often confused with the word 习惯 (habit) in Chinese.

"Habitus" as proposed by Bourdieu is a categorical schema of practice-based perceptions, evaluations, and actions. It has both durability and malleability. Moreover, it stems from social institution and exists in the individual's body (Bourdieu & Wacquant, 1992/1998). When articulating habitus, Chinese scholars have different expressions, but it is commonly understood that habitus works through the individual and the social, objectivity and subjectivity. For instance, Dong Zefang (2015) believes that habitus is a system of habits-abilities and dispositions that social subjects/human beings develop in a constantly evolving social environment. It results from the interactions between individual subjectivity and social objectivity. Bao Yaming (1997) suggests that habitus is a cognitive and incentive mechanism that embodies the impact of social context where individuals are situated. It provides a channel or medium through which information and resources are transmitted to the informed actions. Thus, the interactions between objective contexts and the instantaneous situations where activities unfold are all transmitted through habitus. Both views understand habitus as a product of history and attend to its practice-generating role, while Dong emphasised habitus more as a product of the social and Bao placed more stress on the medium function of habitus. Irrespective of different foci, habitus is completely different from the term "habit" that we often use. "Habit" refers to the outcome of the shaping effect of the external environment on the subject, or the adaptation of the subject to its external environment, whereas habitus focuses more on subjective agency. The relationship between habitus and field is not a linear one between deciding and being decided, but a corresponding relationship of ontology (Xu, Wu, & Zhang, 2014).

Bourdieu's concept of habitus provides a conceptual and methodological tool for educational researchers to delve into educational phenomena that unfold in everyday contexts. Drawing on the concept of habitus, Ma Weina (2003b) worked with teachers, students, and principals to explain the taken-for-granted educational values, behavioural tendencies, and evaluation systems in the school field. She argues that the seemingly ordinary educational values, behavioural orientations, and evaluation systems are constructed through the interactions between habitus and school field. Informed by the concepts of field and habitus, Zhuang Xizhen (2004) analysed the relationships among the position, habitus, and everyday language and behaviour of school administrators. He found a circular, mutually generating relationship: the position of school administrators shapes their habitus, which in turn affects their everyday language and behaviour; meanwhile, the daily conduct further strengthens individual administrative authority; ultimately, school administration overrides teaching, leading to the "administerisation" of school. Jin Shenghong (2007) analysed the forming process of habitus in the school field and its shaping effect on the intention, behaviour, and informal system of the interactions between teachers and students. Jin believes that there are explicit dominance and discipline issues in the educational interactions in the Chinese school field. These interactions may not result from individuals' rational reactions; rather, they manifest a specific habitus in the Chinese educational field. The very type of educational habitus derives from the education system and complex power networks constructed through history. Therefore, positive changes of educational interactions in the school field are dependent not only on changes in educators' attitudes and values, but also the recasting of the education system.

Logic of Practice

Practice is another key concept of Bourdieu that has wide impact on Chinese educational research, particularly in the last ten years. In terms of origin of thought, Bourdieu distinguishes his conceptualisation of practice from Aristotle's concept of "praxis". Bourdieu's theory of practice is closer to that of Marx's. Bourdieu stresses both the subjectivity and the structures of practice in order to surpass a plethora of oppositional binaries – objectivity/subjectivity, inevitability/contingency, regularity/selectivity, rationality/irrationality – in schools of structuralism and constructivism when interpreting practice of human beings.

Bourdieu did not provide a clear definition of practice. What interested him more was how human practice unfolds, what the logic is behind practice, and how agents make decisions during practice. To answer these questions, Bourdieu developed his unique theory of practice. He took into account the urgency of time when analysing human practice. Given that urgency, it is impossible for agents to completely follow general principles or prior plans in the practice process. Instead, they must constantly adjust their practice pathways and strategies according to the ever-changing factors. Due at least in part to the urgency of time, practice is characterised also by ambiguity and uncertainty. In other words, practice does not necessarily result from rational, calculative deliberation. Rather, it is often spontaneously generated by habitus, consciously or unconsciously. Nevertheless, Bourdieu believes that practice is not entirely random or haphazard, but regular and purposive at least to some extent.

Bourdieu's theory of practice has had a profound impact on the understanding of the relationship between practice and theory in Chinese education. Before Bourdieu was introduced to China, Chinese educational research largely adopted the dichotomy of (educational) theory/(educational) practice, and considered that educational theory played a guiding role in educational practice, while educational practice should consciously accept the guidance of educational theory. Due to this dichotomous, hierarchical understanding, some educational researchers have long assumed a superior position to educational practitioners, leading to further tensions and conflicts between educational researchers and educational practitioners. In 2006 however, Shi Zhongying published his paper titled "On the Logic of Education Practice" in the Chinese journal 教育研究. On the grounds of Bourdieu's theory of practice, Shi suggests that practice in the field of education, irrespective of its dramatic differences in forms, has its own general structures or generative principles. In other words, practice has its own logic – oriented by pre-acquired habitus and prepared intent constantly modified by situational factors. Practice is also governed by a one-way temporal structure and the three-dimensional structure constituted by body, psychology, and society. Such governance is both negative and positive. From a negative point of view, this very governance constrains educational practitioners, and hence defines the regularity and rationality of educational practice at least to a certain extent. From a positive perspective, the very same governance can continuously produce substantial educational practice. Shi further proposed:

> Practice is carried out by practitioners, and practitioners, in the face of various, complex objective factors, are not purely rational subjects. Educational researchers cannot understand, explain, and serve educational practice without engaging in practice. As for the role of educational theorists in practice, we are proposers rather than instructors of educational practice; we are partners rather than supervisors of educational practitioners.
>
> *(Shi, 2006, pp. 8–9)*

Shi's paper has sparked increasing interest in Bourdieu's theory of practice among Chinese educational researchers. Since then, Bourdieu's theory of practice has been widely cited in discussions about the relationship between Chinese educational theory and practice (Cheng, 2009; Yu, 2014) and those about the logic of educational reform (Wang, 2009).

Bourdieu's Influence on Chinese Educational Research: Some Comments

Since its introduction to mainland China in the late 1970s, Bourdieu's sociology has had enduring impact on Chinese social sciences research, educational research included. Such impact continues to grow in the new millennium. Over the past four decades, Bourdieu's sociology has had a far-reaching influence on Chinese education across the entire education spectrum – pre-school education, school education, higher education, adult education, vocational education, distance education, and shadow education. Bourdieu's sociology has had an in-depth and penetrating impact on Chinese education because it is not merely a theoretical resource or perspective, but also a theoretical standpoint and creed of some educational researchers. In this light, how to critique Bourdieu's influence on Chinese educational research is a very interesting and important academic topic.

First of all, it is hard to dispute that Bourdieu's sociology has become one of the most influential Western schools of thought in Chinese social sciences research and educational research since the advent of Reform and Opening-Up in 1978. Over the decades, many Western philosophical and sociological perspectives have been introduced to Chinese academia. Significant ones include neo-Marxism, postmodernism, analytic philosophy of education, neoliberalism, neo-pragmatism, post-structuralism, existentialism, and feminism. These schools of thought have influenced Chinese educational theory and practice in various ways and remarkably enriched and broadened the theoretical horizon of Chinese educational decision-making, research, and practice. The extensive introduction and integration of mainstream Western schools of thought, Bourdieu's sociology included, into indigenous Chinese educational theories, practice, and policy analysis would be wholly unimaginable during the Cultural Revolution (1966–76) or the early years of the founding of People's Republic of China (1949–66). The philosophical and social sciences in China then worked diligently to translate and introduce theories of Soviet scholars; this was the so-called "Learning from Soviet Union" movement. The extensive introduction of Western schools of thought to China in recent decades indicates that the Reform and Opening-Up initiated in 1978 goes beyond the economic domain and extends to the social and cultural domains. Without the macro social field of Reform and Opening up, there would have been no introduction of Bourdieu's sociology and other Western thoughts to China, let alone the discussion and employment of these thoughts. Nowadays, to many Chinese educational researchers, Bourdieu is a well-known name, among many others such as Michael Apple, Henry Giroux, Richard Stanley Peters, Michel Foucault, Jacques Derrida, Friedrich Hayek, John Rawls, Gilles Deleuze, Jean-Paul Sartre, Jürgen Habermas, and Nel Noddings, just to name a few here. In contrast, scholars from the Soviet Union who were well known to many during the period between the 1950s and the 1960s have become rather unfamiliar to most young and middle-aged Chinese educational researchers today.

Second, and to restate, Bourdieu's sociology has had significant impact on Chinese educational research. It will be recalled that of all the 1,027 Bourdieusian educational studies collected by the CNKI, an overwhelming proportion was published after 2002, with an average of about 64 articles published every year since 2002. Such an amount of publications is an indication of Bourdieu's popularity among Chinese educational researchers. These publications are largely concerned with educational equity, education reform, teacher education, and the relationship between educational theory and practice. Of all these areas of research, educational equity is the one influenced by Bourdieu the most. As mentioned earlier, since 2002, equality issues, including educational equality, have received increasing attention in China, and such issues have come to the fore of national policy making. At the beginning, the academic debates on equity issues were limited to resource distribution and allocation. Educational equality did not receive due attention. Later on, it was found that educational inequality is an important predictor variable of social inequality. Educational inequality is mainly manifested in the widening student achievement gap between China's eastern and western regions, and between rural and urban areas. When making attempts to unravel educational inequality, Chinese scholars started to recognise the analytical power of Bourdieu's theories of cultural capital and cultural reproduction. Drawing particularly on the three states of cultural capital, Chinese scholars have engaged in much empirical research to understand academic performance of students from different sociocultural backgrounds. Empirical findings indicate the good quality of the fit between Bourdieu and Chinese education. On the grounds of this line of empirical research, Chinese researchers aim to break cultural reproduction and social stratification through enriching student cultural capital within the domestic milieu and recasting student cultural dispositions in schools, and ultimately achieve the policy and ethical goals to break the intergenerational transmission of poverty. In brief, Bourdieu's sociology helps to enhance the sensitivity and depth of Chinese educational research, and contributes to educational reform and innovation in mainland China.

Next, however, the use of Bourdieu by many is selective rather than systematic. Critical review of Bourdieu remains rare. This can be attributed to three reasons. First, when educational researchers aim to understand and solve educational problems, sociological concepts and theories are simply resources for their thinking. They may have neither the capacity nor recognise the necessity to systematically understand Bourdieu's sociology or analyse the similarities and differences between Bourdieu and other European and Western sociologists. Consequently, Chinese educational researchers largely adopt a selective, pragmatic approach to using Bourdieu in their studies. Second, Bourdieu's sociology is fraught with inherent tensions. Bourdieu developed some involute concepts and used nebulous phrases when attempting to transcend traditional dualism, such as "objectification of objectification", "sociology of sociology", "logic of pre-logic", "internalisation of the external", "structured structures", "dominated form of domination". Bourdieu relied on these particular concepts and phrases in his major works to conceptualise his thinking system. Although he constantly expounded and explained these concepts and phrases, readers – especially non-French readers – may be left with many points of confusion. Third, due to their long-established research habitus, Chinese educational researchers hold a non-critical attitude to theories from other disciplines, such as philosophy, psychology, sociology, and economics. They simply transplant these theories to their study, rather than using them critically. Many scholarly articles pre-determine Bourdieu as self-evident and use particular research problems to justify the appropriateness of using Bourdieu. In these articles, there are barely any critiques, challenges, or modifications to Bourdieu's sociology.

Last but not least, although the methodological significance Bourdieu's sociology has been noticed in Chinese educational research, attention to it is far from enough and has not yet informed research practice. With regard to the methodological significance of his theory, Bourdieu has explicitly committed to resolving the oppositions between social physics and social phenomenology, objectivism and subjectivism, collectivism and individualism, and therefore proposed methodological relativism and relationalism. In this vein, Bourdieu's methodology provides in-depth, revolutionary implications for social sciences research in general, and educational research in particular. It is dangerous to hold a static view towards researcher and the researched, research technology and instrument, and research results. It is essential to analyse how they develop within a historical and social field of research and practice. Zhu Zhiyong (2001), in his discussion of the relationship between educational researcher and qualitative research, recognised Bourdieu's methodological significance in educational research. Zhu emphasised that the social world in which research subjects are located and the relationship between research subjects and objects are themselves the object of study. This is what Bourdieu means by participant objectivation, and is also the consciousness and attitude required for conducting research. Sun Yuantao (2009) also pointed out that the relationalist methodology of Bourdieu's reflexive sociology is conducive to helping educational researchers reflect on their arrogance and narcissism, respecting educational practitioners, and constructing a new relationship between researchers and practitioners. In sum, the methodological significance of Bourdieu's sociology has attracted some attention, but has not yet changed the standpoints and attitudes of Chinese educational researchers. Nor has it shaken the research habitus, system, and evaluation of Chinese educational research.

References

Bao, Y. (1997). 布尔迪厄文化社会学初探 [A primary study of Bourdieu's cultural sociology]. 社会科学 [Social Science], 4, 70–73.
Bourdieu, P. (1989). 国家精英：名牌大学与群体精神 [La Noblesse d'État] (Yang Yaping, Trans. 2004). 北京：商务印书馆 [Beijing: The Commercial Press].
Bourdieu, P., & Wacquant, L. D. (1992). 实践与反思—反思社会学导引 [An invitation to reflexive sociology] (Li Meng & Li Kang, Trans. 1998). 北京：中央编译出版社 [Beijing: Central Compilation & Translation Bureau].
Cheng, L. (2009). 教育学的"理论-实践"观 [The "theory-practice" view of pedagogy]. 福州：福建教育出版社 [Fuzhou: Fujian Education Press].
Dong, Z., & Zhao, Y. (2015). 从布尔迪厄文化再生产理论看社会分层与高等教育公平 [Social stratification and higher education equity: A perspective of Bourdieu's theory of cultural reproduction]. 现代大学教育 [Modern University Education], 6, 1–6.

Gao, G., & Lv, G. (2011). 家庭文化资本对藏族学生学业成绩的影响 [The influence of family cultural capital on Tibetan students' academic performance]. *青海民族大学学报 [Journal of Qingdao Nationalities Institute]*, *31*(4), 60–64.

Guo, K., (2005). 文化资本与教育场域—布迪厄教育思想述评 [Capital cultural and educational field—Comments on Bourdieu's educational thought]. *当代教育科学 [Contemporary Educational Science]*, *16*, 33–37.

He, S. (2011). 布尔迪厄的教育追求与知识重建的努力 [Bourdieu's educational pursuit and endeavour on knowledge reconstruction]. *外国教育研究 [Studies in Foreign Education]*, *38*(1), 8–12.

Jin, S. (2007). 学校场域与交往惯习:关于教育交往的对话（二）[School field and habitus: Dialogues on educational communication Ⅱ]. *福建论坛 [Fujian Tribune]*, *8*, 7–9.

Kneller, G. F. (1984). 阶级、文化和教育结构 [Class, culture, and educational structure] (Fan Guorui, Trans. 1991). *现代外国哲学社会科学文摘 [Digest of Modern Foreign Philosophical and Social Sciences]*, *4*, 35–37.

Li, P. (Ed.) (2003). *当代西方文化研究新词典 [New dictionary of contemporary Western cultural studies]*. 长春：吉林人民出版社 [Changchun: Jilin People's Publishing House].

Liu, L. (2014). 教育中的文化资本: 理论、经验与反思[Cultural capital in education: Theory, experience, and reflection]. *现代教育论丛 [The Modern Education Journal]*, *4*, 13–20.

Liu, S. (2006). 论教育场域 [On educational field]. *北京大学教育评论 [Peking University Education Review]*, *4*(1), 78–91.

Ma, W. (2002). 指向"改造性实践"的教育反思 [Educational reflections on "transformative practice"]. *教育研究 [Educational Research]*, *12*, 28–32.

Ma, W. (2003a). 学校场域:一个关注弱势群体的新视角 [School field: A new perspective on disadvantaged groups]. *南京师大学报（社会科学版）[Journal of Nanjing Normal University (Social Science)]*, *2*, 64–70.

Ma, W. (2003b). 惯习:对教育行为的另一种解释路径 [Habitus: An alternative interpretation of educational behaviour]. *江苏教育学院学报（社会科学版）[Journal of Jiangsu Institute of Education (Social Science)]*, *19*(4), 9–13.

Pang, Z., & Ding, D. (Eds.) (2001). *当代西方社会发展理论新词典 [New dictionary of contemporary Western social development theory]*. 长春：吉林人民出版社 [Changchun: Jilin People's Publishing House].

Shi, Z. (2006). 论教育实践的逻辑 [On the logic of education practice]. *教育研究 [Educational Research]*, *1*, 3–9.

Sun, Y. (2009). 布尔迪厄社会科学方法论及其对教育研究的启示 [Bourdieu's sociological methodology and educational research]. *青岛大学师范学院学报 [Journal of Teachers College Qingdao University]*, *3*, 20–23.

Swartz, D. (1977). 皮埃尔·布迪厄：社会不平等的文化传授 [Pierre Bourdieu: Cultural transmission of social inequity] (Xia Xiaochuan, Trans.1979). *外国教育资料 [Comparative Education]*, *3*, 61–69.

Wang, Y. (2009). 教育改革情境中理论与实践关系的再反思 [Re-reflections on the relationship between theory and practice in the context of education reform]. *南京师范大学学报（社会科学版）[Journal of Nanjing Normal University (Social Science)]*, *1*, 81–86.

Wei, H. (2008). 略论"教学时空"的教化意蕴 [Analysing the inculcation of pedagogic time and space]. *教育理论与实践 [Theory and Practice of Education]*, *28*(9), 48–51.

Xu, B. (2003). 教育场域和民主学堂 [Educational fields and democratic learning]. *开放时代 [Open Times]*, *1*, 87–96.

Xu, X., Wu, Q. & Zhang, Y. (2014). 论布迪厄教育社会学思想的理论渊源及理论框架 [Commentary on the theoretical origin and framework of Bourdieu's sociological thought in education]. *辽宁师范大学学报（社会科学版）[Journal of Liaoning Normal University (Social Science Edition)]*, *37*(6), 807–816.

Yu, Q. (2014). 何谓教育实践 [What is education practice]. *教育研究 [Educational Research]*, *3*, 11–18.

Yu, X. (2004). 城乡孩子的语言差异：一种文化资本的传承 [Language differences between urban and rural children: An inheritance of cultural capital]. *南京社会科学 [Social Science in Nanjing]*, *8*, 80–82.

Zhou, H. (2008). 论流动儿童教育公平化的策略：文化资本的视角 [Education equity regarding floating children: A cultural capital perspective]. *教育理论与实践 [Theory and Practice of Education]*, *9*, 23–26.

Zhu, Z. (2001). 教育研究者在质化研究中的"关系"—种反思社会学的思考 ["Relationships" for educational researchers in the qualitative research—A reflection on reflective sociology]. *教育理论与实践 [Theory and Practice of Education]*, *21*(6), 1–6.

Zhuang, X. (2004). 公办中学学校行政人员文化研究—由布迪厄的"惯习"观点说开去 [A cultural study on state-run middle school administrators—Speak from Bourdieu's notion of habitus]. *教育理论与实践 [Theory and Practice of Educational]*, *24*(8), 17–20.

4

"MAKE IT BACK"?

The Social Positioning of the New Generation of Rural Teachers in China

Liang Du

In recent years the rest of the world has witnessed swift and enormous social and economic changes in China. These changes have produced comprehensive and far-reaching consequences in many aspects of Chinese society. New social groups are emerging and growing, while existing social groups being reshaped or appearing in new forms. An increasing body of literature concerns the formation and cultural production of a new middle class in current Chinese society (Tomba, 2004). Much debate has been contextualised in urban spaces, for example, the salaried professionals living in the finer residential communities, or white-collar staff working in the service industry in major cities who recently graduated from vocational schools (Tomba, 2004; Woronov, 2011). Little attention has been directed to the emergence of new social groups in the countryside. This chapter aims to contribute in this regard.

During the past decade, through a large-scale overhaul of the recruiting process of schoolteachers in rural China, a new breach has been opened up in the recruiting system through the Special Post Plan (SPP, 特岗计划, *tè gǎng jì huà*). Since its inception in 2006, the Plan has pushed a large number of young people to thousands of village schools and teaching sites. These teaching posts are located at the furthest end of the tremendous schooling system of the country surrounded by some of the most remote and smallest residential communities in Chinese society. The new generation of rural teachers manifests certain social and cultural characteristics, including relatively high educational levels and stable salary income. It is misleading, however, to treat the SPP teachers as the only source of new rural teachers in current China, as in many places the traditional teacher-recruiting mechanism, and other alternative teacher education programs (see Yin, Dooley, and Mu's Chapter 5 in this volume), coexist with the recently instituted SPP. The Ministry of Education claims that the SPP would eventually become the only channel to recruit regular new rural teachers in less developed central and western China. Demographic data show that the SPP teachers constitute an important portion or even the majority of new rural teachers in many regions (Zheng et al., 2012). Yet the SPP has many challenges. It is worthwhile, then, to address the following questions: how is the new generation of rural teachers, in particular the SPP teachers, channelled into their teaching positions? How do they perceive and reflect on their social trajectory? How is their social trajectory related to broader social structures in contemporary China?

Education, Social Stratification, and Changing Social Grouping in China

In recent years, many researchers have attempted to reveal the processes and mechanisms of social stratification as well as social class formation in relation to education in contemporary China. Although the term "class" has been gradually replaced by "social strata" in domestic context so as to depoliticise new social and economic disparities in China (Anagnost, 2008; Pan & Chen, 2008; Woronov, 2011), social stratification, and emerging social groups nevertheless consistently remain as a focal point of research interest in China (P. Li et al., 2004; X. Lu, 2003). Recently special attention has been paid to the formation of new social classes. Some researchers tend to relate the changing social groupings to schooling and education (M. Li, 2015; Murphy, 2004; Woronov, 2011). Some are particularly interested in the emergence of a new middle class in contemporary China as well as various forms of middle-class culture (Tomba, 2004). Others are concerned with the formation of new groups of working-class people, especially in relation to the massive movement of migrant peasant workers from rural areas to urban centres (Chan & Ngai, 2009; P. Li & Tian, 2011; H. Lu & Ngai, 2014; Pan, Lu, & Zhang, 2010; Shen, 2006; X. Yu & Pan, 2008). Lately the forging of collective identity and class formation among migrant workers have drawn a considerable amount of scholarly attention (Chan & Ngai, 2009; H. Lu & Ngai, 2014; Pan, Lu, & Zhang, 2010; Xiong, 2010). Rapid urbanisation, industrialisation, and marketisation processes, and in association with them the large-scale movement of people between rural and urban areas, have fundamentally changed many aspects of rural population, including their consumption behaviours, beliefs, and value systems (He, 2010; S. Li, 1999; P. Li, 2004).

Although extant studies provide an interesting and informative picture about the changing social map in contemporary China, most of the studies focus on social groups in urban centres, especially in major cities that are booming rapidly in the past decades. Relatively less attention has been paid to the emerging social groups in thousands of county prefectures across the nation, which are usually considered as local centres of "rural regions" in China. Even less attention has been directed to social groups such as village schoolteachers and local government staff, who live in "real" rural areas but nevertheless possess to some degree middle-class characteristics, such as a stable income, respectable profession, and often relatively high levels of education. These groups have been playing, and will continue to play, a crucial role in shaping the social and cultural spheres of rural communities in China. In short, much still needs to be learnt about their social trajectories and positionings – these are the foci of this chapter.

A New Generation of Rural Teachers

Schoolteachers have always been an influential group in countryside (Si, 2009). Rural schools are regarded by some as important social and cultural spaces in local communities (K. Yu, 2014). In recent years, the recruitment process for new rural teachers, especially those in remote and poor rural regions of the country, has undergone a significant overhaul, culminating with the implementation of the Special Post Plan. In 2006, the Ministry of Education, joined by the Ministry of Finance, the Ministry of Human Resources and Social Security, and the State Commission Office for Public Sector Reform enacted the SPP. The key goal of the Plan is to incentivise local governments to recruit rural teachers among newly qualified college and university graduates, through a subsidy scheme provided by the central government. Since its inception, the SPP has become one of the major channels for the renewal of primary and secondary schoolteachers in the rural areas of 22 provinces in central and western China. By 2011, about 235,000 SPP teachers had come into service, distributed in 27,000 schools in over 1,000 counties (Zheng, Du, & Wei, 2012).

In less than ten years, with the inflow of tens of thousands of young, energetic, and well-educated new university and college graduates, the number and composition of schoolteachers in many rural regions of central and western China have been fundamentally transformed. Existing studies about SPP teachers focus on the effects and improvement of the SPP policy. Many researchers report noticeably positive effects of the policy on rural teachers and schools, while observing several major drawbacks of the Plan, including the consistently low income level and subsequent low morale of the SPP teachers, their gender and education disparities, and unclear career identity (Lin & Jin, 2013; Yang & Yang, 2010). Liu (2014), for example, examines the demographic data of 5,014 SPP teachers in Guangxi province in the year of 2012. He concludes that almost all of the new teachers possess a college or university degree, and over 20 per cent of this group are ethnic Zhuang, which is the major ethnic group in the region besides Han Chinese. However, over three-quarters of the group are female,[1] and similarly about 76 per cent of the group were trained in regional teacher training universities instead of comprehensive universities, not to say the prestigious "key" universities.

There is no doubt that the existing studies with a policy focus provide meaningful information about the SPP teachers. But a lack of sociological perspective makes current research of little help to our understanding of the connection between this new generation of rural teachers with the broader social context. So far we know little about how the SPP teachers are channelled to the teaching profession at many rural villages that have gradually become barren and even abandoned during the post-Reform and Opening-Up period while Chinese society has undergone a rapid marketisation process (Du, 2014; Zheng, Du, & Wei, 2012). Although the status of the incoming rural teachers is often considered low by many, the SPP teachers nevertheless constitute one of the best-educated groups, with stable and decent income, in the often poverty-stricken rural areas. Therefore it is meaningful to apprehend the social trajectories and positions of the SPP teachers. Meanwhile, through the institution of the SPP, a group of young people sharing to a large extent some common characteristics make their way into rural schools, located at the very bottom of the school system. These teachers are unique, given their strategic positioning in the educational and social spaces in rural China. In many rural schools, the SPP teachers would be the first generation of schoolteachers that possess college or university degrees, in contrast to most of their older colleagues who were educated at local secondary teacher-training schools. This is also one of the most noticeable results of the readjustments in the teacher-training and recruiting policies and procedures such as the SPP. This chapter attempts to explore the social positioning process of the SPP teachers. To this end, I draw on Bourdieu's framework of field, trajectory effect, and habitus.

A Bourdieusian Approach

Bourdieu's theories were developed in the Western context, particularly in the French social context. This does not mean that his framework cannot be used in social analysis within other societies. Concepts such as field, capital, and habitus provide important analytic tools for our understanding of the social realties in China. As in many Western societies, we believe social forces such as various forms of capital play important roles in structuring the social space in China in which individuals find themselves socially positioned. Of course in a rapidly changing society such as China the theories may have different implications or foci. What we want to particularly bring to researchers' attention is the consequences of the shifting map of various social groups, in particular the emergence of new social groups in China, and thus the trajectory effects that the changes may bring forth to the perceptions and practices of new social groups in relation to their social positions. Bourdieu (1989) understands social positions as follows:

> Agents are distributed in the overall social space, in the first dimension, according to the overall volume of capital they possess and, in the second dimension, according to the structure of their capital, that is, the relative

66 Liang Du

> weight of the different species of capital, economic and cultural, in the total volume of their assets.
>
> *(Bourdieu, 1989, p. 16)*

The notion of capital, therefore, helps to explain the ways in which the total volume and composition of resources possessed by the new generation of rural teachers and their families influence their social positionings and trajectories. Meanwhile, Bourdieu also elaborates upon the concept of habitus, which consists of "schemes of perception, thought, and action" (Bourdieu, 1989, p. 14), contains meanings at both practical and ideological levels, and presents itself in the forms of "generative, unifying principle of conducts and opinions" (Bourdieu & Passeron, 1977, p. 161). According to Bourdieu, habitus is the internalised form of objective conditions and of the conditionings it entails, and at the same time generates and perpetuates the very same objective conditions. The conceptual tool of habitus is helpful to understand and interpret the life experiences of the young rural teachers. However, for Bourdieu, it is not sufficient if one merely looks at the positions (capital) and dispositions (habitus) without understanding simultaneously the "change in these two properties over time" (Bourdieu, 1984):

> The fact remains that one cannot truly understand the sometimes immense differences between categories which are nonetheless close in social space ... unless one takes into account not only capital volume and composition but also the historical evolution of these properties, i.e., the trajectory of the group as a whole and of the individual in question and his lineage, which is the basis of the subjective image of the position objectively occupied.
>
> *(Bourdieu, 1984, p. 453)*

For Bourdieu, practices cannot be completely accounted for solely in terms of the properties defining the position occupied in social space at a given moment. It is also equally important to take into account of the "trajectory effect" because "individuals occupying similar positions at a given time are separated by differences associated with the evolution over time of the volume and structure of their capital, i.e., by their individual trajectories" (Bourdieu, 1984, p. 111). The correlation between a practice and social origin is therefore the result of two effects: the inculcation effect, which is "directly exerted by the family or the original conditions of existence", and the trajectory effect. The latter is the effect of "social rise and decline on dispositions and opinions, position of origin being, in this logic, merely the slope of the starting point of a trajectory, the reference whereby the slope of the social career is defined". The trajectory effect is particular in that it often plays a large part in blurring the relationship between opinions and social origin, "owning to the fact that it governs the representation of the position occupied in the social world and hence the vision of its world and its future" (Bourdieu, 1984, p. 111).

In the current chapter, Bourdieu's framework is informative in two ways. On the one hand, the SPP teachers may not move about in social space randomly and are fully subject to the influences of objective mechanism of channelling or elimination. On the other hand, the SPP teachers who originally possess certain economic and cultural capital are not all destined to an educational and social trajectory leading to a given position, as there are deviations from the socially anticipated, defined, and accepted trajectory. Working through a Bourdieusian lens, I try to comprehend the social positions and positioning of SPP teachers through grasping their social trajectories. We cannot merely grasp their social positions as snapshots at a particular moment. Instead, we need to account for their trajectories over time. In other words, I attempt to take a dynamic approach to understanding how the volume and forms of capital possessed by their original families at some of the most crucial moments in their life histories have shaped the SPP teachers' educational and career trajectories, and channelled them to current social positions. By doing so, it is expected that we can better grasp the trajectory effect on their opinions, practices, and "future".

Research Methods

Data reported in this chapter were drawn from two case counties in Yunnan province, namely Lishan county and Suizhai county.[2] Yunnan province, located in south-western China, is well known for its ethnic diversity. The two case counties are good examples of such ethnic diversity: both comprise large groups of ethnic minority residents. Since 2006 when the SPP was initiated, Yunnan has consistently remained one of the largest provinces in terms of SPP teacher recruitment. This teacher group has constituted the majority of young teachers in many rural schools in the province. Further, the SPP itself actually originated in Yunnan and thereafter was institutionalised nationally by the Ministry of Education (Zheng, Du, & Wei, 2012).

Data reported in this chapter mainly come from two sources. The first source is a full-set demographic data of the new rural teachers in the two counties, which are expected to help us learn the social backgrounds and trajectories of the group. Another source is the qualitative data collected through in-depth semi-structured interviews and focus group discussions with a group of local schoolteachers. The qualitative data offer information about the teachers' life stories and perceptions of their educational and social trajectories and positioning. The demographic background data, originally used for administrative purpose, were provided by the local educational authorities of the two counties. The interviews were conducted by the researcher and a graduate student assistant during their visits to local schools in the two counties.

Interview participants (see Table 4.1), all but one being SPP teachers, were recommended by school leadership team or local educational authority. Their year of participation in the SPP ranged from 2006 to 2014. Mrs. Yang, a non-SPP teacher, was a substitute (代课, *dài kè*) teacher at the time of study. She was working towards obtaining a college degree in the hope of turning herself into a regular teacher. It is expected that her experience and perceptions may provide a different perspective when we look at the social positioning process of the new generation of rural teachers. Each interview lasted about one to two hours, mostly depending on the teachers' schedules. The interviews were conducted in the offices and classrooms at the teachers' schools. In a couple of cases, there were intervals when local educational authority personnel were present during the interviews, which might have influences on the interviewees.

In addition to individual interviews, we also conducted a focus group with three teachers, Mrs. Shao, Mrs. Wang, and Mrs. Li, at Central Primary school, one of the best primary schools in Lishan County. The focus group is expected to offer comparisons between local rural schoolteachers and teachers in the regional centre.

Findings and Discussion

Several findings stood out during data analysis. Most of the new rural teachers were from local rural families with lower to middle socio-economic status. In a sense, they physically come full circle, back to where they started their pursuit of social mobility. Of course, they did to some extent "make it" by following an upward social trajectory. Yet the "circle" in social trajectory was

TABLE 4.1 Participants of interviews and focus group discussions

Name	Gender	Ethnicity	Age	Father's occupation	Mother's occupation
Huang	F	Yi/Han	20s	Peasant	Peasant/temporary worker
Duan	M	Han/Lisu	20s	Peasant/temporary worker	Peasant
Kuang	F	Han	20s	Peasant/temporary worker	Peasant
Hang	F	Han	About 30	Village school teacher	Peasant
Yu	F	Han	About 30	Peasant	Peasant
Guo	F	Han	About 30	Peasant (passed away)	Peasant/small business
Wu	M	Lisu	20s	Peasant	Peasant
Chang	F	Han	20s	County government (passed away)	Schoolteacher
Yang	F	Lisu/Han	30s	Peasant	Peasant

Social Positioning of Rural Teachers   **69**

completed in a highly profound way that involved extremely complicated and delicate processes.

"Make It Back"

Demographic data and personal accounts indicate that the new generation of rural teachers are themselves mostly from a rural origin. Some background knowledge is in order here. The Chinese *hù kǒu* (口, household registration) system officially distinguishes Chinese citizens into rural and urban residents, mostly by their place of birth or origin. A rural/urban dichotomy is one of the most important divisions that the *hù kǒu* system identifies. Although the meaning of being a peasant has dramatically changed in the post-Mao era rife with rapid marketisation, an origin of remote rural area in mid-western China is still widely considered a significant social disadvantage. The demographic data provided by the local Bureau of Education in the two counties do not include the information of *hù kǒu* status or family origin. But during the interview, seven of the eight SPP teachers reported that their parents' families were local villagers, and the same applied to the young substitute teacher. This finding is in accordance with existing research (Zheng, Du, & Wei, 2012), which reports that nearly 80 per cent of SPP teachers nationwide have a family background of rural *hù kǒu*.

Our qualitative data also show that most of the new rural teacher participants had a modest start. Many were born in families with middle to lower economic status even in their own villages. In addition, some rural teacher participants are members of ethnic minority groups, who are often disadvantaged in terms of educational and economic development in comparison with the majority Han group. Consequently, they attended poorly equipped village schools when they were small. Interestingly, as the policies of many local educational administrations attempted to encourage new rural teachers, the SPP teachers in particular, to return to their hometowns to work, many participants literally returned to the very school which they attended years before, or the one at their neighbourhood villages. After years of schooling and the pursuit of upward social mobility, they eventually still returned to a school that was barely different from the one which they attended. In other words, they returned to where their social trajectory started, though as public schoolteachers.

What is noteworthy is that "making it back" is not uncommon among the rural teacher participants, particularly those from the most disadvantaged rural families who lack the economic, cultural, and social capital necessary to support attempts for further upward mobility, such as members of an ethnic minority group from remote villages. For example, teacher Wu was a local Lisu ethnic minority and returned to a teaching site at a small Lisu village in Lishan county, after graduating from a provincial university and making two attempts to pass the SPP qualification exam. During the interview, he recalled that he had six Lisu classmates when he first went to primary school in his village. But later, it turned out that Wu was the only one among the six who moved on to college education, while the rest of the cohort either dropped out in primary or secondary school, or ended up in a low-reputation vocational secondary educational institute. When Wu went to college, he found all his dormitory mates were from highly similar family backgrounds.

> Wu: ... There were six of us in the dormitory, from three or four ethnic groups. There was one Zhuang, one Buyi – no, what is it? ... Bulang? I forget! He is from Yuxi, but he can't speak ethnic language – he just has this ethnic minority label. And the rest three were Han. But few of us had good family economic conditions. There was one who seemed better, but there was no computer at our dormitory! No! So basically everyone was pretty the same.

In fact Wu later recalled that "five out of six of us have become teachers." The only exception is that one of them managed to get into a local bank instead of becoming a schoolteacher. Meanwhile, all six young men went back to work in their hometown counties. Wu's personal experience to some extent manifests a group social trajectory. That is, many individuals from the lower-middle section of rural families in hinterland China who strived for upward mobility through the school systems eventually returned to rural areas instead of migrating to larger cities distant from their hometowns. This is in an interesting contrast to their counterparts who failed in schools and usually ended up in pipeline factories, construction sites, and service economy jobs in big metropolitan centres, especially in the coastal areas of the country. It is obvious that in comparison with their parents' generation who were mostly peasants, the rural schoolteachers have achieved upward mobility in both educational and occupational terms, although many of them found themselves physically returned to their villages.

Wu's experience is echoed by other teacher participants. Another Lisu teacher Yang, for example, was among the brightest students in his primary school before he was admitted to the newly established Ethnic Middle School in the county. According to him, only he and another two classmates out of the approximately sixty graduates of his local village primary school that year got a score high enough to secure admission to middle schools. He continued to do very well in his middle school, and was admitted by the provincial ethnic university after scoring the best in the college and university entrance examination among his secondary school classmates. The ethnic university is considered to be a reputable institute, especially among ethnic minority students. He had now returned as a primary school teacher to his hometown, teaching at the exact village school where he started his education a decade before.

These stories about the social trajectories of the rural teachers suggest that, for some rural regions, the brightest students have "made it" through educational system (Du, 2014). That is to say, they realised upward social mobility by relatively outstanding academic performance. Almost all of them continued to receive their higher education in the regional centres and local cities, and then returned as the new generation of teachers to their hometowns or nearby villages. It is worthwhile, therefore, to point out that their social trajectory is different from the social reproduction process theorised by scholars such as Bowels & Gintis (1976) or Paul Willis (1977), as apparently most of the teachers have acquired a social position that is different from those of their parents' generation. The social mobility that the teacher group has achieved drives us to move beyond the social reproduction theory and instead to explore their subtle living realities and critical life moments, as well as their nuanced social trajectories and the effects of such in complex social spaces.

The Socially Positioned New Generation of Rural Teachers

To some degree, the social trajectory of the rural teacher group is largely shaped by the state and local policies. The SPP, for example, tends to attract teachers who are "willing" to go and stay in rural areas. One of the consequences of this policy is that most newly recruited rural teachers are themselves of rural origins and thus somewhat familiar with the rural teaching positions. Our data also show that the new generation of rural teachers are also channelled to their current school posts – and hence social positions, by various social forces. It is obvious that class, gender, ethnicity, and community ethos played important roles in channelling particular social groups into the rural teaching positions. Due to their lack of economic, cultural, and social capital, many young people from rural families with relatively lower socio-economic status were often channelled to lower-middle sectors of higher educational institutions and consequently were more likely to end up in rural schools. In a Bourdieusian sense, the volume and composition of various forms of capital of the original family – the starting positions in the social space – have largely shaped their social trajectories. But it is simply misleading if we view the social positioning process of the group in a deterministic way. Instead, it is a highly complicated process laden with emotion, conflicts, choices, and possibilities.

One thing that impressed us most during our interactions with the participants was the "regrets" in their lives, especially during "big" moments in their education. The emotional way in which they articulated those moments moved us. "Regret", "pity", or even "sadness" were the words that the teachers used to express themselves. For example, during the interview with teacher Huang, he recalled that if he had attended the No.1 Middle School of the county, instead of the Ethnic Middle School that was recently established and hence less reputed, he would have a totally different life story, apparently for the better. Huang admitted that the choice that he had to make at that time was "mostly based on financial concerns". After so many years, in his own words, he still felt "how sad a thing it is when thinking about it now"!

72   Liang Du

Similarly, teacher Yang expressed her regret, "to a great extent", for being unable to perform well at the nationwide college entrance examination. She believed that she failed to perform at her normal level during the crucial examination and she would have been able to go to a better university had she been given a second chance to take the exam. But she simply did not have the "courage" to ask for a second chance to try the exam:

> I didn't even think about it at that time, because I did not have the courage to ask [my parents to support me] ... You know, I felt shameful if I had to retake the exam the next year, and I dared not to ask for that at home. Because it costs money to retake the exam. And my family had told me beforehand that they would not let me do that even if I failed the exam.

Apparently, in both stories, lack of economic capital was a crucial factor that constrained the participants from furthering attempts for educational and social mobility. According to Bourdieu (1984), the dispositions and practices of a social member is associated with their position in social space, which is in turn decided by the volume and composition of capital possessed by the individual. It is quite clear that the educational choices of the two rural teachers above, whether an economy-based school choice, or giving up retaking a highly crucial exam, were results of the schemes of perceptions and actions of the teachers and their families. On the other hand, the "regret" and "sadness" that the teachers expressed during their reflections, and after they had achieved the social mobility that accompanies being a school teacher – an occupational position associated with different volume and composition of capital from their family – have nevertheless illustrated the dynamics in the visions of the world of the social agents, i.e., part of their habitus. In other words, the experience of upward social mobility may produce a trajectory effect on the participants, which leads them to reflect and regret on their practices at some of their critical life moments, looking back at them not merely as "natural" or "unavoidable".

In addition to the lack of economic capital, the families of many rural teacher participants also lacked cultural and social capital (Bourdieu, 1986). The insufficiency of these resources also caused the lack of support of their families when teacher participants tried to pursuit their social mobility. Teacher Hu recalled how anxious her father was after she received a letter of acceptance from a secondary vocational school that located in another province:

HU: He got a lot of grey hair almost overnight! We got a letter of acceptance from this institute of electronic school in Hunan, but did not hear back from the teacher college (that I applied for).

RESEARCHER: Did you apply for that college?

Social Positioning of Rural Teachers **73**

HU: No. But we were pretty much ill-informed at that time. We didn't know what to do! And then my father was very anxious, and he said I must have been rejected by the teacher college, and what we could do if I had to go to school so far away! He was anxious about all these and got a full-head of grey hair overnight – yeah, his image is still in my head now. We were in this little village. And the ways of our thinking are limited.

As local villagers who had never travelled outside of the province, Hu's parents did not have any knowledge about the school that had sent their daughter a letter of acceptance. Her father's level of anxiety caused by this shortage of information and knowledge is a manifestation of the lack of cultural and social capital required for strategically responding to any unexpected outcome. Such a situation was not unique to teacher Hu. It appeared quite common among the rural teacher participants. As teacher Wu described, "My father did not go to school, and my mother only went to primary school. They could be of little help!"

In comparison, teacher Chang, the only rural teacher participant with an urban family background and whose mother was also a schoolteacher, provided a story that was in sharp but interesting contrast to that of teacher Hu and teacher Wu.

CHANG: I did not do well enough in the entrance exam of high school. So I paid extra to get into a high school, No. 5 high school.
RESEARCHER: No. 5 high school?
CHANG: Yes, I was able to go to No. 1 school! But my mom did the analysis for me: She said my score was not that good . . . uh . . . was very bad. If I went to No.1 school, they had over 70 students in one classroom – My scores would be among the worst. Then the teachers would ignore you, and there would be a mounting pressure. It could have psychological consequence to me. But if I go to No. 5 school, my scores would be among the middle instead of the worst. I would not have that much pressure then. So she decided to let me attend No. 5 school . . . I think it's the right decision!

Teacher Chang's accounts of her experience demonstrate not only the importance of economic capital to crucial life choices, but also the composition of the capital, here the amount of cultural and social capital possessed by the rural teachers and their original families, that could make a difference. In contrast to teacher Wu's and teacher Hu's parents, who were of little help at vital points of their educational paths, Chang's mother, after balancing the advantages and disadvantages, made the best possible school choice for Chang. Even when looking back after so many years, Chang still believed the choice was "correct".

The contrast between the emotional experiences of Chang's satisfaction and Wu and Yu's regrets may bring forth distinct trajectory effects for the individuals. While Chang to some extent followed her mother's career path and looked back at her trajectory with content, the discontent and regrets of the latter two teachers may have illustrated the depth and probably also the long-term impact of their reflection on their trajectories.

In addition to the social positions defined by the quantity and configuration of capital, the social dispositions of rural teachers (e.g., gender, ethnicity) exerted profound influences on their social trajectory. During the interviews, almost all the female rural teacher participants mentioned how their parents' or their own perceptions of gender had affected their educational and/or occupational choices. Expressions such as "as a girl, I should …" appeared in our interviews repeatedly. An emphasis on stability of career and responsibility of taking care of family appeared at the centre of the schemes of perceptions of the female participants. In our interview, teacher Hang, tears in her eyes, recounted why she did not go to high school:

HANG: Now I realise it since it has been in the past! … My parent … my dad was concerned that, as a girl, I might not be able to keep up with the class in high school. Because my school performance was outstanding in the primary school, and among the top two in the middle school. But still he was always worried that I might not be able to keep up with others in high school, and I might fail the college entrance exam.

RESEARCHER: Have you ever considered [working in] places other than Lishan county?

HANG: Never. Because I was told by the teachers that it wouldn't be easy to be out there for a girl like me. And I mentioned to my parents too. If I didn't get the special post teacher position, I would like to leave the province with several classmates to take a look and to see the world outside. But I was told by my parents that it was not a good idea, and the outside world is too dangerous and complicated. So, on the one hand we were not determined enough, and on the other hand we were not confident enough. So it is safer to come back to this place.

Teacher Hang's story was particularly sad. She had to decline the opportunity to continue her study at high school, and subsequently the opportunity of access to universities, simply because of her father's gendered belief that girls could not keep up with the level of learning at high school. Obviously this distrust of her academic capability constituted part of the schemes of perceptions and opinions of her original family, which, according to a Bourdieusian framework, is the result of the total experience of the family and of the social group to which they belong. This gendered classificatory schema tends to attribute superior academic capability to males and inferior academic capability to female students. In addition, it seemed that the parents and Hang's teachers shared a schema of classification when they sent the common message to her that the outside world was too "dangerous" and "complicated" for a simple village girl like her, and consequently quenched her courage and determination of venturing out. After so many years, Hang was still quite upset about her lost opportunity for further education. In her own reflections, she could have been accepted into a university and become "at least a middle or high school teacher" rather than a rural teacher. Again, it deserves our attention that Hang's emotional experience which propelled her to reflect on the critical choice in her life may represent a trajectory effect that has a dynamic and profound impact on her habitus. As she commented during the interview, "now I realise it": she recognised the alternative life opportunities that could have unfolded for her had there not been the limitation in her parents' vision of the world, a recognition that in turn likely to re/shape her current schemes of perceptions and actions.

Participants such as teacher Chang, whose original family's socio-economic status was apparently at a higher level than those of most other participants, also reported a similar experience. As Chang recalled, "The parents – especially the parents at small places such as ours – generally agree on the idea that girls should look for a stable job, such as schoolteachers. It is good!" It seems that the influences of the gendered discourse, which stresses the vulnerability of the female and regards them as "inferior to the male", were applicable to participants across different socio-economic status. However, the trajectory effects might be very different for participants of different socio-economic backgrounds. For most of the schoolteachers who were originally from rural families and who have experienced an upward social mobility, the experience of such a trajectory has governed "the representation of the position occupied by them in the social world" and engendered a vision of their future before them. Therefore they tended to reflect on the emotional moments in their life history that were filled with distress, regret, and, sadness, while they were also getting hold of a new position in the social space and hence building up a new vision of the world with their newly possessed economic and cultural capital that was accumulated along the social trajectory. This trajectory effect, however, is not likely to occur to individuals who experience a horizontal movement in the social space or a collective trajectory of a social group, or modal trajectory.

In association with the gendered habitus, community ethos among the participants exerted a noticeable impact on the self/positioning process of the new rural teacher group. Such a community ethos often puts a particular emphasis on an individual's occupational stability, family responsibility, and geographical proximity to their hometown. Although in many cases such an ethos is interwoven with gendered perceptions, as demonstrated above, the impact of community ethos is not necessarily limited to female participants. While for female participants, the emphasis is often linked to their perceived subordinate role in domestic and social milieus, for male rural teachers it is usually associated with their responsibilities to their original family, their parents, or relatives. For instance, teacher Duan recalled his story of how his ambition to venture outside the province for a promising career opportunity was frustrated by his parents:

DUAN: Yes, I interned at that place for two or three weeks, before I returned to the sales department of Black Dragon company [a large national dairy corporation]. And I spent several weeks there. So I had interned for two or three months in total. And then I was planning to join the Black Dragon company, but this required me to work at its headquarter in Inner Mongolia for a while. I consulted with my family and they didn't agree with my plan. And then they made a lot of calls to me . . .

RESEARCHER: Who was against this at your home?

DUAN: My father . . . Because my two sisters were married, and my parents were kind of – how to say – old fashioned. They insisted I should go back . . . a lot of calls!

RESEARCHER: Why did they want you to come back? To take care of them?

DUAN: They wanted me to take the exams. I took the national civil servant exam, and failed; I took the provincial civil servant exam, and failed; I took the qualification exam for local government-affiliated units, and failed; and I then had to take the special post teacher exam, and didn't succeed either.

After serving as a substitute teacher for a year, in the end Duan was able to secure a special post teacher position exactly at the location where he grew up, as his parents had hoped for. In Duan's reflections, it seems that there existed a mentality – "old fashioned" in Duan's own words – in the local community that young family members should avoid staying too far away from their parents or hometown, especially when there were no other siblings around that could take good care of the parents. Therefore as Duan recalled, he had to interrupt his career venture out of the province, urged by his parents, largely because his two sisters were married off into other families and had hence lost to some degree the capability to take care of their parents.

There is no adequate data here to conclude that this ethos is a product of the intersection of gender, class, and local ethnic culture. But the existence of such a community ethos leaves no doubt that the community ethos intertwines with the complex schema of cognition, such as gendered perceptions, of the participants that result from the positions they occupied and continued to occupy in the social space. Failing to resist the requests by his parents, and the restriction of the "old-fashioned" mentality within the community, Duan eventually returned to his home village as a rural schoolteacher. Yet, he has achieved educational and social mobility and accumulated cultural and economic capital that is far superior to his parents. His reflection and in a way implicit critique of his father's "old-fashioned" way of thinking may have manifested the potential trajectory effects of his upward social experience and could help to shape his vision of the world toward a direction distinct from that of his father's generation.

In addition to socio-economic status and gender, ethnicity also plays an important role in the social positioning process of rural teacher participants. In our interviews, two of the ethnic minority participants specifically recalled how their experiences at the local Ethnic Minority Secondary School impacted their educational and life trajectories. After their graduation from the secondary school, one of them, Duan, continued to complete his higher education at a provincial university for ethnic minorities, which was part of the higher educational systems that is specifically designed to promote the education of ethnic minority groups in China. Afterwards, Duan returned to teach at a village school next to his home village. The schools and universities particularly established in the name of promoting educational opportunities of ethnic minorities are a distinguished feature of the educational systems in China. The experience of the two ethnic minority participants demonstrate that this arrangement has great impact on many ethnic minority individuals who have achieved social mobility through education.

Wu's experience was particularly dramatic and illustrative. He repeatedly failed all his attempts to secure a government-affiliated job position two years after he earned his bachelors' degree from a local provincial college. During his numerous job-seeking attempts, Wu tried almost every type of qualification exams that could lead to civil servant or schoolteacher positions. He actually managed to pass all the written exams during the second year of his job-seeking attempts, but unfortunately was rejected by all the positions after the subsequent face-to-face interviews, for reasons that he could not figure out. Eventually he succeeded in passing the exam for a special post teacher position at one of the most isolated Lisu villages, thanks to the special program initiated by the county educational authority that gave preference to Lisu candidates in the teacher recruitment process for schools that located in predominantly Lisu regions. In other words, it is likely that Wu could not have secured the schoolteacher position were it not for his ethnic minority status and the pressing challenges of ethnic education faced by the local educational authority. Ethnicity has played a critical role in shaping the career trajectory of the minority participants. Meanwhile, the fact that the local policies tend to encourage the returning of ethnic minority students to their communities of origin may have profound impact on local ethnic community ethos.

Conclusions

This chapter explores the social "positioning" process and the social trajectories of the rural teacher participants that led up to their current career positions as rural schoolteachers in some of China's most remote villages. These teachers were channelled to their current teaching posts and thus their social positions by powerful social structural forces functioning at critical life moments both in their education and career. Lack of economic, cultural, and social capital constrained the ways of thinking and the educational choices that the original families made for some of the teachers. Yet participants interacted with the objective structuring mechanism with their "specific inertia" (Bourdieu, 1984, p. 110), that is, a set of embodied dispositions formed through their socio-economic status, ethnicity, gender, gendered perceptions, and community ethos. The conditions of existence of the participants at an early stage can persist in the form of their habitus, and therefore constantly serve as the schema of reference for subsequent educational and career decisions.

The interview accounts of the schoolteachers about their choices and decisions sometimes appeared to be emotive. Participants' emotional moments emerged when they looked back and reflected on their life histories. Such strong sentiments could be important "ruptures" in the living experiences of the schoolteachers, which often propel them to reflect deeply upon their life paths and are likely to have far-reaching impact on their schemes of opinions and actions, or, in Bourdieu's term, "trajectory effects", the effects of vertical movements in social space on dispositions and opinions (Bourdieu, 1984). In other words, the position of a social member in a certain social space at a particular moment should be viewed as part of a dynamic "positioning" process, constituting part of the social trajectory of the individual that subsequently exerts a trajectory effect on his or her opinions and actions. Given the trajectory effects, the changes in their possessed capital and consequently acquisition of a new habitus would not be surprising.

Finally, the institutional arrangements such as the Special Post Plan and local teacher recruitment policies further complicated the social positioning process of the new generation of rural teachers, by singling out and channelling candidates with particular social backgrounds into the rural teaching posts. A notable example of such an institutional channelling mechanism is the local teacher recruitment policy that gave preference to ethnic minority candidates when assigning teaching posts specifically located in ethnic minority communities. Such a policy approach illustrates the significance of ethnicity as an element that contributes to the positioning process of the participants and the ways in which institutional arrangements contextualise this process.

To conclude, this chapter sheds light on not only the social positions but also the "positioning" of the emerging generation of schoolteachers in rural China. In other words, the study helps to better understand the social trajectories of the schoolteacher participants in rural China, and thus to grasp not only their positions as defined by the volume and composition of capitals that they possessed, but also the change of the capitals over their life course and the effects of such changes on the individuals. Such understanding shall subsequently facilitate our comprehension of the schemes of perceptions and actions of the rural schoolteachers, who, given their socio-economic and cultural status in local communities, probably will play a crucial role in shaping rural China in the foreseeable future. In short, by learning more about the rural schoolteachers as a key social group in rural communities, the study is likely to provide some insights into the opinions and practices of the group as well as into the potential social changes in countryside China.

Notes

1 According to the Ministry of Education, the percentage of female full-time teachers nationally is 65.3 per cent at regular primary school level, and 53.5 per cent at regular junior secondary school level; the percentage of full-time ethnic minority teachers nationally is 10.8 per cent at primary school level, and 4.9 per cent at junior secondary school level www.moe.gov.cn/s78/A03/moe_560/jytjsj_2016/2016_qg/index_3. html, accessed on 26 December 2017.
2 The county names, as well as all the names of people and schools appearing in this chapter are pseudonyms.

References

Anagnost, A. (2008). From 'class' to 'social strata': Grasping the social totality in reform-era China. *Third World Quarterly*, 29(3), 497–519.

Bourdieu, P. (1984). *Distinction: A social critique of the judgment of taste* (R. Nice, Trans.). London: Routledge & Kegan Paul.

Bourdieu, P. (1986). The forms of capital. In J. Richardson (Ed.) & R. Nice (Trans.), *Handbook of theory and research for the sociology of education* (pp. 241–258). Westport, CN: Greenwood.

Bourdieu, P. (1989). Social space and symbolic power. *Sociological Theory*, 7(1), 14–25.

Bourdieu, P., & Passeron, J.-C. (1977). *Reproduction in education, society and culture* (R. Nice, Trans.). London: Sage.

Bowles, S., & Gintis, H. (1976). *Schooling in capitalist America: Educational reform and the contradictions of economic life*. New York: Basic Books.

Chan, C. K.-C., & Ngai, P. (2009). The making of a new working class? A study of collective actions of migrant workers in South China. *The China Journal*, 198, 287–303.

Du, L. (2014). *Jiaoshi fengcen, shehui liudong yu jiaoyu zhengce de wanshan: Yi Tegang jiaoshi weili* (Teacher stratification, social mobility, and refining of educational policy: A case study of special post teachers). *Academic Journal of Tachers University of Hebei (Educational Science Edition)*, 1, 11–15.

He, X. (2010). *Xiangcun shehui guanjianci: Jinru 21 shiji de zhongguo xiangcun sumiao (Keywords of rural society: A sketch of China's rural society in the early 21st century)*. Jinan: Shandong renmin chubanshe (Shandong People's Publishing House).

Li, M. (2015). *Citizenship education and migrant youth in China: Pathways to the urban underclass*. New York: Routledge.

Li, P. (2004). *Cunluo de zhongjie: Yangchengcun de gushi (The end of village: Story of the village of Yangcheng)*. Shanghai: Shangwu yinshuguan (The Commercial Press).

Li, P., Li, Q., Sun, L., et al. (2004). *Zhongguo shehui fenceng (Social stratification in China today)*. Beijing: Shehui kexue wenxian chubanshe (Social Sciences Academic Press).

Li, P., & Tian, F. (2011). *Zhongguo xinshengdai nongmingong: Shehui taidu he xingwei xuanze* (The new generation of migrant workers: Social attitudes and behavioral choices). *Shehui (Chinese Journal of Sociology)*, 31(3), 1–23.

Li, S. (1999). *Cunluo zhong de guojia: Wenhua bianqian zhong de xiangcun xuexiao☐ The state in village: Village schools in cultural transformation*. Hangzhou: Zhejiang renmin chubanshe (Zhejiang People's Publishing House).

Lin, H., & Jin, D. (2013). *Minzu diqu Tegang jihua de xianshi kunjing yu pojie lujing - Jiyu 2012 nian Gansusheng xinren Tegang jiaoshi de diaocha* (Practical challenges of Special Post

Plan in ethnic minority regions and the solutions: Based on a survey of the new special post teachers in Gansu province in 2012). *Educational Theory and Practice*, 34, 26–30.

Liu, P. (2014). *Xibu shengyu "nongcun Tegang jiaoshi" laiyuan jiegou ji xiangguan zhengce jianyi - Yi Guangxi tegang jiaoshi weili* (The structure of origins of "rural special post teachers" in western China and policy recommendations: A example of special post teacher in Guangxi province). *Educational Theory and Practice*, 23, 35–37.

Lu, H., & Ngai, P. (2014). *Dangdai zhongguo dierdai nongmingong de shenfen rentong, qinggan yu jiti xingdong* (Self-identity, emotion, and collective action among the second generation of peasant-workers in China). *Shehui (Chinese Journal of Sociology)*, 34(4), 1–24.

Lu, X. (2003). *Dangdai zhongguo shehui jieceng de fenghua yu liudong* (The divisions and changes of contemporary Chinese social classes). *Jiangsu Shehui Kexue (Jiangsu Social Sciences)*, 4, 1–9.

Murphy, R. (2004). Turning peasants into modern Chinese citizens: "population quality" discourse, demographic transition and primary education. *The China Quarterly*, 177, 1–20.

Pan, Y., & Chen, J. (2008). *Jieji huayu de xiaoshi* (The dissappearance of class discourse). *Kaifang Shidai (Open Times)*, 5, 53–60.

Pan, Y., Lu, L., & Zhang, H. (2010). *Jieji de xingcheng: Jianzu gongdi shang de laodong kongzhi yu jianzu gongren de jiti kangzheng* (Formation of class: Labor control at construction sites and the class struggles of construction wokers). *Kaifang Shidai (Open Times)*, 5, 5–26.

Shen, Y. (2006). *Shehui zhuanxing yu gongrenjieji de zaixingcheng* (The social transformation and Reformation of Chinese working class). *Shehuixue Yanjiu (Sociological Studies)*, 2, 13–36.

Si, H. (2009). *Qianru cunzhuang de xuexiao - Rencun jiaoyu de lishi renleixue tanjiu (The school embedded in a village – a historical and anthropological exploration of schooling in Rencun).* Beijing: Education Science Publishing House.

Tomba, L. (2004). Creating an urban middle class: Social engineering in Beijing. *The China Journal*, 51, 1–26. doi:10.2307/3182144

Willis, P. (1977). *Learning to labour: How working class kids get working class jobs.* Westmead, UK: Saxon House.

Woronov, T.E. (2011). Learning to serve: Urban youth, vocational schools and new class formations in China. *The China Journal*, 66, 77–99.

Xiong, Y. (2010). *Diceng, xuexiao yu jieji zaishengchan* (Underclass, school, and class reproduction). *Kaifang Shidai (Open Times)*, 1, 94–110.

Yang, T., & Yang, Y. (2010). *Xibu nongcun xuexiao Tegang jiaoshi xianzhuang diaocha yu sikao: Jiyu Guizhousheng Z zhongxue de ge'an yanjiu* (An investigation and review of current conditions of special post teachers in western China: A case study of Z school in Guizhou province). *Educational Theory and Practice*, 23, 6–18.

Yu, K. (2014). *Zhongguo qianfada nongcun diqu jiaoyu buju jiegou tiaozheng yu gonggong kongjian de tuique – Jiyu jinxi Shilouxian de diaocha* (Redistribution of school locations in less-developed rural regions in China and the retreat of public space: An investigation in Shilou County in Western Shanxi). *Academic Journal of Beijing Normal University (Social Sciences Edition)*, 1, 26–36.

Yu, X., & Pan, Y. (2008). *Xiaofei shehui yu "xinshengdai dagongmei" zhutixing zaizao* (Consumer society and remaking the subjectivities of "new generation of dagongmei"). *Shehuixue Yanjiu (Sociological Studies)*, 3, 143–171.

Zheng, X., Du, L., Wei, M., et al. (2012). *Bluebook of special post teachers in China.* Beijing: Education Science Publishing House.

5

EDUCATIONAL PRACTICE IN A FIELD OF MEDIATION

Elite University Graduates' Participation Experience of an Alternative Program of Schoolteacher Recruitment for Rural China

Yue Melody Yin, Karen Dooley, and Guanglun Michael Mu

Introduction of an Alternative Schoolteacher Recruitment Program (EGRT)

The reform era has seen a widening of the fissure of social and economic development between urban and rural areas in China (Knight & Gunatilaka, 2010). One of the profoundly harmful consequences of this unbalanced development is the gap of teacher quality. The shift from the central planning model that attracted high-achieving but disadvantaged high school students to normal institutions of *shī fàn* (师范, teacher education) and assignment to rural schools has been accompanied by a chronic shortage of teachers – of any calibre – for rural schools (Crowley, 2016; Zhu & Han, 2006).

Internationally, there is also a long history of initiatives designed to recruit teachers to work in difficult-to-staff schools. In many settings around the world, teaching in disadvantaged schools has not been a career of choice for high academic achievers. The most outstanding graduates of traditional teacher education programs are typically snapped up by more advantaged schools, while high-achieving non-education majors are not generally attracted to careers in school teaching at all (Brown, 2015; Haines & Hallgarten, 2002; Tamir, 2009). To supply high-calibre teachers for such schools, some of the more recent initiatives in both traditional university-based teacher education and alternative teacher recruitment programs have made high academic achievement a key selection criterion. The Teach For All network which recruits outstanding graduates for fast-tracked teacher certification or licensing in 46 countries is one of the most widely known of alternative teacher recruitment programs (Scholes et al., 2017). Although Teach

82 Yue Melody Yin et al.

For All programs differ substantially in design and ethos, they all recognise that demonstrated academic capability is a necessary – if not sufficient – accomplishment of high-calibre teachers. As the existence of a diversity of such programs in disadvantaged rural areas attests, China has been a theatre of considerable development in this regard (Crowley, 2016).

This chapter probes this development in teacher recruitment. We report a study of participant experience of one of the programs that recruits high academic achievers from prestigious Chinese universities for service in schools in rural China – the Exceptional Graduates as Rural Teachers program (EGRT).[1] Along with other policy developments of the reform era, programs like EGRT that channel elite graduates from prestigious universities to rural schools are one of several different responses to the teacher shortage. These programs bring social phenomena of considerable sociological interest into being. In these conditions, the essence of EGRT involves connecting two social groups – exceptional graduates from prestigious universities and rural students in disadvantaged schools – who seldom encounter each other in educational interaction given their different positions in socio-educational space (although some exceptional graduates did begin their educational trajectory in disadvantaged schools).

EGRT brings a particular set of educational values to its mission of transcending the social and geographical divide. One of these values entails pursuit of high *sù zhì* (素质, quality) education for students who live and study in disadvantaged conditions. As in the Chinese educational context, 'high quality' education is opposed to 'examination-oriented' education. The term denotes schooling that makes use of student-centred methods with the intent of forming young people who are well-rounded, morally cultivated, rich in skills required by the national economy at a time of intensifying international competition (e.g., higher-order thinking, teamwork, creativity), and nationalistic in identity (Dello-Iacovo, 2009; Wu, 2012, 2016). A second value concerns educational equality across schools in different social and economic conditions. It entails commitment to providing all students with access to high-quality education. A third value relates to the development of teachers and students with entrepreneurial dispositions prized in the global economy – amongst these, leadership in identifying and resolving social problems, and constant hard work and striving to that end. Given their importance in the EGRT culture, these core values constitute the main facets of fellows' identity, which might distinguish them from other teachers. It was cause for consideration, therefore, that in her interactions with EGRT fellows, the first author noticed that while some seemed to apply EGRT values and pursue EGRT goals in their practice in rural schools, others did not seem to do so, in part at least. This observation prompted the investigation reported here. The focus was on the implication of program values in fellows' decisions to join EGRT, perceived disparities between their pre-service assumptions and in-service perceptions, and their enactment of the roles they took up in placement schools.

The study may be of interest in China and beyond. Internationally, research suggests that teachers' practice in the classroom is related not only to their reasons for entering the teaching profession (Chong & Low, 2009; Manuel & Hughes, 2006), but also to disparities between pre-service expectation and in-service experience (DiCicco et al., 2014; Kyriacou et al., 2003). However, programs like EGRT in China have not yet received due scholarly attention: relationships amongst EGRT fellows' enactment of their roles, their initial reasons for participation, and the disparities between pre-service assumptions and in-service experiences remain largely unknown. The EGRT program and its participants are shaped by China's social, political, and cultural particularities; however, the investigation may be of wider interest given global reform transfer (Crowley, 2016) that has seen high academic achievement prioritised as a selection criterion for teacher recruitment in a multiplicity of settings around the world.

In what follows, we use Bourdieusian concepts to provide an overview of EGRT fellows' experiences in three domains: 1) the reasons behind their participation in EGRT, 2) disparities between pre-service expectations and in-service experience, and 3) the way the fellows took up EGRT roles in the rural schools in which they were placed. Then we introduce the empirical study reported here. We then present a quantitative analysis of the relationships amongst the three domains of EGRT fellows' experiences. We conclude the chapter with implications for similar alternative schoolteacher recruitment programs, suggesting that participants might cultivate the practices of reflexive curriculum workers.

A Bourdieusian Overview of the EGRT Program

At first glance, the choice that exceptional graduates from prestigious universities make to teach in rural schools is likely to be considered by many as irrational, unexpected, and surprising. Having graduated from top-tier universities, these young people have acquired an educational qualification recognised universally, knowledge and skills essential for success in neoliberal economic competition within and beyond the nation, as well as social networks likely to be advantageous in the world of work. With all these valuable resources and capacities at their disposal, they enjoy the prospect of career prosperity and status in mainstream society. In Bourdieusian terms, the field of higher education has endowed these young people with symbolic, cultural, social, and potential economic capital adequate to a most favourable position within the field of the high-end labour market. Rural schools, long haunted by deficit discourse, appear to be extraordinarily distant from the life worlds of these advantaged young people. The social chasm between the field of higher education – and the most privileged positions in that field – and the field of rural schooling appears unbridgeable. Therefore, the reasons behind the choice that graduates of prestigious universities make to teach in rural schools constitute a legitimate sociological problem. In her doctoral thesis, Yin (2018) engaged in a nuanced analysis of the reasons behind young people's participation in EGRT. She found that EGRT fellows reported multi-layered and inter-nested reasons for their program participation. Some of these had their provenance, variously, in resistance to conventional life trajectories; demand for a buffer against lost goals and identities; and solutions to life crises. Others seem to be rooted in an instrumental drive arising from the lure of reputation, capacity-building opportunities, and professional development resources available through EGRT, along with an integrative drive resonant with the visions of the educational values celebrated by EGRT (e.g., teaching as leadership, educational quality, and social justice). These latter reasons are the ones we are interested in here.

The Bourdieusian concept of field is useful for our purpose of investigating the decision of young people to join EGRT and their subsequent practice in their placement schools. In conceptualising social space, Bourdieu used the metaphor – drawn from twentieth-century physics – of a force field. Social space warps around agents with the richest resources or capital, that is, those who occupy the strongest positions in the field. Accordingly, the actions of those in the weakest positions are influenced by the existence, strategy and practice of the most powerful agents, even if they seldom – or indeed, never – encounter each other in direct interaction.

As noted earlier, EGRT is predicated on bringing agents from some of the weakest and strongest positions in the broad national field of education into contact. This requires attention to not only the social interactions of these agents, but also the structural positions they inhabit in that field and its sub-fields. To this end, it is useful to understand the EGRT program as a sub-field within the national educational field. This particular sub-field mediates the logic of higher education – prestigious universities in particular, and that of disadvantaged rural schools. We understand the EGRT program as a field of mediation (Mu, 2018) within which there is a confluence of seemingly incommensurable fields, in this case, the field of higher education and the field of rural schooling.

To elaborate, in the EGRT program, the logic of practice mediates the incommensurability between the fields of higher education and rural schooling, as graduates from prestigious universities are channelled into disadvantaged educational contexts. Through layers of competition in the selection process, EGRT bestows a resource-rich opportunity on successful applicants. Selection marks their exceptionality and immediately labels them as excellent and elite educational pioneers. In this respect, successful applicants accrue symbolic capital within the field of EGRT. By dint of its conceptualisation of educational work as leadership, EGRT further enculturates novice graduates from prestigious universities into the neoliberal logic of individualism, performativity, and competitiveness. Working in tandem with this, given its stated mission of promoting educational quality and social justice, EGRT also sparks the altruism of graduates from prestigious universities and charges these young people with the redemptive task of saving the rural world. By multiple means, EGRT speaks to the field of higher education, tailors a program for talented graduates, and successfully convinces them that there is nothing to lose but much to gain when joining EGRT. The EGRT program also speaks to the field of rural schooling, strategically selecting hard-to-staff schools desperately in need of high-quality teachers. Hence, EGRT brings to a confluence the fields of higher education and rural schooling that would not converge in the absence of a field of mediation.

The question remains: why do only some, and not all, graduates from prestigious universities choose to participate in EGRT? If the benefits of EGRT programs are so desirable, why do they appeal to only some of the pool of potential EGRT fellows? Bourdieu (1977) repeatedly reminds us of the match between the habitus of disposition, embodied capital, and classificatory schemes on the one hand, and the field within and for which those elements of habitus were shaped and the value of capital was (arbitrarily) defined. Yin (2018) provides abundant evidence that EGRT fellows tend to be those who have been socialised into a set of dual habituses of entrepreneurship and altruism that 'click' with the logic of EGRT. Their habituses may have grown out of the fellows' early upbringing through primary socialisation within the domestic milieu or/and learning and inculcation through secondary socialisation within powerful institutions such as schools and universities. The parameters of this chapter preclude a more detailed discussion. But it is noteworthy that most, if not all EGRT fellows, reported becoming 'caged birds' (笼中之鸟, *lóng zhōng zhī niǎo*) within the field of rural schooling even though they feel like 'fish in water' (to use the Bourdieusian metaphor) within the field of EGRT. In other words, while all the fellows felt very comfortable within EGRT, they found that rural schools were substantially different from what they had anticipated. Marked disparities between the fellows' pre-service expectations and in-service perceptions epitomised this feeling of being out of place within the field of rural schooling. These disparities manifest in mismatches between their pre-service imaginings of rural students, teachers and schools, and their in-service actualities and teacherly selves (Yin, 2018).

Bourdieusian theory suggests multiple and complex interpretation of the mismatches experienced by EGRT fellows. First, due at least in part to the durability of habitus formed in the field of higher education, EGRT fellows may not be able or willing to counter-train this habitus in order to fit into the field of rural schooling. Second, due at least in part to the field-specificity of capital, that which was once valued in the fields of higher education and EGRT may depreciate, be nullified, or even incur penalty in the field of rural schooling. At first glance, such interpretations seem to be at loggerheads with the argument we have made about the field of mediation in which the fields of higher education and rural education are supposed to converge. This does not necessarily undermine the notion of the field of mediation; rather, it points to its usefulness. To put it simply, the mediation effect of EGRT at the confluence of the fields of higher education and the rural schooling is by definition imperfect.

86 Yue Melody Yin et al.

As a field of mediation, EGRT has not yet been able to, or may never be able to comprehensively prepare graduates from prestigious universities for the teaching profession in rural schools. This argument draws attention to the relative autonomy of the EGRT as a field – in the classic Bourdieusian conceptualisation, fields are distinguished by the particularity and autonomy of their logic of practice, although there may be some heteronomy. In this case, the field of EGRT is not identical to those of higher education and rural schooling. With its own logic, then, EGRT exists as a legitimate field of mediation in its own right. It is therefore not surprising to see the disparities between EGRT fellows' pre-service expectations and their in-service perceptions. It is worth noting that these educational fields are somewhat heteronomous to the extent that neoliberal economic logic underpins practice. This is a point to which we will return in our discussion of findings.

In the context of disparities, a further question emerges regarding the manner in which EGRT fellows play out their roles in rural schools. Yin (2018) discovered that EGRT fellows played diverse roles riven with conflict. In terms of their teacher role, the fellows had to constantly negotiate the tensions between the quality-oriented teaching favoured by the urban middle class and professionals (Dello-Iacovo, 2009) and the examination-based teaching and memorisation required for surviving and thriving in a regimen of high-stakes testing and evaluation. Some fellows chose to give up on the 'hopeless' students while quietly walking through the guilt brought about by a choice that violated their egalitarian beliefs. Beyond the teacher role, EGRT fellows reported that they performed the roles of leaders. Some fellows consciously performed as charismatic leaders to exert their leadership while others seemed to resort to simple corporal punishment as rural teachers. This returns us to our initial question: Why did the fellows demonstrate different enactments of core EGRT values while working in their placement schools?

We have briefly discussed reasons for participation in EGRT, disparities between EGRT fellows' pre-service expectations and in-service perceptions, and the enactment of roles as EGRT fellows. These three aspects unfold across time and space in the course of social practice. The first aspect occurs in the moment when graduates from prestigious universities leave the field of higher education and enter the mediation field of EGRT and subsequently, the field of rural schooling. The second aspect occurs during the transition periods from field to field. The third aspect occurs during the EGRT service period in rural schools. Taking into account the diachronic perspective of Bourdieu's sociology, we grapple with the connections between these three aspects. To this end, we quantitatively analyse the relationships between these aspects.

The Relationship of Participation Reasons, Assumption-Perception Disparities, and Enactment of EGRT Values

The analyses of Yin (2018) began with a theoretically driven thematic analysis (Braun & Clarke, 2006; Holloway & Todres, 2003) of interviews with EGRT fellows. Then a set of questionnaire items was developed to gauge the experience of EGRT fellows in three domains, namely reasons for participation in EGRT, disparities between pre-service assumptions and in-service perceptions, and enactment of EGRT values through educational practices in placement schools. The online questionnaire was completed by 149 respondents. Descriptive statistics pointed to a prominent characteristic of respondents: The EGRT fellows were high academic achievers with little teacher education/training, formally or informally. An overwhelming percentage of the participants were 'academic winners' in high-stakes tests of entrance examination for both senior high schools and universities. Only 20 participants (13.42 per cent) had not attended key point senior high schools; in addition, only 20 had not won admission to a prestigious university in China. Only six participants (4.03 per cent) were students of Education at university.

After the descriptive statistical analyses, Exploratory Factor Analysis (EFA) and Confirmative Factor Analysis (CFA) were applied in order to test whether indicators in the three domains formulated a latent factor/construct. The three domains, it will be recalled, are 1) EGRT-specific participation reasons, 2) disparities between fellows' pre-service assumptions and in-service perceptions, and 3) fellows' enactment of EGRT roles in placement schools. Multiple regression was then performed to examine the relationships among the three domains.

Yin's (2018) qualitative interview analyses found diverse reasons behind EGRT participation. In the current chapter, however, only reasons specifically related to EGRT are included in the analysis. Social-personal reasons (see Yin, 2018) are excluded. EGRT-specific reasons are manifested in two aspects, namely self-benefiting reasons and altruistic reasons. Self-benefiting reasons were measured by five items (shown in Figure 5.1). Exploratory Factor Analysis (EFA) extracted one factor, explaining 54.46 per cent of the total variance of

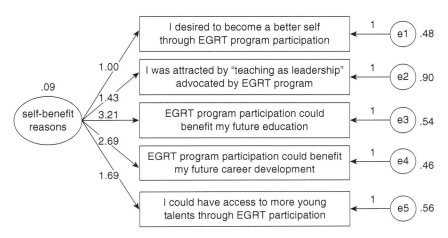

FIGURE 5.1 Measurement model of self-benefiting reasons

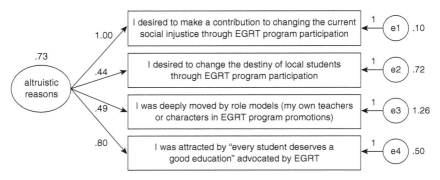

FIGURE 5.2 Measurement model of altruistic reasons

the five items. Altruistic reasons were measured by four items (shown in Figure 5.2). EFA yielded a single-factor solution, accounting for 51.64 per cent of the variance of the four items.

Confirmatory Factor Analysis (CFA) was then used to test the model fit. The five-item single-factor measurement model for self-benefiting reasons fit well (NFI=0.978, RFI=0.935, IFI=0.994, TLI=0.980, CFI=0.993, RMSEA=.053). Cronbach's alpha value (.73) indicates a reasonably high internal consistency reliability within the items. The four-item single-factor measurement model for altruistic reasons also fit well (NFI=1.000, RFI=.1.000, IFI=1.017, TLI=1.051, CFI=1.000, RMASE <.000), with a Cronbach's alpha value of .65.

Yin's (2018) interviews discovered multiple disparities between EGRT fellows' pre-service assumptions and in-service perceptions. Here we focus on fellows' assumption-perception disparities regarding rural students' knowledge base, personal intelligence, learning motivation, and moral behaviour. Paired Samples-T tests show statistically significant difference between fellows' pre-service assumptions and in-service perceptions in all the aforementioned aspects regarding rural students, with pre-service assumptions significantly better than in-service perceptions (see Table 5.1).

The magnitude of the disparities was measured by the score of in-service perceptions after subtracting that of pre-service assumptions. In this way, four variables were created, with each measuring the assumption-perception disparity in one of the aforementioned four aspects.

To gauge the extent to which EGRT fellows performed their roles according the EGRT core values, Yin (2018) drew on her interview findings and developed four items. EFA extracted one factor which explains 53.20 per cent of the total variance of the four items. CFA validated the model fit of the four-item single-factor measurement model (NFI=0.978, RFI=0.960, IFI=1.006, TLI=1.019, CFI=1.000, RMASE <.000). Cronbach's alpha of the four items is .70. The model is shown in Figure 5.3.

TABLE 5.1 Descriptive statistics and paired samples-T Test

Outcome	Assumption M	SD	Perception M	SD	n	95% CI for Mean Difference	t	df	Sig. (2-tailed)
Knowledge base	2.57	.70	2.29	.96	149	.12, .45	3.35	148	.001
Personal intelligence	2.69	.64	2.52	.91	149	-.00, 3.34	1.93	148	.056
Learning motivation	3.46	.86	2.79	.84	149	.48, .88	6.69	148	.000
Moral behaviour	3.58	.67	3.18	.93	149	.22, .57	4.52	148	.000

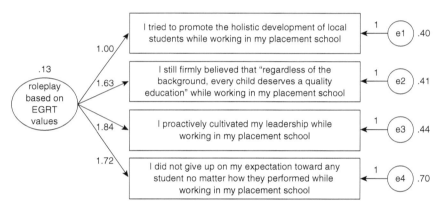

FIGURE 5.3 Measurement model of role play based on EGRT values

Multiple regression was then performed to examine the relationships between reasons for EGRT participation (self-benefiting reasons and altruistic reasons); disparities between pre-service assumptions and in-service perceptions regarding rural students' knowledge base, learning ability, learning motivation, and moral behaviour; as well as EGRT fellows' enactment of their roles in rural schools. Reasons and disparities were treated as independent variables and role enactment according to the EGRT core values was treated as a dependent variable. Regression results (stepwise) show that role enactment based on EGRT values was associated with altruistic reasons, self-benefiting reasons, and disparity regarding assumptions-perceptions of students' intelligence (see Table 5.2). These three predictors together explained 24.0 per cent of the variance of EGRT fellows' role enactment as accordant with EGRT values.

As shown in Table 5.2, both altruistic and self-benefiting reasons for participation in EGRT contribute to fellows' EGRT core value-based role enactment in placement schools. That is, fellows who were more attracted

90 Yue Melody Yin et al.

TABLE 5.2 Regression analysis results of predictors of EGRT value-based roleplays

	B	SE	β	R Square	Adjusted R Square	F
Constant	2.401	.277				
altruistic reasons	.371	.069	.405[***]	.164	.158	28.781
Constant	1.989	.305				
altruistic reasons	.251	.079	.274[**]			
Self-benefiting reasons	.237	.081	.252[**]	.210	.199	19.405
Constant	2.037	.297				
altruistic reasons	.228	.077	.249[**]			
Self-benefiting reasons	.253	.079	.269[**]			
Disparity 2	.131	.044	.214[**]	.255	.240	16.555

$**p<.01$, $***p<.001$

to EGRT due to opportunities for developing the self and helping disadvantaged students were more likely to draw on EGRT values as they performed their roles in placement schools. The disparity between pre-service assumption and in-service perception regarding local students' intelligence was likewise influential. When local students' intelligence perceived by fellows during their in-service years was better than what fellows assumed before they commenced their EGRT service, fellows were more likely to hold EGRT core values when they performed their roles in placement schools, and vice versa. In brief, the degree to which fellows hold EGRT values when performing their roles in placement schools was influenced by their original participation reasons and disparities of pre-service assumption about, and in-service perception of students' intelligence. The question remains, however, as to why these factors, rather than others, influence fellows' EGRT value-based role enactment in placement schools.

Social Dynamics Underlying Different Enactments of EGRT Values

Chinese teachers, especially those in disadvantaged schools (e.g., rural schools in the context of the current chapter), have long been portrayed metaphorically as silkworms who work relentlessly, and as candles that burn themselves out to light students up (Boyle, 2000; Hu, 2002; Ouyang, 2003). Within the field of rural schooling, teachers' altruistic dispositions often accrue high symbolic value. Consequently, the habitus of altruism becomes an embodied form of cultural capital. It is this habitus that may prompt rural teachers to devote themselves to the teaching profession. The field of higher education differs, however, in its neoliberal logic of producing graduates who vie for capitals required for success in the labour market, who strategise to remain competitive within the fields of power and economy, and who pursue entrepreneurial and individual leadership. The habitus of entrepreneurialism may hold the neoliberalised bodies aloof from rural schools. This does not necessarily mean that the field of higher education completely denounces habitus of altruism. Neither does it indicate that the field of rural schooling is fully free of neoliberal intrusion. Our argument here points to the enculturation and socialisation of a particular habitus that aligns with the dominant logic of a particular field – the habitus of altruism of and for the field of rural schooling and the habitus of entrepreneurialism of and for the field of higher education.

The habitus may not always remain a singular form. Construing the program of EGRT as a field of mediation, we observe that the logic of EGRT astutely dissolves a plethora of oppositions between the dominant logic of the field of higher education and that of the field of rural schooling. The logic of EGRT purposefully encourages both altruism and entrepreneurialism, that is, plural habituses. EGRT functions as a magnetic field, the gravitational force of which pulls exceptional graduates from prestigious universities who have plural habituses into this field. Due at least in part to the durability of habituses, EGRT fellows may perform their roles in rural schools according to the core values of EGRT, consciously or unconsciously. Indeed, as the findings of this chapter suggest, EGRT fellows who reported stronger self-benefiting and altruistic reasons for participation in the program are more likely to work in accord with the core values of the program when they perform their roles in placement schools. In summary, during the transition among different fields, from the original field (field of higher education) to the terminal field (field of rural schooling) through the field of mediation (EGRT), the degree of match between fellows from the original field and the field of mediation in terms of capital and habitus largely influences practice in the terminal field.

However, that practice was vulnerable to the effects of classificatory schemes about intelligence buried in the habitus of the fellows. As we noted earlier, when local students were perceived as less intelligent than assumed or even "stupid", then EGRT fellows tended to give up on their previous core educational beliefs and ideals. In doing so, they precluded at least some, if not all of their students, from access to the resources supposed to be made available through EGRT. At the same time, they favoured those whom they deemed academically intelligent. This reproduced an old dynamic: disadvantaged rural students who make it to higher education are themselves likely to have enjoyed the favour of teachers on grounds of their intelligence.

Dominant classes, Bourdieu (1993, 1998) argued, create sociodicies, that work as theodicies of their privilege. Drawing on Weber, Bourdieu's point is that they justify, mystify, and naturalise their own class ascendancy. When the dominant are dependent on academic achievement, as in the case of the students of elite schools in Bourdieu's (1998) work, the justifications are likely to turn on academic capital. Specifically, "merit" or the "natural gift of intelligence" may be read off socio-educational advantage and embedded in the habitus as classificatory systems for imposing intelligence-based divisions on the world. The efficacy of these principles of division arises from their apparently "innate" and embodied quality (Bourdieu, 2001). In consequence, misrecognition is built into reproduction. Academic capital required for school success is arbitrarily and selectively valued, legitimated, and rewarded by schools; and lack of academic capital is often misrecognised as, and mistakenly equated with, an inherent lack of academic intelligence.

Consider the position of the EGRT fellows. Exceptional academic achievements (outstanding GPA) and prestigious university backgrounds were intensively stressed by the program. These "titles" constructed the basis of the injustice of intelligence. The selection criteria of EGRT also denoted other required capitals, such as cultural capital (extracurricular actives and internship), symbolic capital (university honours), and social capital (relations with influential celebrities). With the marketing strategies of emphasis on natural ability and education-based meritocracy, EGRT program participation was regarded as a symbol of distinction in terms of academic and overall capacity by fellows themselves. This sense of superiority had already been revealed by studies of alternative teacher recruitment programs in other countries. In the UK, Teach First participants regarded themselves as "bright, sparkly people" (Smart et al., 2009, p. 38), while in the US, Teach for America participants saw themselves as being intelligent (Straubhaar & Gottfried, 2016).

Based on the selection essence, these successes of the academic race such as the National College Entrance Examination and EGRT enabled fellows to believe that they were selected based on intelligence, rather than other structural factors like family social economic status (Smart et al., 2009). Therefore, the winners in these competitions should be smart/talented. The parallel consequence was that the academic failure of local students was much more likely to be attributed to or misrecognised as lack of intelligence. Aligned with this logic, EGRT further conceptualises fellows as future entrepreneurial and corporate leaders, that future success of EGRT fellows was deserved and inevitable. This, as Bourdieu (1993) argued in another context, "is the language of leaders who feel themselves to be legitimised by 'intelligence' and who dominate a society founded on discrimination based on intelligence" (p.178). The potential vision delineated by EGRT exacerbated the injustice of intelligence, which made them further position themselves as dominant and justified their sense of superiority. It is a tautological and self-reinforcing position and positioning.

If EGRT fellows positioned themselves as smart individuals and bright future leaders, the perceived gulf of intelligence between themselves and local students was further enlarged. In this situation, local students were more easily misrecognised as lacking innate intelligence. It was harder for them to recognise that particular subject knowledges and personal abilities were arbitrarily selected and

Elite University Graduates in Rural Schools **93**

then celebrated in schooling or EGRT contexts. When intelligence was conceptualised as an innate personal ability, born within the body of students, EGRT fellows tended to give up on practice that had been based on EGRT values which they had previously deeply believed in.

EGRT Fellows as Reflexive Curriculum Workers

The findings reported here shed light on similar alternative teacher recruitment programs that seek delivery of high-quality human resources from the original field of higher education to the terminal field of disadvantaged schools. When these programs played the role as a field of mediation to communicate with two distant fields, the original field was usually much more privileged than the terminal field. If the match between the habitus of members in the original field and the mediation field shaped the social practice in the terminal field, the rules and principle of the mediation field bear careful reconsideration. Many studies have criticised similar programs like Teach for America and Teach First for catering for the middle-class values and tastes of agents in the original field, which has the effect of perpetuating or even exacerbating the educational inequalities that such programs purport to address (Anderson, 2013; Smart et al., 2009).

Although strategies of recruiting outstanding academic achievers as teachers have successfully improved overall educational quality in systems such as Finland's, it does not sociologically follow that academic high achievers are the ideal candidates for pedagogues in disadvantaged schools. On the contrary, these high academic achievers with prestigious university educational backgrounds are inclined to easily attribute students' academic failure to innate personal faults or the lack of merit, leading them to easily give up on previously held egalitarian beliefs and values when faced with challenges in schools. In this way, the vigorous advisement and emphasis of EGRT fellow in terms of their personal intelligence and capabilities has the potential to intensify the injustice of intelligence. How might program leaders pre-empt these problems? One solution is for programs such as EGRT to cultivate teachers as reflexive curriculum workers.

Like the reflexive social scientist discussed in the introductory chapter of this volume, the reflexive teacher seeks to identify, in their curricular work, biases that arise from their positions in, and trajectories through, social space (Bourdieu & Wacquant, 1992). For teachers, the professional field in which pedagogies are created and debated is of particular salience in this regard. In this field, a binary opposition between teacher-centred and student-centred pedagogy has long been invoked – Chinese educators' strategic appropriation of the work of John Dewey in the early twentieth century is a case in point (Bevis, 2014). A hundred years on, this binary is implicated in the values of quality education, and equality of access to such, that are at the heart of EGRT. Given the association of student-centred pedagogy with quality, EGRT fellows despaired when teacher-centred, even rote, instruction in foundational cultural knowledge and basic writing skills was necessary (Yin, 2018). How might an alternative response be possible? Is there a more optimistic way to understand the remarkable resilience of traditional pedagogy in the face of progressive or student-centred *doxa* that induced such anxiety in the fellows? This is a problem, encountered in multiple places around the world, and at different moments in the history of modern and mass education. Insights stemming from research with rebellious students in Singapore offers insights into a way forward (Luke, 2008/2018).

Traditional pedagogies, it has been suggested (Luke, 2008/2018), can be understood as a means by which the teacher as master literate and cultural elder within a customary community is able to offer children the intergenerational gift of culturally significant texts and literate technologies. In such a community, academic achievement is gifted by elders to children, not the proof of some supposed natural gift. Yin (2018) conceptualises "localised pedagogic capital" to understand the capacity of rural teachers who skilfully and astutely use traditional pedagogies to enhance the odds of student success in high-stakes tests. Yet the use of more didactic pedagogies need not preclude student-centred pedagogies. The trick is to work out when traditional pedagogies are warranted, and to systematically weave these into the fabric of quality education. This curricular work requires the teacher to be able to identify biases that might stem from occupancy of one or other position in the professional field of pedagogic debate.

The teacher's positions in, and trajectories through, the social spaces of everyday life are also relevant to understanding and resolving the problems identified in the research reported here. Intelligence, as Bourdieu (1993, 1998) argued, can be viewed as an artefact of social experience. For the EGRT fellows, the luck of birth into more privileged urban and (sometimes) rural families, and the lucky accident of encounters with encouraging mentors on the part of those who "showed promise", are some of the social experiences implicated in glittering academic achievement, and thence selection for EGRT (Yin, 2018). In moments of professional stress, the classificatory schema about intelligence buried in the habitus of the academically successful can override their commitment to equality. A reflexive understanding of the social origins of their achievement and classificatory schema is essential if teachers are to put a spanner in the works of schooling as a machine that bestows the symbolic capital of 'intelligence' on some, while exerting symbolic violence on their less advantaged peers. This is cause for consideration not only for alternative programs of teacher recruitment such as EGRT but also for university-based programs – and not only in China. Throughout the world, neoliberal globalisation provides ideal conditions for a flourishing of the injustice of intelligence. Teacherly reflexivity is one means for holding on to and enacting visions of equality of access to quality education.

Acknowledgement

Yin's work in this chapter was supported by China Scholarship Council and Queensland University of Technology.

Note

1 EGRT is a pseudonym created to capture the component of the program that is of interest in this chapter, that is, the use of outstanding academic achievement as a selection criterion. Our interest is in the implications of this criterion for participant experience rather than the program per se.

References

Anderson, A. (2013). Teach for America and symbolic violence: A Bourdieuian analysis of education's next quick-fix. *The Urban Review*, *45*(5), 684–700.

Bevis, T.B. (2014). *A history of higher education exchange: China and America*. New York: Routledge.

Bourdieu, P. (1977). *Outline of a theory of a practice* (Trans. R. Nice). Cambridge: Cambridge University Press.

Bourdieu, P. (1993). *Sociology in question* (Trans. R. Nice). London: Sage.

Bourdieu, P. (1998). *The state nobility: Elite schools in the field of power* (Trans. L.C. Clough). Cambridge: Polity.

Bourdieu, P. (2001). *Masculine domination* (Trans. R. Nice). Cambridge: Polity.

Bourdieu P., & Wacquant, L. (1992). *An invitation to reflexive sociology*. Chicago: University of Chicago Press.

Boyle, J. (2000). Education for teachers of English in China. *Journal of Education for Teaching*, *26*(2), 147–155.

Braun, V., & Clarke, V. (2006). Using thematic analysis in psychology. *Qualitative Research in Psychology*, *3*(2), 77–101.

Brown, J. (2015). The flow of higher qualified new teachers into challenging UK high schools. *Research Papers in Education*, *30*(3), 287–304.

Chong, S., & Low, E.-L. (2009). Why I want to teach and how I feel about teaching – formation of teacher identity from pre-service to the beginning teacher phase. *Educational Research for Policy and Practice*, *8*(1), 59–72.

Crowley, C.B. (2016). Teach For/Future China and the politics of alternative teacher certification programs in China. In L. Lim & M.W. Apple (Eds.), *The strong state and curriculum reform: Assessing the politics and possibilities of educational change in Asia* (pp. 1310–1347). New York: Routledge.

Dello-Iacovo, B. (2009). Curriculum reform and 'Quality Education' in China: An overview. *International Journal of Educational Development*, *29*(3), 241–249.

DiCicco, M., Sabella, L., Jordan, R., Boney, K., & Jones, P. (2014). Great expectations: The mismatched selves of a beginning teacher. *The Qualitative Report*, *19*(42), 1.

Haines, E., & Hallgarten, J. (2002). From ivory towers to chalkface: Recruiting teachers from the elite universities. In M. Johnson & J. Hallgarten (Eds.), *From victims of change to agents of change: The future of the teaching profession*. London: Institute for Public Policy Research.

Holloway, I., & Todres, L. (2003). The status of method: Flexibility, consistency and coherence. *Qualitative Research*, *3*(3), 345–357.

Hu, G. (2002). Potential cultural resistance to pedagogical imports: The case of communicative language teaching in China. *Language, Culture and Curriculum, 15*(2), 93–105.

Knight, J., & Gunatilaka, R. (2010). The rural-urban divide in China: Income but not happiness? *The Journal of Development Studies, 46*(3), 506–534.

Kyriacou, C., Kunc, R., Stephens, P., & Hultgren, A. G. (2003). Student teachers' expectations of teaching as a career in England and Norway. *Educational Review, 55*(3), 255–263.

Luke, A. (2008/2018). Pedagogy as gift. In A. Luke, *Critical literacy, schooling, and social justice. The collected works of Allan Luke* (pp. 272–296). New York: Routledge.

Manuel, J., & Hughes, J. (2006). "It has always been my dream": Exploring pre-service teachers' motivations for choosing to teach. *Teacher Development, 10*(1), 5–24.

Mu, G.M. (2018). *Building resilience of floating children and left-behind children in China: Power, politics, participation, and education.* New York: Routledge.

Ouyang, H. (2003). Resistance to the communicative method of language instruction within a progressive Chinese university. In K.M. Anderson-Levitt (Ed.), *Local meanings, global schooling: Anthropology and world culture theory* (pp. 121–140). Basingstoke, UK: Palgrave Macmillan.

Scholes, L., Lampert, J., Burnett, B., Comber, B.M., Hoff, L., & Ferguson, A. (2017). The politics of quality teacher discourses: Implications for pre-service teachers in high poverty schools. *Australian Journal of Teacher Education, 42*(4), 19–43.

Smart, S., Hutchings, M., Maylor, U., Mendick, H., & Menter, I. (2009). Processes of middle-class reproduction in a graduate employment scheme. *Journal of Education and Work, 22*(1), 35–53.

Straubhaar, R., & Gottfried, M. (2016). Who joins Teach For America and why? Insights into the "typical" recruit in an urban school district. *Education and Urban Society, 48*(7), 627–649.

Tamir, E. (2009). Choosing to teach in urban schools among graduates of elite colleges. *Urban Education, 44*(5), 522–544.

Wu, J. (2012). Governing suzhi and curriculum reform in rural ethnic China: Viewpoints from the Miao and Dong communities in Qiandongnan. *Curriculum Inquiry, 42*(5), 652–681.

Wu, J.T. (2016). Ambivalent 'quality' and the educational sublime: Curriculum reform meets ethnic rural development in Southwest China. In Y. Guo & S. Guo (Eds.), *Spotlight on China: Changes in education under China's market economy* (pp. 67–84). Rotterdam, The Netherlands: Sense.

Yin, Y. (2018). *From university graduates to teachers in disadvantaged schools: A sociological study of participation in an alternative schoolteacher recruitment program* (unpublished PhD), Brisbane: Queensland University of Technology.

Zhu, X., & Han, X. (2006). Reconstruction of the teacher education system in China. *International Education Journal, 7*(1), 66–73. Available online at: https://eprints.qut.edu.au/120080/

6

RURAL CHILDREN'S ACADEMIC SUCCESS, TRANSFORMATIVE HABITUS, AND SOCIAL MOBILITY COST

He Li

Introduction

In the past four decades, the growing gap between the rich and the poor has become a global phenomenon. In China, the disparity between the city and the countryside is notoriously wide. Although polarisation undermines social solidarity, the status quo is less likely to be challenged as long as there is a reasonable prospect of upward mobility (Su et al., 2015). With the substantial decline in the proportion of rural students at Chinese elite universities, the faith in meritocracy is thus under threat. To tackle this issue, Chinese Premier Li Keqiang promised that in order to give rural children hope, their opportunity to enter prestigious universities needs to be gradually increased.

It has to be borne in mind that "the proportion of students from the various classes" in higher education "only very partially reflects the full extent of educational inequality" (Bourdieu & Passeron, 1979, p. 2), if not the wider social and economic injustice. It is particularly true in contemporary China where the rich and the powerful get ahead with education, leaving rural and floating children behind in schools of poor quality. At an age of entrenched inequality and social immobility, people of humble origins find it increasingly difficult to climb up the social ladder. This chapter is based on a study conducted in 2007–08 on students who had rural residency (户口, *hù kǒu*) but have managed to go to a top university against all odds. It is to address two key questions: 1) What makes the exceptions exceptional? 2) What is the cost of social mobility?

The exploration of the "secret" of these "wonder children"[1] in this chapter indeed unpacks the complexity of social mobility. The cost of upward mobility to the self, produced by "hidden injuries of class" (Sennett & Cobb, 1973), are revealed in literature on working-class achievers in the UK and the US, including social and psychological problems such as isolation and disconnections from one's background (cf. Hoggart, 1958; Jetten et al., 2008; London, 1989; Wentworth & Peterson, 2001). The study reported in the current chapter worked with rural achievers at a top Chinese university. Coming from "the least disadvantaged strata of the most disadvantaged classes" (Bourdieu & Passeron, 1979, p. 26), they shouldered a heavy burden of academic success. An analysis of their educational experience indicates that recruiting more rural students to prestigious universities is not an adequate solution to urban–rural disparity and rural crisis. How to break the structural constraints remains a puzzle for most rural students. But first and foremost, why is rural origin a disadvantage in the Chinese context?

Rural Disadvantages

Rural disadvantage is not a mere Chinese phenomenon. In developing countries, the urban–rural relationship represents a major conflict of interest (Lipton, 1977). The dominance of the urban centres "can reduce the possibility of economic development in the periphery" (Nash, 2012, p. 42). Despite the fact that half of the world's population live in rural areas, an almost universal tendency in developing countries is the persistent neglect in development discourses and the lack of appreciation of rural conditions in educational policy (INRULED, 2001).

The case in China is even more pronounced and complicated. Chinese civilisation is in essence rural. However, the countryside has been marginalised in its journey to modernisation. Urban-biased policies, especially the household registration system (*hù kǒu*) established in 1958, have positioned rural dwellers at the lower strata. Since China's economy took off, the government has relaxed its control over geographical mobility, but urban citizens still enjoy substantial advantages in public provisions in general, quality education in particular.

With a firm belief that "urbanisation is modernisation", the government views rural decline as a consequence of globalisation and industrialisation. By the end of 2016, the number of rural workers who had migrated to cities was about 282 million (Xinhua, 2017). Empty villages and vanishing rural life are the concomitants of left-behind children and elders, women and the sick. The situation is deplorable and paradoxical, as China now faces a serious environmental crisis and rising food-safety concerns that particularly threaten powerless rural citizens. Rather than empowering rural residents through education and revitalising rural China, the government sets the lofty goal to "build a highly urbanised, consumer-driven economy" as a remedy (Sheehan, 2017). An important measure is demolishing villages and building new towns and cities so as to relocate villagers and channel migrant workers to lower-tier, usually less developed cities and towns (ibid.). The break-neck pace of urbanisation however creates new problems, such as improper compensation for land appropriation, unstable employment, and a new class of urban poor (Hu & Chen, 2015). Worst of all is the shutdown of nearly three-quarters of all rural primary schools between 2000 and 2015, which actually sets up barriers for left-behind children to access nearby schools (Bagri, 2017). As for the floating children who move to the city with their migrant parents, they experience discrimination and exclusion from urban schools because of their rural dispositions (Mu & Hu, 2016; Mu & Jia, 2016).

To overcome rural disadvantages requires not only more resources and opportunities but also a reverse of rural brain drain. American sociologists Carr and Kefalas (2009) investigated the exodus of young people from America's countryside and found the adults in the community played a pivotal role in rural decline by pushing the brightest young people to leave. Does the same hold true in China? How have the rural children as the first-generation university students broken the spell of social reproduction? What is the implication of their social mobility?

The Bumpy Path to Higher Education

Upward mobility is a narrow and bumpy path for rural children to travel. Remoteness, the lack of educational resources, a shortage of qualified teachers, family poverty, and a high illiteracy rate all constitute an unfavourable environment for rural education. Meanwhile, large-scale closure of rural schools, an urban-biased curriculum, and unequal opportunity to access senior high school further handicap rural students. Indeed, many of them have dropped out of school long before the entrance examination to higher education. On the contrary, students in coastal, urban areas have dramatically greater access to higher education than those in rural areas (Hawks, Jacob, & Wenli, 2008, p. 218). All these challenges rural children encounter can be intimidating. It is reported that among those who quit *gāo kǎo* (高考, University Entrance Examinations), the majority are of rural origin (Zhang, 2013). To overcome these formidable obstacles, rural students need "an unbroken string of miracles" (Bourdieu & Passeron, 1979). Unsurprisingly, the presence of rural students in prestigious universities has substantially dropped in the post-Mao era.

To explain working-class underachievement and middle-class achievement, Bourdieu makes a significant contribution with his social reproduction thesis. For the most disadvantaged classes, he asserts that the process of educational selection "is purely and simply a matter of *elimination*" (Bourdieu & Passeron, 1979, p. 2; original emphasis). Can Bourdieu's theoretical framework also explain those who break the spell, and resist the crushing weight of social conditions by entering into an elite university?

Does Bourdieu's Theory Work Here?

It is well established in academia that disparities in student outcomes cannot be merely attributed to individual variation in genes. Social inheritance also plays a crucial role. It has been found that even when an individual's early life cognitive ability is controlled, parental class, status, and education continue to have significant effects on the educational attainment of the members of the cohort (Bukodi, Erikson, & Goldthorpe, 2014). It is also well established that the persistent link between social origin and educational attainment cannot be simply explained in terms of economic resources. The provision of free secondary education in post-war Europe to remove financial barriers and reduce educational inequalities did not achieve the expected goal (Goldthorpe, 2007). This suggests that it takes more than material resources to succeed in school. Bourdieu's cultural reproduction thesis, formulated in the French context, was then ushered in, and theoretically and empirically adapted elsewhere (cf. De Graaf, Graaf, & Kraaykamp, 2000; DiMaggio, 1982; Lamont & Lareau, 1988; Lareau & Weininger, 2003; Lareau, 2003; Li, 2013; Reay, 1998, 2001; Savage, Warde, & Devine, 2005; Van de Werfhorst, 2010).

In his theoretical framework, Bourdieu (1997) differentiates three types of resources: economic capital, cultural capital, and social capital. They are distributed in a field with an exchange value, transmissible and convertible. As forms of power and objects of struggle, they serve as the source of social classifications and advantages. These resources can be acknowledged by all the competitors in a specific field, and thus bring in honour and recognition, or symbolic capital in Bourdieu's term.

Bourdieu, with his colleague Passeron (1977), privileging symbolic dimensions, proposes that family advantages/disadvantages are transmitted from one generation to another through cultural resources and practices. Children from privileged groups are better prepared for school, because it is their culture and family socialisation that are recognised by, and embodied in, the educational systems. Their advantage thus gained is often misrecognised as natural talent. This forms a contrast with those from underprivileged backgrounds who find the school alien and even hostile. Academic achievements thus produced, although unfair, are seen as meritocratic. Despite the sophistication and elegance of Bourdieu's theory, controversies have arisen over which capital plays a more important role in reproducing social inequalities (Sullivan, 2002). Willis (1983), for example, accused Bourdieu of placing too much emphasis on symbolic relations and downplaying the material ones. It can be argued that Bourdieu does place economic capital at the root of other capitals, and what he highlights is the covert way cultural capital legitimates social dominance.

Cultural capital, as Bourdieu (1997) explains, can be in the objectified state such as books and painting, the institutionalised state as educational credentials, and embodied state such as linguistic competence and manners. It is the embodied form that exerts a hidden influence on social structuring. As the component of habitus, Bourdieu's another cornerstone concept, it is linked to socialisation beginning in early childhood, but often variously and nebulously defined as a "set of dispositions", "tendency", or "inclination" (Bourdieu, 1977, p. 214). Habitus plays a critical role in perpetuating social inequality: the objective circumstances of class, family, and individual experience are internalised into dispositions which in return predispose ways of being, acting, and choice-making in a social space where interaction and transaction occur. In another word, habitus is society "written into the body, into biological individuals" (Bourdieu, 1990, p. 63). It operates "below the level of consciousness", and orients practices and perceptions (Bourdieu, 1984, p. 466). Educationally, the schemes of the dominant social structure tend to convince the disinherited that they owe their scholastic and social destiny to their lack of gifts or merits (Bourdieu & Passeron, 1977), resulting in what Bourdieu (2001, p. 35) calls "self-depreciation or even self-denigration". As a result, the dominated group tends to refuse "what they are refused ('that's not for the likes of us'), adjusting their expectations to their chances ... condemning themselves to what is in any case their lot" (Bourdieu, 1984, p. 471). Bourdieu deploys the Stoic notion of *amor fati* to describe this social inertia (Lane, 2012, p. 130).

If limited to this level of understanding, there would be no surprise that habitus is often accused of being deterministic and even circular, leaving little room for human agency (see Jenkins, 1982; Lamont, 1992; Sullivan, 2002). Class defectors who have achieved social mobility would then go beyond its explanatory power. Bourdieu's own trajectory also contradicts this version of habitus. However, we have to bear in mind that habitus, according to Bourdieu, is a generative system. It can be enabling and transforming, therefore providing space for agency, and allowing conscious freedom (Bourdieu & Wacquant, 1992). It is true that Bourdieu asserts childhood dispositions are "long-lasting; they tend to perpetuate, to reproduce themselves, but they are not eternal" (Bourdieu, 2005, p. 45). As a product of history, it is "durable" and "transposable" (Bourdieu, 1977, p. 85). It can be changed by history, by "new experience, education and trainings" (Bourdieu, 2005, p. 29), shaped and reshaped through the constraints and opportunities individuals experience in the social world (Mahar, Harker, & Wilkes, 1990).

Despite this, Bourdieu's emphasis is still overwhelmingly placed on social reproduction. The *transformative* aspect of habitus, "a propensity for self-improvement" (Reay, Crozier, & Clayton, 2009) under-discussed theoretically and under-employed empirically, is what this chapter tries to explore in relation to rural achievers' experiences of academic success. To grasp the transformative aspect of habitus, we need to work with another vital but often neglected thinking tool of Bourdieu's – *illusio* (cf. Bourdieu, 2000; Bourdieu & Wacquant, 1992). The concept of *illusio*, imbricated with habitus and field, involves "how we are caught up in the game, our belief that it is worth playing, our commitment to it, and our investment in its stakes" without questioning its meaningfulness (Colley, 2012, p. 324). When the under-privileged are excluded and then exclude themselves from the higher education field because of the barriers, what makes these wonder children still invest in stakes in the educational game,

102 He Li

believing in the value of higher education, with the determination to change their fate? Is it a blind decision or a conscious choice?

To address this issue, a real problem then surfaces: An individual's inclinations to change inevitably involve standing back and reflecting on his or her current situation. Bourdieu always focuses on the pre-reflective dimension of action (Reay, 2004, p. 437), asserting that reflexivity only emerges "in situations of crisis". Everyday self-reflection and deliberative judgements are neglected. Working with the concept of habitus therefore needs to "recuperate the reflexive and creative aspects of practice" (Crossley, 1999, p. 658). Bourdieu also insists that his theory "is a temporary construct which takes shape for and by empirical work" (Wacquant, 1989, p. 50). It follows that his concepts need to be anchored in empirical reality, and subject to modification, especially when applied to other cultural contexts. A case in point is Xu's study (2016) on Mainland students in an elite UK university, or Mu and Jia's study (2016) on floating children in China. These empirical orientations and critical engagements help to overcome the Eurocentric tendency which is much alive in Chinese academia, and facilitate the indigenous voice to be heard in theoretical application and knowledge development.

The qualitative study reported in this chapter was conducted at a top-tier university in Beijing from 2007 to 2008. The initial questionnaire was used to obtain their demographic information and gain their informed consent. Interviewing was the major enquiry approach. Gender balance and regional diversity were carefully considered when sampling. This chapter focuses its analysis on the interview data of 52 rural students in an elite university. In-depth enquiry involved descriptions of their educational trajectories from childhood onwards at home and in school, as well as of family locations in their local communities. Interviews were recorded, transcribed, and later analysed using Bourdieu's conceptual tools. Themes were then identified. Their success can be basically expressed in the following formula: Success = family capitals (economic, cultural and social capital) (see also Gofen, 2009) + symbolic capital (stemming from teachers' special attention) + scholastic dispositions (diligence and resilience) + serendipity.

How Are the Miracles Made? The Advantaged Among the Disadvantaged

Bourdieu regards academic successes of the disadvantaged as miracles, claiming that "these survivors have few characteristics in common with their category of origin" (1996, p. 155). His assertion is evidenced in this chapter to the extent that the rural achievers are relatively advantaged among the disadvantaged. The family status of the 52 rural participants varies. A high proportion comes from occupationally "higher-status" families in the rural communities. Five students' parents serve or used to serve in the rural public sectors, two students' parents are entrepreneurs, and 11 students' parents are teachers. Seven of them have both parents as teachers. One student's father used to be a peasant doctor ("barefoot doctor"). Other parents either run small businesses, or work as drivers or chefs (8); or other labouring jobs in cities, towns, or countryside (13); or engage purely in agricultural activities (12).

The profile is, however, still vague, and we need to probe further: Is there anything special in these families that make them stand out in the rural community? The importance of family capitals becomes visible. Before a detailed discussion, the rural ethos as an element of the background is delineated to give an in-depth view of the picture.

Local Ethos and Collective Practice

Choices are always conditioned by objective realities. For rural families, what they encounter is the dilemma of high educational costs and credential devaluation on the one hand, with a shrinking number of white-collar jobs and abundant labouring opportunities on the other. These factors interweave, setting the tone for local attitudes towards education. Despite China's very long tradition of valuing education, the notion that "education is useless" has been prevalent in the countryside in recent years (Yu & Zhang, 2006). As a result, "students asked to leave all the time" in Min's words. Dropping out early and labouring outdoors was a common portrait of the local ethos by my interviewees. Na detailed peasants' risk-avoiding strategies, reasoning why rural children chose to work early in her community. In her accounts, rational calculation, integrating pre-reflexive dispositions, crept into everyday life, working as a disincentive to upward mobility. Considering the high opportunity cost, those who invested in education were likely to be under great peer pressure; as Na said: "If you choose to continue your study, and later go to a less prestigious university, and then can't find a desirable job, your family will become a laughing stock."

Their risk-avoiding strategies stemmed from rural children's slim chances to enter leading universities. Li and colleagues (2013) examined the data of *gāo kǎo* in 2003, and found that poor, rural youth were eleven times less likely to access a prestigious university than urban youth. In peasants' mental structures, higher education was not for "people like them", and manual labouring was their children's wise choice:

> It is very difficult to enter this university, but my rural neighbors just scorn it. "So what?" they would ask. Their own children have laboured outside at a very young age ... Indeed, almost all my classmates in rural junior middle school have been migrant labourers for nearly ten years.
>
> *(Xu)*

In this way, objective conditions were internalised into a rural habitus, which found its expression in self-exclusion from higher education, viewing it as

104 He Li

something undesirable, as "sour grapes" (Bohman, 1999, p. 133). This pervasive ridiculing attitude could compel those who had the "impossible ambition" to give up: "Parents have their concerns in this respect", according to Na. The circle of reproduction is, however, never complete. Not all rural families and children fitted into the milieu, and loved their socially determined fate as a Bourdieusian version of habitus always implies. How did the mismatch of their low social position and their dispositions of aiming high come into being? Most rural participants in this study highlighted their parents' positive attitude toward education. Na also wanted to quit, but her father "insisted that I had another try". This is consistent with Blanden's finding (2006) in the UK context that parental interest in the child's education is very important in understanding why some poor children do better than others at school. However, parental interest in education does not come from nowhere; family resources, albeit limited, play a crucial role, as this study suggests.

Economic Capital Can Make a Difference

Although symbolic resources are stressed in Bourdieu's work, the current research indicates material resources also count a lot in educational achievement in Chinese rural areas. They lay an economic base for, and can be converted into, educational support. Most of these rural university students reported that their economic status was average or above average for their local areas. A well-off family in the countryside, however, can be poor by city standards. As "education costs a fortune" (Xu), "to support us to go to university, almost all our savings are gone, although we are quite rich in the neighbourhood" (Ding). For an average family, the educational cost at the stage of senior middle school can be unafford-able: "When the financial burden became too heavy, my mother had to quit the farm ... to be a migrant worker" (Su). Under such circumstances, economic constraints directly influence family's educational decisions: "Parents wouldn't support you attending a senior middle school unless they are very rich" (Wei).

Family's Cultural Capital and Supportive Attitude

Financial constraints might produce an overt effect on rural parents' willingness to invest in education. It nevertheless cannot explain why some parents were more supportive of their children's education than others, even when they were in a similar economic condition, and why the scholastic yields were so different among children even in the same rural school. The story therefore would be partial if the focus was merely placed on the volume of economic capital a family possesses, without referring to the more hidden but by no means less important embodied cultural capital, expressed by family's attitudes and expec-tations towards education. It may be argued that parental support is decided by their children's promise of academic success. Cause and effect in this case is however by no means clear-cut and the reverse may also be true. Bourdieu (1997, p. 47) attempts to explain the unequal academic achievement by relating scholastic success "to the distribution of cultural capital between classes and the class fractions". It involves parents' educational attainment which is crucial to the transmission of cultural capital in the family. It is also related to parents' habitus, that is, dispositions developed through their past experiences, orienting their attitude toward education.

In the year 2006, only 7.1 per cent of the rural population completed senior middle school in China (OECD, 2009). A stark shortage of well-educated rural dwellers is however not a new phenomenon. China's modernisation can be viewed as a process of draining the rural talent to the city. The only interruption of this process happened to coincide with these rural parents' schooling age. Education reform during the Cultural Revolution (1966–76), which was completely abolished in the post-Mao era, placed much emphasis on rural education, with massive expansion of rural schools, although of poor quality. The expansion led to a significant increase in the number of senior middle school graduates (Han, 2001; Pepper, 1996). In this research, 35 rural interviewees (67.3 per cent) reported that one or both of their parents had been in senior middle school. The relatively well-educated, as my research shows, provided a relatively favourable educational environment for their children. The effect of family cultural capital can be most clearly observed in rural teachers' families, where cultural transmission was conspicuous:

> I was a very naughty boy and always ran home during the class. I got very, very low marks until in the third year I transferred to my mother's class ... And she was very strict with me ... Besides, my mother knew where my weak points were and assigned me some exercises accordingly. She taught me in this way for three years. The effect was obvious.
>
> *(Xue)*

The transmission also involved reading and writing under teacher parents' guidance, which was gradually incorporated into a cultured habitus, resulting in their high achievements. Consequently, "in our rural community, teachers' children, generally speaking, are scholastically successful" (Lin). Similarly, those parents with senior middle school education were also able to better prepare their children for later schooling. The endeavours to enhance their children's academic success were nevertheless confined to only a few. The majority of rural parents, as senior middle school graduates, were perceived to be incompetent in educational involvement, and their support was mainly in the sense of offering money and releasing their children from labour: "If the farm needed hands, I was not required to help them. If I needed some stationary, they would try hard to meet my needs if they could. That's all" (Hao).

106 He Li

In fact, most rural participants denied that their parents had provided any substantial help in their study, maintaining that they had to work on their own. Luo's parents, although better educated, had almost negligible reserves of legitimate, urban-biased cultural capital to bolster her: "In their words, 'it is beyond our ability to help you with your school work. We are very willing to help but don't know how to.'"

What really distinguished more educated parents from other peasants were their high expectations and supportive attitudes, as mentioned. Seven rural interviewees in my research reported that their parents, as senior middle school graduates, had taken to heart their own narrow margin of failure to access higher education. Their past history and dispositions thus shaped were different from other rural residents. The disjunction between habitus and rural field endowed them with reflexive and transformative tendencies (Adams, 2006). Unlike most rural dwellers, they believed that higher education could be for people like them and were committed to ensuring that their children could achieve high and leave the countryside despite the constraints: "My father graduated in 1978 and failed to go to university. He hoped we could fulfil his dreams and required us to do nothing but study, study and study since we were very young" (Xie).

Zhang, described how his father, a barefoot doctor, was different from other rural parents, and had a tight control over him and his siblings for the same reason. To keep them from unwanted influences and distractions, his father adopted almost authoritarian methods to discipline them and even sacrificed his own needs:

> My father wanted us to live in the city, away from the countryside. The only means to achieve this is through higher education. With this idea in mind, he was very strict with us, and always kept a very close eye on us. In order to keep us concentrating on our work and avoid any distraction, my parents didn't buy a TV ... No leisure but study. That was our life. By contrast, other rural children enjoyed more freedom and could play as long as they liked after supper ... So I played outside, too. When my father returned and found me not at home, he brought me back and gave me a good beating.

Parents' transformative propensities and dis-identification with their rural origins supported their children in resisting the collective destiny and achieving upward mobility through extreme diligence, a key disposition of academically successful working-class students in other societies (Reay, Crozier, & Clayton, 2009). High aspirations and educational interest were however not the monopoly of families with culture capital, but were also shared by some illiterate or semi-illiterate parents (of five students in total), who demonstrated a strong desire to help their children escape their social fate. A closer scrutiny reveals that this group consists of migrant workers, ex-soldiers, and small merchants, who were out of the countryside for prolonged time, observing different lives and accessing different ideas. Experiences in the modern urban world influenced their expectations for their children's education: "My father labours outside and knows the benefit of education. Unlike other rural parents who tend to ask their children to drop out early and earn money, he is willing to support us to the end" (Yao).

Encounters with urban culture and better lives, although limited, enabled these rural parents to reflect on their own conditions, recognise alternatives, and devote themselves to their children's schooling. The tension between "the demands of the field and the subjective dispositions" (McNay, 1999, p. 107) resulted in a longing for what is refused rather than a refusal of what is refused. The "unfulfilled longing" (Sayer, 2005, p. 35), which has its genesis in their feelings of frustration and rejection, can be powerful:

> My mother enjoyed reading and studying in her childhood, but her family couldn't afford her education. Suffering from deprivation of opportunity and from the hard life she is leading in running a small business, she hopes we can avoid this and live a different life.
>
> *(Wind)*

So far we have focused on parents' reflexivity and supportiveness which, generated from embodied cultural capital or life experiences, led to a degree of transformation. What also counts is the presence of role models usually in the larger family network, which enhances family capital and promotes rural children's ambition.

Role Models and Social Capital

It is increasingly recognised among researchers that the social capital students access can facilitate their academic success (Goddard, 2003). Social capital deriving from "kinship relations" or "the family group" (Bourdieu, 1997, p. 52), as this research suggests, is of special value to these wonder children, especially in a *guān xì* (关系, networking) society like China where Confucian role relations have been fundamental to traditional social fabric. It is a common theme in rural participants' narrations that their siblings, relatives, and even neighbours who were in higher education served as role models, encouraging them and sharing experiences with them. Or they themselves turned into an example for others to follow. The existence of role models in the big family circle encouraged the rural students to compete for higher education admission despite their disadvantaged positions, convincing them the game "is worth playing; that it is worth the candle" (Bourdieu & Wacquant, 1992, p. 98). Role models can exert enormous power on the followers who are keen to search for recognition, namely symbolic capital:

108 He Li

> One event influenced me profoundly. My sister ranked the third in the whole county in the entrance examinations. We were all very happy. Before that, I had been relaxed and had a low expectation to myself: Being average, neither good, nor bad in my academic performance. After that, I suddenly felt that I ought to work hard.
>
> *(Ling)*

Such an effect not only exists within extended families, but also within the wider rural communities. Role models, operating as incentives, enhance the local aspirations:

> My admission to the university has been a big local event and greatly influenced our local community. Before that, people believed it was extravagant to finish senior middle school or vocational school. Going to university was just beyond their wildest dreams until I succeeded.
>
> *(Dong)*

Bourdieu and his colleague Passeron (1979, p. 26) argue:

> The presence in the family circle of a relative who is or has been in higher education is evidence that these families are in an unusual cultural situation, if only in that they offer a greater subjective expectation of university entrance ... it is their relative unawareness of their disadvantage (based on an intuitive assessment of their educational chances) that frees these subjects from one of the most real disadvantages of their category, namely, the resigned renunciation of 'impossible ambitions'.

This partly explains why rural university students tend to cluster in some extended families and in certain rural communities (Peng, 2007). The role models also demystify the process of social mobility, conveying the message that higher education is achievable for rural children.

Social capital works not only in the symbolic dimension; it also involves substantial support. Many rural participants reported to having urban middle-class relatives or social connections who offered them boarding when in urban middle schools, and facilitated their study in various ways such as giving them advice and helping them out of difficulties: "My aunts and my uncles are all teachers. They always talked about the importance of education. One of my aunts is in charge of a school library, and I immersed myself in the library during summer holidays" (Wei).

In this way, social capital is converted to cultural capital. The combination of economic, cultural, and social resources creates a relatively propitious educational climate and develops high aspirations in a generally unfavourable milieu. This confirms Scherger and Savage's assumption (2010, p. 424) that class dynamics can lay "at the root of some working and intermediate class families displaying more middle class cultural attitudes and educational practices than others".

Misfits and Their Desire to Escape

The majority of my rural participants, as shown above, are members of the relatively better-off groups in rural society. Some have more advantaged family conditions; some have more aspiring parents; some have role models and middle-class connections. This is similar to what Jackson and Marsden (1962) characterised as "sunken middle class families", or those with a particularly aspirational working-class parent whose children did well in grammar school in the UK. Beside family, gender and geography also play a part. Because of the space limitation, I will not elaborate on this point.

There were however still students (seven) in the study who, without any such privileges, also achieved. They differed from their peers who had high aspirations, enabling resources, reflexive and transformative propensities, and ambitious parents. Nevertheless, their social conditions incorporated into habitus had not exerted much constraining power and prevented their entry into university. Bourdieu (2005, p. 31) talks about generative aspects of habitus, which "generate inventions and improvisations but within limits". Then for these students, to what extent has habitus produced unpredictable, creative practices, especially resistance to their social fate?

Bourdieu (2005) describes discrepancy between dispositions and positions as producing "misfits", arguing that "although subjects from the most disadvantaged classes are those most likely to be crushed by the weight of their social destiny, they can also, exceptionally, turn their excessive handicap into the stimulus they need to overcome it" (Bourdieu & Passeron, 1979, p. 25). Bourdieu does not elaborate on what this mysterious force is and how it can translate extreme disadvantages into stimulus. However, misfits in this research give us a clue, as Sun confessed:

> I worked hard just because I didn't know what else I could do if I dropped out. I definitely didn't want to live like other girls: become a waitress in the city, then come back to the village after a few years, get married and raise children, then live a life like my mother had been living.
>
> *(Sun)*

Disgust at their social destiny, feeling "displaced, out of place and ill at ease" (Bourdieu, 2000, p. 157) in the local community was a shared feeling among my interviewees. Bourdieu places *affect* as central to producing social inertia in a lower-class habitus: People desire what their objective conditions allow them to have. Social structure is thus sustained by the love of one's own social destiny.

110 He Li

What is left undiscussed however is its potential for transformation and emancipation (Lane, 2012). As this study reveals, the collective fate was perceived so undesirable by these rural achievers that it became a catalyst to escape, outweighing their concerns about the consequential costs and risks, leading to "an acute sense of self-consciousness" (Crossley, 2001, p. 158), or a feeling of not belonging to their local community.

These children's resistance to their original position or "first habitat" (Sayer, 2005, p. 34) is also related to their strong commitment to their families who had been living in difficulties, and to a sense of unfairness at the hardships they experienced. An aspiration to better their family's life and improve their social status motivated them to work hard. Cheng was propelled by her sympathies with her parents and her wish to ease their suffering:

> My parents had very rough times and bad experiences as migrant workers. Each time it happened, it occurred to me that if I could do better in school, they would be happier, especially my mom . . . Later, I told myself that I should succeed and better their living conditions.
>
> *(Cheng)*

Somewhat differently, Fu was inspired by the contrast between the misery of her family's life and the desirability of (urban middle-class) life on TV:

> When I was a child, in our extended family, only our family condition was poor and my grandparents had nasty attitudes toward us. I felt so wronged and bitter and wanted to fight for our family's dignity. That kind of feeling accompanied me for many years. So my initial motivation derived from a bad environment . . . When I watched TV, I found that sort of [urban] life was what I desired and I knew the only way to achieve was through hard work.
>
> *(Fu)*

Scholastic Habitus and Teachers' Favouritism

These rural children's desire to escape can be also attributed to their initial experience of academic success. Located in the lower stratum in the larger social space, these rural children occupied the top echelon in the enclosed field of rural education. Being "a big fish in a small pond" endowed them with confidence in upward mobility. Their high achievement might be related to their innate ability, but is more likely associated to their family resources. Most interviewees reported enjoying schooling and doing really well from the very beginning. These high achievers tended to believe that their high achievements in the first few years inspired their strong interest in study, which led to further high achievements: "I had been the top student from the very beginning. If you start well, you would like to keep your advantage and reinforce the advantage, then your performance will become better and better" (Tang).

When their identity as successful learners formed and brought accolades, they tried to maintain their top position. This is consistent with Elsner and Isphording's finding (2018) that a student's ordinal rank significantly affects her educational outcomes later in life. Recognition, as a form of symbolic capital, is perceived to be "worthy of being pursued and preserved" (Bourdieu, 1977, p. 182). This reinforced their passion for study. And hard work became a pleasure rather than a chore: "I was very keen to go to school from primary school to junior middle school . . . At that time, the only thing I cared about was schooling (Min).

Capital attracts capital. Their enthusiasm for schooling won their teachers' approval and strong support. China's education has a deep-rooted tradition of focusing its attention on top students. It is particularly so in a local milieu where rural schools' inferior quality and laissez-faire attitude have produced a demoralising effect on rural students: "No one seemed to take study seriously in my school" (Liu); "most students didn't listen and learn" (Sun). Under such circumstances, rural teachers "had to concentrate on these who had good attitudes" (Sun). As my interviewees explained, some rural teachers tried hard to persuade them to leave the "doomed" countryside through working hard. Besides high expectations, they also offered various aids to facilitate these top students' studies:

> In the third year of junior middle school, our leading teacher asked me to move to her accommodation in school because conditions in the school dorm were very poor. I was the first one to live there; later some other good students moved in.
>
> *(Pei)*

Teachers' preferential treatments played an important role in their entry into a key urban senior middle school. The way to success is however a complex and developing process, with teacher's special care, parental support, and children's high achievement interacting with and reinforcing each other. Parents' supportive attitudes enhanced children's educational achievement. Children's high achievement ensured the safety of their family's investment, and invited more resources, such as teachers' attention and parental support, which in return solidified their academic success. Due to the lowered risk, even some highly disadvantaged families became interested in their children's schooling:

> I did quite well in school and was awarded lots of prizes. When teachers met my parents, they usually praised me for my good work. This made my parents very happy. They came to believe I was promising. Since it could make everyone happy, I said to myself that I should remain a top student.
>
> *(Han)*

In this way, family support, teachers' encouragement and students' good performance form a virtuous circle. Rural academic stars' *illusio*, expressed as "a fascinated pursuit of the approval of others" (Bourdieu, 2000, p. 166), grew out of a responsive environment and resulted in their heavy investment in the educational game. Indeed, all participants reported to be high achievers in rural schools. This helped to build their self-confidence and inspired their higher aspirations. A dedication to self-improvement, in order to maintain a competitive edge was then gradually incorporated into a scholastic habitus: "When there are rankings in class, your vanity or competitive spirit will be aroused. You will have a bitter feeling if left behind. If you have been on the top, a lower position will drive you to strive" (Hu); "In senior middle school, it was a pressure I brought to bear on myself. It was to compete with myself, to challenge the very best" (Zhang).

Hu and Zhang demonstrated a strong propensity of "self-scrutiny and self-improvement" (Reay, Crozier, & Clayton, 2009, p. 1103). Once such a habitus is shaped, it is inclined to perpetuate, and reproduce itself (Bourdieu, 2005, p. 29). These students, with high levels of motivation and demand of themselves, kept on track and advanced in their later educational career.

Resilience and "Serendipity": Surviving the Senior Middle School

Rural students' educational advancements were full of challenges, especially at the stage of senior middle school. All the rural interviewees except one survived the very selective entrance examinations and urban-biased admission policies, and eventually entered a key senior middle school located in a city or county town. The quality urban schools turned out to be a strange, hostile place where rural children's initial disadvantages became visible. Financial hardships, a sense of inferiority and fear of failure all constituted sources of stress. But in the face of various difficulties, they demonstrated a high level of resilience, which helped them overcome and succeed.

Their ability to cope with adversity was first of all reflected in their creative ways to manage financial difficulties. The food they ate, clothes they wore, and learning materials they had to purchase all became problematic in senior middle school. In Feng's school, students were required to buy lots of complementary materials:

> I borrowed materials from them [his urban classmates] and read them through until midnight in case they asked for them the next day. You could only use them when they didn't. I was doing things in this way from the first year to the last year and I did well.
>
> *(Feng)*

Economic hardship was only one of the challenges. Cultural distance was also sensed by rural interviewees: "When you compared yourself with urban students, you felt a great distance. These urban children were versatile, capable and could speak very good Mandarin" (Bin).

Bin's sense of inferiority and inadequacy arose when he became aware of his lack of legitimate cultural capital embodied in urban students. Such feelings were intensified when he experienced downgrading in the new educational field: "When I came to the senior middle school, I became invisible ... It took me half a year to adjust. I ranked 43rd in the first term, and then I worked hard, very hard actually, and became 45th."

He was determined to change his strategies, struggling to improve himself through extreme diligence. His adaptability proved to be strong as far as academic achievement was concerned: "When I graduated, I ranked 7th in the whole school".

The rural students' determination to achieve upward mobility is not without price. Families' high expectations, their concerns about the risk of family investment, economic hardships, and strong desires to succeed, placed them under enormous pressure:

> I finally burst out crying bitterly before my parents. The stress was huge ...
> I was the only hope of my big extended family. I had shouldered too heavy burdens and too high expectations. If I failed, they would be very, very disappointed.
>
> *(Xie)*

Despite various adversities, they made it to higher education at a prestigious Chinese university. Their "unexpected" academic outcome, however, was not obtained by serendipity. Rather, it was the aforementioned family capital in economic, cultural, and social forms, coupled with teacher support and role model inspiration, that helped them break the spell of social reproduction. The academic resilience of the disadvantaged, such as the rural achievers in my study, requires theory-building beyond the traditional psychological school. This is what Mu (2018) refers to as a sociology of resilience – an empowering process of socialisation that enculturates the disadvantaged groups into a set of dispositions and capacities required for bouncing back from adversities and achieving success.

Conclusion

The exception proves the rule. To address the question "what makes the exceptions exceptional?" I find that reproduction and transformation are actually two sides of one coin. If we look at the class factor closely, it turns out that the majority of these wonder children were luckily born into families with relative advantages in the rural community. Family capitals of all sorts, although modest, facilitated their study from various aspects. In physically deprived areas, economic resources can guarantee the affordability of children's schooling. Beyond this,

114 He Li

family cultural capital exerted a considerable power, mainly embodied in family members' aspirations and supportive attitude towards education. Meanwhile, the accessible role models in the larger family network, from which stemmed *illusio* – a strong commitment to education – constituted an unusual and favourable cultural atmosphere for these children. Considering the focus of this chapter, factors such as gender, geography have been left undiscussed. If included, it is safe to say it is the advantaged among the most disadvantaged who are more likely to escape their social destiny (see also Wee, 2012 in the UK context) and develop transformative habitus. In this sense, the increasing proportion of rural students in elite universities just makes the myth of meritocracy look real but leave the real problem of inequality unsolved. This also casts doubt on the achievability of educational equality in a highly unequal society.

Family capitals had a positive impact on these rural children's achievement, and their initial academic success was rewarded by symbolic capital from teachers' recognition and parents' high expectations. Their diligence, promoted by their experience of being high achievers, gradually developed into a resilient habitus, orienting them to be dedicated to self-improvement in their later educational career, enabling them to survive an alien environment and generate positive outcomes.

This research benefits from a systematic and contextualised engagement with Bourdieu's thinking tools. When it comes to theoretical implications, we have noted how various types of family capitals work together to influence educational achievement, with cultural capital being highlighted in the Chinese rural context. This means climbing social ladders also requires resources. In this sense, Bourdieu's theory does show considerable relevance, although in a seemingly modified version of reproduction in the disguise of social mobility. However, a major theme of this chapter is to reveal how these wonder children broke the reproduction spell. Transformative habitus and reflexivity then come to the fore. This demands a flexible adaptation of Bourdieu's version of habitus. The chapter indicates that rural participants' determination to achieve upward mobility was triggered early in their formative childhood, mainly inculcated by their aspiring parents, and reinforced by high achievement in schools, and teachers' encouragement. The rural students' aversion to their rural identity and social destiny as migrant workers also played a crucial role (Li, 2015).

The affective response against one's social origins extends our understanding of Bourdieu's notion of habitus. In his self-analysis, Bourdieu uses the term "*habitus clivé*" to describe his ambivalent "perception of self" and "multiple identities" produced by upward mobility (1999, p. 511). Emotions in the form of "shame, humiliation, timidity, anxiety, guilt" are part of the lower classes' habitus, structured by, and also structuring systems of power and domination (Bourdieu, 2001, p. 38). Empirical evidence in this research strongly suggests that "love of one's social fate" and "rejection of collective destiny" can ambivalently coexist: the former is more visible in the local ethos, and the latter in the rural misfits. Therefore habitus, as embodied structure, can be both reproducing and transforming. The hatred of one's low status identity, in line with Skeggs's finding (1997) that working-class women tend to dis-identify with working class, prompts a desire for a different, more respectable life. Lack of harmony between positions and dispositions entailed self-awareness and a transformative tendency. Such a tendency was solidified on these rural children's educational journey by their identity as high achievers, inclining them to strive for changes.

Habitus reveals its complexity in the empirical reality. Weaving "conscious deliberation with unconscious dispositions" (Reay, 2004, p. 438), transformation with reproduction, and freedom with constraints allows for a deeper exploration of social practice. Bourdieu's habitus is often accused of being too ambiguous and overloaded to operate. This feature, however, also means more flexibility in employment, just as this chapter illustrates.

When it comes to policy implications, it is indeed a response to the second question posed in this chapter: What is the cost of social mobility? Upward mobility demands a high price. It means financial burdens. It means disavowing one's rural roots and escaping from their native place. It also means psychic problems. Due to the very high opportunity costs, rural students' desire to rise above their family status placed them under huge stress. This is especially true for those from the most disadvantaged backgrounds.

At the collective level, recruiting a few more rural students to elite universities is not a solution either to educational inequality or urban–rural disparity. These achievers' depreciation of their rural identity and their desire to leave make upward mobility no more than a rural brain drain. This will exacerbate rural decline with empty villages, left-behind children, and disappearing village schools. Rural poverty and marginalisation thus is perpetuated, with a loss of tradition and cultural memory.

So what kind of policy do we need most? We need policies which directly address social and economic inequality at large, rather than solely focusing on social immobility. We need to revitalise the countryside to tackle the rural crisis with more economic and cultural resources. As education is a crucial means to transform rural China, it is important to provide access to quality education as well as training in new technology, with a curriculum which not only appreciates nature and agriculture, but also recognises the rural way of life.

Note

1 Bourdieu and Passeron (1977, p. 227) used the term *miraculé* (translated by Richard Nice as "wonder boys") to describe "the working class child who succeeds against 'all the odds'".

References

Adams, M. (2006). Hybridizing habitus and reflexivity: Towards an understanding of contemporary identity. *Sociology*, *40*(3), 511–528.

Bagri, N. T. (2017). China's rapid urbanisation has caused nearly three-quarters of its rural schools to shut down. Retrieved from https://qz.com/961012/chinasurbanisationhas causednearlythreequartersofitsruralschoolstoshutdown/

Blanden, J. (2006). *Bucking the trend: What enables those who are disadvantaged in childhood to succeed later in life?* Working paper 3. London: Department for Work and Pensions.

Bohman, J. (1999). Practical reason and cultural constraint: Agency in Bourdieu's theory of practice. In Shusterman, R. (Ed.) *Bourdieu, a critical reader* (pp. 129–152). Blackwell: Oxford.

Bourdieu, P. (1977). *Outline of a theory of practice.* Cambridge: Cambridge University Press.

Bourdieu, P. (1984). *Distinction: A social critique of the judgement of taste.* R. Nice (Trans.) Cambridge: MA: Harvard University Press.

Bourdieu, P. (1990). *In other words: Essays toward a reflexive sociology.* M. Adamson (Trans.) Stanford, CA: Stanford University Press.

Bourdieu, P. (1996). *The state nobility: Elite schools in the field of power.* Stanford CA: Stanford University Press.

Bourdieu, P. (1997). The forms of capital. In Halsey, A.H., Lauder, H., Brown, P. & Wells, A.S. (Eds.) *Education, culture, economy and society* (pp. 46–58). Oxford: Oxford University Press.

Bourdieu, P. (1999). *The weight of the world: Social suffering in contemporary society.* Cambridge: Polity Press.

Bourdieu, P. (2000). *Pascalian meditations.* Cambridge: Polity Press.

Bourdieu, P. (2001). *Masculine domination.* Cambridge: Polity Press.

Bourdieu, P. (2005). Habitus. In Hillier, J. & Rooksby, E. (Ed.) *Habitus:A sense of place* (pp. 42–49). Aldershot, UK: Ashgate.

Bourdieu, P. & Passeron, J.-C. (1977). *Reproduction in education, society and culture.* R. Rice (Trans.). London: Sage.

Bourdieu, P. & Passeron, J.-C. (1979). *The inheritors, French students and their relations to culture.* London: University of Chicago Press.

Bourdieu, P. & Wacquant, L. (1992). *Invitation to reflexive sociology.* Chicago: University of Chicago Press.

Bukodi, E., Erikson, R., & Goldthorpe, J. H. (2014). The effects of social origins and cognitive ability on educational attainment: Evidence from Britain and Sweden. *Acta Sociologica, 57*(4), 293–310. doi:10.1177/0001699314543803

Carr, P. J. & Kefalas, M. J. (2009). *Hollowing out the middle: The rural brain drain and what it means for America.* Boston, MA: Beacon Press.

Colley, H. (2012). Not learning in the workplace: Austerity and the shattering of *illusio* in public service work. *Journal of Workplace Learning, 24,* 317–337.

Crossley, N. (1999). Fish, field, habitus and madness: The first wave mental health users movement in Great Britain. *British Journal of Sociology, 50,* 647–670.

Crossley, N. (2001). *The social body: Habit, identity and desire.* London: Sage.

De Graaf, N.D., Graaf, P.M. & Kraaykamp, G. (2000). Parental cultural capital and educational attainment in Netherlands: A refinement of the cultural capital perspective. *Sociology of Education, 73,* 92–111.

DiMaggio, P. (1982). Cultural capital and school success: The impact of status cultural participation on the grades of U.S. high school students. *American Sociological Review, 47,* 189–201.

Elsner, B., & Isphording, I. E. (2018). Rank, sex, drugs, and crime. *Journal of Human Resources, 53*(2), 356-381. doi:10.3368/jhr.53.2.0716-8080R

Goddard, R. D. (2003). Relational networks, social trust, and norms: A social capital perspective on students' chances of academic success. *Educational Evaluation and Policy Analysis, 25*, 59–74.

Gofen, A. (2009). Family capital: How first-generation higher education students break the intergenerational cycle. *Family Relations, 58*(1), 104–120.

Goldthorpe, J. H. (2007). "Cultural capital": Some critical observations. *Sociologica, 2*, 1–23.

Han, D. (2001). Impact of the cultural revolution on rural education and economic development. *Modern China, 27*, 59–90.

Hawks, J.N., Jacob, W.J. & Li, W. (2008). Higher education in China: Access, equity and equality. In Holsinger, D.B. & Jacob, W.J. (Eds.) *Inequality in education: Comparative and international perspectives* (pp. 215–239). Dordrecht: Springer.

Hoggart, R. (1958). *The uses of literacy.* Harmondsworth, UK: Penguin.

Hu, B. & Chen, C. (2015). New urbanisation under globalisation and the social implications in China. *Asia & the Pacific Policy Studies, 2*, 34–43.

INRULED. (2001). *Education for rural transformation: Towards a policy framework.* Baoding: INRULED.

Jackson, B. & Marsden, D. (1962). *Education and the working class.* London: Routledge and Kegan Paul.

Jenkins, R. (1982). Pierre Bourdieu and the reproduction of determinism. *Sociology, 16*(2), 270–281.

Jetten, J., Iyer, A., Tsivrikos, D. & Young, B.M. (2008). When is individual mobility costly? The role of economic and social identity factors. *European Journal of Social Psychology, 38*, 866–879.

Lamont, M. (1992). *Money, moral and manner: The culture of the French and the American upper class.* Chicago: University of Chicago Press.

Lamont, M. & Lareau, A. (1988). Cultural capital: Allusions, gaps and glissandos in recent theoretical developments. *Sociological Theory, 6*, 153–168.

Lane, J. F. (2012). From "amor fati" to "disgust": Affect, habitus, and class identity in Didier Eribon's *Retour à Reims. French Cultural Studies, 23*, 127–140.

Lareau, A. (2003). *Unequal childhoods: Class, race, and family life.* Berkeley: University of California Press.

Lareau, A. & Weininger. E. (2003). Cultural capital in educational research: A critical assessment. *Theory and Society, 32*, 567–606.

Li, H. (2013). Rural students' experiences in a Chinese elite university: Capital, habitus and practices. *British Journal of Sociology of Education, 34*, 829–847.

Li, H. (2015). Moving to the city: Educational trajectories of rural Chinese students in an Elite university. In Costa, C. & Murphy, M. (Eds) *Bourdieu, habitus and social research* (pp. 126–147). London: Palgrave.

Li, H., Loyalka, P., Rozelle, S., Wu, B. & Xie, J. (2013). Unequal access to college in China: How far have poor, rural students been left behind? Working paper 263. Retrieved from reapchina.org/reap.stanford.edu

Lipton, M. (1977). *Why poor people stay poor: Urban bias in world development.* London: Temple Smith.

London, H.B. (1989). Breaking away: A study of first-generation college students and their families. *American Journal of Education, 97*, 144–170.

Mahar, C., Harker, R. & Wilkes, C. (1990). The basic theoretical position. In Harker, R., Mahar, C. & Wilkes,C. (Eds.) *An introduction to the work of Pierre Bourdieu* (pp. 1–25). Basingstoke: Macmillan.

McNay, L. (1999). Gender, habitus and the field. *Theory, Culture and Society, 16*, 95–117.

Mu, G.M. (2018). *Building resilience of floating children and left-behind children in China: Power, politics, participation, and education.* New York: Routledge.

Mu, G.M. & Hu, Y. (2016). *Living with the vulnerability and the opportunities in migration context.* Rotterdam, the Netherlands: Sense Publishers.

Mu, G.M. & Jia, N. (2016). Rural dispositions of floating children within the field of Beijing schools: Can disadvantaged rural habitus turn into recognised cultural capital? *British Journal of Sociology of Education, 37*(3), 408–426.

Nash, R. (2012). *Schooling in rural societies.* New York: Routledge.

OECD. (2009). *OECD rural policy reviews: China 2009.* Paris: OECD Publishing

Peng, Y. (2007). *Higher education and social mobility in rural society.* Beijing: China Renmin University Press.

Pepper, S. (1996). *Radicalism and education reform in 20th-century China.* Cambridge: Cambridge University Press.

Reay, D. (1998). *Class work: Mothers' involvement in children's schooling.* London: University College Press.

Reay, D. (2001). Finding or losing yourself? Working class relationships to education. *Journal of Education Policy, 16*, 333–346.

Reay, D. (2004). "It's all becoming a habitus": Beyond the habitual use of Pierre Bourdieu's concept of habitus in educational research. *British Journal of Sociology of Education, 25*, 431–444.

Reay, D., Crozier, G. & Clayton, J. (2009). Strangers in paradise? Working-class students in elite universities. *Sociology, 43*, 1103–1121.

Savage, M., Warde, A. & Devine, F. (2005). Capitals, assets, and resources: Some critical issues. *British Journal of Sociology, 56*, 31–47.

Sayer, A. (2005). *The moral significance of class.* Cambridge: Cambridge University Press.

Scherger, S. & Savage, M. (2010). Cultural transmission, educational attainment and social mobility. *The Sociological Review, 58*(3), 407–442.

Sennett, R. & Cobb, J. (1973). *The hidden injuries of class.* New York: Vintage Books.

Sheehan, S. (2017). China's hukou reforms and the urbanisation challenge. Retrieved from http://thediplomat.com/2017/02/chinashukoureformsandtheurbanisationchallenge/

Skeggs, B. (1997). *Formations of class and gender: Becoming respectable.* Thousand Oaks, CA: Sage.

Su, Z., Cao, Y., He, J. & Huang, W. (2015). Perceived social mobility and political trust in China. *African and Asian Studies, 14*, 315–336.

Sullivan, A. (2002). Bourdieu and education: How useful is Bourdieu's theory for researchers? *The International Journal of Social Sciences, 38*, 144–166.

Van de Werfhorst, H.G. (2010). Cultural capital: Strengths, weaknesses and two advancements. *British Journal of Sociology of Education, 31*, 157–169.

Wacquant, L.J.D. (1989). Towards a reflexive sociology: A workshop with Pierre Bourdieu. *Sociological Theory, 7*, 26–63.

Wee, S. (2012). Beating the odds? A Bourdieusian reading of working class educational success. PhD thesis, Faculty of Education. Cambridgeshire, UK: University of Cambridge.

Wentworth, P. & Peterson, B. (2001). Crossing the line: Case studies of identity development in first-generation college women. *Journal of Adult Development, 8*, 9–21.

Willis, P. (1983). Cultural production and theories of reproduction. In Barton, L. & Walker, S. (Eds.) *Race, class & education* (pp. 107–138). London: Croom Helm.

Xinhua. (2017). *China has 282 mln rural migrant workers by end of 2016*. Retrieved from english.gov.cn/state_council/ministries/2017/03/.../content_281475595925144.htm

Xu, L. (2016). Mainland Chinese students at an elite Hong Kong university: Habitus–field disjuncture in a transborder context. *British Journal of Sociology of Education, 38*, 610–624.

Yu, H. & Zhang, L. (2006). Focus on the revival of the view that 'education is useless' in rural areas. [in Chinese] *China Youth Study, 2006*(9), 68–72.

Zhang, X. (2013). The rate of Gaokao quitters kept at 10% in the past five years; the majority have chosen to work. [in Chinese] *Jinghua Times (jinghuashibao)* 8 June 2013.

7

RESISTANCE AS A SOCIOLOGICAL PROCESS OF RESILIENCE

Stories of Under-resourced Migrant Families[1]

Guanglun Michael Mu

The exponential growth of urbanisation in China has created rural-to-urban migration on a massive scale. Many migrant parents choose to bring their child (ren) to cities when they move away from their rural hometown. These children, however, not only encounter institutional barriers when accessing free public schooling and social services in cities, but also face social discrimination against their rural dispositions (Mu & Hu, 2016a). As a result, these children are often at risk of undesirable psychological, social, educational, and health outcomes (Mu & Jia, 2016; Mu et al., 2013). The term "floating children" is therefore used to describe the rootlessness of these children in the urban social space. Other migrant parents make the painful choice to leave their children behind in their rural hometown. The caregivers of these children are often grandparents or extended family members in local communities. These children are therefore called "left-behind children", who suffer from no or limited parenting, unsound caregiving, and significant risks across multiple life domains (Hu, Lonne, & Burton, 2014).

The total population of floating children and left-behind children is approaching 100 million (National Women's Association, 2013), accounting for one-third of the total population of children in Mainland China. In the context of massive internal migration, the view of these children as others and underdogs spreads widely and persistently. A sociological approach can denaturalise what is taken for granted (Bourdieu, 2013). This approach is indeed both a theoretical tool and a conceptual conundrum for stakeholders who are socially privileged and who are to engage in working with, and learning from, "othered" young people in ways that are powerful and consequential rather than arbitrary or mandatory. In this chapter, I work through a sociological lens to help stakeholders reconceptualise resilience-building for floating children and left-behind children. I consider these children's resistance to socially defined adversities and desired outcomes as a form of resilience. As the chapter unfolds, it will soon become clear how these children draw on their dispositions, either consciously or unconsciously, and capitalise on resources at their disposal to resist the stereotyped demarcations between the "desired" and the "undesired". In the face of structural constraints, these children demonstrate resilience in the form of self-defined identities and desirables. Before I proceed to the analysis, I briefly argue for a sociological approach to resilience.

Moving Towards a Sociology of Resilience

The notion of resilience originated from a few interrelated disciplines, including, but not limited to, child psychopathology, youth mental health, and child disaster risk reduction. These fields of research traditionally looked into factors implicated in children's psychological "ill-being". The positive psychology movement, however, has initiated a paradigmatic shift in resilience research, looking into children's psychological well-being in precarious conditions. Social psychology pushed resilience research one step further, taking into account ecological and cultural dynamics embedded within "the process of, capacity for, or outcome of successful adaptation despite challenging or threatening circumstances" (Masten, Best, & Garmezy, 1990, p. 426). The discipline of psychology, therefore, has laid a substantial foundation for seminal research on child and youth resilience. Having said that, it is an epistemological fallacy to constrain resilience within the psychological school, as if resilience were an ontogenic trait from within. Therein lie the problems of endogenous approaches to resilience. Such approaches uproot resilience from its nurturing contexts, treating it as an engine without fuel, and mistakenly understanding resilience as a "cause" of "unexpected" positive outcomes in adverse conditions, rather than an effect of the contextual fabric. As a result, such approaches tend to blame vulnerable children for not being resilient in the face of adversity, and commend resilient children for being psychologically or functionally superior in the face of threats and risks.

I do not disavow individual qualities and attributes, especially those tenacious ones that withstand precarious conditions. Yet, in sociological terms, it would be difficult to understand personal capacity, internal cognition, and individual representation without understanding social forms, norms, and structures. It would also be difficult to understand psychosocial resources without understanding social class and power relations, as well as time and space. The portrayal of resilience remains incomplete without taking into account "structural deficiencies" (Seccombe, 2002, p. 385) that systematically place children in adversities. From a sociological perspective, then, it would be difficult to understand resilience as a social process without understanding its relations to histories, cultures, biographies, geographies, and, indeed, social orders that arbitrarily place certain groups of children at a structural disadvantage while endowing others with positions of unquestioned

122 Guanglun Michael Mu

favour. Therefore, resilience-building is unlikely to achieve full success without attending to the rules, principles, and forces that either limit or liberate children's living and learning. Working through a sociological lens, I redefine resilience as a process of socialisation that enculturates children into a set of dispositions (habitus) and endows children with resources (capital) required for rebounding from adversities and performing well across multiple aspects – physical, psychological, social, and educational.

Habitus and capital in combination define a configuration of strategies within the social field where agents are consciously or unconsciously involved in social praxes (Bourdieu & Wacquant, 1992). In precarious conditions, children from different socio-economic backgrounds not only have different levels of access to capital functional to buffer adversities but also have different accretions of habitus that predispose them to certain responses to adversities. In simple words, socio-economic and cultural backgrounds moderate the resilience process and are generative of diverse resilience outcomes. The core message here is that resilience research necessitates sociological understandings. Such understandings remain incomplete without also attending to power relations in research and practice. In sociological terms, resilience is not universal but co-constructed through interactions between the powerless group who are often marginalised, misrecognised, and othered; and the powerful group who control dominant discourses and define what are desired in adverse conditions. Nevertheless, fundamental questions of power, discourse, ontology, or epistemology are rarely raised when discussing child and youth resilience (Ungar, 2010). As a result, resilience often falls prey to "the vagaries of definitional one-upmanship" (Ungar, 2010, p. 6), with the most powerful others having the best privilege to influence the naming of everyday practices as either risk-taking or resilience-building. In other words, risk and (un)desirable outcomes have long been well defined by powerful others through their own epistemology, interest, and logic. The well-established definitions of resilience imposed on children in marginal positions and adverse conditions push these children toward the socially desired directions. The arbitrary language of "risk" and "resilience" of powerful others commits a form of symbolic violence (Foster & Spencer, 2011). This is particularly true when the dispositions, or the habitus of "at-risk" children do not fit the "desirables", or the logic of the dominant social field (e.g., policy, school, media).

Symbolic violence "operates in a much more subtle manner – through language, through the body, through attitudes toward things which are below the level of consciousness" (Bourdieu & Eagleton, 1992, p. 115). As physical force and discipline are something external, and of which people are conscious, it is easier, in a sense, to revolt against them. In contrast, revolt against symbolic violence seems to be difficult, as symbolic domination is "something you absorb like air, something you don't feel pressured by; it is everywhere and nowhere, and to escape from that is very difficult" (Bourdieu & Eagleton, 1992, p. 115). In this respect, domination through symbolic violence "tends to take the form of a more effective, and in this sense more brutal, means of oppression" (Bourdieu & Eagleton, 1992, p. 115). Despite the difficulty of revolting against symbolic violence, disadvantaged young people do not necessarily always succumb to normative societal expectations. Some of them are resistant to the imposed symbolic violence in a resilient way. For example, the resilience of socially disadvantaged Aboriginal and Anglo-Australian girls can manifest in their resistance to negative, stereotyped identities (Bottrell, 2009). For another example, socially disadvantaged students in the UK actively engaged with a reflective process in which they became aware of their need to break with the taken-for-granted social norms and therefore were able to develop certain social, cultural, and specifically, educational capital to successfully negotiate the school-college-university transition (Hernandez-Martinez & Williams, 2013).

With the imposition of symbolic violence, resilience researchers may continue working with stereotypical definitions of "risk" and "desirables" of powerful others, while overlooking the indigenous epistemologies of resilience of children who are arbitrarily made disadvantaged. The aforementioned Aboriginal and Anglo-Australian girls and UK students taught me to purposefully remain episte-mologically vigilant to the danger of unconsciously falling prey to symbolic violence. In this way, the concept of symbolic violence helps to make visible "an unperceived form of everyday violence" (Bourdieu & Eagleton, 1992, p. 112). This is the bequeathal of Bourdieu, known as "participant objectivation" (Bourdieu, 2003, 2013) – the most essential sociological analysis but "the most difficult exercise of all because it requires the break with the deepest and most unconscious adherences and adhesions" (Bourdieu & Wacquant, 1992, p. 253). Following the route of Bourdieu, I approach resilience through often unheard and overlooked stories, focusing on the desirables that floating children and left-behind children envision for themselves and their resistance to mainstream ideologies of education, risk, and positive outcomes. In so doing, I call for the inclusion of marginalised voices originating in communities not yet well heard.

The Portrayal of Xiaobao: A Floating Child, an Early School Leaver

Xiaobao was born into a rural family in Anhui province. His maternal and paternal grandparents and great-grandparents were all farmers, engaging with various back-breaking agricultural work, such as field ploughing, livestock farming, and crop planting. Xiaobao's parents inherited the peasant life. When they were young, they worked on farms in their hometown just like the earlier generations of their family. Nothing changed until 2002 when Xiaobao's parents came to Beijing with folks from their village. The couple also brought Xiaobao to Beijing. At that time, Xiaobao was only three years old.

When the family first came to Beijing, life was very difficult. The couple worked and lived on a construction site. The husband was deployed to a unit responsible for concrete and sand supply for the construction site. He had to work long hours every day, shuttling with a wheelbarrow numerous times between two fixed points within the construction site, transporting concrete and sand from one point to another. This was a tedious and arduous job. Every day Xiaobao's father finished his work at dawn. With his body worn out, stomach hungry, hands dirty, and eyes sleepy, he returned to the shabby temporary cottage at the edge of the construction site – a small shanty that they could call "home" at that time. The wife's job was a hard one too. She was a cook on the construction site. Each time she prepared a meal for the construction workers, little Xiaobao played by her side. Ingredients needed to be washed. In winter time, the cold water from the tap chilled her to the bone. Her wrinkled hands and frostbitten fingers told everything.

The couple worked hard and led a frugal life. Their wages were low so the couple only had nominal savings. Even so, they supported their family in the village by remittance. To save money, they decided not to return to their hometown every Spring Festival because the train tickets during the Spring Festival would cost over one thousand Chinese Yuan (approximately US $150). During their time in Beijing, the couple sporadically talked to their aging parents by long-distance calls. This was the only way to keep the family connected during those years because a mobile phone was an unattainable luxury for them at that time.

Several years of hard work saw some payoffs for the family. Their living conditions improved and the family had more savings than before, though their life was not an affluent one. The couple decided to establish their own business. To do this, they used up their savings and they also had to borrow some money from their relatives and friends. They rented a house in a populated community and opened a small fruit and vegetable shop there. The house was built of bricks, with polished marble floors. There were two rooms in the house. The front room was quite spacious so it was used as the shop. Behind the shop room was a small and sparsely furnished room, where the family lived. I first met them at the shop in 2006. At that time, Xiaobao was seven years old – a conventional age in China to start primary school. There was a public school in the community, which was where Xiaobao studied. Soon after I started my research about floating children, I had an opportunity to talk to the family. Xiaobao's dad recalled:

> It took us a while to get all the documents they [the school] needed, so we just submitted the application and they approved that. How lucky! It's not a good school but it's good enough for us. At least he [Xiaobao] had a school to go to. At least he didn't linger around or mingle with bullies, right? Every day he went to school by himself and came back home by himself after school. We were busy in the shop so we didn't have time to escort him to school, and we didn't have time to pick him up after school either. It's fine as long as he's not led astray by bad boys.

Indeed, Xiaobao was lucky as his application for admission to school was approved. In recent years, policy oscillations have influenced floating children's admission to public schools in cities. Xiaobao went to school in 2006 – at a time when Hu's Government (2003–13) worked with a logic of societal harmony, social inclusivity, and educational equity (Mu, 2018). If he had gone to school in a period when government policies explicitly limited the admission of floating children to urban public schools, Xiaobao might have been excluded from the public school system in Beijing and might have had to study in a migrant-sponsored school.

Let's return to the story of Xiaobao's family. The family's fruit and vegetable shop was the only one of its kind in the community so business was pretty good. Their living conditions continued to improve in subsequent years. In 2013, the couple opened their second business in the community – a small courier company delivering post for the community's residents. The division of labour between the couple was clear. The wife looked after the fruit and vegetable shop and the husband looked after the courier company. The company ran well and the business grew fast. The husband could hardly manage the delivery services by himself.

In 2015, Xiaobao failed his senior high school entrance examination. He gave up school and began to help his dad with the postal delivery. This seemed to work well for the family. Xiaobao worked alongside his dad as a delivery man. With Xiaobao's help, his dad did not have to work to exhaustion as before. By the age of 18, Xiaobao had "successfully" reproduced his parents' social status. Xiaobao's family has survived and thrived in the face of the adversities brought about by migration. The family now owns two cars and seems to enjoy their life in Beijing.

Over the years, I have had considerable contact with Xiaobao and his parents. Sometimes I called Xiaobao's home and sometimes I visited his home after a typical school day. I wanted to understand Xiaobao's school experiences and aspirations for the future. I purposefully asked questions like "What did you do in school today?", "What do you do after school?", "Do you want to go to university?", and "What do you want to do in the future?" (See original data reported in Mu, 2018.) Xiaobao's disengagement in learning is evident through-out our conversation. His failure to pass the exam did not seem to frustrate him. He even did not intend to catch up. He found school was "nothing" but "boring", "chanting", and "repetitive". The only thing he found interesting in school was to toss around chalk and get his teacher mad. His anti-disciplinary practice, according to theories of resistance (e.g., Giroux, 1983a, 1983b), is a typical everyday form of counter-cultural expressions among dominated groups. For example, working-class lads thoroughly rejected school in favour of their own working-class subculture (Willis, 1977) and working-class, immigrant students with limited French literacy rejected school due to "the desire to avoid the humiliation of having to read out loud in front of the other students"

126 Guanglun Michael Mu

(Bourdieu, 1999, p. 61). Xiaobao seemed to be very aware of his dominated and marginalised social position in school: "I don't have *hù kǒu* (户口, urban residency documented in the Household Registration System) so they don't count me in. I would drag down the class mean score". Without the institutionalised cultural capital, urban *hù kǒu* in this case, Xiaobao's studentship was de facto made illegitimate in school. Without the embodied cultural capital required for school success – academic engagement in this case – Xiaobao was marginalised by the neoliberalised pedagogies that celebrate competition and performance in standardised testing.

The neoliberal logic that has infiltrated into the field of education can be understood as a form of symbolic violence imposed on Xiaobao. As a result of this violence, Xiaobao felt "very uncomfortable" in school because he did not "fit the image there". If the symbolic violence remains unchanged and unquestioned, Xiaobao's discomfort would continue. If Xiaobao had no friends in school, he could barely see any point going to school: "I think I go to school because I wanna play with my friends, and that's all." His sense of not belonging to school was governed by his experience of the dominated, marginalised social position that he occupied in the neoliberalised field of education, taking the form of discomfort – an "emotion" or "the unease of someone who is out of place" (Bourdieu, 2000, p. 184). In this vein, the objective limits of neoliberalised schooling have been transformed into Xiaobao's subjective practical responses to the social space in which he was positioned at school. As he confessed, "I don't want to go to school. I don't fit the image there". Citing Bourdieu again, "the space of positions tends to command the space of position-takings" (Bourdieu & Wacquant, 1992, p. 105). The social positions are objectively defined by the quality, quantity, and configuration of capitals at stake, and hence are already there ready to be taken. However, Xiaobao did not take this position haphazardly. Instead, he might have taken the position, either consciously or unconsciously, either willingly or unwillingly, which he was predisposed to take on the basis of his dominated, marginalised position in the neoliberalised field of education. In this respect, position-taking underpins subtle and brutal class politics, hierarchical systems, and unequal structures of the social world.

Social inequalities can be perpetuated through classed pedagogies in school. As Xiaobao noted, "Teachers only care about the good ones in their subjects"; "Teachers said we don't have to worry about that stuff because they are too hard". By using the plural pronoun "we", Xiaobao indicated that he was not alone, but just one of the students who were placed at a structural disadvantage. His teachers seemed to assume that disadvantaged students were doomed to achieve nothing and were not worthy of any help: "Oh if you need help, you'd better get a tutor." In this way, Xiaobao is similar to the North American students who have experienced the most disproportionate school failure and who have been on the receiving end of a pattern of devaluation of identity for generations (Cummins, 2001). For these students, any serious attempt to reverse the imposed stereotype of under-achievement must challenge both the devaluation of identity that these students have historically experienced and the social power structure that perpetuates this pattern.

In Xiaobao's school, then, teachers showed no interest in "populi-culture" but celebrated and canonised "popular culture" (Bourdieu & Wacquant, 1992, p. 82). The former refers to "policies of cultural upgrading aimed at providing the dominated with access to dominant cultural goods" (Bourdieu & Wacquant, 1992, p. 82), while the latter places a "hyperbolic limit" on socially disadvantaged students and entraps them into their historical being of marginalisation (Bourdieu & Wacquant, 1992, p. 82). Behind the popular culture is a "sham inversion of dominant values" and a "fiction of a unity of the social world" (Bourdieu & Wacquant, 1992, p. 83). Although Xiaobao noticed that most teachers smiled at him in school, he doubted that the smiles were wholehearted: "Well . . . most teachers smile at me when they see me in school. But I still think teachers only care about the ones that are good in their subjects.". According to Xiaobao, teachers hypocritically purported educational inclusivity and conferred upon structurally disadvantaged students a nobility only based on their adjustment and submission to the neoliberalised schooling. Unsuccessful adjustment is costly, as it results in subordination, marginalisation, or even exclusion.

Interestingly, Xiaobao's response to the structural constraints brought about by neoliberalised schooling and the popular culture was qualitatively different from adjustment and submission. He did not seem to show interest in improving his school performance. As he noted, "pass [in the exam] is ok". He did not "care about this boring stuff". When asked whether he wanted to go to university, Xiaobao hemmed and hawed: "Maybe . . . if I have money. Hmm . . . probably not, because of my poor grades. Also I am not smart." Here Xiaobao seemed to excuse himself for not having too much educational aspiration − he did not want to go to university because he was not smart enough. Capitals required for school success, according to Bourdieu (1977), are arbitrarily and selectively valued, legitimated, and rewarded by schools. Lack of these capitals is often misrecognised by disadvantaged students, their parents, and their teachers as an inherent lack of academic ability or merit. As Xiaobao confessed, "I am not smart", whether this is true or not. His mum believed that Xiaobao was "not cut out to be a student". The misrecognition was also seen in my interviews with teachers in Xiaobao's school. Consider the excerpt below:

> I usually don't do exercises and items provided by the manual. I also skip the thinking pages. They're way too hard for them [academically disadvantaged students]. They never get it, and they'll never use it because they're lazy. I hate to label them, but they are lazy. In addition, students

here are wild little monsters and have no interest in learning. They don't listen to you in class.

The interview account here evidently shows that educational interactions and pedagogic discourses are never neutral with respect to the messages communicated to students about their value, intellect, and future. The teacher's interview account is fraught with deficit discourses: "They never get it . . . because they are lazy . . . and are wild little monsters." Lack of embodied cultural capital valued by school was misrecognised by the teacher as an inherent lack of academic merit. This misrecognition, according to Bourdieu (1977), was responsible, at least to a certain extent, for Xiaobao's decision to self-exclude from further education. Self-exclusion here also shows Xiaobao's indifference in mainstream schooling. To be indifferent is "to be unmoved by the game" because the game "makes no difference" (Bourdieu & Wacquant, 1992, p. 116). Apart from his indifference, Xiaobao "tossed chalk . . . to get the teacher mad" – a purposeful anti-disciplinary practice against the grain of mainstream schooling. I understand Xiaobao's indifferent, mischievous responses as his resilience in the face of the constraining structures of neoliberalised schooling. Such resilience manifested in indifference and resistance is "a sense of one's place" (Goffman, 1951, p. 297), which, according to Bourdieu (1984, p. 471), "leads one to exclude oneself from goods, persons, places and so forth from which one is excluded". Xiaobao explicitly spoke of his self-exclusion: "I don't want to go to school. I don't fit the image there." This self-exclusion was due, at least in part, to the social exclusion in school: "I don't have *hù kǒu* so they don't count me in". For Xiaobao, self-exclusion from school showed his withdrawal from an arbitrary institution that fails to address diversity and inclusivity.

Bourdieu would consider Xiaobao's indifference and resistance as an ineffective sort of "spontaneist populism", through which "the dominated seldom escape the antinomy of domination" (Bourdieu & Wacquant, 1992, p. 82). This antinomy of domination encompasses two opposite choices. On the one hand, to engage in oppositional school activities "through horseplay, truancy, and delinquency, is to exclude oneself from the school, and, increasingly, to lock oneself into one's condition of dominated" (Bourdieu & Wacquant, 1992, p. 82). In this case, indifference and resistance only further the marginalisation of the already marginalised. On the other hand, "to accept assimilation by adopting school culture amounts to being coopted by the institution" (Bourdieu & Wacquant, 1992, p. 82). The logic of practice here focuses on "adjustment of dispositions to position" that contributes to "submission" of the dominated (Bourdieu & Wacquant, 1992, p. 81). Either way, to oppose or to accept, the dominated groups are condemned to a dilemma of choice when the choices on offer are "two equally bad ones" (Bourdieu & Wacquant, 1992, p. 82). Such a dilemma necessitates the study of the link between school delinquency and the logic of furious competition encouraged by neoliberalised schooling, as Bourdieu, Sapiro, and McHale observed:

especially the effect of a final verdict or destiny that the educational system exerts over teenagers: with a psychological brutality which nothing can attenuate, the school institution lays down its final judgments and its verdicts, from which there is no appeal, ranging all students in a unique hierarchy of forms of excellence ... Those who are excluded are condemned in the name of a collectively recognised and accepted criterion (and thus one which is psychologically unquestionable and unquestioned), the criterion of intelligence. Therefore, in order to restore an identity in jeopardy, students have no resort except to make a violent break with the scholastic order and social order (it has been observed, in France, that it is their collective opposition to school that tends to weld delinquents into gangs) or, as is also the case, to suffer psychological crisis, even mental illness or suicide.

(Bourdieu, Sapiro, & McHale, 1991, p. 651)

By excluding himself from mainstream schooling, Xiaobao would be normally considered to sink deeper into the vicious circle of resistance that amplified "undesirable" outcomes. Nevertheless, Xiaobao's resistance was also a sociological choice in the face of structural constraints – "a paradoxical way to make virtue out of necessity, that is, academic wrongdoing" (Bourdieu, 1999, p. 61). Xiaobao rejected adjustment and submission, and hence did not completely lose his agency. He adopted resistance at the risk of further marginalisation. He was well aware of this further marginalisation. When asked whether he could be anything he wanted in the future, he replied without hesitation: "No. Only rich people can." Xiaobao seemed to fit well to the mainstream knowledge about disadvantaged children – low aspiration, low academic engagement, and hence low academic performance. Indeed, Xiaobao failed in the entrance examination to senior high school and chose to give up and drop out. There is a bulk of evidence that leaving school early can penalise children for a lifetime (OECD, 2012). Interestingly, Xiaobao drew on what I call resilience to question the mainstream knowledge. In my most recent meeting with Xiaobao, I asked about his current status. He replied with delight:

I finally left that damn place, finally don't have to go to school. They treated me like I was really low. As long as you don't ask me to go to school, I'd do anything for you. School for me is not about study. It's more about social stuff, about my buddies, about who I hang out with.

He then jumped into his car and left for delivery in an upbeat mood. Xiaobao's linguistic and bodily responses to my question are telling. To that point in time, he had never regretted leaving school early. In stark contrast, he felt happy about leaving the place where he did not belong. In this way, his resilience attenuated the negative effect of leaving school early, and more importantly, questioned the imposed stereotype of what is desired and undesired.

In this chapter I have reframed the notion of resilience through a sociological lens and construed resilience as habitus. Xiaobao's habitus of resilience was not gained haphazardly. Rather, Xiaobao was enculturated, through socialisation and upbringing within the domestic milieu, into this very habitus of resilience required for resisting structural constraints and rebounding from adversities. When asked about their expectations of Xiaobao, Xiaobao's parents did not feel disappointed about his school failure:

> If he can learn to add, subtract, multiply, or divide, that's good enough. At least, he can help the cashier in the shop after school. If not, I won't worry too much as long as he knows how to manage the shop when he grows up. I really don't have any other expectations if he can read and write and do some simple maths.
>
> *(Xiaobao's mum)*

> Actually people need to look at themselves first. Like I even didn't finish my primary school, how possible is it that my son can become, say, a scientist? That would be a joke! I am fooling myself if I say he can go to university. He just needs to do what he is supposed to do ... What else can we expect? If being a delivery man is good enough for me, it's good enough for my son. He could just do our family business. It's small but good enough for him.
>
> *(Xiaobao's dad)*

Gofen (2009) claims that parents of all social backgrounds typically expect their children to attend university, whereas their capacity varies in terms of translating their expectations into realities. The interview accounts of Xiaobao's parents, however, are at loggerheads with Gofen's claim. Xiaobao's mum would not "worry too much" and did not "have any other expectations" as long as Xiaobao achieved some minimal literacy and numeracy. Xiaobao's dad did not even believe that Xiaobao would be able to continue his study: "I am fooling myself if I say he can go to university." Indeed, Xiaobao performed poorly in exams, engaged in anti-disciplinary activities in class, and left school early. These social praxes would be interpreted as undesired elsewhere, but I understand them as manifestations of habitus of resilience to resist neoliberalised schooling and mainstreaming definitions of "success" (e.g., going to university). Xiaobao might have inherited this habitus of resilience from his parents. The intergenerational reproduction of this habitus was clearly voiced by Xiaobao's dad: "If being a delivery man is good enough for me, it's good enough for my son." In this respect, Xiaobao and his family are very much like the inhabitants of Jonquil Street described by Bourdieu (1999, p. 6): "they started work quite

Resistance and Resilience of Migrants **131**

naturally, often very early, at the age of 14, after a primary school certificate, following their parents' footsteps, and they quite naturally assumed their children would follow them."

Xiaobao may not be consciously aware of his resilience, but his body knew and remembered. Through everyday family socialisation and upbringing, Xiaobao might have already been enculturated into a habitus of resilience. This habitus has been ingrained in his flesh and soul, in his mind and body, in his culture and dispositions. Habitus works "on the basis of the premises established in the previous state" (Bourdieu, 2000, p. 161) and is "linked to individual history" (Bourdieu, 1993, p. 86). Xiaobao's family culture and history formulated the previous state of his habitus. In this vein, the intergenerational reproduction of habitus of resilience happened to Xiaobao by osmosis when "history turned into nature" (Bourdieu, 1977, p. 78), and became "an embodied history, internalised as a second nature and so forgotten as history" (Bourdieu, 1990b, p. 56). As a result, "the active presence of the whole past" became "the active presence" (Bourdieu, 1990b, p. 56) because what historically needed to be durable and transposable through a process of continuous reproduction has now been "inscribed in bodies by identical histories" (Bourdieu, 1990b, p. 59). These identical histories of the family have created a set of dispositions in Xiaobao, seen in his indifference and resistance to neoliberalised schooling and mainstream definitions of "success". For Xiaobao, his habitus of resilience became "a real ontological complicity, the source of cognition without consciousness, of an intentionality without intention, and a practical mastery of the world's regularities" (Bourdieu, 1990a, p. 12).

Xiaobao's resilience *qua* resistance prompts me to question my doxic positionality, which underpins my naïve perception, immediate acceptance, and taken-for-granted certainty of the universal "truth" that Xiaobao should have continued school and gone to university. It is by no means my intention here to claim the appropriateness of leaving school early. But leaving school early does not seem to have been socially fatal for Xiaobao. Had he continued senior high school, would he enjoy it? Would he have gone to university? Would a university degree have opened the door for his upward social mobility? What if he eventually still ended up with the job in his family business after completing university? Would he have collapsed psychically when he realised all his investment and effort were in vain? These are some of the dynamics Bourdieu probed in *The Weight of the World* and other studies of the disappointed students of France. Of course there are no definite answers to these questions as the future is uncertain. But for now, Xiaobao is happy and doing OK. He has shown resilience to resist socially desired outcomes and define his own desirable being and doing. The problem here is not about whether his resilience manages to overturn established social structures of domination and subordination. Neither is it about whether his indifference and resistance manages to break the spell of social reproduction. What merits some rethinking

132 Guanglun Michael Mu

here is what is "desired", what is "undesired", who has power to define them, and how to discover and respect the local, indigenous, marginalised discourses about life success and prosperity that have not yet been fully attended to.

The Portrayal of Xiaoliu: A Left-Behind Child, A Dab Hand at Chores

Nine-year-old Xiaoliu lives in a rural community in Jiangxi province. For the financial benefit of the family, Xiaoliu's parents left their hometown and chose to work in Fujian province, an economically dynamic province in the very south of the Chinese mainland. Like most migrant workers in China, Xiaoliu's parents only return to their hometown once a year during the Spring Festival. It would be unfair to blame Xiaoliu's parents for their "cruelty" of leaving Xiaoliu behind. This was a hard choice from no other better available choices. Xiaoliu's parents are similar to the parents of left-behind children with whom I have worked over the years. Each time I asked them why they left their child(ren) behind in their rural hometown, they always asked me back: "Who doesn't love their own kids? Who doesn't want to live with their own kids and watch them growing up? Who doesn't want to accompany their own kids every day? This is because we don't have any other choices".

Xiaoliu has been brought up by his paternal grandparents as his parents have been unable to live with, look after, and provide caregiving to him. By definition, Xiaoliu is a left-behind child, like many other children in this rural community. He is now living with his grandparents and his five-year-old sister in the household. Xiaoliu has been helping with the chores since he was three years old. He helps with washing up the dishes and cleaning the house. Every morning on his way to school, Xiaoliu escorts his sister to her kindergarten. Xiaoliu's grandfather seems to be very proud of Xiaoliu: "He's only eight years old but he has shouldered a big responsibility for the family."

Xiaoliu's aging grandparents can no longer afford to work on the farm. Neither can they afford to retire early. To reduce the economic burden of the household, Xiaoliu's grandparents take up some casual work in a garment factory located in the town centre. In the rural community where the family lives, there is a market that opens nine times a month. To fully meet daily household expenses, the old couple have to sell wontons at a rented market stall. Every time they work at the market, they have to get up at three o'clock in the morning, preparing ingredients. They usually finish their business around three o'clock in the afternoon when the market closes. Over the years, Xiaoliu has always helped his grandparents at the wonton stall. He has never complained about having to rise early for market work. Instead, he seems to be happy to contribute to the family. Xiaoliu has become a dab hand at making wontons. His wonton-making skills even beat those of his grandparents. His little sister is also contributing at the market stall, often helping clean the dining tables. In October

2016, Xiaoliu became a cyberstar. His story went viral on the Internet when he became famous for being able to make over 10,000 wontons in one day!

Despite the marked difference between Xiaobao's and Xiaoliu's life experiences, both children drew on their resilience to resist the mainstream ideologies about the desirables in life. While Xiaobao showed indifference and resistance to mainstream schooling, Xiaoliu's story complicated socially normalised perceptions about health and well-being. It will be recalled that Xiaoliu often engaged in long-hour, arduous labour work, helping his aging grandparents in their wonton stall, as well as taking on domestic responsibilities, looking after his little sister, and completing routine household chores. Participation in these family work-related activities would be considered a threat to child and youth health and well-being. However, I understand such participation as resilience to socially imposed stereotype of desirables.

It is not uncommon for children to have to engage in chores and sometimes economic activities because such labour may be of functional and financial significance to the children's family. In the international migration context, children of immigrant families worked as carers or surrogate parents to help their family (Valenzuela, 1999). In the internal migration context, many children assumed their responsibility of participating in family work and economic activities (Song, 1999). In the internal migration context of China, some colleagues (e.g., Han, 2004) seem to view children's involvement in housework as a problem, and have contended that such involvement in the labour market might impinge on children's school performance. Such concern is understandable. After all, children's participation in labour, especially excessive labour, is a potential threat to their well-being.

In the current case, Xiaoliu participated in hours-long, arduous work in his family's wonton stall frequently – nine times a month as reported. Such participation would be immediately associated with child exploitation and hence criticised for undermining child safety, health, and rights. The mainstream epistemology about the threatening effect of child labour on child well-being, however, can run into problem when faced with empirical evidence that would suggest otherwise, for example, in Xiaoliu's case. When asked about his experiences of working in the wonton stall, Xiaoliu replied:

> I have long been used to this [working in the wonton stall]. It's not a big deal to get up in the early hours of the morning and chop food stuff. Mum and dad are away and I am the man of the family. I don't want my grandpa and grandma to be too exhausted. I especially don't want them to worry about me … I wish the Spring Festival could come earlier. Mum and dad can only come back home during the Spring Festival. When I grow up, I want to make a lot of money so that I can look after my grandpa and grandma, and mum and dad. I also want to buy beautiful clothes for my sister.
>
> *(Mu, 2018)*

Xiaoliu has "long been used to" the work in his family's wonton stall, as he has learned to do this since he was three years old. Many children would find it a pain to get up at three o'clock in the morning for work. But for Xiaoliu, "it's not a big deal to get up in the early hours of the morning and chop food stuff." Born into a rural village where many young adults choose to work in cities and many children are left behind, Xiaoliu has obtained practical knowledge about "reality": "Mum and dad are away ... and they only come back home during the Spring Festival." This reality may hold true over his childhood. Growing up without parenting and living away from their biological parents would thwart many children. But these domestic dynamics and ecologies have enculturated Xiaoliu into a habitus, a system of internal schemata, and a set of embodied dispositions required for rebounding from adversities, which his body and mind "have long been used to". This is a habitus of resilience, a habitus of know-how, and a habitus of practical epistemology of "shoulds" and "shouldn'ts": "I don't want my grandpa and grandma to be too exhausted. I especially don't want them to worry about me" (shouldn'ts); "I want to make a lot of money so that I can look after my grandpa and grandma, and mum and dad. I also want to buy beautiful clothes for my sister" (shoulds).

Mainstream epistemology would consider children's participation in excessive labour to be age-inappropriate and socially undesired. Xiaoliu and his family seemed to tell a different story. Xiaoliu's grandfather reportedly felt very proud of Xiaoliu: "He's only eight years old but he has shouldered a big responsibility of the family." His story went viral on the Internet due to his extraordinary wonton making skills – over 10,000 wontons in one day! He is known as a dab hand at commercial wonton-making and domestic chores both in the community and in cyber space. Recognition within and beyond the domestic milieu became a form of symbolic capital for Xiaoliu. He himself was very aware of his contribution, responsibility, and significance in his family: "I am the man of the family." This sense of positive self is likely to perpetuate into the future, as Xiaoliu has started to imagine what he should do when he grows up. In this way, resilience was not only a system of dispositions for Xiaoliu but also a set of capacities for accessing capitals and bouncing back from adversities.

Xiaoliu is similar to the adolescents who had to take on additional family responsibilities and coped successfully during the great Economic Depression of the 1930s (Elder, 1974). He is also similar to the children with pleasant work experiences who constructed a stronger sense of identity, subjective well-being, and cohesion with others, and gained recognition for their contribution to others' welfare (Libório & Ungar, 2010). The foundational resilience research led by Werner (1992) over three decades concluded that regular participation in household chores and domestic responsibilities was an important resilience factor that helped high-risk children make successful adaptations in their adult life. Xiaoliu's resilience differs, however, in two ways. First, he had positive responses to excessive labour that would otherwise erode child well-being. He did not take his fate lying down but manoeuvred a resilient approach to coping with the now and aspiring for the future. Second, he showed resistance to mainstream ideologies about social practices that inhibit well-being and those that facilitate well-being. As a left-behind child, Xiaoliu would be commonly defined as an at-risk child. However, he drew on his resilience to positively respond to adversities and resist the socially imposed stereotype.

Putting Xiaobao's and Xiaoliu's stories together, I consider resistance to be a form of resilience when no other resources (e.g., schooling, social support, money) are made readily available and accessible to children in highly adverse conditions. Such resilience is a process of socialisation that enculturates Xiaobao and Xiaoliu into a system of dispositions (habitus) and endows them with a set of resources (capital) required for rebounding from adversities. Resilience *qua* resistance is empowering in situations where mainstream ideologies are taken as universal truth without question. It is equally empowering in situations where imposed stereotypes are mistakenly understood as social norms. Resilience *qua* resistance, therefore, calls for more attention to local, indigenous epistemologies, and urges a rethink of what are traditionally taken for granted as (un)desirable and what are arbitrarily defined as (un)acceptable. Xiaobao's and Xiaoliu's stories are informative. Questions remain, however, about how to interpret resilience *qua* resistance in a larger picture. To address this question, I now present a quantitative analysis of the resilience of left-behind children and floating children.

Disengagement in Mainstream Schooling and Deviation from the Stereotyped Desirable Future

The sample for the current quantitative analysis was drawn from my larger project about student resilience and well-being in China (Mu & Hu, 2016b). This sample is composed of 486 floating children and 222 left-behind children. For the purpose of analysis here, the sample was divided into two groups: one group consisting of 194 children exposed to at least three risk factors, and the other group consisting of 514 children exposed to less than three risk factors.[2] Three constructs included in the analysis are: child and youth resilience, academic engagement, and aspiration for the future. Reliability and validity of the three constructs have been justified through a psychometrically robust process (Mu, 2018; Mu & Hu, 2016b).

The analysis encompasses two stages. In the first stage, simple linear regression was used, treating resilience as a predictor/independent variable, and academic engagement and aspiration for the future as outcome/dependent variables. Resilience has a statistically significant contribution to aspiration for the future ($t = 9.26$, $p < .001$; $F = 85.80$, $p < .001$), explaining 10.8 per cent of the variance of aspiration for the future. In a similar vein, resilience has a statistically significant contribution to academic engagement ($t = 7.94$, $p < .001$; $F = 62.98$, $p < .001$), explaining

136 Guanglun Michael Mu

7.3 per cent of the variance of academic engagement. Results indicate that, in general, floating children and left-behind children who are socialised through a resilience process are more likely to be academically engaged and show aspiration for the future. This finding is known knowledge and largely fits the "mainstream" image of adversity, resilience, and "desired" outcomes.

In the next stage, resilience was treated as an independent variable, and academic engagement and aspiration for the future were treated as dependent variables, with the grouping variable (exposure to adversity) added to the model as a moderator. The first model, resilience-exposure to adversity-academic engagement, fit well ($F = 26.83$, $p < .001$), with exposure to adversity demonstrating a statistically significant moderating effect ($F = 5.78$, $p = .017$) on the relationship between resilience and academic engagement. The second model, resilience-exposure to adversity-aspiration for the future, also fit well ($F = 24.83$, $p < .001$), with exposure to adversity demonstrating a statistically significant moderating effect ($F = 5.32$, $p = .021$) on the relationship between resilience and aspiration for the future. The interaction of adversity and resilience has a significant negative effect on academic engagement ($b = -0.19$, $t = -2.40$, $p = .017$). This means that the contribution of resilience to academic engagement becomes weaker for children exposed to at least three risk factors, compared to that for those exposed to less than three risk factors. By the same token, the interaction of adversity and resilience has a significant negative effect on aspiration for the future ($b = -0.42$, $t = -2.31$, $p = .021$). This means that the contribution of resilience to aspiration for the future becomes weaker for children exposed to at least three risk factors, compared to that for those exposed to less than three risk factors.

In general, floating children and left-behind children who are socialised through a resilience process tend to demonstrate higher levels of academic engagement and aspiration for the future. Interestingly, the "magic" resilience effect on academic engagement and aspiration for the future seems to fade when floating children and left-behind children are faced with multiple adversities (at least three risk factors). It would be empirically wrong, however, to claim that these children are not resilient. Such an empirical fallacy may result from lack of reflexive analysis of quantitative data. This irreflexivity in the face of "hard" evidence can immediately fall prey to persistent, despicable deficit thinking, as Luke and Goldstein (2006) have long warned us that the use of large-scale psychometrics without due consideration of, and statistical adjustment for, social diversity gives the deficit model new legs – the good intentions of measurement scientists and many liberal policy makers notwithstanding. Therefore, responding to the "hard" evidence of underperformance requires serious, reflexive rethinking of the known, mainstream knowledge. Mindful of Luke and Goldstein's warning, I argue that floating children and left-behind children exposed to multiple risks may have been socialised into a resilience process qualitatively different from the "mainstream" epistemologies of resilience that define academic engagement and aspiration for the future as socially desired outcomes. It is by no means my intention to claim that academic engagement and aspiration for the future are not important for these children. But the data here show some evidence that floating children and left-behind children, when faced with multiple adverse conditions, may have their own worldviews about what they want to engage and to what they should aspire, which may deviate from the mainstream epistemological paradigm.

For floating children and left-behind children plagued by multiple adversities, staying in mainstream schools would mean continuous suffering from the conflicting aspirations that schools open and close for them at one and the same time. On the one hand, school seems to incline these children to reject dominated social positions, engage in socially anticipated adaptations, and break the "natural" cycle of working-class reproduction "by provisionally setting them apart from productive activities and cutting them off from the world of work" (Bourdieu, 1999, p. 185). On the other hand, school leads these children "to reject the only future accessible to them but without giving any guarantee for the future that it seems to promise" (Bourdieu, 1999, p. 185). Therefore, resistance to mainstream schooling and stereotyped definitions of desirables represents a form of resilience in the face of structural constraints. In this respect, floating children and left-behind children are different from the subproletariat described by Bourdieu (1999, p. 185) as "fated by lack of power over the present" with "an absolute uncertainty about the future". On the contrary, these children engage in a resilience process that enables them to choose their present and define their future in powerful ways that are different from the socially desired life pathways.

Resistance, Resilience, and Sociological Implications

Mainstream ideologies would portray Xiaobao as an undisciplined student, a low academic performer, and an early school leaver who did not have the cultural and social capital required for life success. As a result, he had to end up as a post-delivery man in his family business. Yet Xiaobao refused to submit to the socially imposed stereotype. He purposefully deviated himself from school where he did not belong and happily engaged in gainful employment in his family business right after he dropped out of school. Xiaobao did not have a sense of social impotence although he left school and started working much earlier than most of his peers. In this respect, early school leaving and early entry into the labour market were Xiaobao's strategic life choices, demonstrating his resilience in the face of structural constraints. Xiaobao is similar to the "troubled teens" whose patterns of deviance are healthy adaptations that permit them to survive unhealthy circumstances (Ungar, 2002). Although Xiaobao's life choices were deviant from socially

138   Guanglun Michael Mu

desired life trajectories and hence could be interpreted normatively as indicative of failure, incapacity, or lack of aspiration, he constructed an alternative pathway to well-being through which he redefined life satisfaction, social belonging, and power. In this vein, Xiaobao's resistance to the imposed stereotype manifested his hidden resilience that would often be overlooked and misrecognised by mainstream ideologies.

In a similar vein, mainstream ideologies would portray Xiaoliu as a disadvantaged left-behind child engaging in long hours of arduous labour of an exploitative nature. Living and growing up in a suboptimal child-rearing environment normally undermines young people's well-being. Yet Xiaoliu rejected any arbitrary labelling scheme of vulnerability or risk. Despite having been born into an impoverished rural family and having to grow up without parenting, Xiaoliu has developed into a confident social person and a significant member who has made valued, recognised contributions to his family. He drew on his resilience to protest against pejorative ascribed identities and access symbolic capital beneficial for rebounding from adversities. Xiaoliu's resistance to identity prescription and ascription vocalised the alternative views from the margins, and hence can be acknowledged as a resilience approach to counteracting "what he has been told" and questioning the established mainstream understanding of health and risk.

Consistent with the qualitative work, the quantitative analysis in this chapter indicates that floating children and left-behind children, especially those living in highly unfavourable circumstances, tend to engage in purposeful living that demonstrates patterns of resilience different from socially valorised ones. Stories of these young people urge a rethink of the open dichotomies of problem and performance, of resistance and resilience. The structural dichotomies fail to encapsulate the lived experiences of marginalised children, underestimate their capacities for controlling their own present and designing their own future, and overlook the ways in which they construe and define themselves. Unless their insights are voiced, respected, and legitimised, their alleged vulnerability and imposed marginalisation are likely to continue and prevail. Reframing resistance as resilience helps to recognise the resources of the marginal cultures, the power of the socially defined vulnerable groups, and the values of indigenous voices. Indeed indigenous peoples have long taught us to reframe resistance as resilience through their tribal epistemology. See a quote from James Clairmont – a Lakota spiritual elder:

> The closest translation of "resilience" is a sacred word that means "resistance" ... resisting bad thoughts, bad behaviours. We accept what life gives us, good and bad, as gifts from the Creator. We try to get through hard times, stressful times, with a good heart. The gift is the lesson we learn from overcoming it.
>
> *(cited in LaFromboise et al., 2006, p. 194)*

Resistance and Resilience of Migrants **139**

In response to the indigenous wisdom, floating children and left-behind children draw on their resilience *qua* resistance, and turn out to be what Bourdieu calls "extraordinary practical analysts":

> Situated at points where social structures "work", and therefore worked over by the contradictions of these structures, these individuals are constrained, in order to live or to survive, to practice a kind of self-analysis, which often gives them access to the objective contradictions which have them in their grasp, and to the objective structures expressed in and by these contradictions.
>
> *(Bourdieu, 1999, p. 511)*

Of course floating children and left-behind children were not born with these practical analytical skills. Instead, these have been enculturated into a habitus of resilience through family upbringing and socialisation. Such resilience helps me to understand why Xiaobao hated school with a passion, why he did not regret leaving school early, and why these outcomes were socially accepted within his family. Such resilience also helps me to understand why Xiaoliu could bear the hard, almost unceasing, work at his family's wonton stall for long hours, to ensure support for his grandparents; and why his grandparents were so proud of his contribution to the family. Their resilience also encompassed a set of capacities and capitals valued by themselves and their families. Their populism, stoicism, and optimism give me a better understanding of from where their resilience emanates, of how they can survive and thrive in the face of adversities so great that would have pressed many young people to collapse. Although resilience can emerge from various sources, family seems to be the primary source of resilience of Xiaobao and Xiaoliu.

In the face of structural constraints, not all floating children and left-behind children succumb to symbolic violence, or have their social agency completely oppressed. Xiaobao and Xiaoliu, together with many floating children and left-behind children with whom I have worked over the years, have led a life in ways that they and their families could see as good. In the face of the symbolic violence of the neoliberal expectations of social success and performance, many floating children and left-behind children reject stereotyped *doxa* and classed identities. They question the predetermined common sense. They claim their ordinariness in a way of just being themselves. Their ordinariness is an attribute of being honest to a normative everydayness, rather than fooling themselves with "bad faith" – "one's own lies to oneself" (Bourdieu, 1999, p. 205). They are tantamount to the white working-class boys with a deeply engrained habitus of "loyalty to self" (Stahl, 2015, p. 72) – the discomfort in acting like something they are not or performing an identity that they perceive to be inauthentic. These children constantly remind people in power of the power from the margins.

140 Guanglun Michael Mu

In this respect, their resilience is manifested in their resistance to neoliberal prerogatives of schooling and normative societal expectations.

Nevertheless, floating children and left-behind children might have been labelled elsewhere as at risk, vulnerable, or problematic. If such arbitrary labelling does not leave the scene, child and youth resilience research would remain haunted by devils of deficit thinking. The deficit model lays an epistemological basis for problem-based analysis of children and adolescents – a "scientific paradigm" of which governments and policies are particularly in favour. This is understandable because young people are framed as adults-in-the-making and problem-based analysis of these young people lends itself to the prediction, and hence prevention, of future problems. The problem-based approach legitimates prevention as a socially desired way of managing and governing young populations. Although the approach has undoubtedly improved the lives of certain young people at certain times, it is largely built on the grounds of predetermined "good" and "bad" outcomes, and "desired" and "undesired" futures. When such an approach diagnoses certain young people as sliding towards "bad" outcomes and "undesired" futures, these young people are immediately put in jeopardy and labelled as at risk in a universal sense, based on the problem-based analytical logic that, if intervened with, corrected, or saved early on, they will achieve a "good", "desired" future, instead of becoming depraved adults.

The problem-based approach understands young people as adults-in-the-making, rather than social agents for now and in their own right. Such an understanding often misses, or even misrecognises, the nuances and dynamics of young people's lived experiences. Some young people draw on their resilience to resist the socially desired way of being and doing, and hence falsify any arbitrary claims about their present and prospective life. When marginalised young people consider mainstream options to be constraining and opt for their own desirables, their resistance may at times further marginalise themselves from mainstream social space and further deviate themselves from conventional success. However, their resistance is also indicative of their resilience in terms of recognising and realising their own values and worldviews, and breaking the delimiting boundaries set by others. Their resistance here has nothing to do with cynicism or nihilism. It instead points to the very reality and complexity of the social world that is fraught with clashing interests, orientations, and lifestyles. Consequently, resilience research and practice require an approach of what Bourdieu (1999, p. 3) calls "the multiple perspectives" to replace the "simplistic and one-side images"; to "relinquish the single, central, dominant, in a word, quasi-divine, point of view that is all too easily adopted by observers – and by readers too"; to "correspond to the multiplicity of coexisting, and sometimes directly competing, points of view"; and to articulate "a complex and multi-layered representation" and "the same realities but in terms that are different and, sometimes, irreconcilable".

Notes

1 This piece was originally published in my monograph Mu (2018). *Building resilience of floating children and left-behind children in China: Power, politics, participation, and education.* London: Routledge. See Chapter 4: Resistance as a sociological process of resilience: Indigenous voices from under-resourced migrant families (pp. 104–129). The piece is reprinted here with permission of Taylor & Francis.
2 See a full description of the sample in Mu (2018) –*Building resilience of floating children and left-behind children in China: Power, politics, participation, and education.*

References

Bottrell, D. (2009). Understanding "marginal" perspectives: Towards a social theory of resilience. *Qualitative Social Work, 8*(3), 321–339.

Bourdieu, P. (1977). *Outline of a theory of practice* (R. Nice, Trans.). Cambridge: Cambridge University Press.

Bourdieu, P. (1984). *Distinction: A social critique of the judgment of taste* (R. Nice, Trans.). London: Routledge & Kegan Paul Ltd.

Bourdieu, P. (1990a). *In other words: Essays towards a reflexive sociology* (M. Adamson, Trans.). Stanford, CA: Stanford University Press.

Bourdieu, P. (1990b). *The logic of practice* (R. Nice, Trans.). Cambridge: Polity Press.

Bourdieu, P. (1993). *Sociology in question* (R. Nice, Trans.). London: Sage.

Bourdieu, P. (1999). *The weight of the world: Social suffering in contemporary society* (P. P. Ferguson, S. Emanuel, J. Johnson, & S. T. Waryn, Trans.). Cambridge: Polity Press.

Bourdieu, P. (2000). *Pascalian meditations* (R. Nice, Trans.). Cambridge: Polity Press.

Bourdieu, P. (2003). Participant objectivation. *Journal of the Royal Anthropological Institute, 9*(2), 281–294. 10.1111/1467-9655.00150.

Bourdieu, P. (2013). Participant objectivation (D. Fernbach, Trans.). In T. Yacine (Ed.), *Algerian sketches* (pp. 265–279). Cambridge: Polity Press.

Bourdieu, P., & Eagleton, T. (1992). Doxa and common life. *New Left Review,* I/191 (January-February), 111–121.

Bourdieu, P., Sapiro, G., & McHale, B. (1991). Second lecture – The new capital: Introduction to a Japanese reading of state nobility. *Poetics Today, 12*(4), 643–653. 10.2307/1772707.

Bourdieu, P., & Wacquant, L. J. D. (1992). *An invitation to reflexive sociology.* Cambridge: Polity Press.

Cummins, J. (2001). Empowering minority students: A framework for intervention. *Harvard Educational Review, 71*(4), 649–675.

Elder, G.H. (1974). *Children of the Great Depression: Social change in life experience.* Chicago: University of Chicago Press.

Foster, K. R., & Spencer, D. (2011). At risk of what? Possibilities over probabilities in the study of young lives. *Journal of Youth Studies, 14*(1), 125–143.

Giroux, H.A. (1983a). Theories of reproduction and resistance in the new sociology of education: A critical analysis. *Harvard Educational Review, 53*(3), 257–293. 10.17763/haer.53.3.a67x4u33g7682734.

Giroux, H.A. (1983b). *Theory and resistance in education: A pedagogy for the opposition.* New York: Bergin & Garvey.

Gofen, A. (2009). Family capital: How first-generation higher education students break the intergenerational cycle. *Family Relations, 58*(1), 104–120.

Goffman, E. (1951). Symbols of class status. *British Journal of Sociology*, *2*(4), 294–304. 10.2307/588083.

Han, J. (2004). Survey report on the state of compulsory education among migrant children in Beijing. *Chinese Education & Society*, *37*(5), 29–55.

Hernandez-Martinez, P., & Williams, J. (2013). Against the odds: Resilience in mathematics students in transition. *British Educational Research Journal*, *39*(1), 45–59. 10.1080/01411926.2011.623153.

Hu, Y., Lonne, B., & Burton, J. (2014). Enhancing the capacity of kin caregivers and their families to meet the needs of children left behind. *China Journal of Social Work*, *7*(2), 131–144.

LaFromboise, T.D., Hoyt, D.R., Oliver, L., & Whitbeck, L.B. (2006). Family, community, and school influences on resilience among American Indian adolescents in the upper midwest. *Journal of Community Psychology*, *34*(2), 193–209.

Libório, R.M.C., & Ungar, M. (2010). Children's perspectives on their economic activity as a pathway to resilience. *Children & Society*, *24*(4), 326–338. 10.1111/j.1099-0860.2009.00284.x.

Luke, A., & Goldstein, T. (2006). Building intercultural capital: A response to Rogers, Marshall, and Tyson. [Online supplement to Rogers, T., Marshall, E., & Tyson, C.A. (2006). Dialogic narratives of literacy, teaching, and schooling: Preparing literacy teachers for diverse settings. *Reading Research Quarterly*, *41*(2), 202–224].

Masten, A.S., Best, K.M., & Garmezy, N. (1990). Resilience and development: Contributions from the study of children who overcome adversity. *Development and Psychopathology*, *2*(4), 425–444. 10.1017/S0954579400005812.

Mu, G.M. (2018). *Building resilience of floating children and left-behind children in China: Power, politics, participation, and education*. London & New York: Routledge.

Mu, G.M., & Hu, Y. (2016a). *Living with vulnerabilities and opportunities in a migration context: Floating children and left-behind children in China*. Rotterdam, Boston, & Taipei: Sense Publishers.

Mu, G.M., & Hu, Y. (2016b). Validation of the Chinese version of the 12-item child and youth resilience measure. *Children and Youth Services Review*, *70*, 332–339. 10.1016/j.childyouth.2016.09.037.

Mu, G.M., & Jia, N. (2016). Rural dispositions of floating children within the field of Beijing schools: Can disadvantaged rural habitus turn into recognised cultural capital? *British Journal of Sociology of Education*, *37*(3), 408–426. 10.1080/01425692.2014.939264.

Mu, G.M., Zheng, X., Jia, N., Li, X., Wang, S., Chen, Y., He, Y., May, L., Carter, M., Dooley, K., Berwick, A., Sobyra, A., & Diezmann, C. (2013). Revisiting educational equity and quality in China through Confucianism, policy, research, and practice. *The Australian Educational Researcher, 40*(3), 373–389. 10.1007/s13384-013-0113-0.

National Women's Association. (2013). 我国农村留守儿童、城乡流动儿童状况研究报告 [*The national report of the current status of left-behind children and floating children*]. Beijing: National Bureau of Statistics Press.

OECD. (2012). *Equity and quality in education: Supporting disadvantaged students and schools*. Paris: OECD Publishing.

Seccombe, K. (2002). "Beating the odds" versus "changing the odds": Poverty, resilience, and family policy. *Journal of Marriage & Family*, *64*(2), 384–394.

Song, M. (1999). *Helping out: Children's labour in ethnic businesses*. Philadelphia, PA: Temple University Press.

Stahl, G. (2015). *Identity, neoliberalism and aspiration: Educating white working-class boys.* Abingdon, UK & New York: Routledge.

Ungar, M. (2002). *Playing at being bad: The hidden resilience of troubled teens.* Lawrencetown, Nova Scotia: Pottersfield.

Ungar, M. (2010). What is resilience across cultures and contexts? Advances to the theory of positive development among individuals and families under stress. *Journal of Family Psychotherapy, 21*(1), 1–16. 10.1080/08975351003618494.

Valenzuela, A. (1999). Gender roles and settlement activities among children and their immigrant families. *American Behavioral Scientist, 42*(4), 720–742. 10.1177/000276429904 2004009.

Werner, E. E. (1992). The children of Kauai: Resiliency and recovery in adolescence and adulthood. *Journal of Adolescent Health, 13*(4), 262–268. 10.1016/1054-139X(92)90157-7.

Willis, P. (1977). *Learning to labour: How working-class kids get working-class jobs.* Farnborough, UK: Saxon House.

8

ACADEMIC COMPETITION AND PARENTAL PRACTICE

A Study of Habitus and Change

Xu Zhao, Robert L. Selman, and Allan Luke

Bourdieu's sociological theory examines the underlying structures of social life by analysing "the social (or more precisely, political) construction of reality as it appears to intuition" (Bourdieu, 1993, p. 181). This chapter is a study of how the reality of academic competition in China's secondary education is co-constructed by anxious parents and the social conditions within which they function. These parents live in an emergent market economy which generates open unemployment, inequality in capital, and the dominant perception that under-achievement in education is linked to the threat of poverty and imminent feelings of shame. Drawing from Bourdieu's model of field, habitus, and capital, our aim here is to demonstrate first how parents have formed a habitus of individuated competition in response to the rules of exchange and discourses of the emergent new market structure of Chinese education. In addition, our analysis shows how different kinds and levels of capital are linked to positioning (e.g., structural determinations) and position-taking (e.g., degrees of agency) within the field: while economic and educational capital works to provide some middle- and upper-middle-class families with levels and degrees of autonomy from the market mechanism, for others the absence and lack of capital leaves the majority of Chinese students and parents, especially those from working-class families, with seemingly no choice but to focus on test-preparation for economic survival. Our analysis also points towards a broader historical trans-formation in Chinese families and society: whereby long-standing cultural traditions of education as the principal ladder of social ascendancy are now being challenged by youth in the context of the emergence of new patterns of child-parent relationships. Our case here is that we are observing and docu-menting nothing less than the construction of a new Chinese habitus: *Homo economicus* in sociological and psychological formation (Bourdieu, 2008).

Although we call on a recent analysis of historical shifts in the views of Chinese policy makers on the purposes of education (Zhao, 2016), our discussion is mainly based on an empirical study, qualitative in design and method. This study was conducted in 2015 and 2016 with over 70 Chinese parents and students from two Chinese cities (Jinan and Shanghai) and a wide range of socio-economic backgrounds. We take two interpretive approaches to analysing the empirical data which include both interviews and focus groups. First, we take a theory-driven approach, using Bourdieu's three main "thinking tools" (Wacquant, 1989, p. 50), namely, the concepts of habitus, capital, and field to examine Chinese students' and parents' constructions of what counts as good education and the strategies they use to achieve their educational goals. Secondly, we take an inductive approach to identify salient cultural practices and themes that shape habitus but are not necessarily captured by Bourdieu's initial theorisation. This fits one of the key aims of this volume: to augment and critique Bourdieu's sociological models where they might run up against anomalous cultural, social, and economic phenomena that are distinctive to the new China.

Combining the theory-driven and inductive approaches, we begin with a characterisation of a shared habitus that is cultivated in the field of Chinese education and the broader social, cultural, political, and historical conditions of Chinese society. By investigating the differences in the educational practices of the families who possess different kinds and levels of social, economic, and cultural capital, we consider how habitus, capital, and field are expressed and their combinatory interaction in the Chinese game[1] of academic competition, and, thereby, differential ways in which social structures are internalised, embodied, and appropriated. Finally, by demonstrating how social fields and institutional relations may function as self-reinforcing and self-annulling sources of repression and entrapment, we explore the educational question that has been consistently raised in response to Bourdieu's models of intergenerational reproduction (Yang, 2014): Wherein lies the hope for escape and change?

The study described here proceeds from both a participant-based analysis of the perspectives of children and parents who inhabit different strata of the social hierarchy (emic) and a third-person objectivistic analysis of parental practice (etic) (Morris et al., 1999). The emic approach investigates how children and parents think, feel, and act in relation to academic competition; the etic approach serves the purposes of (1) comparing patterns across different groups to understand habitus, social position in field, and change, and (2) investigating the practical relations of exchange that shape habitus, including documenting connections between individual psychology, family relationships, and broader social and historical processes. Together, the two analytical moves cast light on the mutually structuring relationships between the emergent habitus of competition and contemporary conditions of Chinese education, economy, and society. They also point out where and how long-standing elements of traditional habitus

146 Xu Zhao et al.

are in a process of social and cultural disruption, potentially setting the grounds for further change in Chinese education. Our case is that Bourdieu's theory provides a generative sociological framework but requires elaboration to capture the social psychological and cultural complexities involved in this current reshaping of habitus. In particular, we describe four processes that are essential for understanding the mutually structuring relationships and interaction between habitus and field in a changing society such as China. These processes sit in four interconnected and nested levels: individual psychology, traditional values and patterns of family relationships, national-level ideology and policy, and collective memory and historical experience.

We organise this chapter by roughly following Bourdieu's "three-moment" approach to data analysis: (1) analysing "the position of the field vis-à-vis the field of power"; (2) mapping out the objective structure of the relationships between the positions occupied by agents and institutions competing in the field, and (3) analysing the habitus of agents (Bourdieu & Wacquant, 1992, pp. 104–105). We begin with an analysis of the *second* moment, considering the structural topography of the field of secondary education in China. We briefly introduce how preparing for the test- and competition-based Chinese College Entrance Exam, or the *gāo kǎo* (高考), is the ultimate goal of teaching and learning in Chinese secondary education. We explain those forms of capital that are rare, valued, and sought after as signs of distinction by all players in the field. We then move to the *third* moment of analysis to consider the practice of the actual individual agent within the field. Here, we present our analysis of the empirical data. Our key research questions, then, are as follows. In the Chinese game of academic competition, what characterises and distinguishes the habitus of the different players in the field, namely, the students and parents from the different social positions? What forms of capital do they possess and use to gain an edge in academic competition? What conflicts and contradictions exist in the participants' beliefs and practices? Finally, in the discussion section, in line with Bourdieu's *first* moment of analysis, we locate the empirical findings in the broader field of power, namely, the social, political, and historical contexts of Chinese society. The chapter concludes with summary comments on the value and limitations of Bourdieu's sociological frameworks for explaining contemporary Chinese education and society.

Academic Competition in China: Who/What Is to Blame? Who/What Is the Game Changer?

Each year in June, about 10 million 12th graders in China take the college entrance exam, or the *gāo kǎo*, to compete for 6.5 million seats in universities and, out of those, fewer than 1 million seats at the "first-category" research universities. In order to succeed on the *gāo kǎo*, students spend most of their waking hours on test-preparation, and parents spend a tremendous amount of money and energy on selecting regular schools, tutorial schools, and private tutors to put their children in the best position to succeed (Kwok, 2010). This educational structure selects high-achieving students for higher education. It has to date been a key institutional mechanism and human capital framework for economic growth and poverty amelioration. However, by the turn of the twenty-first century, the negative impact of competition-related stress on children's mental and physical health had begun to raise serious concerns among parents, educators, and policy-makers. Our previous research shows that the desire to gain an edge in academic competition pervades everyday family life; it influences children's peer relationships in school (e.g., their social capital and relations of trust with friends); it governs parent-child interactions; and, due to its long-term impact on social stratification and individuals' attitude toward others and society, it has profoundly shaped the future social, moral, and civic landscapes of Chinese society (Zhao, 2015; Zhao et al., 2014).

In an attempt to reduce academic competition, since the late 1990s the government has issued new policies on a regular basis that aim to change what schools and parents do. However, these policies have set the context for schools and parents to invent new local strategies to continue the game of academic competition (Zhao, 2015). While schools and parents typically blame each other[2] for the pressure to push students to work harder, we have argued in previous work that an effective intervention should be coordinated across multiple social entities, targeting changes in systems (i.e., education and legal systems), cultural discourses (i.e., informed social awareness about morality and civic participation), and both individual and collective senses of social agency and efficacy (Zhao, Selman, & Haste, 2014). However, we also believe that interventions focused on the identification of the levers that can change parents' and students' beliefs and that such practices may have some effect on ameliorating the situation. Here we ask: What aspects of individual disposition, belief, and position-taking can be changed through cognitive and behavioural intervention? What aspects are necessary responses to structuring forces of the field and cannot be changed through such post-hoc intervention alone? Empirical investigations of these questions, even if partial and incomplete, are important for understanding the durability of existing practices and, indeed, potential avenues for shifting the social and educational fields of exchange. These investigations can also help us understand how much scope there is for reshaping knowledge and belief (as forms of cultural capital) and agentive "position taking" (Bourdieu, 1983) of individuals and communities, and what roles preventive interventions, as a bottom-up strategy, can play in altering relations of exchange.

This study was undertaken in Jinan and Shanghai in 2015 and 2016 respectively, as part of an ongoing research and intervention project on academic stress in Chinese students. The initial aim of the empirical study was to understand how parents and students from different socio-economic backgrounds perceive the state of academic competition, what motivates them to

148 Xu Zhao et al.

invest in it, what concerns them, and how they consider and deal with issues ranging from major decisions on school choice to daily routines and practices. We describe how we have collected the empirical data and how Bourdieu's sociology provides a framework for interpreting our findings. We then move on to discuss how the psychological and cultural themes we have identified may contribute to further elaboration of Bourdieu's models in Chinese education.

Empirical Study with Parents and Students from Two Cities

The study involved more than 70 parents and students from Jinan and Shanghai. Jinan is the capital city of Shandong province, two hours drive from Qufu, the birthplace of Confucius. In Shandong province, one of China's most economically diverse and robust areas, Confucian tradition maintains a high-profile influence on the social norms and conventions, especially regarding family life and interpersonal/intergenerational relationships. In Jinan, we collected in-depth interview and focus group data from three schools, which represented high-achieving, middle-achieving, and low-achieving schools (based on conventional test scores). As shown in our previous work in China, school types and achievement levels are always closely associated with students' socio-economic backgrounds, indicated by parental educational level and occupation (Zhao, 2015; Zhao et al., 2014). Social class clearly matters in the new China, with advanced tertiary education in China and study overseas a clear marker of distinction. In the present study, the parents from Jinan included university professors with doctoral degrees, professionals and administrative staff with college degrees or higher, as well as blue-collars workers who never finished high school. Their ages ranged from late 40s to early 50s, and their children were in grades 6–10.

In Shanghai, historically and currently the most cosmopolitan city in China, we organised a focus group with eight mothers who have studied overseas and have now returned to live and work in Shanghai. These individuals are commonly called "overseas returnees" (海归 hǎi guī) in China. They shared the characteristics of having a college degree or higher from North American or European countries, speaking fluent English as a second or third language, and currently or previously holding high-income management positions in international corporations in Shanghai. Their children were attending either international schools or some of the most elite public schools in Shanghai.

Data collected from parents included two focus groups (5–6 parents in each group) and nine interviews from Jinan, and one focus group (8 mothers) from Shanghai. We also tried to understand the issue from students' and teachers' perspectives. Data from students included six interviews and nine focus groups (4–6 participants in each group) from Jinan. In both interviews and focus groups, we asked the participants to share their thoughts about academic competition and pressure, and what they do to deal with pressure and achieve

Academic Competition and Parental Practice **149**

their goals. We also asked them to comment on concrete scenarios that involve different perspectives and choices related to academic competition.

The analysis reported here aims to understand how Chinese families operating under different socio-economic conditions differ in their educational beliefs, practices, choices, and strategies. For this purpose, we compared the data from three groups: the white-collar parents who were professors, professionals, or administrators in Jinan, the blue-collar parents who were factory or service workers in Jinan, and the eight mothers from Shanghai who were returnees from European or North American countries. Without accurate information on their income levels, we believe the three groups – distinguishable in terms of educational achievement and distinction – can be safely classified as high-, middle-, and low-income families on the national level. Before reporting our findings, we first explain what we perceive as the major features of Bourdieu's empirical approach and how we have conducted our analysis informed by both Bourdieu's concepts and critiques of Bourdieusian empiricism in the sociological literature.

Understanding Habitus in the Chinese Field of Academic Competition

Habitus refers to human subjects' overall dispositions and sensibilities, including the cognitive structures that individuals implement in their practical knowledge of the social world. These are internalised and embodied social structures (which are objectified and institutionalised social conditions and cultural practices). Our data analysis has aimed to identify the links between habitus and field. Hence the question: What has been internalised and embodied by the Chinese participants in relation to their goal of survival and distinction in the field of academic competition? Since Bourdieu defines habitus as a system of dispositions which generate perceptions, appreciations, and practices (Bourdieu, 1990, p. 53), we coded the data using beliefs, perceptions, values, practices, strategies, and choices as proxies of habitus, but also included data on a broad spectrum of ways of acting, feeling, thinking, and being (Grenfell, 2014). We then compared the three groups of parents from the different social positions and examined the connections between habitus, field, and capital. In this way, our design worked recursively from selection and formation of the cohort to data which was then used to test and instantiate the initial cohort formation.

Next, our analysis took into consideration critical perspectives on Bourdieu's structuralism. For example, Lamont (1992) has convincingly argued that Bourdieu's theorisation of habitus focuses exclusively on proximate structural conditions (e.g., the material *conditions* of existence characteristic of a class *condition*), but neglects the impact of broader structural features (e.g., international-level geographic conditions and political system) and cultural resources (e.g., cultural models) available to individuals from different nations. This is where the context of Chinese political economy, state ideology, and cultures explicitly come into play. In response to such

150 Xu Zhao et al.

critiques, we took an inductive approach to data analysis to identify themes emerging from the data that point to the broader structural and cultural forces that shape habitus but might not be fully anticipated in Bourdieu's structuralism.

In the following section, we first introduce the multiple themes that we have identified from both the etic (researchers' perspective informed by Bourdieu's theory) and emic (participants' perspective) approaches of data analysis. To describe the habitus in relation to academic competition, we follow the pattern of moving from introducing the "old" (traditional, familiar, and widely shared) to the "new" (reflection, resistance, and change) patterns of parental practice. These capture, we would add, the relationships between what Williams (1978) referred to as "residual" and "emergent" cultures, a distinction particularly salient in the context of the radical and dynamic socio-economic transformation of Chinese society. We also provide evidence to demonstrate how the various themes of the habitus are related to the structure of the education system. In the concluding discussion section where we contextualise the empirical study within the broader societal context, we will return to examine this mutually structuring relationship between habitus and field in the Chinese context, from both a Bourdieusian sociological perspective and a social psychological perspective that takes into consideration the ideological and historical processes that shape habitus.

What Has Been (Most Deeply or Broadly) Internalised and Embodied?

Bourdieu's concern with habitus is the problem of how the "outer" (the social) becomes "inner" (the internalisation process) and how habitus as a "collective consciousness" is expressed in objectified forms such as lifestyle choices (cultural styles, artefacts, and practices), and in different degrees and forms of actual cultural capital (embodied practices) (Grenfell, 2014). In line with this perspective, our analysis here suggests that, within a long tradition of seeing education as the ladder for social ascendancy (dating back to the sixth century AD) and in a contemporary competition-based education system, many Chinese parents and students share the belief that competitive success in education is the singular and exclusive path leading to a decent life. Even though resistance to this mainstream belief exists among rural families (Mu, 2018; Mu & Hu, 2016) and each year about 1 million Chinese 12th-graders gave up on the *gāo kǎo*, either to take jobs or go to overseas colleges (Wang, 2013), the vast majority of Chinese students have to prepare for the *gāo kǎo* in order to go to college in China. Previous research (e.g., Fong, 2004) and the present study both show that, for urban working-class families, their children's academic success is often viewed as the sole hope for the family's future financial security. For many middle- and upper-middle-class parents, academic success is the way to maintain the social positions and the sense of social status that older generations (going back to one or multiple generations) have worked hard to

Academic Competition and Parental Practice **151**

obtain. This is not a simple matter of rational belief or social ideology – it is multigenerational, embodied Han Chinese cultural practice.

Consider, for a moment, the implications of a social field of exchange construed through the metaphor of a ladder: hierarchical, linear, with limited access and space at each rung; status, height, and progress, further, is publicly visible from a distance and, importantly, to those on the ascent. This reality is often construed as parents and children having "no choice" but to focus on test-preparation to gain an edge in academic competition. Related to this construction of reality is parents' view of children and their educational outcomes as comparable products, the quality of which depends on the raw material (their superior or inferior innate capacity), but more on parents' investments of time, energy, and resources on their improvement. Consequently, students' academic achievement is closely linked to parents' sense of success and failure, the rungs that their children appear to occupy, and affiliated feelings of pride or shame.

In this section, we first present examples demonstrating how these basic assumptions about education, life, and the *malleable* nature of children, especially in childhood, are shared by parents across different social positions and how they are linked to the education system and broader social, economic, and political conditions. Second, we illustrate how these assumptions are expressed in the strategies that parents use to promote their children's academic success, and how the strategies express different kinds and degrees of capital. In our discussions of these issues, we provide examples showing individuals' reflections on and resistance to the shared assumptions and common practices. Working from the perspective of Western systems, Hirschman (1970) makes the prototypical case that parents as "consumers" in educational markets have the options of exit, voice, or loyalty in response to their perceptions of the quality of the system. Emergent patterns of parental "choice" in the new Chinese educational marketplace is the study of considerable current research (e.g., Liu, 2018; Yochim, 2014). Our question concerns the "ladders" of contemporary Chinese education: Which families and parents have and experience such volitional alternatives and choices? Which do not?

No Choice: Good Education and Good Life

Competing to obtain relatively rare educational qualifications is taken as the only way for individuals to gain financial security, respect from others, and access to the good life. This logic is used by parents from different social positions to reflexively make meaning of their own life trajectories, and it is used intergenerationally as a guiding principle governing child-rearing goals and activities. The working-class parents from Jinan make the link based on their past experiences (i.e., deprivation of educational opportunities), and their current lack of job security and class position. In contrast, the parents who are university employees in Jinan and the overseas returnee parents from Shanghai

152 Xu Zhao et al.

make the link based on their past educational success as outstanding students, subsequent professional achievement, and financial success. The parents all try to pass on a single message to their children. That is, only through working hard today to gain competitive educational success can they have a good life tomorrow.

The construction of the reality that students and parents have no choice but to do everything they can to go to a good university is reflected in the following comment from a father, who is a university administrator from Jinan:

NING (MIDDLE-CLASS FATHER): I would tell my son to look at the factory workers who are laid off, those unemployed, and the street sweepers. Guess what he said? He said it is not bad to be a street sweeper, and it is an honour to work and serve. My son is like that. But I think China has so many people competing for jobs. This is a realistic issue. Parents have a lot of pressure, more pressure than our children . . . I myself got out of the rural area because of education. I have a good job, but I see how hard it is to get a good job [today]. If my son doesn't go to a good university, cannot find a good job, what would he live on? I am concerned about his future. All I want to tell him is: with so many people in China, so many college graduates, his only choice is to prepare for the *gāo kǎo*, go to a good university, and get a good job. That is the logic of most parents.

The need to be "realistic" is a shared view among the students and parents from Jinan. As shown through Ning's account, the reality is constructed that individuals in a highly competitive society have no choice but to compete for the more desirable educational qualifications in order to survive. Ning's son, in his likely rhetorical response to his father's teaching, seems to suggest that his father is being socially snobbish rather than economically realistic in his denial of the value of blue-collar jobs. However, Ning's observation is actually shared by the blue-collar parents themselves. The following excerpt is from a focus group discussion with six working-class parents whose children were attending a low-achieving junior high school in Jinan:

GUO: I feel very anxious. My son is already in grade eight, just one more year before the High School Entrance Exam. I don't have any idea about his future.

SUN: As parents, we don't know what kind of future our children can have and what we can do to help them. We are all very anxious.

WANG: It is like . . . whenever I see [my daughter] is relaxing, I would ask her, "Why couldn't you do some homework?"

GUO: Why am I so anxious? Think about the education system. If my son doesn't do well in school, and his total score cannot be within the first 140 in his school's ranking, he won't be able to go to a high school, not even a common high school [middle- or low-achieving]. He can only go to a vocational school. He cannot learn anything there.

Academic Competition and Parental Practice **153**

These working-class parents, mostly migrant workers from rural areas, define good education as having a high school degree (the product that indicates good education and respectability in society) and learning the skills of reading and writing (the indicators that validate the worth of the product). For them, even a high school degree is beyond their reach. Reflected in the example above are working-class parents' shared feelings of uncertainty and anxiety about their children's (and their own) future. Their anxiety is grounded in their feelings of helplessness in improving their families' economic circumstances and their social positions within the current social hierarchy. Their concerns about survival underline the impact of extant social and economic fields on individuals' educational beliefs and practices, particularly the lack of state pension and health care systems that can provide families from lower social classes with some degree of autonomy or protection from the market. In the following excerpt, the same working-class parents talk about these deeper roots of their education-related anxiety:

INTERVIEWER: What kind of life do you want your children to lead in the future?
WANG: I hope she doesn't have to lead a hard life like mine, and she will have a better life.
GUO: I want my son to go to a high school. I tell him that when he has a job in the future, his colleagues may do the same job, but if they have a high school education, they will have more knowledge. They will know how to say things, do things, and write things. Without a high school education, I tell my son, he won't know how to write articles.
SUN: It is important to learn more knowledge. Use me as an example. I only completed elementary school. Now, I get paid for the days I work. [On the days] I don't work, I get nothing. In the future, the single-child generation will need to take care of four elderly parents [one's own parents and in-laws], and maybe grandparents too. Now we have three or four siblings [to share the burden]. Their burden will be much heavier than ours. If they don't have a good education ... honestly, sweeping streets is a job, being the mayor is also a job. But their differences are heaven and earth. If their parents are seriously ill and need help, what can they do to help them when they must go to work everyday [to bring food to table]? You cannot say they are not good to their parents. If they don't have a good education, and can only sweep streets to make a living, they cannot even take care of themselves. What happens when the parents are ill?

Here, good education is linked to gaining more job skills and working in better conditions than the older generation, as a classical element of intergenerational social mobility. This assumption that the primary purposes of education are job opportunities and financial security actually departs from the Confucian humanistic tradition of seeing the primary goal of education as self-cultivation. This

154 Xu Zhao et al.

concept of "a good education" is in line with the Bourdieusian perspective that individuals' educationally acquired cultural capital, verified through the institutional capital of credentials and achievement, is longitudinally exchangeable for economic capital (i.e., convertible goods, income, wealth), social capital (institutional access, networks), and, indeed, further cultural capital (additional skills, knowledges, beliefs, and credentials) (Luke, 2018). Indeed, for the working-class families, it is about gaining the required educational credentials (institutional capital) and job skills (embodied capital) for economic survival; for the middle-class families, it is about economic survival but also about the production, reproduction, and intergenerational sustainability of distinctive social position.

Academic Achievement and Filial Duty

Traditional moral teachings and family values are part of a primary socialisation whereby families shape individual habitus from infancy (Bourdieu & Passeron, 1990). We found a powerful influence of the sense of filial duty on the educational practice of some children and parents. This influence is particularly reflected in the data from Jinan, close to Confucius' birthplace of Qufu. Students and parents from Jinan often mention children's responsibility to take care of their parents in the future. Gaining the ability to provide their parents with a good/better life is an important motive for many of the students to work hard in school. In the following example, 11th-grader Hao talks about what motivates him to work hard:

HAO (BOY): What motivates me? Very simple: a better life in the future. Also, my biggest motivation is to give my parents a better life. My parents' income level is not very high, in the middle range. I don't want my parents to worry about me and suffer for me. I should care for them. So I must work hard. Honestly, only when you have a good job, can you have the money to take good care of your parents. Some people may tell you examples of ancient people who lived a life free of the pursuit of fame and wealth. Today we need to be realistic. Without money, you can do nothing [to help your parents]; with money, you can support your parents.

Hao is from a working-class family. He is clearly concerned about the financial security of his parents and is determined to improve the family's economic situation through his educational efforts. His concerns about the future of his parents and his emphasis of being "realistic" echo Ning, the middle-class father who is concerned about the future of his son. Here, embodied cultural traditions (filial duty) interact with the conditions of the economic and social field (the requirement of educational qualification on a competitive job market) to contribute to the entrenched belief that children and parents have no choice but to climb the ladder, to enter the playing field of the game of academic competition.

Challenges from the Younger Generation

While the traditional and common practice of linking educational qualifications to success in life and to the fulfilment of filial duty is deeply entrenched, it is also under challenge. The overseas returnee parents with educational qualifications, high-paying jobs, and the "good life" that the working- and middle-class families aspire to, also struggle with the question of what constitutes a good education and a good life for their children. These parents have previously defined their values and aspirations for their children in the same way as the middle- and working-class parents. One mother emphasised, "That is what our generation did. We changed our life through *dú shū* [读书, reading/working hard in school] and going to a good university." Another said, "We have a family tradition to become well-educated engineers and medical doctors. I tell my daughter, 'You will have more opportunities when you have a good college degree.'" But this experience-based belief is being challenged by their children. One mother was asked by her daughter, "Why should I go to the best university in the world? What differences will it make in my life? People who have high school degrees can be successful too."

The questions from the younger generation can be seen as existential attacks on the well-constituted habitus of these parents, which are well adapted to the field of Chinese education in the 1970s–80s. The questions challenge the parents' basic assumptions about how to live a good life, how to orientate themselves toward the future, and even "how to be". One interpretation is that the level of economic capital that these families possess has the effect of freeing their children from the need to support their aging parents in return of the sacrifice they have made. Children from these better-off families only need to consider their own future when making educational choices and decisions, as reflected in the rhetorical question mentioned earlier: "What differences will it make in *my* life?" That is, their overall economic capital sets the conditions for an alteration of long-standing and durable intergenerational practices. From a different perspective, it can also be argued that the overseas returnee parents are socialising their children in a new way: towards an emergent "possessive individualism" (Apple, 1990), affiliated with Western middle-class nuclear families and consumer culture. This individualistic view moves away from the traditional emphasis on filial duty and the self as a member of the family who should put the interest of the family collective first, a belief that still has a strong hold on Jinan students and parents.

In either case, it is not hard to imagine that these parents have proudly told themselves and their children that, because of their own educational and professional success, their children will not be burdened by the responsibility of taking care of their aging parents, and that they will have the freedom to pursue a good life, even though what constitutes a good life remains a question affiliated with the material and cultural conditions in the new China, a socio-historical field in formation. Here, despite the parents' own habitus, their

156 Xu Zhao et al.

possession of higher levels of economic and cultural capital (higher levels of education and new approaches to child-rearing presumably sourced from exposure to different cultural models) provides opportunities for the next generation to form a different habitus. In effect, this amounts to a material historical change and transformation in the intergenerational social, economic, and cultural reproduction described by Bourdieu & Passeron (1990), a model which, we noted at the onset of this chapter, has been critiqued precisely because it does not readily account for significant intergenerational change and social transformation through education and pedagogic action.

Children as Comparable Products to be Improved

Assumptions about the nature of children and the tasks of child-rearing constitute a distinctive parental habitus related to academic competition. It has been argued that a key feature of Chinese parents' educational practice is their emphasis on children's efforts rather than their innate ability (Stevenson et al., 1990). Accordingly, Chinese parents play an active role in making sure their children work as hard as they can to achieve their (or parental and familial) goals. *Guǎn* (管, training) is a well-documented practice considered as characterising Chinese parenting across different social and economic contexts (e.g., Bond, 1998; Chan, Bowes, & Wyver, 2009; Chao, 1994; Chen & Luster, 2002; Gorman, 1998; Pearson & Rao, 2003; Stewart et al., 2002). Our analysis here suggests that, given the Chinese education system that evaluates academic success based on measurable products (standardised tests, exams, students' rankings), parents' efforts are actually based on the view that children themselves are products whose quality is defined through comparison with peers, and the products' improvement relies, to a large extent, on parents' effort to ensure their children make the best effort themselves. In this way, the competitive ladder actually functions as a kind of feedback loop for parents, reinforcing and verifying beliefs about the efficacy of collective effort.

The Practice of Upward Social Comparison

Associated with the view of children as malleable products, our interviews with students from Jinan documented a common set of strategies that parents use to motivate their children. We grouped them into three categories: *lecturing, monitoring*, and *comparing*. *Lecturing*, or nagging (叨叨, *dāo dāo*) in the students' words, typically involves talking with children about the parents' past educational experiences and emphasising young people's responsibility to work hard in school so that they will not repeat the life struggles of their parents. It also involves reminding children, at all given opportunities, of the importance of paying close attention to teachers' lectures and working hard on their homework. *Monitoring* involves a surveillance system, whereby parents are continuously checking, usually both in the evening and during weekend, whether their children are actually studying in their own room, whether they finish their homework on time, and whether they have done extra reviewing before going to bed. *Comparing* involves talking with one's own child about the achievements and good qualities of other children (often known and local) to urge him or her to catch up with those exemplars.

The following excerpt shows how a group of seventh-graders, all from working-class families, talk about how their parents use the strategies of lecturing, monitoring, and comparing to make them work harder:

LING (GIRL): Usually I do the reviewing work in school. I spend all the self-study time on reviewing the materials. Getting home, I only need to do my homework. Then I do a bit more reviewing before going to bed. But my mother always says to me, "Think about the kids who rank number one in your grade. They all study until late night. You are going to bed so early. Isn't it foolish?" I don't think it is that foolish. I have reviewed all of the materials of the day, and my mother still thinks I am foolish by going to bed early. There is a bit of problem with their method [of parenting].

INTERVIEWER: What time do you go to bed that is too early for your parents?

LING (GIRL): After 10 p.m. . . . we get up really early in the morning, around 5:30 a.m.

MING (BOY): The students ranked number one in the grade go to bed really late.

TONG (GIRL): The monitor of my class gets up at 4:30 a.m., and goes to bed really late. I don't know what time. My mother always tells me to work hard. She always tells me to memorise some articles and new words after finishing homework. She just nags, saying if I don't listen to her, she will tell the teacher, and the teacher will discipline me. So I just do whatever they tell me to do.

LING (GIRL): My mom is strict with me. She always says, "[as a child] I wanted to learn but didn't get the opportunity. I have been disadvantaged by that and spent many years to catch up. So I want you to work hard when you are young." So she always tells me, "Work hard to prepare for the tests. When you do well in the tests, you will have the opportunity to enter xxx." Stuff like that. She says this every other day. Sometimes I just listen to her. Sometimes she doesn't stop, and I become really annoyed. I would say to her, "It is not like I am not doing my best. If I have too much pressure, I will feel nervous, and I won't do well in the tests."

INTERVIEWER: What do you think about parents' comparing their children with other children?

LING (GIRL): I don't know whether to laugh or to cry about it. My parents always compare me with other kids. Once it was just too much and I got annoyed. I said to my mom, "Why don't you learn from the better parents? Why do you always ask me to learn from the better kids?" She said a sentence that I didn't know whether to laugh or to cry. She said, "You can go to the better parents to be their children!" I wanted to say, "Why don't you have the better children to be your own?" The thing is that parents want us to be like other kids, but they don't try to be like other parents. This is not fair for us. I know they are parents, but I think in today's society, parents also need to learn to use good methods. It is not like the old days when children must listen to our parents no matter what. We should listen to them, but we also need to help them improve. This comparing and competing habit of thinking is not healthy. This is not good for children's psychological health.

This is how the myth that high-performing students go to bed later and get up earlier than everybody else is reinforced among students and parents, and further exacerbates their feelings of anxiety and inadequacy. For Ling's mother, Ling is being foolish by going to bed at 10 p.m., because the higher-achieving students go to bed at a much later time. This works as a kind of self-fulfilling prophecy, which, if repeated enough, becomes a benchmark of practice and of everyday strategies to enforce, rationalise, or even evade the practice. Even though Ling says she disagrees with her mother, she still feels the need to explain to the interviewer that her family gets up early in the morning in order to justify her going to bed at the early time of 10 p.m. Ming and Tong both confirm the idea that the high-achieving students go to bed at a very late time, even though they do not really know what time those students go to bed. There is pressure on students to stay up as late as possible, and it is never late enough when compared with the higher achievers.

Comparing one's own children with their higher-performing peers is sometimes a strategy that parents consciously use to motivate their children to work harder, but it has also become of a *habit* of thinking and behaviour. The students we interviewed are often annoyed by their parents' lecturing and monitoring, but they especially resent their parents' habit of comparing. The "comparing and competing habit of thinking" that Ling observed is so common among parents that the expression "other parents' kids" (人家的孩子, *rén jiā de hái zi*) has become a popular catch phrase used by students to refer to the high-achieving and perfect kids whom their parents praise with envy and want their children to emulate. From the parents' perspective, it is a way to stimulate their children to work harder and do better on tests. But many parents admit they do it out of a habit and in an unconscious and even uncontrollable manner. Ning, a middle-class father from Jinan, recalled that once he tried to point out his son's "weak points" in comparison with other children's "strong points", as parents often do to motivate their children. His son responded in the same way as Ling did, asking him to adopt those better kids as his own. Ning says he just stood there, speechless and thinking: "Why does my son have no motivation to do better (上进, *shàng jìn*)?"

This practice of upward social comparison (comparing oneself with people who perform better than they do) may be a feature of individuals from a collectivist tradition (Chung & Mallery, 1999). In sociological terms, it might be framed as an ongoing quest for distinction by the positing of an ideal type of student habitus. It may even be an influence of the Confucian moral teaching: "When we see men of worth/virtue, we should think of equalling them." However, it is not hard to see the link between this competing and comparing habit of mind and the competition-based education system. In addition to the *gāo kǎo*, high school promotion is also based on competitive success on standardised tests. The city of Jinan implemented a quota policy in 1997 to reduce academic competition and educational inequality at the junior high school level. Based on this policy, the best high schools in Jinan must accept a certain number of students from each of the junior high schools in the city. The number of students who can be promoted to the best senior high schools is decided based on the total number of enrolment in a junior high school, which is decided based on local government's evaluation of the quality of teaching in the school. The students whose ranking position is not within a certain number in his or her school would have no choice but to attend a vocational high school. For example, in one of the junior high schools we studied, there are a total of 600 students in grade nine. The two best senior high schools in Jinan have 70 seats available for students from this junior high school. In order to be promoted to one of these two high schools, parents need to make sure their children work hard to maintain their top 50 ranking positions. The institutional field of secondary education, then, works through a system of limits, thresholds, and scarcity of exchanges; that is, there are only so many rungs on the metaphorical ladder. Those who hold lower positions will go to low-achieving high schools. The students with the lowest ranking positions can only go to vocational schools, and lose their opportunity for higher education. Our interviews with the working-class parents suggest that a great source of anxiety for these parents is the worry that their children will go to a vocational high school, work blue-collar, low-paying jobs, and struggle in life like they do themselves. Therefore, this system *structures* parents' thinking and behaviour by making comparison between children's academic performance a necessity, as it is the most reliable way for parents to evaluate their children's capacity to succeed in the competition-based system and to adjust their expectations and make plans accordingly.

The New Parent–Child Relationship and the New Self

These systems are not airtight but are subject to historical challenge. There is some evidence that middle-class parents critically reflect on the practice of seeing children as comparable products and on the habitual upward social comparison. What was previously implicit in parental practice is being made explicit, and what has been semi-automatic is being reflected upon and critically examined. In the following example, Dong, a 7th-grade boy from Jinan,

160 Xu Zhao et al.

describes his relationship with his parents who are professionals working with troubled children:

DONG (BOY): My parents are agreeable. When I want to do something, I can talk to them and let them know how I think about it. Unless they think I am going too far, they will let me do what I want to do. There are not a lot of conflicts between us ... As long as I am not going too far, like spending too much time playing, they are okay. They tell me it is my own responsibility to make sure I do well in school, as long as I believe what I am doing is justifiable (问心无愧, *wèn xīn wú kuì*). They don't directly compare me with other kids. They only tell me to learn from others. I don't want to learn from others. I am myself. I am not a thing that can be made out of a mould.

The above example documents a parent–child relationship that no longer follows the traditional hierarchical pattern, but acknowledges degrees of children's agency and autonomy. It also shows some middle-class parents' reflecting on their approaches to promoting their children's academic success and their roles in shaping their children's development and future life. Dong's parents do not "directly" compare him with other kids, only telling Dong to learn from the kids who presumably demonstrate qualities that are desirable to Dong's parents. But even this suggestion is rejected by Dong, who has a firm belief in his individuality. His claim, "I am myself. I am not a thing that can be made out of a mould", suggests the emergence of a new discourse about the self among middle-class Chinese families. This is a new habitus shaped by the primary socialisation of Chinese middle-class homes. The following example shows how Qin, a university lecturer, considers the right method of *guǎn* (管, training):

QIN (MIDDLE-CLASS MOTHER): Parents need to develop a good way to communicate with children when they are at the stage of elementary school. [This will] help children cultivate a good attitude and habit toward school work. It would be too late to discipline children by the time they reach junior high school. So we now emphasise strict monitoring (严管, *yán guǎn*) at the elementary level, and give children more autonomy after that. I am trying to influence the parents in my daughter's homeroom group. Many of them understand *guǎn* as control. This kind of *guǎn* means "whatever I say, you must listen, because I love you and I do what I can for your benefits." Teenage children won't accept this. The Chinese word "*guǎn*" is interesting. It can mean to control (管制, *guǎn zhì* or 管控, *guǎn kòng*). It can also mean to manage (管理, *guǎn lǐ*). Parents need to learn from managers, giving their children the freedom they need.

The two examples above show the search for new metaphors about the nature of children and the roles parents should play. Neither Qin nor the mother of

Academic Competition and Parental Practice **161**

Dong is free of the comparing and competing habit of thinking and behaviour, but they are more aware of modernist discourses around the need to protect children's psychological and emotional health, and both take the approach of encouraging rather than criticising their children. It is particularly interesting that Qin refers to the need for parents like herself "to learn from managers", in effect arguing that child-rearing can follow tenets from the fields of business and work. The overall orientation of these parents is to emphasise their children's autonomy, and to be respectful of their children's thinking and decision-making. They emphasise the importance of communicating with their children and are more aware of respecting individuality.

Like these two mothers, many of the middle-class parents in our study often feel they know what they should do, in contrast to the working-class parents who explicitly express their sense of a lack of knowledge about how to guide their children in navigating the education system and a changing society. Middle-class parents' educational background and professional and social environment provide them with expanded opportunities to critically weigh the impact of the education system on their children and to reconnoitre what they as parents should do in their children's best interests. While they often use the same default strategies of lecturing, monitoring, and comparing to motivate their children to work harder, they generally tend to be critically reflective about their parenting practice.

Who Has Choices? Capital and Strategies

Habitus is the composite cultural capital that individuals possess and embody. But cultural capital sits in relationship to available social capital (networks, access, relations, communities) and economic capital (convertible material wealth), and requires recognition and acknowledgement (symbolic capital) within a social field (e.g., the school, workplace, community) in order for it to have viable exchange value. Our analysis shows a strong link between social position and the range of strategies that parents deploy to promote their children's academic success. The middle-class and overseas returnee parents use a broader range of strategies within the system than the working-class parents. These strategies entail the exchange of social capital: for example, using social media to network with other parents, strengthening communication with teachers, monitoring school practices, investing in tutoring schools, making informed decisions about school, and using social connections to place their children in the most advantageous school and homeroom group. Qin, for example, a middle-class mother, used her social networks to enrol her daughter into a good junior high school and to be assigned into a homeroom group that has the best teachers in the school. Gang, a middle-class father, wanted to find a way to help his son stop playing computer games and focus on his schoolwork. In the last two months before the high school entrance exam, Gang and other parents organised an evening self-study group for their children, under the supervision of volunteering parents. It worked very well for his son: "In such an environment, everybody is working hard together. The kids could not walk around or do anything else but focus on their schoolwork."

Even when their children are attending a high-achieving high school with the best teachers to prepare them for the *gāo kǎo*, middle-class parents continue to invest in after-school tutoring classes (Zhang & Bray, 2014). According to Gang, there are very few students in his daughter's school, the best in Jinan, who are not attending tutoring classes. Tutoring classes cost up to a thousand yuan [US$150] per week, not affordable for working-class parents. Middle-class parents can also use their social connections to arrange for their children to take classes in a school with better teachers and later go back to their own school to take the *gāo kǎo*. As Gang commented, offering his own version of social analysis: "Children's educational success is actually a test of parents' financial and social capacities." As we can see in these cases, this entails a whole-scale mobilisation and exchange of families' economic, social, and cultural capital on behalf of the child's education. All bets are off in the quest for distinction, which constitutes a deliberate, strategic set of parental actions, investments, and exchanges.

In the end, when middle-class children cannot go to a high-achieving high school and the chance of going to a good university in China becomes limited, better-off parents have the option of sending their children to an international program to prepare them for overseas colleges. The international programs not only open doors to overseas universities but also open their eyes about qualities for a successful life:

YING (MIDDLE-CLASS FATHER): My son is not the type of kid who works hard on schoolwork. It worries me. He likes sports. He is very compassionate, very kind, and honest. He is too honest and can be taken advantage of in society. But his teacher at the international program totally surprised us by saying my son will be the second most successful person in the program. The first is a kid who is academically strong and knows what he wants to do. The teacher says my son will be the second most successful, whether in China or overseas. He has a great personality. He is very self-disciplined and always tries to help others. The teacher's comments give my son a lot of confidence in himself. The teachers always encourage the kids. I very much appreciate this approach.

In the above example, the teacher uses the familiar expression of "number xxx" in her rank-order prediction of students' future success. Her evaluation, however, is not based on academic achievement only, but incorporates students' personal and social qualities. Teaching in an international program, rather than within the test-based Chinese education system, the teacher is able to take a different perspective about what individual qualities predict future success. This helps Ying, the father, to take a different perspective about his son.

Academic Competition and Parental Practice   **163**

In fact, the overseas returnee parents in our study are all preparing their children for education in North America, Europe, or Australia. During the focus group discussion, one mother, having shared her concerns about the Chinese education system putting too much pressure on children, asked herself and the group, "Shall we move to Australia to give my children more space to grow up?" Another mother answered her question indirectly by saying, "I hope my daughter can study in the US. There is too much pressure in China on girls and women." With these concerns, the parents all agree that leaving China is the way to provide their children with a good education and a good life. Their search for overseas alternatives is, in itself, a critique and commentary on the current Chinese educational field. For those parents who have received overseas education and credentials, it also marks a resetting of the parameters of inter-generational cultural and economic reproduction.

A Shared Feeling of Anxiety

Anxiety has become a habitual state for many Chinese parents. Despite the different levels of capital they possess, the working- and middle-class parents from Jinan and the upper-middle-class parents from Shanghai share a deep feeling of anxiety, anxiety about their children's academic success, future job competition, financial security, and social positions, but also about how to define the good life and its requisites. Anxiety creates a huge gap between what parents believe they should do and what they actually do. For the middle-class parents, even though they know the flaws of the field, they cannot act otherwise. For example, middle-class father Ning shares his struggle in dealing with his son's poor performance:

NING (MIDDLE-CLASS FATHER): Honestly, I don't want my son to care too much about his scores. I would rather he is healthy and grows up happily. I have medical training and work in a medical school. I see many students at my university, who are good students and attending a good university. But they are under so much pressure. Every year there are students who jump to their death from a high building. Many have psychological problems. I don't want my son to be like them. I hope he is happy. But I understand the parents who worry so much about their children's school performance. I am also worried about my son's scores. Really worried . . . I have a colleague, who is a very high-achieving professor at my university. Her son didn't do well in the High School Entrance Exam and was at the bottom of his school's ranking. The mother was really worried. She said, "It would be better if he just die!" When facing situations like that, parents should not lose their temper. They should sit down to analyse the situation with their children, encourage them and talk about what to do next. But it is easy for me to tell my colleagues what to do. When I face my own son's scores . . . I know what I should do, but I just cannot control my temper.

164 Xu Zhao et al.

Despite their knowledge of the harmful impact of academic pressure on children's health and psychological well-being, Ning and his colleague find themselves in a state of complete anguish when their children's test results fail to meet their expectations. It is even worse for working-class parents, whose feeling of anxiety is often combined with a sense of helplessness due to their lack of the kinds of social, economic, and cultural capital that, we saw earlier, is central to the educational strategies of middle- and upper-middle-class families. This dilemma, indeed, is similar to that of French working-class students and families described by Bourdieu & Passeron (1990): the school as a social field effectively rewards those who come to school with cultural, economic, and social capital, and often misrecognises or devalues the cultural capital of working-class children.

In the following example, Mei, an 11th-grade girl at a boarding school recalls her experience with her self-employed parents, after she performed poorly on the High School Entrance Exam:

MEI (GIRL): I had a very hard time after the High School Entrance Exam. My parents scolded me every day, and I cried every day. I didn't want to sleep. I blamed myself. I felt completely lost and empty. I couldn't get out of those feelings. I stayed at home, eating and then sleeping, sleeping and then eating. When my dad told me to go to see my grandma, I just cried, feeling too ashamed to go. I didn't leave our apartment for the whole month during the summer. Even now, when my parents come to school to see me, they still mention that exam and my poor score. They say it in a sarcastic way to make me feel bad. My dad always says he was a good student and saved my grandma a lot of worries. But now he has a daughter like me ... One day, it was too much for me and I argued with him. That was bad for our relationship. Now, our relationship is better, but whenever we talk about my test scores, my dad is very harsh. He is very anxious/worried (急, *jí*). He would point to the question where I made a mistake, keep poking the sheet of paper, and talk in a very loud voice. I am very scared. He was so harsh to me. For a while I thought he didn't love me. Then, during that summer, I saw he was so worried about my not being able to go to a good high school. He made phone calls to everybody he knew to see if they had some *guān xì* (关系, network) to get me into a good school. My dad aged very quickly, and he also had heart problems. I realised he loves me.

Mei's description foregrounds her parent's, especially her father's, strong feelings of anger, anguish, and anxiety in response to her performance in the high-stakes High School Entrance Exam. While Mei was feeling lost, empty, ashamed, scared, and socially withdrawn, her parents did not know what to do except scold her every day and try desperately to find social connections that could help enrol Mei into a good senior high school.

Academic Competition and Parental Practice **165**

What are the social and cultural bases of parents' shared feeling of anxiety? As shown in the examples we provided earlier, Chinese parents' anxiety has its roots in both social and economic structures (e.g., a huge income disparity and the lack of a functioning social security net in Chinese society; school systems that systematically advantage those with extant capital; a market system that offers alternative pathways for upper-middle- and upper-class children) and the cultural practices and beliefs of the educational field that we have described here, a field fraught with traditions, mythologies, and self-fulfilling and habituated practices. A middle-class father in our study also describes the problem to a "materialistic" and "narrow-minded" view of life generated in a market economy:

TING (MIDDLE-CLASS FATHER): The market economy promotes the idea of so-called "career success". Following this materialistic way of thinking, the most promising, the easiest, and the guaranteed path to success is either to become a government official or to make a lot of money. People don't think about other options. This [practice] creates many social problems: problems of social morality, education, family relationships, and general mental health problems.

Ting further points out that the combination of a competition-based education system and over-protective parents who constantly emphasise to their children the importance of protecting their self-interests tragically creates a generation of Chinese children who are selfish and who are not capable of collaborating with others – another version of the 'possessive individual'.

The feeling of anxiety also exists among the overseas returnee parents, despite their possession of higher levels of social, economic, and cultural capital. One mother observed, "Gradually, the expectation increases: the pressure of society on children to achieve high, to go to the best universities in the world, and the pressure from teachers on children to go to the best high schools." Speaking English during the discussion, these mothers said they struggle to answer basic questions such as: What is a good education for my children? Is it about extracurricular activities or academic work? What kind of life should I guide and support my children to live? Where should we draw the line between supporting their educational success and harming them by putting too much pressure on them? These questions suggest an emergent "logic of practice" (Bourdieu, 1990) that sees children's future lives as different and separate from their parents' immediate lives and childhood experiences. These parents see their children through a different lens: as independent individuals living in a still-in-formation historical and cultural moment the parameters and implications of which none of them have yet to fully grasp. This is a new game in formation. They do not link their children's educational and career success to their own future security and happiness. Having achieved desired educational and professional successes themselves, these parents are anxious about the more

166 Xu Zhao et al.

fundamental question of what a good education and a good life means for their children. At the same time, they base their deliberations and strategies on their own experiences as part of this new generation of Chinese middle- and upper-class parents with higher education, overseas training and sojourns, and their understandings of the unprecedented economic and social changes occurring around them. This is at once an intergenerational moment of reproduction *and* counter-reproduction, or tradition and change. It marks out an emergent new logic of practice and, indeed, the making of a new Chinese habitus.

Beyond Bourdieusian Structuralism: Four Additional Processes for Understanding the Formation of Habitus

Bourdieu's emphasis on individual action as emerging from a practical anticipation of profit (improvement of social positions) has been criticised by scholars as determinist, pessimistic, and fatalist (Grenfell, 2014; Grenfell & James, 1998). Yet we have found his critical perspective useful for documenting and understanding parental educational practice in China. There are important analogies between the Chinese education system today and the French education system described by Bourdieu (cf. 1984, pp. 133–134; 2000, p. 227). Here we refer to the rapid expansion of higher education and the consequential devaluation of academic qualifications, the widespread perception of the scarcity of educational resources and benefits, increased competition on the job market, and middle-class parents' increased investment of surplus capital in educational resources and services. These educational phenomena are occurring in the context of a climate of global economic volatility, an increased disparity of wealth (Wang, 2014) and the documented exploitation of workers in particular regions and sectors. In this contemporary context, Bourdieu's critical social theory is a valuable tool in revealing how society and education can be sources of the domination and entrapment for human vision (cognition) and agency (behaviour), and how the acquisition and exchange of knowledge can be a mechanism of social division and inequitable stratification.

As noted earlier, one of the strongest critiques about Bourdieusian structuralism is provided by Lamont (1992), who argues that Bourdieu's theorisation of habitus focuses exclusively on the influences of material conditions but neglects the impact of broader structural features and cultural resources. Our analysis here suggests that Bourdieu's model is a useful framework for the study of Chinese education, but, given the complexity and newness of Chinese social and economic conditions, it cannot wholly account for the psychological, cultural, and political complexities involved in the reshaping of individual disposition and practice. We identified four processes that are key for understanding the mutually structuring relationships and interactions between individual and collective habitus and the field of Chinese society and education. These processes rest on four levels: Individual psychology and agency, family relationships, national-level ideology and policy, and collective memory and historical experience.

First, change in Bourdieu's theory is explained through the concept of "hysteresis", or the incongruence between the forces within a structure. Our analysis, however, highlights the powerful impact of individuals' psychological struggle and their conscious efforts to reconstruct their habitus by: reflecting on their own cultural traditions in defining good education and good life; learning new ideas from others (often from those occupying a higher social position), and by borrowing cultural models that do not derive from their own life experiences (e.g., Western child development and educational axioms). What is striking about many of the commentaries offered by the middle- and upper-middle-class parents is the degree to which they are engaged in an inner dialogue within families that oscillates between a traditional focus on competitive success and distinction and emergent discussions about what might count as the 'good life' for their children in the future, the latter a central focus of traditional Aristotelian ethics. This appears to us much more a matter of dialectical (and intercultural) change – with broad onto/phylogenetic scope and depth – than a matter of structural determination where habitus is formed by reference to shaping and determining field.

For example, research during the 1990s often described Chinese adults as insensitive to children internalising their problems, such as loneliness, and often seeing the primary task of socialisation as helping children develop the capacities for controlling personal desires and emotions (Desjarlais et al., 1995). By contrast, our comparison of the three groups here suggests that while this finding still holds for our sample of working-class parents, it is changing among well-educated middle-class parents, particularly those who have overseas educational experiences and have been exposed to discourses about the importance of protecting children's social and emotional health. Some of the middle-class parents, having cultivated a well-constituted habitus themselves to play the game of academic competition, challenge themselves with questions about what constitutes a good education and a good life for their children. For these parents, what is at stake is not only their children's competitive success, but also what is "good" for their children and what, indeed, might count as "success" in the first place. Here, their children's happiness and health is under consideration.

Our view is that this marks the emergence of a new habitus. It is facilitated by a higher level of autonomy from the control of market mechanisms, gained from the possession of higher levels of economic capital and by different, emergent forms of cultural capital. But it is not simply a matter of Westernisation or the imposition of external values; our interpretation is that these commentaries of parents and their children are artefacts of a complex, dialogic process of exchange, between generations, between cultural values and paradigms of childhood, and, that they are characterised and informed by varied and often incisive analyses and discussions of emergent economic and social conditions in the new China. In line with Lamont's aforementioned critique of Bourdieu's theory for

168 Xu Zhao et al.

neglecting individuals' moral commitment in their choice of lifestyles, our analysis shows that parental beliefs and practices are not just motivated by the desire to gain a competitive edge, but that they also have genuine concerns about the happiness of their children in and of itself. Their decisions about and with their children indeed often appear as reproductive decisions based on blends of cultural tradition, folkloric knowledge about the "system" and social mobility, and accepted practices and mythologies about what it takes to succeed. But they also are based on what for them are new insights about childhood, about the longitudinal value of childhood and education, experience and autonomy, and their readings of changing institutional and market forces. Some of these families are quite consciously and deliberately making choices that mark out the formation of this new habitus, without precedent in their families, their histories, or Chinese education.

Secondly, our analysis points to the sustained importance of traditional cultural values, as well as of simultaneously emerging changes to these values, including the emphasis of filial duty on individuals' educational practice and their orientations toward the future. Previous research has shown that in cultures influenced by the Confucian tradition, doing well in school is a demonstration of filial duty; consequently, adolescents' academic stress partly arises from the desire to please their parents and to bring honour to their families (e.g., Cheung & Pomerantz, 2012). Reflected in the present study, students also have a strong sense of responsibility to do their best in school in order to return the care of their parents and avoid deep feelings of guilt toward their parents. In addition to the strong sense of responsibility to provide financial support to their elderly parents in the future, filial responsibility also means working hard in school to avoid disappointing one's parents and making them lose face in front of other parents. The students from Jinan also avoid directly criticising their parents. When they do talk about conflicts with their parents, they often contribute them to parents' well-intended but "incorrect methods" of parenting, and do not forget to express their deep gratitude for their parents' sacrifice. Bourdieu's models of the inculcation of the habitus in early childhood and the efficacy of primary socialisation offer an explanation of this durable traditionalism, which remains central to almost all analyses of Chinese education past and present. However, it stops short of capturing the complex dialectics of continuity and change, traditionalism and the critical re-appropriation of tradition here occurring in an emergent Chinese middle class with unprecedented levels of cultural, economic, and social resources at their disposal.

Thirdly, we concur with Bourdieu's general sense that national-level ideological and related policy processes can be formidable field forces that actively and forcefully shape collective habitus (e.g., Bourdieu, 1998). Education in China functions to provide skilled labourers for the economy, but it also has the officially stated task of (re)shaping Chinese individuals' collective consciousness in order to increase the nation's strength and power on the global market and to maintain social and political stability within its borders. For example, from the late 1980s to the early 1990s, the Chinese central government initiated educational reforms to introduce competition mechanisms (竞争机制, *jìng zhēng jī zhì*) into secondary education and promote competition consciousness (竞争意识, *jìng zhēng yì shí*) among teachers and students. We have argued that, while this reform was in line with the global rise of neoliberalism that promotes the ideas of building a competitive market system in education, it also arose from the distinctive economic, social, and historical context of China in the late twentieth century, particularly in relation to the reinstallation of the competition-based *gāo kǎo* system in the late 1970s (Zhao, 2016).

Considered a relatively fair system, the *gāo kǎo* is designed to provide equal opportunities to students from all backgrounds. In 1977, when the Chinese Cultural Revolution ended and the *gāo kǎo* system was reinstated, test scores gradually replaced political and family backgrounds as the criterion for college admission. In this historical context, the reinstallation of the *gāo kǎo* system was considered as a representation of the reinstallation of the values of meritocracy, fair competition and the respect of knowledge in Chinese society. It was widely acclaimed as a history-making event that changed the fate of millions of Chinese youth and the country (Barendsen, 1978). Since the collectivist system in the 1950s and 1960s effectively reduced income gaps at least within urban and rural societies, and the marketisation of secondary education only began in the mid-1980s, the *gāo kǎo* in the late 1970s and 1980s was indeed a relatively fair system for students from different socio-economic backgrounds. Many of the parents in our study succeeded in the *gāo kǎo* during this period and attribute their professional success to individual effort and achievements.

Forty years later, however, the social and economic contexts of the *gāo kǎo* have changed (Guo & Guo, 2014). Following the marketisation of secondary education in China in the 1980s, educational resources related to school choice and tutoring classes became commercial goods to be purchased by, or exchanged among, those who have the necessary levels of social and economic capital (Liu, 2018). Parents must rely on the social, cultural, and economic capital they have gained as a result of their own educational success to make sure their children are advantaged rather than disadvantaged in academic competition. Academic competition is, as pointed out by a parent in the present study, a competition of parents' possession of social and economic resources. It is therefore the combined pressure of the two levels of competition, competition between children based on test scores, and competition between parents drawing on differential levels and kinds of social, economic, and cultural capital that contributes to the formation of an overlapping social field of education, childhood, and parenting, which structures and is structured by a parental habitus that is built around competition, the quest for distinction, and near-continuous anxiety about their children's and family's futures. As much as the *gāo kǎo* governs Chinese students' and parents' educational practices, it also

170 Xu Zhao et al.

shapes their collective consciousness *qua* cultural habitus, particularly their dispositions toward the future and their social, cultural, and political interest and behaviour. For the majority of Chinese young people, individualistic competition for survival and distinction is a core element of the new cultural habitus, an ultimate teleological focus of life.

Finally, from a psychological perspective, we argue that habitus must be understood from the perspective of collective memory and historical experiences of war, violence, deprivation, and loss. While Bourdieu's early doctoral studies focused on the durability of cultural tradition, memory, and practice amongst the Kabyle in North Africa, his later corpus of work outlines the operations and consequences of synchronic social structures and institutional fields. It is our view that the shared feelings of anxiety about academic and economic competition and the competing and comparing habits of mind among Chinese parents are to some extent the impact of trauma and traumatic stress from the collective Chinese memories of war and famine, individuals' direct or indirect experiences of violence, political persecution, economic chaos, and material and information deprivation during the Cultural Revolution (1966–76) (Dikötter, 2016; Song & Gong, 2016; Yang, 2016), as well as the more recent experience of collective layoffs, loss of benefits, and the feeling of social degradation and exclusion by the urban proletarians of the state-owned factories during the restructuring of the 1980s and 1990s (Chen, 2003; Hassard, 2007; Solinger, 2002). A rich body of research literature with populations from across the world have shown that the experience of high-stress events such as war, famine, genocide, political prosecution, material deprivation, and social exclusion can have traumatic multi-generational impacts on individuals' cognition, emotion, and behaviour, leading to unconscious, semi-conscious, or very conscious feelings of anxiety, anger, uncontrollable worries, and feelings of helplessness (Desjarlais et al, 1995; Joop & de Jong, 2002). Individuals from economically and culturally marginalised communities are at a higher risk of acquiring emotional disorders compared with their higher socio-economic status counterparts (de Jong, 2006; Lorent et al., 2003). Poverty, marginalisation, and exclusion always has a history, histories that are at once political, economic, cultural, sociological and, indeed, embodied, psychological, and ontological.

Understanding the impact of collective memory, trauma, and their intergenerational reproduction requires the integration of a sociological perspective, such as that of Bourdieu's, and a psychosocial/cultural/historical perspective. For any theory to make a difference in the context of the current globalisation of systemic threats to youth and families, it needs to speak to those aspects of the human condition that have been articulated in well-respected conceptual frameworks across many disciplines within the broader social sciences, especially in fields with a strong commitment to understanding the nature and nurture of human development. These include sociocultural models of literacy (Lewis, 2007), social cognitive models of human agency (Bandura,

Academic Competition and Parental Practice **171**

2008), personological models of psychology (McAdams, 1988), sociological models in philosophy (Allen, 2002), evolutionary models of human nature (Bowlby, 1969), and cultural/developmental models of social communication and interaction (Selman, 2007). These conceptual frameworks point to three fundamental human needs constantly requiring fulfilment: a need for affiliation (e.g., a sense of cultural identity, place, and moral empathy), a need for safety (or to have the power to protect), and a need for agency (to be effective in meeting one's goals, both individual and collective). Therefore, we ask of Bourdieu's sociology: To which of these three needs does it speak directly?

We think Bourdieu's theory speaks to all three needs, but, ironically, it has less to say about human agency than it does about safety and affiliation. If we historicise Bourdieu's work, it is itself the historical product of a stolid, durable European class system. Bourdieu's sociology is a model that explains cultural continuity, structural force and power, and, ultimately, cultural, economic, and social reproduction (for example, his explorations of intergenerational continuity amongst the Kabyle in North Africa, the post-war class/Catholic systems of France, and the aspirations of the 1968 student movement in Paris). It does not wholly account for the dynamic and unprecedented economic, cultural, social, and psychological processes in China that are contributing to the emergence of the new Chinese subject. Our view is that this historical formation cannot be accounted for in conventional binaries of East and West, or traditional/communal and bourgeois individualism. For the families we have worked with here, the new Chinese subject is being shaped, and constructed dynamically in relation to individual and collective memories of the past, experiences and analyses of the present, and dreamings of the future.

Everything about recent Chinese history – the Great Leap Forward campaign, the Cultural Revolution, the One Child policy, the Reform and Opening-Up, Socialism with Chinese Characteristics, major poverty amelioration and significant economic and cultural inequality, and the emergence of an economic and geopolitical superpower within a half century – speaks to a different onto/phylogenetic moment, one unprecedented in Eastern or Western social science and philosophical explanation.

Notes

1 "Game" here is used in the Bourdieusian sense of a competitive sport in which at any given moment players in different social positions use capital and strategies to improve their social positions.
2 Teachers on Weibo order parents to undertake onerous tasks; parents bribe teachers to give their children preferential treatment.

References

Allen, A. (2002). Power, subjectivity, and agency: Between Arendt and Foucault. *International Journal of Philosophical Studies*, 10(2), 131–149.

172 Xu Zhao et al.

Apple, M.W. (1990). *Education and power.* London: Routledge.

Bandura, A. (2008). Toward an agentic theory of the self. *Advances in Self Research,* 3, 15–49.

Barendsen, R.D. (1978). *The 1978 National College Entrance Examination in the People's Republic of China.* Washington, DC: Department of Health, Education, and Welfare, Office of Education.

Bond, M.H. (1998). Chinese dimensions of parenting: Broadening western predictors and outcomes. *International Journal of Psychology,* 33(5), 345–358.

Bourdieu, P. (1983). The field of cultural production, or: The economic world reversed. *Poetics,* 12, 311–356.

Bourdieu, P. (1984). *Distinction: A social critique of the judgment of taste.* Cambridge, MA: Harvard University Press.

Bourdieu, P. (1990). *The logic of practice.* Trans. R. Nice. Stanford, CA: Stanford University Press.

Bourdieu, P. (1993). *The weight of the world: Social suffering in contemporary society.* Stanford, CA: Stanford University Press.

Bourdieu, P. (1998). The essence of neoliberalism. *Le Monde diplomatique.* December. Trans. J. Shapiro. https://mondediplo.com/1998/12/08bourdieu

Bourdieu, P. (2000). *Pascalian meditations.* Stanford, CA: Stanford University Press.

Bourdieu, P. (2008). *Political interventions: Social science and political action.* Trans. D. Fernbach. London: Verso.

Bourdieu, P. & Passeron, J.C. (1990). *Reproduction in education, society and culture.* Trans. R. Nice. London: Sage.

Bourdieu, P. & Wacquant, L.J.D. (1992). *Invitation to reflexive sociology.* Cambridge: Polity.

Bowlby, J. (1969). *Attachment.* New York: Basic Books.

Chan, S.M., Bowes, J., & Wyver, S. (2009). Chinese parenting in Hong Kong: Links among goals, beliefs and styles. *Early Child Development and Care,* 179(7), 849–862.

Chao, R.K. (1994). Beyond parental control and authoritarian parenting style: Understanding Chinese parenting through the cultural notion of training. *Child Development,* 65(4), 1111–1119.

Chen, F. (2003). Industrial restructuring and workers' resistance in China. *Modern China,* 29(2), 237–262.

Chen, F. M., & Luster, T. (2002). Factors related to parenting practices in Taiwan. *Early Child Development and Care,* 172(5), 413–430.

Cheung, C. S.-S., & Pomerantz, E.M. (2012). Why does parents' involvement enhance children's achievement? The role of parent-oriented motivation. *Journal of Educational Psychology,* 104(3), 820–832.

Chung, T., & Mallery, P. (1999). Social comparison, individualism-collectivism, and self-esteem in China and the United States. *Current Psychology,* 18(4), 340–352.

de Jong, J. (Ed.) (2006). *Trauma, war, and violence: Public mental health in socio-cultural context.* New York: Kleuwer Academic/Plenum Publishers.

Desjarlais, R., Eisenberg, L., Good, B., & Kleinman, A. (1995). *World mental health: Problems and priorities in low-income countries.* New York: Oxford University Press.

Dikötter, F. (2016). *The Cultural Revolution: A people's history, 1962–1976.* New York: Bloomsbury Publishing

Fong, V.L. (2004). *Only hope: Coming of age under China's one child policy.* Stanford, CA: Stanford University Press.

Gorman, J.C. (1998). Parenting attitudes and practices of immigrant Chinese mothers of adolescents. *Family Relations,* 47(1), 73–80.

Grenfell, M. (Ed.) (2014). *Pierre Bourdieu: Key concepts* (2nd Edition). Bristol, CT: Acumen.

Grenfell, M., & James, D. (1998). *Bourdieu and education: Acts of practical theory*. Taylor & Francis E-Library.

Guo, S., & Guo, Y. (Eds.). (2014). *Spotlight on China: Changes in education under China's market economy*. Rotterdam: Sense.

Hassard, J. (2007). *China's state enterprise reform: From Marx to the market*. New York: Routledge.

Hirschman, A.O. (1970). *Exit, voice, and loyalty: Responses to decline in firms, organizations, and states*. Cambridge, MA: Harvard University Press.

Joop, T.V., & de Jong, M. (2002). Public mental health, traumatic stress and human rights violations in low-income countries. In *Trauma, war, and violence: Public mental health in socio-cultural context* (pp. 1–91). New York: Springer.

Kwok, P.L.Y. (2010). Demand intensity, market parameters and policy responses towards demand and supply of private supplementary tutoring in China. *Asia Pacific Education Review*, 11(1), 49–58.

Lamont, M. (1992). *Money, morals, and manners: The culture of the French and the American upper-middle class*. Chicago, IL: Chicago University Press.

Lewis, C. (2007). *Reframing sociocultural research on literacy: Identity, agency, and power*. Mahwah, NJ: Lawrence Erlbaum Associates.

Liu, S. (2018). Neoliberal global assemblages: The emergence of 'public' international high-school curriculum programs in China. *Curriculum Inquiry*, 48(2), 203–219.

Lorent, V., Eaton, D., Robert, A., Philippot, P., & Ansseau, M. (2003). Socioeconomic inequalities in depression: A meta-analysis. *American Journal of Epidemiology*, 157(2), 98–112.

Luke, A. (2018). *Critical literacy, schooling and social justice: Selected writings*. New York: Routledge.

McAdams, D.P. (1988). *Power, intimacy, and the life story: Personological inquiries into identity*. New York: Guilford Press.

Morris, M.W., Leung, K., Ames, D., & Lickel, B. (1999). Views from inside and outside: Integrating emic and etic insights about culture and justice judgment. *Academy of Management Review*, 24, 4. doi:10.5465/AMR.1999.2553253.

Mu, G.M. (2018). *Building resilience of floating children and left-behind children in China: Power, politics, participation, and education*. New York: Routledge.

Mu, G.M., & Hu, Y. (2016). Coming into an inheritance: Intergenerational social reproduction through class-based pedagogies. In G.M. Mu & Y. Hu (Eds.), *Living with vulnerabilities and opportunities in a migration context: Floating children and left-behind children in China* (pp. 47–77). Rotterdam: Sense Publishers.

Pearson, E., & Rao, N. (2003). Socialization goals, parenting practices, and peer competence in Chinese and English preschoolers. *Early Child Development and Care*, 173(1), 131–146.

Selman, R.L. (2007). *The promotion of social awareness: Powerful lessons from the partnership of developmental theory and classroom practice*. New York: Russell Sage.

Solinger, D.J. (2002). Labour market re-form and the plight of the laid-off proletariat. *China Quarterly*, 170, 304–326.

Song, Y., & Gong, Z. (2016). *Guangxi wen ge ji mi dang an zi liao [Secret archives about the cultural revolution in Guangxi, classified documents.]*. Deer Park, NY: Guo shi chu ban she; 国史出版社.

Stevenson, H., Lee, S., Chen, C., Stigler, J., Hsu, C., & Hatano, G. (1990). Contexts of achievement: A study of American, Chinese, and Japanese children. *Monographs of the Society for Research in Child Development*, 55(1/2), 1–119.

Stewart, S.M., Bond, M.H., Kennard, B.D., Ho, L.M., & Zaman, R.M. (2002). Does the Chinese construct of guan export to the West? *International Journal of Psychology*, 37(2), 74–82.

Wacquant, L.J.D. (1989). Towards a reflexive sociology: A workshop with Pierre Bourdieu. *Sociological Theory*, 7 (1), 26-63.

Wang, L. (2014). Widening urban rural divides: Examining social exclusion and educational inequality in Chinese schools. In S. Guo & Y. Guo (Eds.), *Spotlight on China: Changes in education under China's market economy* (pp. 313–329). Rotterdam: Sense.

Wang, S. (2013, July 8). Giving up on "Gaokao." Asian society. http://asiasociety.org/northern-california/giving-gaokao-0

Williams, R. (1978). *Marxism and literature*. Oxford: Oxford University Press.

Yang, G. (2016). *The red guard generation and political activism in China*. New York: Columbia University Press.

Yang, Y. (2014). Bourdieu, practice and change: Beyond the criticism of determinism. *Educational Philosophy and Theory*, 46, 1522–1540.

Yochim, L. (2014). Navigating the aspirational city: Processes of accumulation in China's socialist market economy. In S. Guo & Y. Guo (Eds.), *Spotlight on China: Changes in education under China's market economy* (pp. 329–348). Rotterdam: Sense.

Zhang, W., & Bray, M. (2014). Shadow education: The rise and implications of private supplementary tutoring. In S. Guo & Y. Guo (Eds.), *Spotlight on China: Changes in education under China's market economy* (pp. 69–86). Rotterdam: Sense.

Zhao, X. (2015). *Competition and compassion in Chinese secondary education*. New York: Palgrave Macmillan.

Zhao, X. (2016). Educating competitive students for a competitive nation: How and why the Chinese discourse of competition in education has rapidly changed within three decades? *Berkeley Review of Education*, 6(1), 5–28.

Zhao, X., Haste, H., Selman, R. L., & Luan, Z. (2014). Compliant, cynical, or critical: Chinese youth's explanations of social problems and individual civic responsibility. *Youth & Society*, 49, 1123–1148.

Zhao, X., Selman, R. L. & Haste, H. (2014). Academic stress in Chinese schools and a proposed preventive intervention program. *Cogent Education*, 2(1). doi: 10.1080/2331186X.2014.1000477.

9

CAPITAL CONVERSION AND SCHOOL CHANGE

A Bourdieusian Analysis

Ning Jia and Guanglun Michael Mu

Introduction

This chapter is a case study of how the capital portfolio of one Chinese school principal motivated and set the grounds for school development and change. Drawing from elements of Bourdieu's sociological framework, the chapter reports a longitudinal case study of a Beijing primary school and delves into the dynamic process of school change in the current Chinese educational context. It documents how the principal brings to the field of a particular institution his cultural and social capital to shape a distinctive logic of practice within school administration. Through reconfiguring the administrative culture and the campus culture of the school, the process documented here is one where the principal's personal capital is converted into various forms of a specialised kind of school capital, here termed as "organisational capital". In sum, this is an instance of how capital exchange leads to a structural reconfiguration of the school field: a case study of Chinese school leadership, reform, and change.

The case being made here is that there may be a distinctive element of Chinese school and institutional culture that has not been widely documented in the conventional Western literature on principalship and school reform: The exchange of a principal's cultural and social capital, specifically the conversion of personal social and academic networks, reputation, and distinction, as part of a leadership style and capacity developed over an extended period, into organisational capital for the school, an aggregate form of symbolic capital. This collective form of institutional resources reforms the school's reputation, status, and distinction; its expanded floor area, more teaching buildings with advanced IT resources, and additional funding; its strengthened connections with parents,

176 Ning Jia and Guanglun Michael Mu

communities, and government sections; and its campus and administrative culture reshaped through the process of capital conversion.

Policy Context

Nearly three decades have passed since radical reforms of basic education in China were promulgated in the 1985 policy, *Decision of the Central Committee of the Chinese Communist Party on the Reform of Educational System*. The result has been a quasi-marketisation of the education system in China, gradually supplanting central control and micromanagement. This has seen schools receive more education funding and, perhaps more importantly, greater autonomy for the principals who administer them. These changes are consistent with the larger structural reforms of the economic system (Guo & Guo, 2016). A succession of laws and regulations has ensued, providing the grounds and procedures for the ongoing modernisation, expansion, and decentralisation of compulsory education in China.

State Guidelines for Medium- and Long-term Education Reform and Development Plan (2010–2020) was a policy attempt to address many of the core problems facing Chinese education. This includes a focus on improved educational provision and outcomes for floating children in urban China (Mu et al., 2013), unattended left-behind children in rural communities (Mu, 2018), and children in diverse new family configurations (e.g., single-parent families). A further problem has been the degree to which conditions of educational inequality have been exacerbated by the politics of school selection and school quality, the increased provision of private or marketised schooling, and regional disparities in funding.

Recently, the modernising agenda was extended through the policy framework of *Key Competences of Chinese Students* (2016), which aims to refocus curriculum and teaching in response to the emergent demands of both economic globalisation and ongoing national modernisation. This has broad parallels in current transnational curriculum reform. More recently, *Modernisation of Chinese Education 2030* (exposure draft) proposes a key index system for monitoring educational development, in effect putting in place elements of a contemporary governance system for establishing an open, modern education (Drafting Group, 2017). Currently, the Ministry of Education is updating the 2030 document and developing a framework for the modernisation of Chinese education (2035), again focusing on overall regulation, local autonomy, and accountability.

Taken together, these Chinese educational policies are extensions of the original paths of basic educational reform and development. A streamlined administration structure would give schools increased local autonomy and freedom, with higher levels of funding and expanded school-level resources and infrastructure. Yet the efficacy of these modernisation strategies is contingent upon local schools' development of educational planning and vision. An effective locally governed school system requires highly professionalised school leadership who can manage issues of initiative and agency, accountability and regulation. Against this policy backdrop, what follows is a longitudinal case study of a local principal and a school in transition. It reports on a fragment of the longitudinal study and examines the following questions:

- How is the principal's personal capital converted into the school's organisational capital?
- How does capital conversion relate to school change?
- How might school principals make a greater impact on school development?

Answers to the first two questions emerge directly from our data analysis. The last question takes up the normative implications of the study for school leadership and development.

On School Leadership: A Bourdieusian Perspective

Classical studies on capital originated from Marx (1885/1978), who defined and divided capital into two forms: Circulating capital and fixed capital. While Bourdieu (1986) did consider material forms of capital to be the root of other forms of symbolic resources, he complemented Marx's economic approach to material and monetary forms of capital and their relation to class structure and class struggle. In this vein, Bourdieu refocused on capital in its symbolic forms and cultural practices, showing how social position and cultural distinction are objectively defined by capital. Bourdieu (1990b) describes the processes whereby material capital is converted into symbolic capital and then returned through conversion to material capital. Symbolic capital, he explains, is an acknowledgement or credit from others within a social field, the equivalent to fame and honours, which, once established, enables and enhances further conversion of other forms of capital.

Bourdieu's conceptualisation of capital has been widely applied to educational studies for over three decades. In the area of school administration and leadership, discussions of capital typically do not engage with sociological models of exchange. Ekinci (2012) emphasised mutual trust among staff as a core dimension of a school's social capital, which was found facilitative of information sharing within school. This indicates that an enabling and sustainable social network within a school can develop into social capital for that institution. Although school social capital benefits from organisational stability, that form of capital can enhance a school's responsiveness to reform and change (Holme & Rangel, 2012). In settings where they are regarded as more conventionally defined human capital, that is, as productive resources (Young, Reimer, & Young, 2010), school principals are often identified as key actors of school change and school performance. In case studies, "forms of transformational leadership" of principals have been found to enhance teacher social capital and collective efficacy (Minckler, 2014). Moreover, through disciplined professional collaboration, principals are able to sustain and create social capital for organisational change (Jones & Harris, 2014).

There has been a long-standing call to advance theory in the field of school administration by using Bourdieu in the case study of educational leadership (Lingard et al., 2003). Yet the call has only been sporadically taken up in the research literature. In the US and England, much of the field has focused on the combination of decentralisation and parallel push for national standards and accreditation systems, with standards that have reified extant roles and practices (English, 2012). There is also evidence on head teachers' ambivalence about change and their retention of professional *doxa* in the face of policy agenda focused on school leadership (Gunter & Forrester, 2010). The interesting tension here is between a proposed reconceptualisation of the transformative disposition of principal/school leader and her/his capacity to translate this into instructional reform, on the one hand, and a sociological focus on the durability of pedagogic action and structures of reproduction, on the other. To date, there has been little published work on the conversion and mobilisation of individual leaders' forms of capital as central to the processes of local organisational change and the restructuring of the school culture. The focus of the chapter, then, is on the forms of capital deployed by one Chinese principal and how these personal resources are converted into school capital and transformed into school change.

The Current Study: Principal Capital, School Capital, and School Change

This chapter reports on a longitudinal project conducted in a primary school located in Haidian district of Beijing. The school was established in 1957 and the present principal has been working there for nearly two decades. The case school was identified and selected as typical of its area and community, but also because it was known as a site for an ongoing reform process which had yielded visible improvements in school performance and achievement. When established in 1957, the school was known as X central primary school. Over the decades, the school has undergone a series of renamings, from Y central primary school in 2003, through the affiliated primary school of Z University in 2010, to the school group affiliated to Z University in 2015. Through its renaming strategy, the school has gradually accrued symbolic capital given the prestige of the University to which the school was affiliated. It is simplistic, however, to attribute the school's improvements and its reputation growth only to the renaming strategy. The longitudinal project was therefore developed and conducted to unveil the sociological dynamics behind school improvement.

Longitudinal qualitative data were collected in the forms of semi-structured interviews, critical incident interviews, storytelling, and classroom and activity observations. Many kinds of print materials were provided voluntarily such as teachers' teaching notes and journals, principal's addresses, and policy documents. A total of 30 interviews was conducted; all took place on campus and lasted approximately 20–60 minutes each. Interview participants included the school principal, former principals, former and present school leaders, teachers, students, parents, community workers, and government officials. During the interviews, participants were invited to discuss the school culture, the principal and his leadership, and their perceptions of school change (if any).

The school principal, Mr. Song, was also asked to talk about his leadership. He was chosen to be the principal in 1999 when he was 29 years old. Interestingly, he did not take immediate action to change the school but waited for three years. He narrated during one of the interviews:

> When I became the principal, there were lots of seniors and doyens who devoted their entire life to the school. Hence, they did not want any change of work circumstance. I had less experience at that time and everything was not ready for change yet. Three years later, nearly all of the doyens had retired and the staff and teachers were almost all young. I tried many ways to practise my new ideas. To reframe school structure and to integrate resources, I actively communicated with the superintendents to ask for more money to develop school buildings. After that my colleagues and I went to the streets to distribute flyers to introduce our school to the community and to attract more students and parents.

Over a period of a decade, the principal has deliberately built and accumulated his cultural and social capital. He returned to university and completed an Ed.D. degree – fully deeming and institutionalising his available cultural capital. He has also proactively and actively built a social network of local influential colleagues and community members. Here the expansion of social networks, including engagement with people of status and reputation is part of the Chinese ethos of *guān xì*[1] (关系, networking) – an essential element of social capital in the Chinese context. Using these networks, the principal invited community leaders and university professors to participate in the school's cultural construction program.

Well advanced into this program of reform, Song and his school were confronted with a critical moment when the community around the school was rebuilt. A new high-quality villa community replaced the bungalow-style accommodation of the past. This set the terms for a major demographic and cultural turnover of residents. The new population consisted of residents of high socioeconomic status who could choose the school to which their children went. Song saw community rebuilding as an opportunity to facilitate school development:

> I recognise that [the rebuilding] may be a chance to transform our [population of] students although I didn't know how to make them [the

parents] send their children to my school. Then I got information that the University would like to establish an affiliated school as its research partner school. I wrote a plan and talked with some knowledgeable and resourceful people at [an elite university]. Following their advice, I expressed interest in the cooperation with the University to a super-intendent but he said it was impossible for a non-selective school to be an option for the University. I despaired at first but I didn't give up. I expressed my interest in the cooperation again and again. In contrast to my positive attitude, the selective school [expected to take part in the cooperation] hesitated and declined to work with the University. Finally, I got the chance and changed the school name to the Affiliated Primary School of the University. I felt so excited about it and gained much more sense of achievement. I felt like [it was now possible] to be hopeful for the school's future and to be capable of attracting and keeping students from surrounding communities.

What emerged from narratives like the one above was an entire process of the principal's cultural capital and social capital transferring to the school's distinction and public profile. Through the conversion of capital, school culture was reshaped. Accordingly, the school accumulated organisational capital, and further, there were both inter-capital-conversion and cross-capital-conversion. The former pattern of capital conversion refers to the convertibility of a particular form of capital into other forms. The latter pattern refers to an escalated mechanism of capital conversion, that is, the convertibility of individual level capital into organisational level capital. The succeeding sections report on these findings from two streams: first, the growth in quantity of capital as a result of the demographically changed status quo, and second, the system of capital conversion in the school.

School Capital Growth in Quantity

Intuitively, school statistics provide evidence in changes relating to the school's organisational capital. Since the school became an affiliated school of the University, it has gained increasing popularity in its community and neighbour-hood communities. Student enrolment grew dramatically from 160 in 2010 to 3,800 in 2015. Some background knowledge is in order here. In China, student enrolment number is the grounds of allocation of educational funding, establishing the base for economic capital inputs for school operation and function. With a marked growth in student numbers after the school's renaming, the school received significant material investment from the government, with its floor area expanded from 24,000 square meters to 60,000 square meters. Material investment also saw consistent growth of the book collections in the school library. As the school librarian corroborated in an interview:

> I think the principal takes seriously the number of books in the school library. But there was no money to buy new books until recent years. After our school name changed I got RMB 100,000 [approximately US $15,000] every year to buy books. Well, I don't see any difference in the students.

The economic capital – school funding – was immediately converted to material and objectified forms of assets, the land and the books in this case. But consumption of objectified cultural capital requires embodied cultural capital, which takes time to accumulate. This might be the reason why the librarian had yet to see any change in student performance at the time of the interview.

The growth in the school's economic and symbolic capital saw a gradual change of parent and student profiles, with more students from high SES families. Parents became more engaged in school activities and kept a tight rein on their children's academic achievement and key competence. Consequently, teachers felt more challenged as they were pressed to enhance their knowledge and skills in order to better address parents' demands and students' needs. Interestingly, interviews and observations, in general, did not reveal teacher burnout. On the contrary, teachers tended to connect with students and their parents for the purpose of nurturing students both inside and outside classrooms. These positive changes are laudable: Student delinquency seemed to decline; parents were more engaged; teachers became more supportive; school culture became more welcoming and enabling; the school's reputation was further built upon, and school funding was markedly increased. All these positive changes helped to accrue the school's organisational capital, which in turn brought more positive changes. A virtuous circle was formed.

Mechanism of Capital Conversion

Overall, data analysis revealed that Song was engaged in a transformational leadership role in the process of school change. Although elsewhere research suggests that transformational leadership is less likely to be perceived by teachers in low-performing schools (Minckler, 2014), the current study seemed to suggest the opposite. Teachers in this once relatively low-status school commonly reported experiencing the principal's transformational leadership, and its associated school change. See a teacher's interview account as an example: "Working with him [the principal] I experience an amazing adventure. Many new ideas continuously come out and I must keep pace with him." School change through Song's transformational leadership, however, did not break out all at once but unfolded in several stages, from personal capital formation, through personal and school capital development and conversion, to exponential growth in school capital. How was the principal's individual capital developed and converted to the school's organisational capital? Three essential elements of capital conversion repeatedly emerged from the data analysis. These elements were: time, a significant person, and a critical moment.

Capital Conversion as a Temporal Project

First of all, capital conversion was found to be a temporal project and was achieved over time. When established in 1957, the school was located on the outskirts of Beijing. Students were commonly from neighbouring rural communities. Parents' educational qualifications and socio-economic status were strikingly low. The school had limited deployable resources, and a low quantity and quality of capital. As a result, the school was positioned on the margins of the educational market in Beijing. The hard work of three generations of school principals saw the original X central primary school successfully transformed into today's school group affiliated to Z University with three campuses, one of which was established as a junior high school. At the time of this study, the school has acquired spacious, modern teaching buildings with advanced IT resources; hosted numerous regional, national, and international visitors; and received countless rewards at various levels. Teacher and student quality as well as parental socio-economic status were greatly enhanced. The transformational shift in the quantity and quality of the school's organisational capital objectively defined the school in a more favourable position in the education market. This transformation, however, took 60 years to happen. As Bourdieu (1986) claims that social world is accumulated history, capital conversion is an accumulation period, a journey. Time is not only a mediator of transmission of capital, but also a precondition of accumulation of capital.

Significant Persons in Capital Conversion

In the school's first 40 years, two generations of school principals reportedly worked really hard. There had been some improvements, but nothing major or revolutionary. No remarkable achievement was made until Song took principalship in 1999. This pointed to the second essential element of capital conversion, the significant person; in the current case, it was Mr. Song, the principal with a transformational leadership style. When Song first came to the school, there were many senior leaders safeguarding the old school ethos. He understood their safeguarding role as a significant barrier for any school reform. Mindful of their conservative power, he did not rush to initiate any change. Instead, he patiently worked as an observer and thinker, pondering over potential pathways to school change, while took time building his own capital. His attainment of an Ed.D. was just one example.

When the old senior leaders retired, Song saw the chance for change. His understanding of the previous organisational dynamics within his school are evidence of his cultural capital – his astute analysis of the conservative school

Capital Conversion and School Change   **183**

culture and his strategic patience of waiting for the chance for change that eventually came up, as he had hoped. Once again, it could be seen immediately that control of the time of reform is valuable for both the individual and the organisation. Both educational problem-solving and school turnaround need time within which principals can act strategically according to the promptings of their feel for the game.

When the old power figures retired, Song drew on his transformational leadership to reshape power relations and social positions in the school field. Once the school was a conservative, centralised social space manipulated by old, senior staff; it has now become less hierarchical and more equal, suggesting that Song has transformed the social landscape of the school field. Interview accounts regarding this change were numerous. This teacher's comment is an example:

> Once there was a big decision-making [process] and we had a discussion. We could argue intensely without considering our position [in the hierarchy]. Big decisions were always made through a democratic process. Teachers vote to make decisions. Like the name of school buildings was decided by teacher and student votes.

Song also drew on his social capital that gave him access to the critical information about the University's plan to establish an affiliated school. His sense of acquaintance towards persons in positions of institutional authority was an invaluable resource in this regard. Song approached the superintendent and made consistent efforts, all of which proved rewarding when he successfully gained the opportunity to affiliate his school with the University.

Song became a significant person during school change as he converted his personal capital – practical analysis of the internal politics, transformational leadership style and capacity, and strong *guān xì* with resource-rich authorities in powerful institutions (e.g., universities, governments) – into school capital in material and symbolic forms. His significance was corroborated throughout the interviews with stakeholders. See a typical comment from the previous school principal:

> Song is a smart guy and loves reading very much. All the time, he has been much more passionate to the job on education, and never changed. At the beginning, the other superintendents and I chose him to be a principal of a small village school. We felt a little worried about his relative inexperience. After a while, we visited his school without prior notice. And we felt really happy to find the school had become better and we recognised that we had made the right choice. Maybe three years later, I recommended him to the superintendent for appointment as principal of this school. You see, I found a capable talent and felt thankful for his job in succession of mine.

Critical Moment in Capital Conversion

Time and personal impact were essential but may not fully complete the process of capital conversion by themselves. There were some critical moments that helped to realise capital conversion despite the potholes and distractions along the way. These critical moments therefore became the third essential element of capital conversion. Over an extended period of school development, two critical moments occurred that seemed to have contributed to capital conversion. First, the school's culture was wholly reshaped through the School Culture Construction Program. Second, the school became the affiliated school of the University.

The former was Song's innovative achievement. Song developed a program that aims to maintain children's nature rather than producing children as commodities in the educational market. Here Song seemed to value what Hilgenbeger (1993, p. 654) meant by "the natural liveliness of the child", that is, an interest in the world and other human beings. The program soon became the signature program of the school, which in turn made the school increasingly popular among parents, particularly middle-class parents. See an example drawn from a parent's interview account:

> I transferred my daughter to this school after considering a large number of famous schools in Beijing. Instead of comparison with other children on material things such as cars, houses, and the like, I want my daughter to become a naïve and happy child. This is exactly what's happening here.

The program was also widely welcomed by the teachers. Comments like the following one were common: "In my opinion, the turning point of our school is school culture construction." Song's initiative of constructing a school culture to nurture children's nature had a positive effect on student moral behaviour. The librarian noted, "Previously I had to lock the door before I left for lunch. Otherwise books would be lost. It's not a problem now."

The second critical moment was the strategic renaming of the school after the school became the University's affiliated school. Capitalising on the reputation of the University, Song enhanced the symbolic capital of his school. His strategy was rewarded, as the school's augmented symbolic capital was then converted into economic, cultural, and social capitals, which were then further exchanged for symbolic value. This is a virtuous cycle indeed.

Doxa, Time, and School Change

School change requires agents to be in for the long haul. This is because the school as a social organisation and a powerful institution has the tendency to reproduce, in its own specific logic, its own beliefs. When there is a quasi-perfect

Capital Conversion and School Change **185**

correspondence between the objective orders and the subjective principles of organisation and institution, the school beliefs appear as self-evident. The self-evidence of belief is what Bourdieu means by *doxa*. As *school doxa* largely remains unquestioned and taken for granted, school change is often hard to occur. This is particularly true in well-established schools with a long history, for example, in the case school analysed in this chapter, where school leadership and teaching force have internalised the *doxa* further to carry on the collective rhythms. As Bourdieu (1977, pp. 165–167) explained to us:

> In a determinate social formation, the stabler [*sic*] the objective structures and the more fully they reproduce themselves in the agents' dispositions, the greater the extent of the field of *doxa*, of that which is taken for granted … Moreover, when the conditions of existence of which the members of a group are the product are very little differentiated, the dispositions which each of them exercises in his [*sic*] practice are confirmed and hence reinforced both by the practice of the other members of the group (one function of symbolic exchanges such as feasts and ceremonies being to favour the circular reinforcement which is the foundation of collective belief) and also by institutions which constitute collective thought as much as they express it, such as language, myth, and art. The self-evidence of the world is reduplicated by the instituted discourses about the world in which the whole group's adherence to that self-evidence is affirmed. The specific potency of the explicit statement that brings subjective experiences into the reassuring unanimity of a socially approved and collectively attested sense imposes itself with the authority and necessity of a collective position adopted on data intrinsically amenable to many other structuration.

The self-evidence of *school doxa* does not necessarily exclude school change. The principal could influence *school doxa* with capital drawn from stakeholders, as well as their own capital. Then the whole group begins to perform in accordance with a new system of collective rhythms. School restructuring is only possible when principals "have the material and symbolic means of rejecting the definition of the real that is imposed on them through logical structures reproducing the social structures (i.e. the state of the power relations)" (Bourdieu, 1977, p. 169). In the case of this school, the principal spent time in accumulating his own cultural, social, and symbolic capital that empowered him to reject the old power, though not in an immediate manner. More importantly, he envisioned the new *doxa* in daily administrative life. Using his own wit, connection, and persistence, he affiliated his school to the University and changed the school name. In so doing, he converted his individual capital to the school's organisational capital, and added valued to it by virtue of the symbolic capital of the University. All capital conversion lifted

186 Ning Jia and Guanglun Michael Mu

the school's social position in the education market. According to the practice of the case school regarding capital conversion, the chapter interprets an effective pathway in Chinese educational context in order to exemplify for other school principals, who should also "derive their power from their capacity to objectify unformulated experiences, to make them public – a step on the road to officialisation and legitimation – and, when the occasion arises, to manifest and reinforce their concordance" (Bourdieu, 1977, pp. 170–171).

Yet capital conversion and school change require both serendipitous chances and deliberative action and position-taking by the "rational" habitus. In this case study, the two critical moments were somewhat serendipitous. Without the community rebuilding, middle-class families might not choose to move to the community, and hence the new school culture would not be popular. Without the selective school declining the opportunity to work with the University, Song's attempt to affiliate his school with the University might have failed. In these ways, the reshaping of the school field was only possible with two structural reorganisations (see Chapter 2): the demographic change in this Beijing community wrought by urbanisation and gentrification, and the larger marketisation of teacher employment and school governance. In this way, Song's case is a metaphor for many of the larger restructurings occurring across the field over this historical period.

Having said that, serendipity itself may not spontaneously work to convert capitals. Song was a significant person with enough volume of capitals to recognise and use the critical moments to accomplish capital conversion. His possession of capitals was required "in order to seize the 'potential opportunities' theoretically available to all" (Bourdieu, 1990b, p. 64). When Song first came to the school, his disposition of transformational leadership collided with the old school field, guarded by conservative gatekeepers. Such a collision is what Bourdieu (1990a, p. 108) referred to as "situations of crisis which disrupt the immediate adjustment of habitus to field". But Song did not adjust his habitus to the field. What emerged from the crisis, for Song, was a rational habitus and conscious computation to look for opportunities for change. It therefore became necessary for Song "to undertake the work of conscious systematisation and express rationalisation which marks the passage from *doxa* to *orthodoxy*" (Bourdieu, 1977, p. 169). Song's rational habitus and the seemingly serendipitous opportunities emerging from contingent social conditions can be summarised by the following quote from Bourdieu (1990b, p. 64):

> In short, the art of estimating and seizing chances, the capacity to anticipate the future by a kind of practical induction or even to take a calculated gamble on the possible against the probable, are dispositions that can only be acquired in certain social conditions. Like the entrepreneurial spirit or the propensity to invest, economic information is a function of one's power over the economy. This is, on the one hand,

Capital Conversion and School Change   **187**

because the propensity to acquire it depends on the chances of using it successfully, and the chances of acquiring it depend on the chances of successfully using it; and also because economic competence, like all competence (linguistic, political, etc.), far from being a simple technical capacity acquired in certain conditions, is a power tacitly conferred on those who have power over the economy or (as the very ambiguity of the word "competence" indicates) an attribute of status.

As school change requires both serendipity and rationality, position-taking and positioning, the principal needs to identify and encode the school genes in an embodied state so that the conversion of capital from the principal individually to the group, then to the school, can occur after a period of time devoted to school organisation. Therefore, a school organisation can be taken as an organic group structure, the operation of which has a logic as a biological weapon. Capital is efficacious, for Bourdieu, "both as a weapon and as a stake of struggle, that which allows its possessors to wield a power, an influence, and thus to exist" (Bourdieu & Wacquant, 1992, p. 98). A school organisation has its own law of growth and multiplication. The principal, with transformational leadership and capital at disposal, reads, interprets, and employs this law when faced with adaptation to an environment externally and integration internally, as biological DNA does.

The "school DNA", then, is a coding of a particular school can survive, evolve, and thrive. *School doxa* is equivalent to School DNA, and works as a technological mechanism of capital conversion. Here we think of school DNA as coded information, as an historical trace and institutional memory that is manifest in explicit action, habituated practice, and institutional rules. In this regard, it is similar to what educational ethnographers refer to as school ethos – a coded, at times visible, at times invisible, effable yet ineffable pattern that reflects an acquired, historical, habituated "essence", that is durable and always sociologically constructed.

Principals need time to recognise the *doxa* of the school so that they can adjust the pace to lead and adapt to *school doxa*. To this end, principals spend time accumulating their own capital for the transformative task at hand, and then can engage in building, embedding, and evolving the school's organisational capital. The organisational capital of the school increases, eventually reaching a critical mass sufficient to leading school growth and attracting more teachers and students with a high quality and quantity of capital. It is a positive loop of capital attracting capital and is consistent with Bourdieu's theorem of capital conversion:

> The real logic of the functioning of capital, the conversions from one type to another, and the law of conservation which governs them cannot be understood unless two opposing but equally partial views are superseded:

188 Ning Jia and Guanglun Michael Mu

> on the one hand, economism, which, on the grounds that every type of capital is reducible in the last analysis to economic capital, ignores what makes the specific efficacy of the other types of capital, and on the other hand, semiologism ... which reduces social exchanges to phenomena of communication and ignores the brutal fact of universal reducibility to economics.
>
> *(Bourdieu, 1986, pp. 252–253)*

Particularly in the case of the building of relationships as part of the process of school change and institutional reorganisation, it would be problematic to see changes in the codes, rules, and policies – forms of semiologism – as indexical of the remaking of *school doxa*. In Song's case, we have suggested, school change and reform is a process of capital exchange, entailing multiple, overlapping forms of capital in dynamic relationship. If we view this as a matter of capital exchange (rather than codes, messaging, and semiosis per se, as much of the educational leadership literature does), such a process of exchange requires extended time, labour, and position-taking. Bourdieu goes on:

> The universal equivalent, the measure of all equivalences, is nothing other than labour-time (in the widest sense); and the conservation of social energy through all its conversions is verified if, in each case, one takes into account both the labour-time accumulated in the form of capital and the labour-time needed to transform it from one type into another ... the transformation of economic capital into social capital presupposes a specific labour, i.e., an apparently gratuitous expenditure of time, attention, care, concern ... From a narrowly economic standpoint, this effort is bound to be seen as pure wastage, but in the terms of the logic of social exchanges, it is a solid investment, the profits of which will appear, in the long run, in monetary or other form. Similarly, if the best measure of cultural capital is undoubtedly the time devoted to acquiring it, this is because the transformation of economic capital into cultural capital presupposes an expenditure of time that is made possible by possession of economic capital.
>
> *(Bourdieu, 1986, pp. 252–253)*

Implications for Policy, Principal Training, and School Change

What emerged from the data analysis here are three nested, mutually beneficial moments with the school transformation. First, Song paid time for accumulating his own capital. At the same time, he analysed the old school authority and culture, identifying the barriers for school change and looking and waiting for opportunities for change. Second, he built in steps to new norms around authority and drew on his transformational leadership and power to impel

Capital Conversion and School Change **189**

teachers and staff to work together and identify school culture. As school cultural capital was elevated, even though this was largely an invisible conversion, Song promoted teachers' job satisfaction, engagement, and organisational commitment. Third, Song maintained the capital conversion through communicating with outside stakeholders for assistance and support. By means of government and University capital as well as that of his own, Song led an acceleration of the pace of capital accumulation. The school's economic capital, social capital, cultural capital, and especially, symbolic capital increased. The enhanced organisational capital of the school attracted more students with high family SES, which in turn, further enhanced the school's organisation capital. After a historical development, the school has gradually become mature and capital conversion came true.

This chapter has attempted to assess the results of the importation of the capital concept and its classification into the study on Chinese school educational administration. The chapter discovered the mechanism of capital conversion through an organisational sociological interpretation. This interpretation rests on two perspectives. The first is codified in the work of Bourdieu's conceptualisation of capital, and conversion of different forms of capital needs to be taken into account for using these concepts. Nevertheless, the paths of capital conversion might be missing from Bourdieu's theories and thus not adequate to address Chinese modern school reform. Therefore, we have integrated a second alternative interpretation to assert the process, logic, and principle of capital conversion, not only on inter-capital-conversion, but also on cross-capital-conversion from individual forms to organisational forms. This stresses the importance of examining cross-interactional processes whereby organisational capital can evolve and develop on the grounds of the transformation of individual capital into collective capital. The specialised skills required for cross-capital-conversion are internalised in the principal's individual cultural capital and transformational leadership to decode and reshape School DNA or *doxa*. Cross-capital-conversion demands time, enabling structural conditions, what we have here referred to as serendipitous conditions, and the accumulated capital resources, agentive action, and position-taking by individuals like Song.

We conclude this chapter by offering some advice to principals and educational administrators. This case study is a microcosm and exemplar from the period of educational reform and decentralisation described across this volume, capturing some of the larger structural dynamics, local community demographic and economic changes, and where and how individual agents' position-taking can reshape institutional exchange and lives. The school is both a sociological field of exchange and an organic organisation with its own growth rhythm and DNA or *doxa*. Principals need time to accumulate and build their own capital and identify school DNA. At the same time, the institutional conversion of capitals, however it might appear in a structural field, is a diachronic process that can occur over decades, as in the case of this Beijing school. This is consistent with Bourdieu's emphasis on the amount of time devoted to capital accumulation, capital conversion, and capital reproduction. Current policy-making and the educational administration status quo in China have an air of urgency, a policy impatience for anything less than immediate change. In addition, particular evaluative criteria have long been affected by bureaucratic conventions. What this case study shows is that change at the local school level requires a combination of structural conditions in communities, enabling policy conditions, and leadership with the initiative to build and utilise their own capital resources. As simple as this may seem – Song's case shows that the making, implementing, and using policy for local change requires a rare confluence of time and patience, the availability and mobilisation of available resources, and social fields that are receptive and enabling of such exchange and reform.

Note

1 Relationship building may both result from and result in the exchanges of favours and connections that are mutually beneficial for the parties involved in the exchanges. The exchange requires strategies and initial connections. It is time consuming and complex. Beneficiaries of the exchange are expected and obliged to return the favour. The exchange is not a one-off transaction, but an ongoing investment.

References

Bourdieu, P. (1977). *Outline of a theory of practice* (R. Nice, Trans.). Cambridge: Cambridge University Press.

Bourdieu, P. (1986). The forms of capital. In J.G. Richardson (Ed.), *Handbook of theory and research for the sociology of education* (pp. 214–258). New York: Greenwood.

Bourdieu, P. (1990a). *In other words: Essays towards a reflexive sociology* (M. Adamson, Trans.). Stanford: Stanford University Press.

Bourdieu, P. (1990b). *The logic of practice* (R. Nice, Trans.). Cambridge: Polity Press.

Bourdieu, P., & Wacquant, L.J.D. (1992). *An invitation to reflexive sociology*. Cambridge: Polity Press.

Drafting Group, P.R.C. (2017). *Chinese education modernisation 2030 (exposure draft)*. Shanghai: Drafting Committee.

Ekinci, A. (2012). The effects of social capital levels in elementary schools on organisational information sharing. *Educational Sciences: Theory & Practice*, 12(4), 2513–2520.

English, F.W. (2012). Bourdieu's misrecognition: Why educational leadership standards will not reform schools or leadership. *Journal of Educational Administration and History*, 44(2), 155–170. doi:10.1080/00220620.2012.658763

Gunter, H.M., & Forrester, G. (2010). New Labour and the logic of practice in educational reform. *Critical Studies in Education*, 51(1), 55–69. doi:10.1080/17508480903450224

Guo, S., & Guo, Y. (Eds.). (2016). *Spotlight on China: Changes in education under China's market economy*. Rotterdam: Sense.

Hilgenbeger, N. (1993). Johann Friedrich Herbart. *Prospects*, 23(3), 649–664. doi:10.1007/bf02195141

Holme, J.J., & Rangel, V.S. (2012). Putting school reform in its place: Social geography, organisational social capital, and school performance. *American Educational Research Journal*, 49(2), 257–283. doi:10.3102/0002831211423316

Jones, M., & Harris, A. (2014). Principals leading successful organisational change: Building social capital through disciplined professional collaboration. *Journal of Organisational Change Management*, 27(3), 473–485. doi:10.1108/JOCM-07-2013-0116

Lingard, B., Hayes, D., Christie, P., & Mills, M. (2003). *Leading learning*. Milton Keynes, UK: Open University Press.

Marx, K. (1885/1978). *Capital: A critique of political economy* (D. Fernbach, Trans., Vol. 2). London: Penguin.

Minckler, C.H. (2014). School leadership that builds teacher social capital. *Educational Management Administration & Leadership*, 42(5), 657–679. doi:10.1177/1741143213510502

Mu, G.M. (2018). *Building resilience of floating children and left-behind children in China: Power, politics, participation, and education*. London: Routledge.

Mu, G.M., Zheng, X., Jia, N., Li, X., Wang, S., Chen, Y., . . . Diezmann, C. (2013). Revisiting educational equity and quality in China through Confucianism, policy, research, and practice. *The Australian Educational Researcher*, 40(3), 373–389. doi:10.1007/s13384-013-0113-0

Young, P., Reimer, D., & Young, K.H. (2010). Effects of organisational characteristics and human capital endowments on pay of female and male middle school principals. *Educational Administration Quarterly*, 46(4), 590–616. doi:10.1177/0013161x10375608

10

USING ENGLISH AT AN INTERNATIONAL DOCTORAL WORKSHOP

A Three-level Field Analysis

Guanglun Michael Mu, Liwei Livia Liu, Wangqian Fu, Dongfang Hao, Ning Jia, Yimei Qin, Hongmei Sziegat, Xiaodong Wang, and Xueqin Wu

Human history is not short of evidence relating to the widespread use of one language as a medium of communication in a regional or global context. Two thousand years ago, the grand prosperity of Chinese culture and science saw Japanese and Koreans learn the Chinese language and import lashings of Chinese characters to their own language systems. Eight hundred years ago, Latin was privileged as the sole language of scholarship across Europe prior to the rise of German, which then became the mainstream language of scientific communication in Europe and in the world at large. In France, the higher education sector started to respond to the Germanic influence in the early twentieth century (Bourdieu, 1988). This was followed by the unstoppable rise of English in the 1930s. Since then, English has replaced German as the dominant language of scientific communication. The value disparity between English and German in international academia is not difficult to justify: There is growing inclination on the part of German scholars to publish in English and a gradual decline in the use of German as the language of publication for non-German scholars (Ammon, 2006). Today, German, French, Spanish, and Italian are still used as international scientific languages alongside English, but their usage is constrained within certain niche subjects such as archaeology, musicology, philology, and theology. Irrespective of discipline, many scholars tend to publish "their best in the west, offering more minor works for local publication" (Swales, 1997, p. 378). At present, it is difficult to empirically dispute that English is in widespread use as the language of international academia.

To further understand the power, politics, and participation entailed by the use of English in international academia, our research question here is: What are the sociological dynamics behind using English at an international doctoral workshop series from the perspectives of native Chinese-speaking participants? Centring on this research question, this chapter unfolds in several stages. First, we provide a panoramic overview of the Chinese policy context that nurtures the rise of English in Chinese academia. Second, we establish the empirical basis of our study by a discussion of the major schools of thinking that are concerned with the superiority of English to other academic languages. We also review the literature regarding the widespread use of English in globalising higher education. Third, we introduce the context of the chapter by describing the history and organisation of the international annual doctoral workshop series. This is followed by a succinct discussion of Bourdieu's sociology that constructs the theoretical underpinnings of our study. Next, we engage in Bourdieu's field analysis to debunk the sociological conundrums associated with using English at the doctoral workshop. Finally, we conclude the chapter with some reflections on future research and practice.

The Rise of English in Chinese Academia: Context and Policy

Within Chinese academia, Mandarin enjoys a predominant position. This predominance can be seen in the use of Mandarin as the mainstream medium of communication for all academic purposes. However, the predominance of Mandarin does not necessarily exclude foreign languages, in particular Russian and subsequently English, from gaining a certain symbolic value. According to the National Bureau of Statistics data, during the period between the establishment of the People's Republic of China in 1949 and the commencement of the Cultural Revolution in 1966, 10,698 national scholarship students were sent to study in socialist/communist countries, 78 per cent of whom were sent to the Soviet Union given the close political, economic, and educational ties between the two countries. During this period, Russian functioned as the medium of "international" scientific exchange and communication for China. During the same period, very few scholarships were arranged to support study in Western countries, and self-funded overseas study was de facto not possible given the strict government control over human mobility. During the Cultural Revolution (1966–76), the national scholarship program was suspended. It was not resumed until 1978 when Deng Xiaoping came into power and promulgated the Reform and Opening-Up Policy.

Deng's claim of leadership was a critical historic moment – China broke away from the Soviet Union, relaxed its relationship with the West, and desperately demanded conversation and cooperation with the outside world. At the end of 1978, the first cohort of national scholarship students was sent to the US and the Ministry of Public Security started to approve self-funded

194 Guanglun Michael Mu et al.

overseas study. In 1981, to further unshackle the limits on self-funded overseas study, the State Council promulgated the *Provisional Regulations for Self-Funded Overseas Study*. In the early 1980s, the State Council started to support the organisation of international academic conferences in China in order to facilitate knowledge exchange (in English). At the same time, the Ministry of Education defined English as a compulsory unit of study at universities, irrespective of student major. In 1987, the national College English Test came to the fore as the most frequently used English test in China. Through a series of policy shifts, English gradually replaced Russian as the first foreign language, and accrued symbolic value in Chinese academia.

The rapid advancement of reforming and opening-up, coupled with subsequent supportive policies, has dramatically ushered in the internationalisation of Chinese higher education. Such internationalisation has intensified in the new century. In 2010, the State Council promulgated the *State Guidelines for Medium- and Long-Term Education Reform and Development Plan (2010–2020)*. The *Plan* spends a whole chapter on the internationalisation of higher education, explicitly urging governments, universities, research institutes, and tertiary education sectors to cultivate intellectuals with an international horizon. Following the promulgation of the *Plan*, the internationalisation of higher education has seen an exponential growth in joint research, joint degree programs, joint establishment of institutions, faculty and student exchange programs, curriculums designed in English, and representation of foreign academics. According to a recent survey (China Education Association for International Exchange, 2015), 2.9 per cent of the academics at 985 universities[1] were foreign passport holders; 11.8 per cent of the Chinese academics at these universities gained their PhD overseas; and 3.7 per cent of the units at these universities were taught in English. These figures are expected to rise as the internationalisation of higher education was stressed in *The 2017 Key Work Objectives of the Ministry of Education*. Such internationalisation institutionalised through government policies largely assumes English to be the major medium of international communication and hence will continue to gain marked significance in Chinese academia.

It is clear that the status of a particular language as an academic lingua franca is defined largely on the grounds of macro-level social orders. Politics, policies, and power all come to inform the rise and fall of such a language. Less clear, however, are the micro-level politics and tensions associated with language users in academia. The current chapter aims to contribute in this regard. English stands at the apex of the linguistic hierarchy in international academia. In this chapter, it is by no means our intention to either defend or challenge the dominant position of English. Rather, our intention is to grapple with the social practices of using English in a micro-level academic community. Specifically, we set the scene of our study at an international annual doctoral workshop series. We analyse the perspectives of native Chinese-speaking participants in

Using English at a Doctoral Workshop **195**

relation to their use of English at the workshop. Before introducing the doctoral workshop, we discuss the literature regarding the use of English in international academia.

English as a Carnivore that Engulfs Other Academic Language Denizens?

The use of English in every layer of the academic domain is so amply debated in the literature that it only requires a brief revisit here. Currently, English is used as a scientific meta-language for all functions: "for publishing, information gathering (reading), conferences or guest lectures, for informal written and oral correspondence and face-to-face communication" (Ammon, 2006, p. 2). The power of English advantages major English-speaking academic systems – the US, the UK, Australia, and bilingual Canada included. These academic systems spend a predominant proportion of global research funds, house a myriad of leading universities in the world, edit most top-tier scholarly publications, and host a large percentage of the world's international students (Altbach, 2007). Such indicators seem to suggest the mutually empowering relationship between English as an academic lingua franca and the academic power of English-speaking systems.

The origin of the unbridled spread of English can be attributed to a series of social vicissitudes, from British colonialism, through the fall of Germany and France in the two World Wars, to the contemporary ingrained economic, political, and scientific power of the United States (Ammon, 2006; Earls, 2013; Mauranen, 2003). Academic superpowers like the US and the UK astutely ensure English as the scientific lingua franca in order to further consolidate their hegemony in the scholarly world. The UK/US Study Group (2009), for example, aims to collaboratively assert the primacy of the US and the UK in the realm of higher education and further increase their competitiveness within the global educational market. According to this group, the two countries will plant firmly the ideals of *liberty and democracy* and encourage the development of multidisciplinary networks of *international* scholars *through the medium of English*. Here we see the Study Group's ideals of inclusive international networking on the one hand and its exclusive stress on academic power of English on the other.

Although the use of English as a lingua franca would seem to benefit the globalisation of scholarship, voices about the threats of English to linguistic diversity in the scholarly world are loud and strident. The predominance of English challenges other academic systems or even snuffs out those small ones that do not use English as their native language (Ammon, 2006; Coulmas, 2007; Enrique Hamel, 2007). The gain of English in the scientific field occurs at the cost of research work that is equally important but disseminated in other languages (Altbach, 2007; Ammon, 2006). In this vein, English is described as a *hyper-central language* (Swaan, 2001), a *killer language* (Skutnab-Kangas, 2003),

196 Guanglun Michael Mu et al.

and a *Tyrannosaurus rex* in the academic Jurassic Park (Swales, 1997). These phenomena have been discussed and theorised within schools of thought concerned with *Englishisation* (McArthur, 1992), *linguistic imperialism* (Phillipson, 1992), and the *cultural politics of English* (Pennycook, 1994).

Elite domains like higher education are often the first to see the shift towards English (Berg, Hult, & King, 2001) and are at risk of *domain loss* (Ljosland, 2007). Such loss has become increasingly visible in Nordic countries where there are expanding domains of English and corresponding contracting domains of Scandinavian languages. For example, the academic language shift towards English has been markedly observed among young Finnish academics (Brock-Utne, 2001). In Sweden, there has been a significant drop in doctoral theses published in Swedish and a dramatic growth in doctoral theses published in English (Berg et al., 2001). The same phenomenon has occurred in Norway where doctoral candidates consider English to be of higher value than Norwegian when writing their thesis (Ljosland, 2007). However, Ferguson (2007) argues that the threat of English is less dire than is claimed in the domain loss discourse. He contends that the situation is not best characterised as *diglossia* where English is prioritised over other languages. Rather, the situation is one of *academic bilingualism* where dual language systems serve different purposes across different disciplines albeit with the increasingly intrusive role of English.

Contra Ferguson (2007), the English "take-over" in Nordic and international higher education sectors is very real and present. Coleman's (2006) prophecy that English will become the language of higher education seems to be proving true. The Englishisation of higher education has seen rampant development of English-medium programmes (Earls, 2013). An increasing number of universities in non-English-speaking countries have started to offer more courses in English to capture the profits in the market, with this trend particularly noticeable in countries where the use of English is widespread, such as the Scandinavian countries (Brock-Utne, 2001; OECD, 2017). Many universities in mainland Europe are also driven by the economic rewards of international student recruitment. These universities have worked diligently to develop English programmes to attract fee-paying international students, to enhance the university's international prestige, and to develop the English-language skills of their staff and students (Ferguson, 2007).

In the Chinese context, responses to the internationalisation of higher education are emerging. Wang & Zhao (2004) advocate the use of English so that Chinese scholars can contribute their share to global scholarship. However, the visibility of Chinese scholars of social sciences and humanities in international English publications is strikingly low, due to their inadequate academic language competence (Flowerdrew & Li, 2009). The language barrier can be an insurmountable one, particularly in social sciences and humanities where academic English requires a very high level of competence that is difficult to attain in a foreign language (Ammon, 2006). Another response to the internationalisation of Chinese higher education is the growing quality and quantity of international conferences held in China. At these conferences, however, it is not unusual to see English usage tower over Chinese (Xiao & Peng, 2008). The use of English at international conferences indicates China's respect for international convention (China Association for Science and Technology, 2008), but challenges remain. For example, Chinese participants with lower English proficiency were found to be less interactive in discussion and hence less content with their conference participation experience (Xiao & Peng, 2008).

In response to the aforementioned challenges, many colleagues (e.g., Gagan & Wallace, 2001; Wallwork, 2010) have provided a detailed manual and an exhaustive list of strategies to help non-native English-speaking participants to better present in English at international conferences. The good intention of these colleagues is commendable, but the accommodationism and the assimilationism behind such an approach tend to blame non-native English-speaking participants for their inadequate English proficiency. In contrast to the accommodationism and assimilationism approach, some colleagues call for reflections from native English-speaking participants on their use of English at international conferences. Native English-speaking presenters are usually more attentive to their presentation content than to their English structures, vocabulary, and pronunciation, which impede the effectiveness of their presentations because audiences, particularly non-native English-speaking ones, "cannot understand them well" (Hashemi & Hokmabadi, 2011, p. 2111). In these situations, non-native English-speaking audiences, more often than not, are like the ones who sit through presentations in charitable silence with politeness and patient tolerance that approach the heroic, as described with amazement by Jay (1970).

In summary, it is hard to overemphasise the utility of English in the globalising higher education. That said, the predominant use of English tends to encourage a monolingual ethos in the academy, and erode linguistic diversity. Extensive macro-level debates have engaged with the use of English as an academic lingua franca. These debates largely centre around four models, involving: (1) a call to reject the encroachment of English through linguistic imperialism, domain loss, and Englishisation; (2) the discourse of equity, inclusivity, and diversity that calls for academic multilingualism; (3) the accommodationism and assimilationism approach in complicity with the deficit model that blames the incapability of non-native English speakers, and (4) the postcolonial guilt that shows sympathy to the English-colonised academic communities. Despite these macro-level debates, non-native English-speaking participants' first-hand, micro-level experiences of using English at international academic meetings such as conferences, seminars, and workshops are barely heard. Herein lies the merits of our work. We use Bourdieu's theory as method and draw on his approach of field analysis to weave the macro-level social orders and the micro-level language practices. We analyse the perspectives of native Chinese-speaking participants in an international annual doctoral workshop and use Bourdieu to take stock of the sociological dynamics behind their use of English at the workshop. Before

198 Guanglun Michael Mu et al.

we proceed with the analysis, we provide an introduction to the doctoral workshop and an overview of Bourdieu's sociology.

The Doctoral Workshop as A Social Space of Struggle: A Three-Level Field Analysis

Over the past decade, Beijing Normal University, China and Queensland University of Technology, Australia have co-organised and co-funded an annual doctoral workshop series. The University of Calgary in Canada joined the network in 2015 on the occasion of the tenth anniversary of the bilateral doctoral workshop series. Since then, the three partner universities take turns hosting the annual workshop at which four to six doctoral candidates and one to two academics from each partner university meet for approximately a week. The workshop programmes are designed for relevance to emerging scholars in China, Australia, and Canada. Although workshop programmes have evolved over the years, key components include: (1) pre-workshop sessions in each country on participation information and logistics, introduction to participants across the three universities, and student presentation rehearsals; (2) workshop sessions in the host country that include student presentations, guest lectures, academic writing seminars, school visits, and cultural tours, and (3) face-to-face and online post-workshop collaborative writing and ongoing discussion of joint research possibilities. Throughout these activities, English is always used as the working language and this will continue. As the doctoral workshop connects academics and doctoral students from increasingly culturally diverse backgrounds, it is time to rethink the linguistic homogeneity at the workshop. We take the opportunity to critically reflect on the use of English from the perspectives of native Chinese-speaking workshop participants.

We theorise the workshop as a social space within the field of higher education and the field of power. To clarify, *field* refers to a social space of conflict and competition where agents vie, consciously or unconsciously, for species of resources to establish monopoly and claim authority – "cultural authority in the artistic field, scientific authority in the scientific field, sacerdotal authority in the religious field" (Bourdieu & Wacquant, 1992, p. 17). In this respect, the field is composed of a structured configuration of objective relationships of inequalities, whether constant or permanent, between different positions of agents (Bourdieu, 1998a). These positions, as explained by Bourdieu & Wacquant,

> are objectively defined, in their existence and in the determinations they impose upon their occupants, agents or institutions, by their present and potential situation (situs) in the structure of the distribution of species of power (or capital) whose possession commands access to the specific profits that are at stake in the field, as well as by their objective relations to other positions (domination, subordination, homology, etc.).
>
> *(Bourdieu & Wacquant, 1992, p. 97)*

According to Bourdieu's field theory, the relative positions of native and non-native English-speaking participants in the doctoral workshop can be objectively defined by the distribution of resources – English, amongst other academic resources in this case – within the social space of the doctoral workshop. According to Bourdieu's theory of social practice (Bourdieu, 1977), certain manners of being and thinking, routine behaviours, and patterns of sociocultural activities of the doctoral workshop participants can result from the relations between the *resources* at participants' disposal and the *dispositions* embodied in their mind and body within the particular social arena of the doctoral workshop. The resources are what Bourdieu (1986) means by *capital* – a set of accumulated assets that have the potential to produce profits and reproduce themselves in an identical and expanded forms. The dispositions are what Bourdieu (1998b) means by *habitus* – a set of durable and transposable bodily and cognitive structures that consciously or unconsciously direct social agents to certain strategic responses to given situations.

Informed by Bourdieu's conceptual triad of capital, habitus, and field, we delve into the sociocultural dynamics behind our use of English at the doctoral workshop. We are nine native Chinese-speaking workshop participants from the three partner universities. This chapter is an example of the post-workshop collaborative publishing activity across the three universities promoted by the annual meeting. In preparing this chapter, we produced qualitative data from two sources during the time of the doctoral workshop: Focus groups and individual reflections. In both ways, we had opportunities to document our experiences of using English at the workshop. The frequency, length, time, and venue of the focus groups were collectively decided based on our convenience and availability. In addition, each of us wrote an individual reflection on our perspectives and experiences of using English at the workshop. Our dataset was composed of three audio-recorded focus groups and nine individual reflections.

To make meaning out of these data, we draw on Bourdieu's field analysis that "involves three necessary and internally connected moments" (Bourdieu & Wacquant, 1992, p. 104): (1) the analysis of the field vis-à-vis the field of power; (2) the analysis of relations between positions occupied by agents competing for legitimacy in the field, and (3) the genesis and manifestations of habitus that generate agents' practices. At the first level, we analyse our perceptions of how macro-level power and politics come to define the role of English in the field of higher education. At the second level, we map out the micro-level relations of linguistic power amongst workshop participants within the social space of the doctoral workshop operating as field. At the third level, we unearth the systems of dispositions that workshop participants have internalised through the socially anticipated and accepted use of English at the doctoral workshop. The three-level field analysis aims to address our core research question: What are the sociological dynamics behind the use of English at the doctoral workshop? We treat Bourdieu's theory as method and

200 Guanglun Michael Mu et al.

use his theoretically based approach to field analysis to discuss English in fields of higher education and power, the social positions of English users at the doctoral workshop, and the dispositional praxes of using English at the workshop.

English in the Fields of Power and Higher Education

Throughout our reflections and focus groups, we had a unanimous view that English has become the language of scholarship. Many of us spoke of the widespread use of English for communication at international conferences, publication in high-impact scholarly journals, and access to Western knowledge and theories. Terms such as "dominance", "superiority", "lingua franca", and "mainstream" were repeatedly used to describe the authority of English in international academia. These terms seem to indicate the symbiotic relationship between language and power. The origin of the power of English was one topic discussed in our focus groups. We talked about "the historical power of British colonialism" and "the contemporary dominance of the US in the power fields of economy, politics, and science". Such superpowers, previous or present ones, contribute to the dominant position of English.

No field is fully autonomous and fields may be heteronomous, that is, affected by other fields to at least some extent. As a consequence, the logics within the field of power can infiltrate into the field of higher education. Workshop participant BHM briefly mentioned, "The role of English was further strengthened by global competition. In order to perform well, both policy makers and higher education institutes regard English as a tool of building world-class universities and internationalising higher education", while CXQ seemed to consider the field of higher education to be heteronomous of the field of policy:

> After the Reform and Opening-Up Policy in the 1980s, the Chinese government promulgated the national foreign language education policy and defined English as one of the major subjects to be tested at the university entrance examination and taught at universities. University graduates who pass the national English proficiency test are more competitive in the labour market. The purpose of these policies is to train intellectuals to learn science and technology from the Western countries and to advance China's development.

Both BHM and CXQ explained English education at universities, looking at how the field of higher education can be influenced by the field of power – the political and policy power of government and the economic power of the labour market. UGM also noted in his reflection, "As far as I know, at many universities, financial awards for English publications and Chinese publications differ. This further strengthens the academic dominance of English." The different financial award policies indicate the nexus between the field of higher education and the field of power, in the latter of which accumulation of economic capital is the dominant principle of hierarchisation (Bourdieu & Wacquant, 1992). In this case, the logic behind the financial award for English publications at many universities resonates with the principles of economic competition and calculative investment in the field of power. Dominant agents or institutions in field of power have in common the possession of the capital necessary to occupy dominant positions in other fields (Bourdieu, 1996). The logic of higher education, which values scientific reputation and scholastic knowledge, would seem to be adulterated by economic logic which enters the field of higher education through its agents who are also in the field of power. For example, UGM reflected:

> English-speaking countries, the US and the UK in particular, own most of the scholarly journals in social sciences. Their editors and reviewers were mostly trained through the Western education system. They have inherited Western academic rules and applied these rules to their edit and review work, and hence strengthen the position of Western scholarship.

Here UGM talked about the monopoly of English-speaking systems in producing English-speaking editors and reviewers who, using English academic conventions, wield symbolic violence to reproduce the authoritative position of English-speaking academic systems in the field of higher education. The authority of English undergirds and guides the strategies of occupants of authoritative positions – who "seek, individually or collectively, to safeguard or improve their position and to impose the principle of hierarchisation most favourable to their own products" (Bourdieu & Wacquant, 1992, p. 101). The products of the field of higher education dominated by English can be English-speaking academics, who are also the producers of the field where English is "the capital of instruments of expression" required for producing "a written discourse worthy of being published" and "presupposing appropriation of the resources deposited in objectified form in libraries" (Bourdieu, 1991, p. 57). In this way, English-speaking systems have made their power official and legitimate in the field of higher education.

English-speaking academics can compete for a favourable position due to their possession of English as linguistic capital (Bourdieu, 1991). It should be acknowledged that Bourdieu (1991) draws on the notion of linguistic capital to theorise the symbolic value of socially legitimate ways of using a particular language. We extend this notion by analysing the different values accrued by different languages (see Gogolin, 2002; Mu, 2016). Linguistic capital has value in the relationships between the field of higher education and the field of power. The external determinations (e.g., the logic of the field of power) that bear on agents situated in a given field (e.g., academics in the field of higher education) never apply to

202 Guanglun Michael Mu et al.

these agents directly, "but affect them only through the specific mediation of the specific forms and forces of the field" (Bourdieu & Wacquant, 1992, p. 105). In other words, English as linguistic capital plays a mediating role in the relationship between the field of higher education and the field of power.

As a social space within the field of higher education, the doctoral workshop unsurprisingly gave high value to English. Throughout our reflections and focus groups, there was a consensus that this was not unusual in the academic field: "Whether at our doctoral workshop or international conferences elsewhere, English is widely used as a lingua franca" [TLW]. "A prerequisite for participation in the doctoral workshop was a submission of an English paper. That is to say, a Chinese paper is not qualified. To participate in the workshop, the use of English is the first condition" [NYM]. By virtue of the consensus on the use of English at the workshop, we defended the linguistic market of English and preserved the linguistic logic in the field of higher education. Behind this logic are dynamic, nuanced power relations between occupants of different positions within the social space of the doctoral workshop. We now turn to the analysis of these relative social positions.

The Social Positions of English Users at the Doctoral Workshop

Much discussion in our reflections and focus groups was centred on the social positions constructed through the doctoral workshop. For instance, NYM wrote, "In contention for a space in an academic area, we need to follow English scholarly paradigms and frameworks when conducting research, and stay more closely to English expressions." The words "follow" and "stay more closely" indicate the relative positions of "domination" and "subordination" (Bourdieu & Wacquant, 1992, p. 97) and the inequality between "people who dominate and others who are dominated" (Bourdieu, 1998a, p. 40), between those who lead and those who follow, and between those at the centre and those who intend to stay closer to the centre. The words "English scholarly paradigms and frameworks" as well as "English expressions" are what Bourdieu (1991, pp. 57–58) means by "rhetorical devices, genres, legitimate styles and manners and, more generally, all the formulations destined to be 'authoritative' and to be cited as examples of 'good usage'".

Given the unequal positions between English-speaking systems and others, we commonly used terms like "difficult", "challenging/ed", "confusing/ed", "clueless", "unintelligible", "non-proficient", "weak", "inappropriate", and "laborious" to describe our feeling of using English at the workshop. These terms have a connotation of inequality objectively defined by language speakers' "present and potential situation in the structure of the distribution of species of power" (Bourdieu & Wacquant, 1992, p. 97). Here, the situation refers to the unequal distribution of linguistic capital or the legitimate English competence required for academic communication at the doctoral workshop. Lack of linguistic capital reportedly resulted in multifarious sociocultural praxes that included admiring, staying silent, and feeling ignored.

UDF wrote in his reflection with envy, "Watching them [native English speakers] speaking freely, the only thing I can do is to admire." At this very moment, UDF did not have the linguistic capital (Bourdieu, 1991) – English in this case – to converse as freely as native English speakers. UDF came into contact with a community in which he was not able to, but wished to, participate. He admired the native English speakers who had the required linguistic capital. Nevertheless, lack of this capital objectively defined his low social position, from where he could only look up at those whom he admired but might never manage to become.

Silence was another sociocultural response of Chinese participants to the use of English at the doctoral workshop. As BXD wrote, "Sometimes we could not express our opinions in English so we had to keep silent at the workshop." Similarly, NWQ wrote, "It's observable at the workshop that those who asked questions were often native English speakers. The frequency of Chinese students asking questions was markedly low." The silence of Chinese participants at the workshop was also observed by native English-speaking participants, as UGM recalled, "At the workshop some Australians and Canadians came to me, saying Chinese students were somewhat silent." In situations where inadequate linguistic capital inhibits full participation, silence seems to be a common social praxis. As Bourdieu (1991, p. 55) suggests, "Speakers lacking the legitimate competence . . . are condemned to silence" in the social domains where this competence is required. In situations where those lacking linguistic capital feel left out by occupants of it, a sense of being ignored may appear. As CXQ lamented:

> When I saw [how] English became the dominant language and Chinese students were not actively involved in the conversations, I had a feeling all non-native English speakers in the room were somewhat ignored and put at a disadvantaged position . . . Many a time I would still have a feeling of being an outsider especially when I am the minority and the native speakers throw in some jokes, idioms, or slangs, the meaning of which I have no clue about.

UGM had a similar account:

> Sometimes I noticed native English speakers were completely indulged in academic discussions in English. Of course this is nothing wrong . . . But it inadvertently ignored Chinese participants and made them passive and silent. This is a phenomenon of "linguistic ignoring" . . . Nobody deliberately ignored us but we were in fact ignored.

Because of the inadvertent linguistic ignoring, NWQ wished with a euphemism that native English speakers "could have considered more the Chinese

204 Guanglun Michael Mu et al.

participants during workshop presentations and discussions". In situations of linguistic ignoring, the quantity and quality of linguistic capital (English in this case), can distinguish insider and outsider. In "structured systems of sociologically pertinent linguistic differences" (p. 54), we could be "*de facto* excluded from the social domains" (p. 55) where the required command of English went way beyond our reach. Interestingly, our sense of inequality resulting from lack of linguistic capital was mitigated in certain situations. See the excerpt from our focus-group discussion.

UWY: I felt I learned more when I talked to them [native English speakers] privately, because I can talk to them about topics I am really interested in, like very focused topics.

BHM: I think maybe it's because private conversation is a kind of informal communication. It makes you feel very relaxed so you can more freely express some good ideas.

CXQ: Probably we need more of this kind of free time for private or small-group discussion.

BHM: Like an informal meeting where we chat.

NWQ: And we have different interests, like the topics that interest you. So one-to-one is better.

BXD: I think through this kind of conversation one major point is to find differences, differences between Chinese and Western culture. This is a very interesting thing we are interested in and they are interested in. This is a common point, I think.

CXQ: So except for formal presentations, informal communications are actually very important.

The magic of the informal clearly emerged from the above excerpt. In an informal situation, those lacking English competence reportedly felt more relaxed, talked more freely, and expressed better. This is because the dominant linguistic competence is more likely to function as linguistic capital in a more formal situation, which "is able to impose by itself alone the recognition of the legitimacy of the dominant mode of expression, converting the optional variants (at least on the level of pronunciation) into imperative rules" (Bourdieu, 1991, p. 70). This very formality was manifested in the workshop presentations of native English-speaking participants whose "academic jargons daunted us". Conversely, the authority of English speakers diminished as the degree of informality increased. In informal situations, lack of linguistic capital "tends to become less unfavourable to the dominated" (p. 71).

Of course, Chinese participants did not exclusively depend upon situational change that counteracted their linguistic disadvantage. Many of us rose up to the challenge and engaged in "reading English scholarly journals", "writing English papers", and "doing research presentations in English", Although admiration, silence, and marginalisation were commonly reported sociocultural dynamics involved in using English at the doctoral workshop, Chinese participants were not necessarily always illegitimate onlookers. Instead, some of us were competing for better positions in the field of higher education by accumulating linguistic capital. In the next section, our discussion shifts from Chinese participants' positions to their dispositions. We decipher the nuanced, dispositional praxes of using English at the workshop – the habitual praxes through which participants took certain positions within the social space of the workshop.

The Dispositional Praxes of Using English at the Doctoral Workshop

> In this game, the trump cards are the habitus, that is to say, the acquirements, the embodied, assimilated properties ... the inherited assets which define the possibilities inherent in the field. These trump cards determine not only the style of play, but also the success or failure in the game.
>
> *(Bourdieu, 1993, p. 150)*

The social space of the doctoral workshop is like a game. To understand our game-playing at the workshop, it is useful to decipher our habitus, which can manifest in various transmutable dispositions. The complexity behind our dispositional praxes of using English at the workshop was evidenced in the data. On the one hand, the doctoral workshop took place in China so we "felt like hosts to Australian and Canadian visitors". Our cultural sentiments of showing "respect", "politeness", and "hospitality" to visitors predisposed us to "accommodate the linguistic needs of foreign visitors". We did not expect them to *do as Romans do when in Rome*. Instead, we "felt obliged to speak their language [English]" and "give up using Mandarin". This long-established Confucian virtue of obliging others is a habitus of *Chineseness* (Mu, 2016). The obligation was not our rational choice because habitus comes from "the source of cognition without consciousness, of an intentionality without intention" (Bourdieu, 1990a, p. 12). On the other hand, we were "keen to grasp each possible opportunity to communicate with native English speakers" and wanted to "become confidently engaged in scholarly discussions with them". Such a disposition of confidence seemed to differ from the habitus of Chineseness. It is a new form of habitus emerging from the globalising higher education field in which we wish to actively and confidently participate.

The sense of obligation and the sense of confidence demonstrate a habitus of two quite distinct sorts – the Confucian tradition and the international horizon. To understand ambivalent and contradictory dispositions, Bourdieu (2007, p. 67) talks about "*cleft habitus*", which is a "cleft, tormented habitus bearing in the form of tensions and contradictions" (Bourdieu, 2000, p. 64). Bourdieu (2005) tends to adopt a negative framing of cleft habitus which is "torn by contradiction and internal division, generating suffering" (Bourdieu, 2000,

206 Guanglun Michael Mu et al.

p. 160). Our habitus, however, does not seem to involve painful negotiations between the old and the new, the traditional and the international. Instead, it indicates the ways in which our habitus draws upon the internalisation of seemingly incommensurate structures to morph in accordance with the demands and expectations of both the Chinese and the international academic spaces. In this respect, our habitus is not a cleft, but a conflation.

Another observed form of embodied dispositions of Chinese participants was embarrassment. As UDF confessed, "Sometimes it's hard to understand [the discussion]. Watching them [native English speakers] talking happily, I just embarrassedly smiled." UGM also shared his embarrassed moment:

> Sometimes when native English speakers noticed the silence of Chinese participants, they asked in a caring way, "I found our Chinese participants very silent. Do you have any particular ideas you want to share with the group?" At this moment, everyone looked at the Chinese participants. I had the exact experience. At that time, I felt like I had to say something, willingly or unwillingly. This is a phenomenon of "linguistic spotlighting". When we didn't want to say anything, our names were called and we were put in the spotlight. We felt embarrassed.

During these embarrassed moments, UDF and UGM were aware of the unequal relationships due to their "practical, bodily knowledge" (Bourdieu, 2000, p. 184) of their present and potential unfavourable position in the social space. The practical, bodily knowledge conferred by the sense of placement takes the form of emotion – "the unease of someone who is out of place". This sense of being out of place governs the "experience of the place occupied, defined absolutely and above all relationally as a rank". Therefore, the capital-defined ranks/positions in a field and the practices, expressions, and stances/position-takings in the field are "methodologically inseparable" because "the space of positions tends to command the space of position-takings" (Bourdieu & Wacquant, 1992, p. 105). In other words, the unfavourable social positions of UDF and UGM led to their embarrassment, fraught with bodily unease. This is what Bourdieu (2000, p. 169) means by bodily emotion – "the practical recognition through which the dominated, often unwittingly, contribute to their own domination by tacitly accepting, in advance, the limits imposed on them", often taking the forms of "shame, timidity, anxiety, guilt, blushing, inarticulacy, clumsiness, and trembling".

By tacitly accepting, in advance, the imposed limits, the bodily emotion of embarrassment seemed to predispose us to take unfavourable positions within the social space of the doctoral workshop. Such a sense of inferiority can be "the products of dominated linguistic habitus" (Bourdieu, 1991, p. 71). This habitus, as a set of bodily dispositions and cognitive schemata, is the generative principle of unconscious "being, seeing, acting, and thinking", or "structures of perception, conception, and action" (Bourdieu, 2005, p. 43). The unconsciousness in our predisposed practices of using English at the workshop is not hard to justify, as none of us has ever rationally questioned the widespread use of English before we engaged in the current research. Since the sense of inferiority was the product of a *modus operandi* (Bourdieu, 1977) of which we were not the producer and had no conscious mastery, this sense often outran our conscious intentions.

Interestingly, native English-speaking participants seemed to be predisposed to take a superior position within the social space of the doctoral workshop, due to their linguistic advantage. Since we did not collect data directly from them, we draw on our own understandings of their position-takings. In our focus-group discussions, we mentioned their "high language speed during presentations", "use of difficult words we failed to understand", "underestimation of our language barriers", and "joyfulness of them talking freely together while we are frustrated to catch up". It is by no means our intention to blame them. Instead, we completely understood that "they didn't mean to frustrate us." They just spoke in the normal way. At the very moment of them speaking, they seemed unaware that their linguistic advantage was exactly our linguistic disadvantage.

The "undisputed, pre-reflexive, naïve, native compliance with the fundamental presuppositions of the field" (Bourdieu, 1990b, p. 68) is *doxa* – "the relationship of immediate adherence that is established in the practice between a habitus and the field to which it is attuned, the pre-verbal taking-for-granted of the world that flows from practical sense." This practical sense of taking-for-grantedness is "social necessity turned into nature, converted into motor schemes and body automatisms", and "informed by a common sense" (p. 69). The dominant linguistic habitus of native English- speaking participants is fortuitously (for them) attuned to a field that legitimises English. When their habitus encountered a social world of which the habitus was the product, they found themselves "as fish in water" (Wacquant, 1989, p. 43). They did not have to consciously feel the weight of the water or rationally reason about their fish-in-water practice; hence they took the practice for granted. As a result, their possibly unintentional use of rapid speech and possibly inadvertent choice of difficult words were socially accepted and anticipated linguistic practices of which they might have been unaware.

The social praxes of using English at the doctoral workshop seemed to go without saying because they came without saying and hence were largely taken for granted. These social praxes constitute a spectrum of habitual dispositions acquired through internalising the culturally normal and socially anticipated structural conditions. Habitus is an accretion of internalised lessons that we have learned over the course of our life history and our socialisation at the workshop.

Conclusion and Discussion

To unearth the sociological dynamics behind using English at the doctoral workshop, we drew on Bourdieu's field analysis to grapple with the superiority of English in fields of power and higher education, the relative social positions of English users at the workshop, and the dispositional praxes of using English at the workshop. Existing debates consistently attribute the dominance of English to the historical power of British colonialism and the contemporary power of the US in global economy, politics, and science. Similarly, our study discusses the power of economy, policy, and government that comes to define the superiority of English in higher education, although from within a Bourdieusian perspective. Extant studies (e.g., Flowerdrew & Li, 2009; Jiang, Borg, & Borg, 2017; Wang & Zhao, 2004; Xiao & Peng, 2008; Yang, 2005) also discuss Chinese scholars' language choice and general experience of using English. Our study differs, however, in its analysis and theorisation of the subtle, multilayered language practices at an international annual doctoral workshop and the nuanced, interconnected positions and dispositions of workshop participants. What has emerged from our data are unequal social positions manifested in social praxes of admiring, staying silent, and feeling ignored. Lacking linguistic capital, we could be described in Wenger's (1998, p. 165) graphic words as "catching, as we peek into foreign chambers, glimpses of other realities and meanings". We are also akin to those second-language learners in the imagined communities who did not have required linguistic proficiency for real classroom participation (Norton, 2001; Pavlenko & Norton, 2007). That said, we do not resist using English or despair in the English-speaking environment. In stark contrast, we strategically choose to participate in the workshop and use English as much as possible for the benefits of ourselves and our native English-speaking peers.

Schools of linguistic imperialism, Englishisation, and domain loss problematise the uneven globalisation of higher education, questioning English-speaking academic systems that wield their symbolic power to engage in "Anglophone gate-keeping practices" (Swales, 1997, p. 380) or/and to coerce other/ed systems to take a stance with respect to English as the academic lingua franca (see Phillipson, 1992). These schools are widely present in the literature but less convincing in the face of our findings of the largely unconscious position-takings of superiority or inferiority. The unconsciousness is similar to that of Norwegian doctoral students in Ljosland's (2007) study, whose choice of English in thesis writing seemed to be self-evident, socially normal, and hence taken for granted. This taken-for-grantedness may wake up from its epistemic sleep when crisis disrupts the routine adjustment of position-takings to positions. In crisis circumstances "when rational choice may take over" (Bourdieu & Wacquant, 1992, p. 131), self-evidence is practically destroyed.

The crisis does not have to be a revolutionary social event. It can be a critical learning moment in a routine context where the undiscussed is brought into discussion. In this context, what once was a covert, implicit, and connotative state of latency has shifted to an overt, explicit, and denotative strategy of practice. What historically was unconsciously buried in mind and body has become a consciously carried epistemology at present and in future. This is a sociological phenomenon of "habitus realisation" (Mu & Dooley, 2015; Mu &

Hu, 2016; Mu et al., 2016). The doctoral workshop is a critical learning moment that realises our habitus. We noted in the reflections and focus groups that the issue of language choice and usage as well as its associated complexities have never come into our mind until we participated in this research. The social position of being a non-native English speaker subliminally directed us to unquestioningly take the socially anticipated position. Participation in this research has become a "crisis" for us to rationally mull over this acquiescence. We also hope that this chapter can become a "crisis" for others, especially for native English-speaking colleagues, to realise their habitus and rethink their taken-for-granted use of English in international academia. By dint of the crisis, our doctoral workshop becomes an empowering social space to engage in critical linguistics that enables doctoral students and educators to grapple with foundational questions about how language uses and choices "shape a version of material, natural, and sociopolitical worlds ... and establish relations of power" (Luke, 2012, p. 8). More importantly, we consider the crisis to be a gainful opportunity for doctoral educators and students to engage in reflexive work that helps to transform linguistic habitus into what Luke (2019, p. 160) conceptualises as "intercultural capital", that is, "the capacity to engage in acts of knowledge, power, and exchange across time/space divides and social geographies, across diverse communities, populations, and epistemic stances".

We also have some practical reflections. First, it is important for non-native English-speaking academics, ourselves included, to feel comfortable at international academic meetings (e.g., conferences, seminars, and workshops). We should confidently express our identities as who we are, rather than feel marginalised on account of our "non-standard" accents, inadequate English proficiency, or culture-specific communicative styles. We have great bilingual colleagues and open-minded monolingual colleagues who appreciate our proficiency in another language. Second, it is important for native English-speaking academics to take seriously the taken-for-granted authority of English in the field of higher education. We have made every possible effort to become academically literate in more than one language. However, the bulk of our native English-speaking colleagues seems to make little effort in this regard. The number of monolingual Anglophone academics is noticeable, and perhaps growing (Ammon, 2006). Having said that, we do not expect the linguistic dominators to speak the language of the linguistic minorities. Rather, we suggest the linguistic dominators to engage in reflexive sociological work, to reflect on their assumed and often misrecognised superiority, and most importantly, to modify their linguistic habitus. At international academic meetings, it is not uncommon for us non-native English speakers to receive comments like "Wow, you speak good English!" from our native English-speaking colleagues. We acknowledge such compliments, but we argue that this moral condescension is no different from patronising us. We would like our native English-speaking colleagues to engage more with our scholarship rather than our linguistic attributes. We also hope that these colleagues would consider adjusting their speech and making their slides and handouts more linguistically facilitative. The overuse of visuals and underuse of words make their presentation fancy but less helpful and useful for conveying their ideas to non-native English speakers. Third, it is important for conference program planners to create opportunities for informal communication between conference participants. Such informal communication, as our data shows, has strong potential to reduce inequality brought about by uneven distribution of linguistic capital – English in this case – in formal communication (e.g., conference presentation).

The contemporary dominance of English is, in all probability, a time-bound phenomenon. Other lingua francas may replace English in the future. Therefore, linguistic dominance of whatever language will continue to challenge international academia. Within the field of higher education, how can we do justice to *all* linguistic communities? Real solutions will take time but warrant effort. Although we are not very clear about what to do, we are clear about what not to do. We should, for all practical purposes, deviate from linguistic imperialism. Neither is it a good solution to close ourselves within our own national school, because linguistic chauvinism is as dangerous as linguistic imperialism. Equally problematic is academic multilingualism which is too expensive to achieve. That said, academic communities with bi/multilingual potential, such as Hong Kong, Singapore, and Scandinavia, are at a good place to lead this work. Our sociological study calls for a bottom-up approach. At the individual level, colleagues who read this chapter may rethink the widespread use of English in international academia. At the institutional level, we hope that universities, research institutions, governments, funding agencies, potential bi/multilingual academic communities, and powerful international organisations (e.g., OECD, UNESCO) will all engage in discussions of using English in international academia.

We want to make a final remark before we conclude this chapter. The epistemological logic behind our use of Bourdieu is very much like that behind our use of English at the workshop. It is not a coerced but a co-opted use. We are not colonised by Western theories and languages. Instead, we are social agents with epistemological aptitude who are able to use Western tools according to our own interest and understanding. In an era when power relations between the East and the West are shifting, the West no longer towers over the East. Postcolonial concern and guilt about Westernisation is not necessary. Neither is it necessary to panic about the Western "invasion". By virtue of the epistemological aptitude, we are able to critically engage in, and respond to, Western tools.

Note

1 In May 1998, the Central Government initiated a project to promote the development of world-class universities in China. This is the so-called "985 Project". The Project provides significant financial support to a cohort of selected universities (currently 39).

Reference

Altbach, P.G. (2007). The imperial tongue: English as the dominating academic language. *Economic and Political Weekly*, *42*(36), 3608–3611.

Ammon, U. (2006). Language planning for international scientific communication: An overview of questions and potential solutions. *Current Issues in Language Planning*, *7*(1), 1–30. doi: 10.2167/cilp088.0.

Berg, E.C., Hult, F.M., & King, K.A. (2001). Shaping the climate for language shift? English in Sweden's elite domains. *World Englishes*, *20*(3), 305–319.

Bourdieu, P. (1977). *Outline of a theory of practice* (R. Nice, Trans.). Cambridge: Cambridge University Press.

Bourdieu, P. (1986). The forms of capital. In J.G. Richardson (Ed.), *Handbook of theory and research for the sociology of education* (pp. 241–258). New York: Greenwood Press.

Bourdieu, P. (1988). *Homo academicus* (P. Collier, Trans.). Stanford: Stanford University Press.

Bourdieu, P. (1990a). *In other words: Essays towards a reflexive sociology* (M. Adamson, Trans.). Stanford: Stanford University Press.

Bourdieu, P. (1990b). *The logic of practice* (R. Nice, Trans.). Cambridge: Polity Press.

Bourdieu, P. (1991). *Language and symbolic power* (G. Raymond & M. Adamson, Trans.). Cambridge: Polity Press.

Bourdieu, P. (1993). *The field of cultural production*. Cambridge: Polity Press.

Bourdieu, P. (1996). *The rules of art: Genesis and structure of the literacy field* (S. Emanuel, Trans.). Stanford: Stanford University Press.

Bourdieu, P. (1998a). *On television* (P.P. Ferguson, Trans.). New York: The New Press.

Bourdieu, P. (1998b). *Practical reason: On the theory of action* (R. Johnson, Trans.). Cambridge: Polity Press.

Bourdieu, P. (2000). *Pascalian meditations* (R. Nice, Trans.). Cambridge: Polity Press.

Bourdieu, P. (2005). Habitus. In J. Hillier & E. Rooksby (Eds.), *Habitus: A sense of place* (2nd ed., pp. 43–49). Aldershot: Ashgate Publishing Limited.

Bourdieu, P. (2007). *Sketch for a self analysis* (R. Nice, Trans.). Chicago: University of Chicago Press.

Bourdieu, P., & Wacquant, L.J.D. (1992). *An invitation to reflexive sociology*. Cambridge: Polity Press.

Brock-Utne, B. (2001). The growth of English for academic communication in the Nordic countries. *International Review of Education*, *47*(3/4), 221–233.

China Association for Science and Technology. (2008). 学术会议过程与使用语言研究 [The process and language use at academic conferences]. Beijing: China Science and Technology Press.

China Education Association for International Exchange. (2015). *Internationalisation of higher education in China 2015*. Beijing: China Education Association for International Exchange.

Coleman, J.A. (2006). English-medium teaching in European higher education. *Language Teaching*, *39*(1), 1–14. doi: doi:10.1017/S026144480600320X.

Coulmas, F. (2007). English monolingualism in scientific communication and progress in science, good or bad? *AILA Review*, *20*(1), 5–13. doi: 10.1075/aila.20.03cou.

Earls, C.W. (2013). Setting the Catherine wheel in motion: An exploration of "English-ization" in the German higher educastion system. *Language Problems & Language Planning*, *37*(2), 125–150.

Enrique Hamel, R. (2007). The dominance of English in the international scientific periodical literature and the future of language use in science. *AILA Review*, *20*(1), 53–71. doi: 10.1075/aila.20.06ham.

212 Guanglun Michael Mu et al.

Ferguson, G. (2007). The global spread of English, scientific communication and ESP: Questions of equity, access and domain loss. *Ibérica, 13*(Spring), 7–38.

Flowerdrew, J., & Li, Y. (2009). English or Chinese? The trade-off between local and international publication among Chinese academics in the humanities and social sciences. *Journal of Second Language Writing, 18,* 1–16.

Gagan, M., & Wallace, R. (2001). *Making a presentation in English at a European conference.* Aveiro: Federation of European Chemical Societies.

Gogolin, I. (2002). Linguistic and cultural diversity in Europe: A challenge for educational research and practice. *European Educational Research Journal, 1*(1), 123–138.

Hashemi, M., & Hokmabadi, M. (2011). Effective English presentation and communication in an international conference. *Procedia – Social and Behavioral Sciences, 30*(2011), 2104–2111.

Jay, A. (1970). *Effective presentation: The communication of ideas by words and visual aids.* London: Management Publications Limited.

Jiang, X., Borg, E., & Borg, M. (2017). Challenges and coping strategies for international publication: Perceptions of young scholars in China. *Studies in Higher Education, 42*(3), 428–444. doi: 10.1080/03075079.2015.1049144.

Ljosland, R. (2007). English in Norwegian academia: A step towards diglossia? *World Englishes, 26*(4), 395–410.

Luke, A. (2012). Critical literacy: Foundational notes. *Theory into Practice, 51*(1), 4–11. doi: 10.1080/00405841.2012.636324.

Luke, A. (2019). *Educational policy, narrative, and discourse.* London: Routeldge.

Mauranen, A. (2003). The corpus of English as lingua franca in academic settings. *TESOL Quarterly, 37*(3), 513–527.

McArthur, T. (1992). *The Oxford companion to the English language.* Oxford: Oxford University Press.

Mu, G.M. (2016). *Learning Chinese as a Heritage Language: An Australian perspective.* Bristol: Multilingual Matters.

Mu, G.M., & Dooley, K. (2015). Coming into an inheritance: Family support and Chinese Heritage Language learning. *International Journal of Bilingual Education and Bilingualism, 18*(4), 501–515. doi: 10.1080/13670050.2014.928258.

Mu, G.M., & Hu, Y. (2016). *Living with vulnerabilities and opportunities in a migration context: Floating children and left-behind children in China.* Rotterdam: Sense.

Mu, G.M., Jia, N., Hu, Y., Hughes, H., Shi, X., Zhang, M.,. . . Xia, H. (2016). Generating benefits and negotiating tensions through an international doctoral forum: A sociological analysis. *International Journal of Doctoral Studies, 11,* 63–85.

Norton, B. (2001). Non-participation, imagined communities and the language classroom. In M.P. Breen (Ed.), *Learner contributions to language learning: New directions in research* (pp. 159–171). Essex: Pearson Education.

OECD. (2017). *Education at a glance: OECD indicators.* Paris: OECD Publishing.

Pavlenko, A., & Norton, B. (2007). Imagined communities, identity, and English language learning. In J. Cummins & C. Davison (Eds.), *International handbook of English language teaching* (pp. 669–680). New York: Springer.

Pennycook, A. (1994). *The cultural politics of English as an international language.* Harlow: Longman.

Phillipson, R. (1992). *Linguistic imperialism.* Oxford: Oxford University Press.

Skutnab-Kangas, T. (2003). Linguistic diversity and biodiversity: The threat from killer languages. In C. Mair (Ed.), *The politics of English as a world language: New horizons in postcolonial cultural studies* (pp. 31–52). Amsterdam: Rodopi.

Swaan, A.D. (2001). *Words of the world: The global language system*. Cambridge: Polity Press.

Swales, J. M. (1997). English as Tyrannosaurus Rex. *World Englishes, 16*(3), 373–382.

UK/US Study Group. (2009). *Higher education and collaboration in global context: Building a global civil society*. London: UK/US Study Group.

Wacquant, L.J.D. (1989). Towards a reflexive sociology: A workshop with Pierre Bourdieu. *Sociological Theory, 7*(1), 26–63.

Wallwork, A. (2010). *English for presentations at international conferences*. Dordrecht: Springer.

Wang, S., & Zhao, W. (2004). English and the humanities in China. In Q.S. Tong, W. Shouren, & D. Kerr (Eds.), *Critical zone 1: A forum of Chinese and Western knowledge* (pp. 69–78). Hong Kong: Hong Kong University Press.

Wenger, E. (1998). *Communities of practice: Learning, meaning, and identity*. Cambridge: Cambridge University Press.

Xiao, J., & Peng, G. (2008). 国际学术会议的语言及其效果研究 [Language use and its effectiveness in the international academic conferences]. In C.A.f.S.a. Technology (Ed.), *学术交流质量与科技研发创新* [Academic exchange and science and technology innovation] (pp. 93–101). Beijing: China Academic Journal Electronic Publishing House.

Yang, R. (2005). The Chinese professoriate in comparative perspective: Self-perceptions, academic life, gender differences and internal differentiation. In A.R. Welch (Ed.), *The professoriate: Profile of a profession* (pp. 179–192). Dordrecht: Springer.

11

LEARNING TO THEORISE FROM BOURDIEU

Using *Zhōng wén* (中文) in English for Research Publication Purposes

Michael Singh

Introduction

Across every discipline in many countries where researchers' first language is not English, there is pressure on them to disseminate their research through publications in academic English (López-Navarro et al., 2015; Rezaeian, 2015). As Bourdieu and Passeron (1994/1965, p. 8) reminded us, "academic English" is no one's "mother tongue". Fifty years later, this is a significant point given that postcolonial migrants, post-Cold War refugees, and international students have increased the number of students capable of translanguaging practices in English-medium universities. Now, education is about the tensions between imposing provincial English-only habits onto these students, and translanguaging practices that offer the potential for enhancements in research and knowledge production (Verran, 2001).

However, English-medium universities have not moved in the direction of post-English-only approaches that add value to students' translanguaging practices. Disseminating research through English-medium publications has become a marker of researchers' academic performance and worth, to the neglect of their translanguaging practices. *Higher degree researchers* (HDRs) are encouraged to do likewise as part of their candidature. The pressure from the state and universities for English-medium publications now surpasses researchers' professional desire to disseminate their research to global scholarly communities (Ge, 2015). Comparative ratings of nation states' knowledge-producing capacity sustain innovations which put English first, as do international rankings of universities and the international marketing of English-medium education.

Methods of research writing are difficult even for researchers working in their first language. For researchers in *Zhōng guó* (中国, China), their efforts to publish in English can be perplexing. Even rewriting research already published in *Zhōng wén* (中文, Chinese language) for publication in international English-medium journals can be a struggle (Cargill, O'Connor, & Li, 2012). Researchers who use *Zhōng wén* in their everyday academic work can find disconcerting the challenges to meet the academic English requirements of journal editors, reviewers, and readers. These challenges include the added intellectual demands of translating concepts from *Zhōng wén* and writing research in academic English, with its peculiar register and genres, thus demanding a large investment of time (e.g., Bai, Millwater, & Hudson, 2012; Kim & Lim, 2013; Yang, 2013).

Not surprisingly, the pressure for researchers in *Zhōng guó* to contribute to global knowledge production by writing for English-medium research journals has created an opportunity for monolingual English-medium universities to market a new field of knowledge. In Australia, the long-term disinvestment in funding public university education by a serial coalition of Labour–Liberal governments drives this commodification of English. The problems many researchers from *Zhōng guó* face in producing papers acceptable for publication in such journals, and the pressure on them to comply with their university's publication performance requirements, have led to the creation of *English for research publication purposes* (ERPP). The government of *Zhōng guó* invests public taxes in funding ERPP training programs for its researchers. The focus of ERPP training is on putting into practice the principles for writing research in academic English (Corcoran & Englander, 2016).

ERPP training sees researchers learning strategies to make papers readable in academic English through creating coherent and cohesive structures. They learn to demonstrate their original contributions knowledge by indicating how findings differ from those currently available in English-language literature (Wallwork, 2011). Likewise, they make improvements in their English-medium research papers by actively reading publications in English in their own disciplines. Active reading entails underlining archetypal phrases that express various formulaic language functions, noting the structuring of research papers, and using segments of published papers as templates.

Research into ERPP training programs reports increases in researchers' competence in writing in academic English (Geiger & Straesser, 2015). However, a major concern is evident in the case made for ERPP. Corcoran and Englander (2016) explained that the rationale for ERPP is "the increasing demands on many [post-English-only] scholars outside the centre(s) of scientific knowledge production to publish their research in international [English-medium] scholarly journals" (p. 1). In other words, ERPP imposes English as the dominant language for disseminating the world's research and uses its dominance in global knowledge production to reinforce that dominance. In Bourdieu's (1999) terms, ERPP entails "the imposition of the dominant principle of domination" (p. 227). Publishing research in English is largely (but not exclusively) for monolingual English-speaking editors, reviewers, and

216 Michael Singh

readers, situated in reference to research already published in English. Now that English commands the attention of governments, universities, and researchers throughout the world, the problem is that as "an 'authorized language,' invested with the authority of [largely monolingual English-speaking researchers], the things it designates are not simply expressed but also authorized and legitimated" (Bourdieu, 1977, p. 170).

Three characteristics of monolingual English-speaking researchers are relevant to this study. First, they work with research published in English, the language of knowledge production. Second, some have a "monolingual mindset" (Creagh, 2017; Ndhlovu, 2015), seeing research through what they insist are the norms of academic English, or holding this to be the only language in which worthwhile research is produced and disseminated, or opposing the use of any other language for research. Third, some monolingual English-speaking researchers contest monolingual English-only instruction, research, and management. This move entails working to add value to knowledge production through inviting HDRs to employ knowledge from their own languages to create meaning and explore what such "translanguaging practices" (García & Wei, 2014) mean for learning transformation. Together, these ideas inform a proposal for what a post-English-only approach to ERPP could look like for researchers from *Zhōng guó*. Likewise, for monolingual English-speaking researchers, translating their research into other languages makes possible its dissemination to a diversity of scholars (Hoffecker & Abbey, 2017).

Emerging trends in global knowledge production contradict the imposition of English as the dominant principle for research dissemination, and thus the dominant vehicle for generating advances in knowledge (Hollingsworth, Müller, & Hollingsworth, 2008). *Zhōng guó*, for instance, is now a knowledge-producing superpower, making advances in science and technology (Gupta, 2016). Researchers in Australian universities conduct world-leading projects with researchers from *Zhōngguó* in artificial intelligence, supercomputing, driverless cars, and military technology (Iggulden, 2017). That researchers from Australia and *Zhōng guó* report on their research in English-medium journals ignores the asymmetry in global knowledge production, especially that being generated in *Zhōn gwén*. In part, the rationale for teaching students throughout the world how to learn *Zhōng wén* is to engage with *Zhōng guó* as a knowledge-producing superpower.

Some researchers working in fields related to ERPP have raised concerns about the imposition of English-medium research publications as the dominant principle for dominating global knowledge production (Alatas, 2006; Chen, 2010; García & Wei, 2014; Rancière, 2015). This research provides resources to guide disruptive innovations in using ERPP. This chapter addresses possibilities for post-English-only approaches to ERPP. Here, "post-English-only" refers to researchers extending their capabilities for theorising by using their full linguistic repertoire when publishing research in English. Such approaches make a theoretical advantage of researchers' translanguaging capabilities while accommodating the norms governing research writing in English, given the tensions posed by the asymmetrical press for global production and dissemination of knowledge in English. With an estimated 6,000 languages throughout the world, most countries have multilingual populations. Like Australia, *Zhōng guó* is a multilingual country (Liang, 2014). Many researchers in *Zhōng guó* speak *Zhōng wén*, English, and other minority or international languages. A minority of the world's researchers practice English-only monolingualism.

This chapter arises from a longitudinal investigation into a post-English-only approach to ERPP (Singh, 2018). Securing legitimacy for theorising in *Zhōng wén* in English-medium universities requires positioning within scholarly tradition. This study is situated in reference to Bourdieu's (1977, 1993, 1999, 2004) efforts to share his French concepts with monolingual English-speaking academics, albeit with the aid of translators. Bourdieu (1991) understood languages to be socio-linguistic phenomena, which are differentially valorised, with educational proficiency in languages being defined by institutionalised mechanisms rooted in linguistic hierarchies that structure the production and communication of human knowledge. By considering the dissemination of Bourdieu's French concepts in English-medium publications, it is possible to discern lessons for using analytical tools in *Zhōng wén* through research publications in English to report something new or distinctive. Taking a theory-building perspective (Swedberg, 2017), this study was designed to extend the capabilities of HDRs for theorising by using aphorisms in *Zhōng wén* as analytical tools when writing research for publication in English. This study provides grounds for considering what such a post-English-only ERPP program could look like in the context of *Zhōng guó* being a global knowledge-producing superpower.

French Conceptual Tools in English for Research Publication Purposes

For me, the importance of Bourdieu's research lies in how he engaged in theorising, more than his analytical concepts (Singh, 2010; Singh & Han, 2010). However, this research was undertaken when my knowledge was slight; with the extension of my studies, this chapter brings forward and reworks these ideas from that research (Singh & Huang, 2013). The significance of Bourdieu's theorising resides in "the manner in which he produced, uses, and relates … concepts, substantive theories, methodological prescriptions, or empirical observations" (Wacquant, 1992, p. ix). Practically, theorising entails using metaphors as conceptual tools to generate propositions that provide insights into a given phenomena (Swedberg, 2017). Rather than applying a predetermined theory, Bourdieu used metaphors as tools to analyse and enrich the meaning made of phenomena he investigated. This section considers lessons from Bourdieu's efforts to have the conceptual tools he produced in French disseminated via English-medium research publications by HDRs using aphorisms in *Zhōng wén*.

218 Michael Singh

Collective Contributions to Theorising

For Bourdieu (2004), theorising relies "on collective experience regulated by norms of communication and argumentation" (p. 72). Theorising benefits from the collective knowledge-producing capabilities of the world's post-English-only researchers regulated by norms of translanguaging practices for communicating and making scholarly arguments for the conceptual resources generated through their research. Thus, theorising involves a "reflexivity reflex" (Bourdieu, 2004, p. 89), whereby the meaning made of evidence and counter-evidence serves to generate and test analytical tools. To mediate if not mitigate complacency, self-indulgence, and narcissistic reflexivity, one's scholarly community, both locally and internationally, subjects researchers' analytical concepts to critiques. As Bourdieu (2004, p. 83) explained, theorising involves

> collective process performed before an audience and subject to rules ... a peer group that is both very critical—the group for whom one writes, and the most daunting of audiences—and very reassuring—the group that underwrites and backs up (with references) and provides guarantees of the quality of the products.

Challenging Bourdieu's (2004) conceptual tools accords with his own scholarly ethos of mobilising collective critique to test and improve researchers' theorising. Not surprisingly, critiques have been advanced against Bourdieu's (1977) research (e.g., Goodman & Silverstein, 2009; Silverstein, 2004; Yacine, 2004). These critiques question the practice of collecting data in countries such as *Zhōng guó* and making exclusive use of theories disseminated in English (or those translated from French) for data analysis (Alatas, 2006; Chen, 2010).

Alternative approaches are possible. Scribner and Cole's (1981) study indicated that Vai literacy learners in Liberia have the capability for theorising, evident in tasks involving logic, reasoning, taxonomic categorisation, and metalinguistic reflection on knowledge about language. Rejecting any presumed divide between data collection and theory generation, post-English-only literacy education can extend these capabilities. Further, Street's (1984) study of Iranian villagers showed that literacy is a socially grounded practice, challenging mistaken assumptions that reduce literacy to mechanical or technical skills. Economic, political, and social factors adhere to literacy practices, which are affected by the mobilisation for changes in these domains. For English-medium universities enrolling ever more post-English-only HDRs, this research suggests that extending their capabilities for theorising is as important as learning mechanical techniques. Through translanguaging practice, they can use their linguistic repertoire to deepen their capabilities for theorising, capabilities needed for making original contributions to knowledge.

However, literature on ERPP says little about enabling flows of theoretical knowledge from the field of production in one language for dissemination in

Learning to Theorise from Bourdieu **219**

English-medium research publications (Corcoran & Englander, 2016; Wallwork, 2011). For Bourdieu (1999), the reason is that "competitors ... often have a hidden interest in not understanding, or even in preventing understanding from taking place in others" (p. 221). It is not in the interest of ERPP programs to incorporate theoretical knowledge from other languages because of the competitive market advantage to be had in preventing understanding that theorising occurs in other languages. Intellectual competitors, Bourdieu (1999) contended, "constantly peddle prejudices, stereotypes, received ideas, and hastily simplistic representations which are fuelled by ... misunderstandings, general incomprehension, and wounded pride" (p. 220). A focus on HDRs' technical research skills fuels incomprehension of theory and theorising (Swedberg, 2017), while reinforcing prejudices against theorising in other languages (Shusterman, 1999).

Bourdieu (1999) understood that the theoretical resources he generated in French are used in English in ways such that what they say does not matter, "so much as what they can be made to say" (p. 224). In the international competition for knowledge production and dissemination, ERPP comprises "the imposition of the dominant principle of domination" (Bourdieu, 1999, p. 227). For researchers in *Zhōng guó*, the dominant principle of domination is that English-medium journals are the vehicle for publishing their research, provided it references theories disseminated in English. Innovations that shore up the academic value of research published in English sustain the dominant principle of domination. Domination is effected through assigning status by ranking journals, identifying needs of researchers in *Zhōng guó* for training in how to publish research in English-medium journals, promoting new commodities such as ERPP training, and struggling to protect the dominant position of English within the international education market. However, the commoditisation of Australian education due to the coalition of Labour–Liberal governments' disinvestment in funding its universities undermines their capability to resist threats to their integrity by local and international corporate and political interests.

Translating Conceptual Tools

Scholars confront challenges in translating Bourdieu's concepts from French to English. Focusing on cross-sociolinguistic similarities and overlapping principles of theorising establishes plausible bridgeheads for translanguaging. The translation of French concepts into English alters their meaning as much as the socio-historical changes associated with the time delays taken for translations. These socio-historical effects strain contextual differences in understanding Bourdieu's concepts. This is evident in the 30-year delay between the 1965 publication in French of *Rapport Pédagogique et Communication* and its publication in English as *Academic Discourse: Linguistic Misunderstanding and Professional Power* (Bourdieu, Passeron, & Martin, 1994/1965). The evident changes in the titles suggest that conceptual divergences are more important than any literal or direct translation.

220 Michael Singh

Likewise, Bourdieu's use of the French word *méconnaissance* challenged the translator, given that "misrecognition" does not capture its rich meaning. To express this term as an analytical concept in English, the translator gave it a "specific scientific sense" (Nice, 1977b, p. xxvi) by making recurrent use of *méconnaissance* throughout *Reproduction in Education, Society and Culture* (Bourdieu & Passeron, 1990).

Written in academic French, Bourdieu's (1999) theories contributed to, and bore the marks of France's intellectual traditions, scholarly arguments, and public policy debates. Specially, the field of production for Bourdieu's early French conceptual tools was imperial France and its colony, Algeria. Scholarly and public debates in France saturated the field of knowledge production, some of which Bourdieu, his translators, and readers overlooked, or took for granted. The lack of details about the context of theory production can pose challenges. Consider, for example, *Outline of a Theory of Practice*, a product of Bourdieu's (1977) early empirical studies:

> Fieldwork in Kabylia which provided the ethnographic basis for this text and the starting-point for its reflections was carried out amid the tragic circumstances of the Algerian war [which] brought to a head the contradictions inherent in the ethnologist's position.
>
> *(Nice, 1977a, p. vii)*

Although the theorising in *Outline* was a product of Bourdieu's position in France's war against Algeria's national liberation, this is not necessarily evident in the book itself. Bourdieu (1977) undertook his research in the Algerian resettlement camps to which the French military moved the Kabyles. However, *Outline* does not refer to Bourdieu being part of the 400,000-strong French military involved in the Algerian War of Independence that ended France's 130 years of colonial rule. Bourdieu produced his theorising about the Kabyles' experiences in the context of the many anticolonial wars fought by imperial France (Goodman & Silverstein, 2009; Silverstein, 2004). However, *Outline* did not engage the Kabyles' theorising about imperialism, colonialism, militarism, nationalism, liberation, or independence (Lane, 2000; Yacine, 2004).

Outline is "open to misreading" (Nice, 1977a, p. viii) for various reasons, in part because details of the context of production are not included in the translated text. Originally published in French in 1970, *Reproduction in Education, Society and Culture* (Bourdieu & Passeron, 1990), wrote *against* the structural Marxism advanced by Althusser (1969). Bourdieu's innovative efforts to transcend or otherwise break out of Althusserian theorising appear contradictory and eclectic (Nice, 1977a, p. viii). While intending to combat the structuralist perspective, it ensnared Bourdieu's theorising, especially with their international circulation in English. His theorising amounted to no more than the claim that institutions of the state, schools, and universities function to reproduce the viability of capitalism.

Monolingual English-speaking Scholars' Reception of French Analytical Concepts

Integral to the publication of analytical concepts in French or *Zhōng wén* in English-medium research journals is their reception and engagement by monolingual English-speaking editors, reviewers, and researchers. For example, monolingual English-speaking researchers questioned Bourdieu's (1977) concept of habitus by drawing attention to the problematic relationship between concepts generated in another language and their dissemination in English-medium research publications. For Lane (2000), the Bourdieusian concept of "habitus" means that the Kabyles had a disposition to position themselves as tradition bound, and this habitus structured their sense of "what can or cannot be achieved based on intuitions gained through past collective experience" (p. 25). Likewise, Fowler (1997) understood habitus as meaning that the Kabyles "choose actively what they are objectively constrained to do. Thus, they make a virtue out of necessity" (p. 18). In effect, Bourdieu's (1977) concept of habitus positions the Kabyles as relying on their past collective experiences to sustain innovations in their traditions because French colonialism made it necessary for them to do so.

Bourdieu (1977) used the concept of habitus to explain that the Kabyles needed to satisfy their immediate material demands for subsistence. Their habitus was characterised by "temporal immediacy", constraining them to focus on their daily needs (Lane, 2000). Hence, the Kabyles had no time for theorising their conditions of existence under French colonialism. They had no time to theorise what they had come to know of imperial France over the past century or more, or to theorise innovations that might disrupt French colonialism. The "temporal immediacy" of the Kabyles' habitus meant they were bereft of time for "constructing a rational political project for the future" (Lane, 2000, p. 163).

Further, the habitus of the Kabyles made the "cultural reproduction of domination inevitable" (Bohman, 1999, p. 141), irrespective of whether that domination be French or Arab. Moreover, the Kabyles' habitus meant they were unaware of how they themselves reproduced French colonial domination. This lack of awareness meant that they were unable to theorise how to "transform their social world through willed praxis" (Lane, 2000, p. 96). The habitus of the Kabyles constrained them to reproducing their subjugation, such that any self-generated "innovation and transformation [was] improbable and dependent on external social conditions" (Bohman, 1999, p. 141). They had to rely on Bourdieu's (1977) theory to understand the limitations of their habitus and transformative possibilities. However, there are problems in taking habitus to mean that the Kabyles do "not have the capacity for rational calculation which would enable [them] to become a revolutionary force" (Robbins, 1991, p. 26).

The problem here is that forgoing interpretations of Bourdieu's (1977) concept of habitus make it difficult to "account for the emergence of an indigenous liberation movement which [proved] powerful enough to provoke

222 Michael Singh

the downfall of a French Republic" (Lane, 2000, p. 16). Moreover, the rise of the anticolonial liberation movements against France in Algeria (and in Cameroon, Madagascar, Vietnam, and Western Sahara) indicate that some colonised people made the time to theorise imperialism and liberation, even while addressing their immediate needs. Their theorising informed the planning and enactment of their preferred futures outside the French empire. In other words, Algerian anticolonialists suspended their "investment in the immediate self-evidence of everyday life in order to make a rational calculation of possible future gains" (Lane, 2000, p. 21).

A danger in Bourdieu's (1977) *Outline* is reading it as granting colonial researchers capabilities for theorising, while denying colonised peoples the intellectual agency they have for theorising (Bohman, 1999; Fowler, 1997). For example, Bourdieu did not give the Kabyles' aphorisms any "specific scientific sense" (Nice, 1977b, p. xxvi), using them instead as data to advance his own theorising (Yacine, 2004). Importantly, Bourdieu did not have an "ethnocentric belief in a congenital difference between the primitive and the modern mentalities" (Lane, 2000, p. 32). He also attributed the same lack of capability for theorising to the French working class. In contrast, Goodman and Silverstein (2009) and Margolis (1999) contended that theorising is a capability of all peoples. Bourdieu's concept of habitus cannot fully explain the Kabyles' theorising, which produced the innovations, which disrupted French colonialism, and contributed to changes in their conditions of life, problematic though these remain (Roberts, 1982).

Bourdieu (1991, 1999, 2004) along with his translators invested considerable effort to have the conceptual tools he generated in French disseminated via English-medium research publications. His efforts to do so provide useful insights for HDRs from *Zhōng guó* interested in developing their intercultural self-confidence through introducing analytical concepts in *Zhōng wén* into English-medium research publications. To meet the scholarly sensibilities of monolingual English-speaking academics, post-English-only researchers in *Zhōng guó* might consider how they can give metaphors in *Zhōng wén* the sense of being analytical concepts in English-medium journals. To aid the dissemination of concepts produced at a given time and place in *Zhōng wén* via English-medium publications, readers benefit from knowing the relevance of the socio-historical field of conceptual production and understanding how the translation has been produced to accommodate a different time, place, and language.

Here it is important to avoid the genetic fallacy of assuming that the socio-historical context of production decisively determines the meaning and uses of concepts. Specifically, it is a mistake to read Bourdieu's theorising as absolutely determined by French imperialism, colonialism, militarism, and structuralism. This fallacy ignores the challenges of theorising the complexities of a given situation faced by all researchers, given that "there is no position from which to do an objective, detached study of one's own sense of reality" (Dreyfus & Rabinow, 1999, pp. 92–93). Neither past collective experiences of HDRs from *Zhōng guó* nor the objective constraints of today's English-medium research publications deny them using aphorisms in *Zhōng wén* to develop intercultural self-confidence for theorising in *Zhōng wén*, a position from which they can pursue disruptive innovations in ERPP.

The investment made here in debating Bourdieu's (1977) framing of the Kabyles' habitus has been necessary for drawing lessons that might inform HDRs from *Zhōng guó* about developing their intercultural self-confidence through using analytical tools from *Zhōng wén* in ERPP. Bourdieu conducted his research in collaboration with formidable Kabyles intellectuals. His co-researchers and authors included Abdelmalek Sayad, Mouloud Feraoun, and Mouloud Mammeri, who were variously a sociologist, and teachers, poets, and novelists. Designated as informants, they were dependent on the patronage of Bourdieu; their relationship with him bore the scholarly non-reciprocity inherent in French colonialism.

There are, however, two important lessons to be drawn from accounts of these Kabyles intellectuals (Silverstein & Goodman, 2009). First, HDRs from *Zhōng guó* should question Bourdieu's concepts and theorising wherever warranted. These Kabyles intellectuals criticised Bourdieu's ethnographies for lacking attention to the specificities of the Kabyles' uses of their oral traditions and history in responding to their socio-political concerns. Likewise, their rich, textured accounts of the specificities of the Kabyles' life stood in marked contrast to Bourdieu's, even though his own theorising was derivative of scholarly conversations with them. Second, HDRs from *Zhōng guó* should extend their own proclivities for theorising in *Zhōng wén* and English. These Kabyles intellectuals' anti-colonialist theorising about the Kabyles' intellectual culture and modes of critique was informed by the classics produced by ancient Mediterraneans from Greece. Through researching protests and strikes, they theorised about the French colonial occupation as a sociocultural rupture, recognising that postcolonial liberation would not create a *tabula rasa* free of the double yoke of patriarchy and religious authority. A challenge for HDRs from *Zhōng guó* is to mobilise forms of theorising through which they recognise themselves, promote their intellectual flourishing, and build their intercultural self-confidence. The next section briefly considers methods for investigating a pedagogical intervention through which they could learn to invest their research with the added value that comes with theorising.

Notes on Research Methods

This chapter arises from a longitudinal pedagogical study which, beginning in 2006, entailed working with HDRs from *Zhōng guó* to deepen their capabilities for theorising by using their full linguistic repertoire for research publications produced in English (e.g., Gao, 2012; Huang; 2011; Lu, 2017; Meng, 2012; Qi, 2013; Shen, 2017). The coexistence of hundreds of languages in English-medium universities produced through migration and internationalisation

224 Michael Singh

presents opportunities for translanguaging knowledge-producing practices. To do so, it was necessary to explore with these HDRs expected uses of their languages in producing and disseminating knowledge via English-medium publications to an international readership. To engage with the normative constraints that categorise languages as bounded vehicles for knowledge production and dissemination, this educational intervention began by inviting the HDRs' consideration of possibilities for supplementing their labelling as being of "non-English-speaking backgrounds" or as speaking "home" or "community" languages. Labels are sociolinguistic practices used to intervene in and to give effect to the constitution and shape of research.

In response to the force of these insubstantial and elusive labels, they considered what "post-English-only HDRs" might mean for their production of analytical concepts from their full linguistic repertoire to make meaning of the evidence they were analysing. This multiplication of the labels available for these HDRs brought their translanguaging capabilities up against the university's dominant principle of domination expressed through English-medium instruction, research, and management. Strategies used in this educational intervention invited these post-English-only HDRs to extend their creative capabilities for writing research publications that used largely English along with *Zhōng wén*. Moving recursively, they accounted for the productive value of interrelationship among languages, identified the presence of loanwords in English and *Zhōng wén*, and explored divergences in concepts across these languages.

The HDRs who volunteered to participate in this study engaged in an ERPP training program, which was based on four presuppositions (Singh, 2010, 2011). First, the intellectual culture of *Zhōng guó* provides a portfolio of resources – aphorisms, metaphors, and images – which can be given the sense of analytical concepts. Second, HDRs from *Zhōng guó* can extend their capabilities for theorising through using these resources in *Zhōng wén* to analyse the evidence they generate through research conducted largely in English. Third, they can use *Zhōng wén* in research reported in English-medium publications in ways that appeal to the sensibilities of editors, reviewers, and readers. Fourth, for intellectual freedom to have meaning in Australian universities, HDRs who elect to use translanguaging practices to extend scholarly debates should not be restricted, punished, or ostracised. These HDRs explored ways of verifying these presuppositions by drawing insights from Bourdieu's (1977, 1999, 2004) uses of French concepts in English-medium publications. The goals addressed here concerned the place of theorising within the international research community, especially the distribution of the capabilities for theorising within that community, and the relationship between making an original contribution to theorising and publishing in English-medium research journals.

The rationale for researching this educational intervention in ERPP draws on two interrelated fields of research. First, scholars who focus on interrupting academic dependency on theories produced or disseminated in English informed this method (Alatas, 2006; Chen, 2010). The problem of academic dependency, which is driven by English-medium instruction, research, and management, is that it mistakenly assumes the "world as a whole has one permanent centre from which culture changing ideas tend to originate" (Battiste, 2008, p. 184). In other words, the dominant principle of domination produces academic dependency on theories disseminated in English among post-English-only researchers. For HDRs from *Zhōng guó* to think critically about their academic dependency, they can learn from Bourdieu's use of French concepts in English-medium publications, to extend their uses of concepts from their complete linguistic repertoire.

Second, historical evidence of the circulation of Asian and African theoretical ideas throughout Europe informed this research. The intellectual connections throughout *Zhōng guó*, Arabia, and Europe span the centuries (Hobson, 2004). Historical studies indicate that the uneven knowledge flows throughout Eurasia have produced far-reaching heterogeneity in the intellectual assets used for theorising (Goody, 2010). The historical record provides warrant for rejecting claims that Europe or *Zhōng guó* have totally separate homogeneous categories of knowledge (Clarke, 1997). As in the past, *Zhōng guó* has connections to global knowledge-producing networks. As a knowledge-producing superpower, *Zhōng guó* is the focus of intellectual and linguistic desires from beyond its borders. An appreciation of the history of alternations in global flows of knowledge production, dissemination, and appropriation (Goody, 2010; Gordin, 2015; Hobson, 2004) gives warrant to innovations in ERPP that affect translanguage knowledge flows. These disruptions include deepening post-English-only HDRs' capabilities for theorising using their full linguistic repertoire, and mobilising the multiplicity of theoretical resources available across humanity's intellectual cultures and languages.

Bourdieu (1977) used over ninety Kabyle aphorisms as data, analysing them to sustain arguments using his French concepts. Rather than reproducing this approach, this study focused on giving aphorisms in *Zhōng wén* a specific scientific sense as conceptual tools. The aims were to demystify theory and theorising for these HDRs from *Zhōng guó* and to build their intercultural confidence for contributing to international scholarly debates through generation theoretical tools in *Zhōng wén*. A key question for the HDRs who volunteered to participate in this study was what theoretical sense could aphorisms in *Zhōng wén* be given for research publications reported in English. To deal with this quandary, they began by using *chéngyǔ* (成语) or idioms (Mah, 2002) as conceptual tools to analyse evidence generated through their own research. The excerpts presented below indicate their uses of translanguaging practices (García & Wei, 2014) to extend their theorising capabilities. Through translanguaging practices, the post-English-only HDRs made use of their full linguistic repertoire, explicitly integrating *Zhōng wén* and English into their research studies, bringing their translanguaging capabilities and the knowledge it provides them access to out of the shadows. The importance of these excerpts is that they contribute to

226 Michael Singh

evidence of post-English-only HDRs' intellectual enrichment through engaging the dominant principle of domination in ERPP.

Using Zhōngwén Concepts in English-medium Research Publications

For the HDRs in this project, producing theoretical tools from aphorisms available in *Zhōng wén* and using them in research publications produced in English were intellectual challenges. The following excerpt provides insights into reasons for this, including the misrepresentation of the intellectual culture of *Zhōng guó* and prejudice against creating analytical concepts from resources available in *Zhōng wén*:

> I had various concerns about the value of conceptual knowledge from *Zhōng guó* for my research produced in English. These concerns emerged from my knowledge about the importance to me and *Zhōng guó* of undertaking education abroad and doing so in English … By analysing these concerns I extended my disposition towards using conceptual tools from *Zhōng guó* in my research which was undertaken abroad and largely reported in English.
>
> I acquired knowledge from abroad when I started to learn English; I was six years old then. This English-language learning was extended during my studies at a British university in *Zhōng guó* where I was immersed in theoretical knowledge from abroad. When writing essays as a student at that university, I was not encouraged to use theoretical sources from *Zhōng guó*. Too many citations to *Zhōng guó* references led to a minus mark. All students were discouraged from using *hàn zì* (汉字, written script) and concepts in *Zhōng wén*.
>
> *(Mù Tián, 目田)*

This excerpt suggests that as a field of knowledge production, *Zhōng guó* produces no analytical concepts that are worthy of scholarly essays, let alone publication in English-medium research journals. Positioning *Zhōng guó* as a data-mining site makes English the vehicle for sourcing theories for its analysis. Often HDRs from *Zhōng guó* accept this positioning; the expectation is that they do so. In those universities in *Zhōng guó* where education is conducted within an English-only monolingual mindset, students' intercultural confidence in using *Zhōng wén* as a language for theorising is undermined. English-medium instruction fails to extend their capabilities for using conceptual assets in *Zhōng wén* as analytical tools.

However, through study abroad, some HDRs from *Zhōng guó* learn they can make an advantage of their translanguaging capabilities in what are ostensibly English-medium universities. They find that translanguaging practices enable them to work with concepts they know in *Zhōng wén* and then make strategic use of them in research produced largely in English. The following two excerpts theorise how this English-only monolingual mindset imposes constraints on education conducted in *Zhōng guó* and abroad, undermining the intellectual freedom required for using *Zhōng wén* analytical tools:

> 我用了 "traditional" 来形容中国的教学法, 用 "new" 来形容CLT。这个用词也暗示了 我对中国的教学法"没有信心," 因为 traditional 有点贬义在里面, 而 new 又有一点宣扬褒义的成分。在 [British university in China], Chinese knowledge 是不受到推崇的。所以在一个西方国家做学术也好, 教书也好, 我都是很谨慎的运用中国的知识。中国的知识也经常被打上 traditional 的标签, 而西方兴起的教学法常常是 "new"。这可能也是 globalisation 给我们灌输的意识。所以, 我现在本身就是一个矛盾体。

When HDRs developed their ideas in *Zhōng wén*, they included these in their research publications along with their elaboration of these ideas in English. Instead of making a direct or literal translation of the above, this HDR used the preceding ideas as a stimulus to make meaning of the educational dilemma she had come to recognise. She brought these ideas together to extend her entry-level capabilities for theorising:

> Rather than look for research reporting innovative teaching in *Zhōng guó* I used the terms "traditional" to conceptualise the methods for teaching in *Zhōng guó*, and "new" for imported ideas about communicative language teaching. On reflection, this hierarchy suggests my *misrecognition* (Bourdieu, 1977) of theorising in *Zhōng wén* about language teaching as "inferior" to the language education theory produced and disseminated in English. When I was studying at a British university in *Zhōng guó*, knowledge in *Zhōng wén* was refused recognition. *Zhōng wén* and the conceptual tools it provided access to, were rendered unrecognisable, being denied any place in our assignments. Therefore, thinking of knowledge in *Zhōng wén* as inferior became deeply rooted in my mind, my habitus (Bourdieu, 1977). When studying abroad, I was conservatively cautious when it came to producing conceptual tools in *Zhōng wén* for my research. It went without saying that writing and theorising in English was "natural". Knowledge from *Zhōng guó* is always labelled pejoratively as "traditional", while knowledge in English is often labelled approvingly as "new". This idea is informed by the globalisation of knowledge in English. Paradoxically, my research embodied these contradictory elements.

Here, a challenge for HDRs in this study was to verify the presupposition that *Zhōng wén* provides concepts for incorporation into English to make meaning of the evidence they had collected. They had to critically reflect on their

228 Michael Singh

knowledge of aphorisms in *Zhōng wén*, their appropriateness in speaking to the scientific sensibilities of monolingual English-speaking editors, reviewers, and researchers, and the conditions that might make it possible for them to be expressed as analytical tools in research published in English. Understanding that neither English nor French are the world's only sources of analytical concepts tools (Gordin, 2015) built their intercultural confidence in using *Zhōng wén* as analytical concepts and extended their sense of intellectual freedom.

To avoid obscuring the specific scientific sense of an ordinary French word for monolingual English-speaking researchers, Nice's (1977b) strategy was to use Bourdieu's concept of *méconnaissance* without translation. When extracting concepts from their field of production in *Zhōng wén* to give the sense of being analytical tools in English, the HDRs provided additional details as a necessary part of their elaborated translations. The following excerpt illustrates the moves required to use *Zhōng wén* conceptual tools in a largely English-medium research report:

> Philosophical concepts in *Zhōng wén* provided important analytical tools for making sense of evidence about the Australian school culture in which I worked as a volunteer teacher-researcher. To make sense of this situation I used the concept, *yīn dì zhì yí* 因地制宜. Here 因 (*yīn*) means "according to", 地 (*dì*) means "location, places or earth", 制 (*zhì*) means "making" and 宜 (*yí*) means "appropriate plans or measures".
>
> Historically, this concept, *yīn dì zhì yí* 因地制宜, once referred to an agricultural strategy (*dì* means earth). In twenty-first century *Zhōng guó*, this concept has been given a specific urban sense, with *dì* now understood as the natural, sociocultural, and economic environments. Thus, the concept *yīn dì zhì yí* now means that an appropriate plan always has to take local conditions into consideration.
>
> In terms of education in *Zhōng wén*, there is a similar concept, *yīn cái shī jiào* 因材施教 which encapsulates the importance of learners. 因 (*yīn*) means "based on, according to". 材 (*cái*) literally means "the wood which is used as material for building", but is a metaphor for "students". 施 (*shī*), a verb, means "conducting" and 教 (*jiào*) means "education" or "teaching". Thus, students need to be educated to make a contribution to their country – and now the world – just as wood needs to be shaped for building a house. As a whole, the concept *yīn cái shī jiào* means that teachers should conduct their teaching in accordance with students' characteristics and capabilities so they can contribute to their country (e.g. Australia, *Ào dà lì yà*, 澳大利亚) and the world in which *Zhōng guó* is a knowledge-producing superpower. *Yīn dì zhì yí, yīn cái shī jiào* (因地制宜,因材施教) can be used to make sense of possibilities for localising the contents, teaching/learning methods and modes of assessment in teaching Australian school students how to learn *Zhōng wén*.
>
> *(Mi Tu, 米兔)*

To accommodate the distance the aphorism had to travel across languages and intellectual cultures, a little of the field where it was produced was provided as part of the process of elaborating its specific scientific sense. The practice of theorising involves explaining a particular aphorism in *Zhōng wén* in a way that develops its sense as an analytical tool. The sensibilities governing monolingual English-speaking researchers who regard themselves as authorities on what constitutes theorising in English, despite well-established debates, provide the point of reference for these moves (Choi, 2010; Guo & Beckett, 2007). By using such aphorisms as analytical concepts, the HDRs extended their intercultural confidence and capabilities for theorising in *Zhōng wén* and English. They furthered their understanding of the structures, including those governing intellectual freedom, which enabled their production of theoretical tools in *Zhōng wén* for use in English-medium research publications.

The work of educating HDRs from *Zhōng guó* in universities, which privilege English-medium instruction, research, and management, provides evidence and a starting point for thinking critically about the contradictions inherent in this position. There are HDRs from *Zhōng guó* who can theorise about their positioning within the international education market and the positions available to them through the historically informed international education policy of *Zhōng guó*:

> The Government's education policy in Australia claims to realise the importance of its students knowing key regional Asian neighbours. One reason for this is that *Zhōng guó* is Australia's largest trading partner. However, it remains to be seen just how essential monolingual English-speaking researchers in Australia see the need to better understand the theoretical assets of *Zhōng guó*.
>
> The concept *zhī jǐ zhī bǐ, bǎi zhàn bù dài* (知己知彼，百战不殆) is especially relevant here. 知 (*zhī*) means "to know, understand or meet". 己 (*jǐ*) means "myself" and 彼 (*bǐ*) means "other people, a partner or opponent". Thus, the first part of this concept means: "Know the characteristics of one's self, as well as those of one's partners or opponents." 百 (*bǎi*) means "hundred", 战 (*zhàn*) means "war or fighting in a war", 不 (*bù*) means "no or none", and 殆 (*dài*) means "risks". Thus, this part of the *chéngyǔ* 成语 means: "You could fight a hundred times with no failure." However, you should not become involved in fighting a hundred wars. Having its origins in military theory produced in *Zhōng guó*, this aphorism proposes that if people want to win, they must know themselves as well as they know their opponents. That *Zhōng guó* and Australia are trading partners gives import to this proposition.
>
> *Zhōng guó* invests heavily in Australian export commodities such as agriculture, education, energy, technology, and tourism. In this context, the aphorism, *zhī jǐ zhī bǐ, bǎi zhàn bù dài* (知己知彼，百战不殆) means that Australia should know that its key international partner, *Zhōng guó*, has

230 Michael Singh

theoretical tools for explaining global patterns in language-and-knowledge production and dissemination. It should avoid the misrecognition of these. For Australian universities knowing *Zhōng wén* so as to engage in Australia/ *Zhōng guó* theorising is likely to increase mutual understanding.

(Wéi Guān, 围观)

This excerpt indicates that HDRs from *Zhōng guó* are capable of theorising the illusions specific to English-medium universities, which make international education a commodity that works for economic-specific interests. The marketing of monolingual English-medium commodities such as ERPP is but one instance of this agenda. The economic importance of Australian universities being successful in their market engagement via education with *Zhōng guó* is undeniable. International education is a billion-dollar industry, being a mainstay of Australia's economy and a vital part of the Government's economic plans (Australian Government, 2015).

Bourdieu (1993) misrecognised the Kabyles' theorising about France's imperial, colonial, and military power in Algeria and so did not engage with it. Likewise, the Australian Government misrecognises the warrant for intellectual engagement with *Zhōng guó*, which asserts its own agency through international education to become a knowledge-producing superpower. The Australian Government's (2015) international education policy is a mechanism for compensating for its disinvestment in the education of its public. HDRs from *Zhōng guó* apprehend the misrecognition evident in this Australian Government policy. Some theorise about its limitations and contradictions. Of course, Australian researchers are under no illusions about the specific motivations of Australia's government and the manifold shortcomings of its international education policy (Deloitte Access Economics, 2016; McCrohon & Nyland, 2018). Importantly, HDRs from *Zhōng guó* can multiply the positions available for an interested study of internationalising education through ERPP, inserting post-English-only knowledge production into this agenda.

In sum, HDRs from *Zhōng guó* can engage in theorising using conceptual tools they can access in *Zhōng wén* for dissemination in English-medium research publications. Through drawing on their full linguistic repertoire for ERPP, post-English-only researchers can be "reflexive in ways that are crucial for their ability to become aware of and change the conditions under which they act and speak" (Bohman, 1999, p. 140). Through their awareness of the theoretical resources available in *Zhōng wén*, the tensions posed by English-medium instruction, and their capabilities for giving a specific theoretical sense to aphorisms in *Zhōng wén*, they contribute to changing the conditions for publishing research produced in English.

Heterodoxy and Orthodoxy

Here, Bourdieu's (1977) concepts of heterodoxy and orthodoxy are helpful in making sense of ERPP as a field that brings together research education, languages, and theorising through research dissemination. The preceding account suggests that HDRs from *Zhōng guó* can provide leadership for engendering post-English-only approaches to building intercultural self-confidence in theorising in English and *Zhōng wén*. Doing so entails two interrelated moves. First, the heterodox possibilities of researchers using their full linguistic repertoire to make original contributions to knowledge have to be explored. Second, the tensions posed by the orthodoxy of English-only research education and publication have to be investigated in reference to English being both necessary and insufficient for global knowledge production.

Opening up the portability of theoretical assets in *Zhōng wén* entails making it possible for them to move across intellectual cultures, languages, and education institutions. Specifying the analytical sense of aphorisms in *Zhōng wén* for English-medium research publications involves a heterodox string of innovations that disrupt any monolingual mindset. The selection of aphorisms in *Zhōng wén* takes into consideration the explanation required for journals produced for largely monolingual English-speaking researchers. Giving aphorisms in *Zhōng wén* the sense of being analytical tools is integral to appealing to reviewers' sensibilities.

Monolingual English-speaking research educators in English-medium universities can sponsor post-English-only theorising in English-medium research publications. However, this stance means not joining the relatively homogeneous group of agents who control and sustain the power of orthodox English-only monolingualism and who oppose learning transformations that might disrupt the "dominant principle of domination" (Bourdieu, 1999, p. 227). For example, Corcoran and Englander (2016) recommended innovations in ERPP that sustain this orthodoxy, whereby "journal editorial committees ... embrace diverse and divergent forms of English-language research papers" (p. 5). Inserted into the orthodoxy of English-only monolingualism, ERPP is a field occupied by agents who hold positions of power that take writing and theorising in English as the only acceptable ways of contributing to global knowledge production. The professional authority of heterodox agents of post-English-only approaches is stripped away from orthodox elites who impose limits on the languages used for theorising and critical thinking.

However, while orthodox English-only monolingualism is dominant, it does not exist in a state of innocence, but rather it exists only in relation to humanity's linguistic heterodoxy. In many places throughout the world, this orthodoxy has not managed to secure itself as natural or normal, as being above and beyond question, except with violence. Migrant and international education provokes contact with the languages of diverse intellectual cultures that question ERPP. Such contact invites a suspension of innovations to sustain monolingual English-only modes of knowledge production and dissemination. Critiques of English as the dominant principle of theoretical domination echo critiques of English-only hegemony (Alatas, 2006; Chen, 2010). The conventions governing monolingual

232 Michael Singh

English-medium instruction, research, and management are questioned (Macedo, Dendrinos, & Gounari, 2015). The globalisation of *Zhōng guó* provides a necessary condition for questioning the ERPP orthodoxy. However, in itself this is not sufficient for producing post-English-only theorising and research publications. Beyond questioning the orthodoxy of ERPP, there remains the work of publishing much more post-English-only research in English-medium journals for acceptance of this new academic convention.

In Bourdieu's (1977) terms, the state of heterodoxy at play in a world of English-language imperialism (Choi, 2010; Guo & Beckett, 2007) and its associated theoretical colonisation (Alatas, 2006; Chen, 2010; Singh, 2015) signifies the presence of already existing choices. Given dissatisfaction with English-only monolingualism, the existing heterodoxy of humanity's languages sees some post-English-only researchers using their intellectual agency to conduct research which prioritises disruptive innovations necessary for changing the prevailing orthodoxy. The concept of *zhī jǐ zhī bǐ, bǎi zhàn bù dài* (知己知彼，百战不殆) makes explicit an understanding in *Zhōng guó* about the hundreds of possibilities for competition in the world's established educational order. The following propositions might usefully inform moves to do so, as they point to the disruptive rather than reproductive uses of the Kabyles' knowledge for theorising.

For the Tamazight-speaking Kabyles, the following axiom expresses intellectual equality, "The [person] who has no enemies is a donkey" (Bourdieu, 1977, p. 11). Thus, challenging post-English-only researchers to extend their capabilities for theorising by using their full linguistic repertoire "is to credit [them] with the dignity of [scholars] of honour, since the challenge, as such, requires a riposte and therefore is addressed to [researchers] deemed capable of playing the game of honour, and of playing it well" (Bourdieu, 1977, p. 11). Languages make theorising possible. Highly specific versions of languages give form to theories. Theorising can be usefully analysed and better understood in relation to the languages in which researchers produce and receive such knowledge. From Bourdieu's work, researchers from *Zhōng guó* learnt that theorising entails transforming ordinary words into academic language through specifying their definition, context, and use. Forming and informing researchers capable of making positive uses of their full linguistic repertoire contributes to the struggles over languages in English-medium universities, which sanction negative processes for distancing themselves from *Zhōng wén*.

The Kabyles dismiss as dishonourable a challenge to anyone who is incapable of engaging with it: "Better that he should strip himself . . . than that I should unclothe him" (Bourdieu, 1977, p. 11). Thus, monolingual English-speaking researchers dishonour themselves when challenging post-English-only researchers to engage in theorising, but deny them the use of their translanguaging practices. The international languages market incorporates inequalities, sanctions, and censorship which define what languages can and cannot be used for knowledge production and reception. To argue for disruption to the professional learning of monolingual English-speaking research educators and then to challenge a researcher for using pseudonyms in *Zhōng wén* to anonymise the names of Australian schools where she conducted her doctoral studies is an act of bad faith. There is more to the bad faith inherent in this challenge; naming *Zhōng wén* in relation to an imagined monolingual English-only Australian valorises an unnamed linguistic hierarchy. Such bad faith contains Australia's linguistic diversity so as not to disrupt or undermine the domination of English-only monolingualism. The expectation was for the researcher to adjust her intellectual ambition to realise her goal of theorising in *Zhōng wén* and English by wanting what the field of English-only research publication offers her. Through peer review, classifications governing linguistic hierarchies are "translated" into seemingly disinterested academic judgements of merit while reinforcing as unquestionable the legitimacy and maintenance of English-only academic research, processes, and products. However, making apparent the linguistic diversity of Australia's schools through using *Zhōng wén* pseudonyms makes monolingual English-only prohibitions appear less axiomatic or natural. The monolingual mindset is delegitimised. The arbitrariness of seeing English-only research publications as the way of doing research and the way researchers ought to do it is recognised.

For the Kabyles, "the prudent, circumspect [person] does not get involved with [a senseless challenge]" (Bourdieu, 1977, p. 12). Only critical analyses "coming from an equal in honour deserves to be taken up . . . for there to be a challenge, the [researcher] who receives it must consider the [researcher] who makes it worthy of making it" (Bourdieu, 1977, p. 12). Making orthodox English-only monolingualism the "dominant principle of domination" (Bourdieu, 1999, p. 227) evident in ERPP opens its hierarchical order of languages for theorising to challenge. Post-English-only researchers' capabilities for using their full linguistic repertoire to theorise gains legitimacy through them making their experiences of theorising in *Zhōng wén* evident in English-medium journals. Theories are both intellectual currency and educational commodities in the international academic marketplace, where English currently holds a legitimate place in the world's linguistic hierarchy. The manipulation of researchers' linguistic resources contributes to the current domination of English in theorising and research publication. Rather than being unwitting partners, among the dominated are those willing to learn from those who currently dominate global knowledge production in order to compete for this distinction. The educational marketing and consumption of ERPP makes theorising an intrinsically sociolinguistic practice. Questions about the uses of languages in knowledge production and exchange always bring into play multidirectional relations of power and authority, governing the price for making such profitable contributions. Tamazight and *Zhōng wén* are among the world's unequally positioned languages, constituted through competitive struggles over the production, dissemination, and uses of knowledge and the processing of theorising.

"Post-English-only" research, theorising, and publication names practices of translanguaging which exist namelessly in the shadows of English-medium

234 Michael Singh

universities. Post-monolingual ERPP explicitly addresses the need for post-English-only researchers to use conceptual resources from their various languages in English to extend original knowledge production, to deepen their theorising capabilities in those languages, and to publish in sophisticated academic genres in languages othered by English. Centres of global knowledge production exist beyond those in the world's dominant language. Post-English-only researchers can use translanguaging practices to publish their research in international English-medium scholarly journals. Instances of post-English-only theorising which can command attention through publication are invested with the authority of their scholarly community – editors, reviewers, journals, readers, and those who cite the works. The *British Journal of Sociology of Education* and *Compare* are among those English-medium research publications in which theorising in *Zhōng wén* has been expressed (Singh & Han, 2010; Singh & Huang, 2013).

Post-English-only research publications gain legitimacy from the scholarly communities which authorise their dissemination. These innovations in ERPP also engender scholarly communities through the disruption of orthodox English-only monolingual knowledge production and dissemination. Post-English-only researchers verify their claims on intellectual equality from their capability to formulate instances of post-English-only theorising. In offering a means for expressing what is usually repressed, the mobilisation of their translanguaging capabilities announces what they can do, say, and be. Doing, saying, and being a post-English-only researcher rests on a dialectical relationship between those with the power to make English the authoring language for research publications and groups which supplement this position by authorising post-English-only research, theorising, and publication.

Conclusion

Unequal language/theory power relations are evident in the disjunction between humanity's linguistically divergent knowledge production and its asymmetrical dissemination via the use of ERPP. Academic English is not the first or preferred language of the majority of the world's researchers. Post-English-only researchers have a long-term interest in challenging the dominance of English-only instruction, research, and management in universities. To bring their HDRs' translanguaging practices out of the intellectual shadows, monolingual English-speaking academics encourage post-English-only education, despite university management turning against them.

This chapter has guided readers through an inherently complex argument via recursive moves using Bourdieu (1977) to encourage both critical thinking about Bourdieu's work and research informed by the spirit of Bourdieusian theorising. The argument is that translanguaging practices make a post-English-only approach to ERPP an educational possibility in English-medium universities. This is especially so where this approach is used as a vehicle for extending HDRs' theorising capabilities. Australia's English-medium universities have yet to confront willingly their failings in this regard.

Existing approaches to ERPP operate within an English-only monolingual mindset. Even so, such approaches warrant supplementation with more fulsome consideration of the possibilities post-English-only approaches offer researchers tasked with the challenge of publishing their research in English. There is need for further research by post-English-only researchers and their monolingual English-speaking colleagues into using the pressure for ERPP as a vehicle for extending their capabilities for theorising, using their full linguistic repertoire.

Inequities in original knowledge production are growing due to increasing English-language hegemony and homogeneity in using theories produced in English. It is important to understand the changing approaches of those responsible for driving and enacting policy and pedagogy in *Zhōng guó* and abroad. There is a need for studies of the disruptions by post-English-only researchers to the inherently unequal relations of power within global research-driven knowledge production. Future theorising is likely to benefit from extending the collective knowledge-producing capabilities of post-English-only HDRs regulated by norms of translanguaging practices for communicating scholarly argumentation. Using concepts in *Zhōng wén* in English-medium research publications can contribute to the intercultural self-confidence necessary to counter the standardisation and homogenisation of the world's intellectual culture that is being aided by ERPP.

References

Alatas, S. (2006). *Alternative discourses in Asian social science.* New Delhi: Sage.

Althusser, L. (1969). *For Marx.* London: Verso.

Australian Government. (2015). Draft national strategy for international education (For consultation). https://internationaleducation.gov.au/International-network/Australia/InternationalStrategy/Documents/Draft%20National%20Strategy%20for%20International%20Education.pdf

Bai, L., Millwater, J., & Hudson, P. (2012). Chinese teaching English as a foreign language (TEFL) academics' perceptions about research in a transitional culture. *Journal of Higher Education Policy and Management, 34*(1), 91–102.

Battiste, M. (2008). The decolonization of Aboriginal education. In P. Dasen & A. Akkari (Eds.), *Educational theories and practices from the majority world* (pp. 168–195). New Delhi: Sage.

Bohman, J. (1999). Practical reason and cultural constraint. In R. Shusterman (Ed.), *Bourdieu* (pp. 129–152). Malden: Blackwell.

Bourdieu, P. (1977). *Outline of a theory of practice.* Cambridge: Cambridge University Press.

Bourdieu, P. (1991). *Language and symbolic power.* Cambridge: Polity Press.

Bourdieu, P. (1993). *The field of cultural production.* Cambridge: Polity Press.

Bourdieu, P. (1999). The social conditions of the international circulation of ideas. In R. Shusterman (Ed.), *Bourdieu* (pp. 220–228). Malden: Blackwell.

Bourdieu, P. (2004). *Science of science and reflexivity.* Cambridge: Polity Press.

236 Michael Singh

Bourdieu, P., & Passeron, J. (1990). *Reproduction in education, society and culture*. London: Sage.

Bourdieu, P., & Passeron, J. (1994/1965). Language and relationship to language in the teaching situation. In P. Bourdieu, J. Passeron, & M. Martin (Eds.), *Academic discourse* (pp. 1–34). Cambridge: Polity Press.

Bourdieu, P., Passeron, J., & Martin, M. (1994/1965). *Academic discourse*. Cambridge: Polity Press.

Cargill, M., O'Connor, P., & Li, Y. (2012). Educating Chinese scientists to write for international journals. *English for Specific Purposes, 31*(1), 60–69.

Chen, K. (2010). *Asia as method*. Durham, NC: Duke University Press.

Choi, P. (2010). Weep for Chinese university. *Journal of Education Policy*, 25(2), 233–252.

Clarke, J. (1997). *Oriental enlightenment*. London: Routledge.

Corcoran, J., & Englander, K. (2016). A proposal for critical-pragmatic pedagogical approaches to English for research publication purposes. *Publications*, 4, 6. doi:10.3390/publications4010006.

Creagh, S. (2017). Multiple ways of speaking back to the monolingual mindset. *Discourse, 38*(1), 146–156.

Deloitte Access Economics. (2016). *The value of international education to Australia*. Canberra: Australian Government.

Dreyfus, H., & Rabinow, P. (1999). Can there be a science of existential structure and social meaning? In R. Shusterman (Ed.), *Bourdieu* (pp. 84–93). Malden: Blackwell.

Fowler, B. (1997). *Pierre Bourdieu and cultural theory*. London: Sage.

Gao, T. (2012). Shake your amazing body. (Master's thesis). Penrith, NSW: Western Sydney University.

García, O., & Wei, L. (2014). *Translanguaging*. London: Palgrave Macmillan.

Ge, M. (2015). English writing for international publication in the age of globalization. *Publications, 3*(2), 43–64.

Geiger, V., & Straesser, R. (2015). The challenge of publication for English non-dominant-language authors in mathematics education. *For the Learning of Mathematics, 35*(3), 35–41.

Goodman, J., & Silverstein, P. (2009). *Bourdieu in Algeria*. Lincoln: University of Nebraska Press.

Goody, J. (2010). *The Eurasian miracle*. Cambridge: Polity Press.

Gordin, M. (2015). *Scientific babel*. London: Profile Books.

Guo, Y., & Beckett, G. (2007). The hegemony of English as a global language. *Convergence, 40*(1/2), 117.

Gupta, S. (2016). Science superpowers find common ground. *Nature, 539*(7629), S6–S9.

Hobson, J. (2004). *The Eastern origins of Western civilisation*. Cambridge: Cambridge University Press.

Hoffecker, L., & Abbey, D. (2017). From English to Chinese, Japanese, and Russian. *Journal of the Medical Library Association, 105*(1), 49–54.

Hollingsworth, J., Müller, K., & Hollingsworth, E. (2008). China. *Nature, 454*(7203), 412–413.

Huang, X. (2011). *A self-study of a Chinese teacher-researcher's practice of transnational knowledge exchange*. (Master's thesis). Sydney: University of Western Sydney.

Iggulden, T. (2017, December 15). Australian universities accused of sharing military technology with China. *CNN News*. www.abc.net.au/news/2017-12-15/universities-sharing-military-technology-with-china/9260496

Kim, L., & Lim, J. (2013). Metadiscourse in English and Chinese research article introductions. *Discourse Studies*, *15*(2), 129–146.

Lane, J. (2000). *Pierre Bourdieu*. London: Pluto Press.

Liang, S. (2014). *Language attitudes and identities in multilingual China*. Dordrecht: Springer.

López-Navarro, I., Moreno, A.I., Quintanilla, M.Á., & Rey-Rocha, J. (2015). Why do I publish research articles in English instead of my own language? *Scientometrics*, *103*(3), 939–976.

Lu, S. (2017). Chinese modes of critical thinking. (Doctoral thesis). Sydney: University of Western Sydney.

Macedo, D., Dendrinos, B., & Gounari, P. (2015). *Hegemony of English*. London: Routledge.

Mah, A. (2002). *A thousand pieces of gold*. London, England: Harper.

Margolis, J. (1999). Pierre Bourdieu. In R. Shusterman (Ed.), *Bourdieu* (pp. 64–83). Malden: Blackwell.

McCrohon, M., & Nyland, B. (2018, January 12). The perceptions of commoditisation and internationalisation of higher education in Australia. *Asia Pacific Education Review*, 1–10. https://link.springer.com/article/10.1007/s12564-018-9515-z

Meng, H. (2012). *Democratising Australian, Anglophone research education in the face of Eurocentric knowledge transfer*. (Doctoral thesis). Sydney: University of Western Sydney.

Ndhlovu, F. (2015). Ignored lingualism. *Australian Journal of Linguistics*, *35*(4), 398–414.

Nice, R. (1977a). Translator's foreword. In P. Bourdieu (Ed.), *Outline of a theory of practice*. Cambridge: Cambridge University Press.

Nice, R. (1977b). Translator's note. In P. Bourdieu & J. Passeron (Eds.) (1990), *Reproduction in education, society and culture*. London: Sage.

Qi, J. (2013). Critique-based multilingual knowledge co-construction. (Doctoral thesis). Sydney: University of Western Sydney.

Rancière, J. (2015). *The method of equality*. Cambridge: Polity Press.

Rezaeian, M. (2015). How to write and publish a scientific manuscript in English. *Journal of Human Health*, *1*(3), 61.

Robbins, D. (1991). *The work of Pierre Bourdieu*. Buckingham: Open University Press.

Roberts, H. (1982). The unforeseen development of the Kabyle question in contemporary Algeria. *Government and Opposition*, *17*(3), 312–334.

Scribner, S., & Cole, M. (1981). *The psychology of literacy*. Cambridge, MA: Harvard University Press.

Shen, H. (2017). Translanguaging for bilingual educational theorising in higher degree researcher education. (Doctoral thesis). Sydney: University of Western Sydney.

Shusterman, R. (1999). Introduction. In R. Shusterman (Ed.), *Bourdieu* (pp. 1–13). Malden: Blackwell.

Silverstein, P. (2004). Of rooting and uprooting. *Ethnography*, *5*(4), 553–578.

Silverstein, P. & Goodman, J. (2009). Introduction. In J. Goodman & P. Silverman (Eds.), *Bourdieu in Algeria* (pp. 1–62). Lincoln: University of Nebraska Press.

Singh, M. (2010). Connecting intellectual projects in China and Australia. *Australian Journal of Education*, *54*(1), 31–45.

Singh, M. (2011). Learning from China to internationalise Australian research education. *Innovations in Education and Teaching International*, *48*(4), 355–365.

Singh, M. (2015). Against Asia-centric methods. In H. Zhang, P. Chan, & J. Kenway (Eds.), *Asia as method in education studies* (pp. 144–162). New York: Routledge.

Singh, M. (2018). Post-monolingual research methodology. In R. Erwee, M. Harmes, & P. Danaher (Eds.), *Postgraduate education in higher education, university development and administration* (pp. 1–28). Singapore: Springer.

Singh, M., & Han, J. (2010). Peer review, Bourdieu and honour. *British Journal of Sociology of Education, 31*(2), 185–198.

Singh, M., & Huang, X. (2013). Bourdieu's lessons for internationalising Anglophone education. *Compare, 43*(2), 203–223.

Street, B. (1984). *Literacy in theory and practice.* Cambridge, UK: Cambridge University Press.

Swedberg, R. (2017). Theorizing in sociological research. *Annual Review of Sociology, 43,* 189–206.

Verran, H. (2001). *Science and an African logic.* Chicago: University of Chicago Press.

Wacquant, L. (1992). Preface. In P. Bourdieu & L. Wacquant (Eds.), *An invitation to reflexive sociology* (pp. ix–xiv). Chicago: University of Chicago Press.

Wallwork, A. (2011). *English for writing research papers.* New York: Springer.

Yacine, T. (2004). Pierre Bourdieu in Algeria at war. *Ethnography, 5*(4), 487–509.

Yang, Y. (2013). Exploring linguistic and cultural variations in the use of hedges in English and Chinese scientific discourse. *Journal of Pragmatics, 50*(1), 23–36.

12

RE: APPROPRIATING BOURDIEU FOR A SOCIOLOGY OF CHINESE EDUCATION

Guanglun Michael Mu, Allan Luke, and Karen Dooley

Since its foundation in 1949, the People's Republic of China has undertaken successive fundamental changes across the fields of politics, public culture, economy, and education. These fields exist as conjoined and semi-autonomous social spaces, each with its own "logic of practice" (Bourdieu, 1990, p. 80), "functioning in accordance with rigorous mechanisms capable of imposing their necessity on the agents ... who are in a position to command these mechanisms" (Bourdieu, 1977, p. 184). Although agents within a field command the mechanisms of the field, they are rarely constrained altogether within a singular field, neither socially nor temporally, physically nor in geo-location. Human subjects live and work across multiple fields simultaneously. Consequently, despite whatever relative autonomy and boundaries are established in policy or practice, social fields are interlocking, enabling multilayered "cross-field effects" (Lingard & Rawolle, 2004). If we historicise cross-field effects in China, we see the shift of logic of one field leading to fluctuations of another, sometimes by deliberate plan, at times in unintended ways. These concluding remarks recontextualise the analyses of the educational field in this volume in relation to the larger currents of change across contemporary Chinese society and everyday life.

Historically, the ideological and geopolitical alliance between China and the Soviet Union created a practical alignment between the two countries' political systems, economic models, and educational systems. In the field of education, the Chinese tertiary sector was once analogous to that of the Soviet Union. Chinese universities were specialised in particular disciplinary and applied fields (e.g., agricultural, forestry, engineering universities, normal universities) and the works of Soviet theorists like Vygotsky and Kairov were widely used by Chinese educationists (Deng, 2016), who were either fluent in Russian or had ready access to Chinese translations. However, the China/Russia political relationship was ruptured in the 1960s and China's relationship with the West was gradually altered in decade following. It was a historical moment when Chinese higher education began to open to Western theories and schools of thought, with increasing access to original and translated work by Western writers in the sciences, social sciences, and humanities.

Of all Western theorists introduced to China, Pierre Bourdieu is amongst the most influential. Substantive discussion of Bourdieu's sociology by Chinese scholars emerged in the early 2000s, as documented by Shi and Li (Chapter 3) in this volume. Bourdieu's work was initially introduced to China in the late 1970s with the conclusion of the Cultural Revolution and the promulgation of the Reform and Opening-Up Policy. The state had officially declared the Maoist class struggle over, and any social and cultural superiority was claimed to have been eliminated through relentless violence, sweeping revolution, the redistribution of the means of production and, indeed, the ideological purification of the educational system. The belief that China was effectively classless and cultureless was embodied in the new Chinese habitus and state ideological *doxa*. Marxism was reiterated as the theoretical foundation of the Chinese communist revolution and social development. At that historical moment, the dominant claim was that no other Western schools of thought, Bourdieu's sociology included, were needed as priority shifted to economic development.

By his own account, Bourdieu undertook three major economic studies (on the economy of honour in Algeria, and credit and single-family housing in France) (Robbins, 2009; Swedberg, 2011). However, throughout his lifetime, he was better known for his transposition of economic discourse into sociological concepts (e.g., capital, interest, investment, market) in order to theorise hierarchical cultural distinction and social classification. Not surprisingly, in the then officially cultureless, classless, and economy-driven China, Bourdieu's strong focus on the reproduction of distinction, capital and social class, was not considered of particular explanatory power or relevance.

The new ethos of economic development was led by Deng's famous dictum "let some people get rich first". This was a diametric shift from Mao's egalitarianism. Deng's leadership, while conducive to economic growth, set the conditions for the emergence of a *nouveau riche* while the poor struggled in the market economy. There is a widening gap between the urban and the rural, the coastal and the inland, a Han Chinese majority and many cultural minorities, and indeed the rich and the poor. This is viewed as an increasing threat to China's social stability. Hence, the imperatives to address inequality and the achievement of equity have come to the fore of the state agenda (Mu, 2018). While the field of national policy once stipulated economic development as the sole priority, it has now turned towards a view of economic growth *and* social equity – and hence, prosperity with order and stability – as its dual priorities. The change was mirrored in the scholarly field. Over the past decade, much of the debate within Chinese universities and affiliated social science academies has re-centred on the economic bases of social and cultural problems and conflict. Accordingly, Bourdieu's sociology has been put to work in theorising and empirically studying structural inequality and the reproduction and conversion of capital in Chinese society.

Our view is that to understand reproduction and social change requires the empirical study of their interdependence within the fields of the family and the educational system. Our view is that it is not a matter of simply applying or mapping Bourdieu's concepts, models, and ideas upon a distinctive and unique historical, cultural, and social context. This is not a question of getting Bourdieu right, so to speak, or of checking the fidelity of Chinese uses and applications of Bourdieu to date by reference to his originary intents or claims. Although Bourdieu engaged with the classic sociological problem of social reproduction, stasis, and change, his sociology was forged in a half century of research on the decolonisation of Algeria, the social and revolutionary movements in the West of the 1960s, the modernisation of rural France, the massification and diversification of French higher education, and, for the last several decades, the ascendance and crises of neoliberal capitalism. Equally complex upheavals have occurred in China over the past century, and the complexity and ambiguity of social and economic change continues since Xi came into power in 2013. But these events have unfolded from very different historical, cultural, and political economic bases, with different genealogies and patterns.

The concluding notes in this chapter review some of these distinctive issues and differences. What follows is a composite of our discussion notes as we worked through these essays, from our continuing dialogue with our contributors and co-authors, and from our diary exchanges during ongoing lectures and seminars in China. While our work begins from Bourdieu's sociology, this is an opportunity for a parallel reconsideration of Bourdieu's work in the light of reproduction and transformation in Chinese education. Our aim here is a reflexive sociology that weaves between theory and context, the sociological imagination and the facticity of the social and material realities of the new China. Here we explore the grounds for expanding, critiquing, and re-appropriating Bourdieu's ideas as part of the project of a new critical sociology of education in China. With all respect to the field and our Chinese colleagues, this is but a first collective attempt to build new theory and to table new premises, deliberately polemical and speculative, historical and wide-ranging.

On Reproduction and Transformation

The intergenerational transmission of cultural values and normative practices forms the mechanism by which specific social resources and capacities (e.g., class, power, wealth, assets, knowledge, network, reputation) remain durable

242 Guanglun Michael Mu et al.

and sustainable over time (Bourdieu, 1993a). The systems of exchange instantiated by the institutional practices of social reproduction assume and confer, and thereby reassert the power of agents whose authority is used to rationalise that reproduction. At the same time, in part because of the arbitrary nature of this authority, the process "condemns those agents whose province is most limited to a state of perpetual emergency" (p. 123). In contrast to a classical economic determinism, Bourdieu made the case that social reproduction occurs through hidden socialisation and cultural practice, and hence does not operate solely on formal transmission and legal inheritance. It is accomplished in a manner in which participants are not always conscious, even while they are deeply engaged in its logic and quotidian practices, principally through domestic life, kinship relations, and schooling.

It is worth noting that case-based and quantitative sociological studies of reproduction in the West have tended to focus on the field of the school and on pedagogic action – with less extensive empirical study and more general reference to the family as part of the home/school transition, often in relation to cultural and linguistic minorities.[1] This reflects in part the ethical and practical difficulties of the study of everyday domestic and community life, and the relative accessibility for educational researchers to the interactional fields of schooling. But it is also, we would speculate, an artefact of the degree to which the unmarked normative nuclear family, the middle class family, the migrant and minority family, and even its blended millennial, alternative structures are subliminally consecrated fields in the West – positioned as beyond the direct intervention and control of the liberal state and its institutions, especially given a traumatic history of genocidal interventions of the state with Indigenous peoples in North America and Australia, the state-sanctioned White ownership of African-American slaves and now, the forcible break-up of migrant families. Implied relationships between family structure, socialisation, and formation of the habitus leading to unequal and stratified social reproduction – particularly of the minority and socio-economically marginalised habitus – are taken to run the risk of illiberal deficit models, moral and non-secular judgement about the adequacy of parents, parenting and particular family configurations. We raise this as a key point of contrastive analysis – for it would not be possible in China to discuss intergenerational social and economic reproduction, the formation of the habitus, and the making of advantage, privilege, and distinction without talking about the systematic reformation and refashioning of the family by an illiberal, strong state.

According to Bourdieu, family is the primary social site that constructs "one of the major conditions of the accumulation and transmission of economic, cultural and symbolic privileges". He argues that

> The family plays a decisive role in the maintenance of the social order, through social as well as biological reproduction, i.e. reproduction of the

structure of the social space and social relations. It is one of the key sites of the accumulation of capital in its different forms and its transmission between the generations. It safeguards its unity for and through this transmission. It is the main "subject" of reproduction strategies. That is seen clearly in the transmission of the family name, the basic element in the hereditary symbolic capital. The father is only the apparent subject of the naming of his son because he names him in accordance with a principle of which he is not the master, and in transmitting his own name (the name of the father) he transmits an *auctoritas* of which he is not the *auctor*, according to a rule of which he is not the creator. The same is true, mutatis mutandis, of the material heritage. A considerable number of economic acts have as their "subject" not the individual *homo economicus* but collectives, one of the most important of these being the family; this is as true of the choice of a school as of the purchase of a house. For example, in property purchases the decision often involves a large part of the lineage (e.g. the parents of one or the other of the spouses, who lend money and in turn have the right to give advice and influence the economic decision). It is true that, in this case, the family acts as a kind of "collective subject", as commonly defined, and not as a simple aggregate of individuals. But this is not the only case in which it is the site of a kind of transcendent will manifesting itself in collective decisions and in which its members feel required to act as parts of a united body.

(Bourdieu, 1996, p. 23)

We return to this issue of the family, principally and particularly because the traditional Chinese patrilineal extended family – violently disrupted through the Cultural Revolution, then reconstructed into a hybrid nuclear/extended mode through the one child policy, and further spatially reorganised with the coming of the *hù kǒu (户口)* system – is the field of emergence for the new *Homo economicus* of the individuated worker/consumer/citizen. In this regard, the Chinese habitus is a product of the new version of what Bourdieu here refers to as the "collective subject", especially where the combined motive force of traditional Chinese patriarchy and kinship, newly founded private/family "property", urban working parents and absent rural parents, and other forms of individuated capital converge on the formation of the *singular individuated child*, with all that that might imply. There are, further, additional issues of sexism and gender equity raised by the traditional patrilineal preference for the single *male* child, and by the current shift to preference for the *female* child by urban families due to high economic cost of rearing a male child whose family is expected to provide housing as bride price for marriage. Taken as a whole, this social reality underlines the primacy of the social field of the family: that is, as a site where intergenerational relations are defined and structured directly by the strong state, through the law of the father, as well as through the macroeconomic

244 Guanglun Michael Mu et al.

fields of the market economy. This obviously has direct positioning and structuring impacts on the cultural capital brought to (or excluded from) the field of schooling. But moreover, it speaks to the social ontogenesis of relations of power, insofar as the strong state and its doxic blend of socialism and neo-Confucianism rely upon an isomorphism of relations of power in the simultaneous fields of family/school/state/party – now extended in the market economy to include the workplace/enterprise/corporation.

The state, therefore, has engaged in an official consecration of the ethos of the single child, the sole focus of multigenerational home socialisation and, where available, emergent middle class surplus income – as much as the "floating" and "left behind" and "*shǎo shù mín zú*" (ethnic minority, 少数民族) child. These children – with their new second child policy siblings – comprise the new combinatory disposition who enters and leaves, is recognised and misrecognised, is granted access to and/or disbarred from the fields of pedagogic action of the school.

According to Bourdieu, schooling assumes a monopoly over the consecration of previous works and claims hegemony over the production of cultural consumers, only by according that very "infallible mark of consecration, the elevation of works into 'classics' by their inclusion in curricula" (Bourdieu, 1993a, p. 123). Any classics included in the curriculum thus become the hidden curriculum, the structural inertia of which contributes to the maintenance of a routinised and rationalised scholastic culture. The logic of the hidden curriculum "allows it to wield a monopoly over its own reproduction" (p. 123). Bourdieu describes the nature of education:

> The education system reproduces all the more perfectly the structure of the distribution of cultural capital among classes ... in that the culture which it transmits is closer to the dominant culture and that the mode of inculcation to which it has recourse is less removed from the mode of inculcation practiced by the family. Inasmuch as it operates in and through a relationship of communication, pedagogic action directed at inculcating the dominant culture can in fact escape (even if it is only in part) the general laws of cultural transmission, according to which the appropriation of the proposed culture (and, consequently, the success of the apprenticeship which is crowned by academic qualifications) depends upon the previous possession of the instruments of appropriation, to the extent and only to the extent that it explicitly and deliberately hands over, in the pedagogic communication itself, those instruments which are indispensable to the success of the communication and which, in a society divided into classes, are very unequally distributed among children from the different social classes.
>
> *(Bourdieu, 1973, p. 80)*

This would certainly apply to the children of the educated middle class, and those of elite property owning and managerial classes, who arrive at the school with requisite capital intact, recognisable and, where available, enhanced by access to the durable goods of the private and shadow educational economies and, in other cases, by the returning cultural capital of overseas university credentials.

> An educational system which puts into practice an implicit pedagogic action, requiring initial familiarity with the dominant culture, and which proceeds by imperceptible familiarisation, offers information and training which can be received and acquired only by subjects endowed with the system of predispositions that is the condition for the success of the transmission and of the inculcation of the culture. By doing away with giving explicitly to everyone what it implicitly demands of everyone, the educational system demands of everyone alike that they have what it does not give. This consists mainly of linguistic and cultural competence and that relationship of familiarity with culture which can only be produced by family upbringing.
>
> *(p. 80)*

This notion of a dominant culture and its hierarchical relationships to marginalised and minoritised cultures can be taken up at multiple levels, vis-à-vis the unmarked possession of the combinatory capital of Han Chinese compared with that of *shǎo shù mín zú* (ethnic minority) cultures, languages, dialects, accents, and vernacular dispositions, and, in other instances, by reference to the hegemonic power of urban culture whereby the symbolic capital affiliated with Shanghai, Beijing, and other capital city elites has optimal social and economic exchange value.

Following Durkheim, Bourdieu's case is that social reproduction is accomplished first through family inculcation, and second, through school education: "The success of all school education, and more generally of all secondary pedagogic work, depends fundamentally on the education previously accomplished in the earliest years of life" (Bourdieu & Passeron, 1990, p. 43). Yet Zhao and colleagues' work (Chapter 8) complicates Bourdieu's "sequential delineation" (Sriprakash, Proctor, & Hu, 2016, p. 439) of social reproduction, which presupposes a movement from primary *to* secondary socialisation. Their case studies of families of different social classes depict the mutually constitutive effect of family, parenting, and schooling. This effect is at once cross-field, synchronic and speaks to the "structural isomorphism" (Luke, 2018b) of family, schooling, and the strong state. On the one hand, family functions to minimise the social distance between the habitus that it inculcates and the pedagogic practice of schooling. This includes, obviously, culture specific background knowledge, fluency in the *lingua franca*, emergent biliteracy and digraphia with

246 Guanglun Michael Mu et al.

both writing systems (Liu, 2005); but as well, the habits and compulsions of hard work, self-discipline, and time management, respect for authority.[2] On the other hand, high-stakes testing and the examination system set the grounds and incentives for middle and upper-middle class parents to adopt corresponding strategies essential for children's successful competition in the education market and, in cases, for the exploration of offshore alternatives. Even amongst many working class families who lack the surplus income to hire private tutors or, for example, to purchase online English learning resources, the press for success in schooling is used to structure and rationalise the everyday practices, time management, and spoken axioms that guide everyday family life, even in very early childhood.

Bourdieu's reproduction theory is viewed by many as circular and tautological: "My work is often read – misread in my eyes – as deterministic and fatalistic" (Bourdieu & Wacquant, 1992, p. 210). Particularly given the radical economic and cultural shifts that have occurred across the immediate past two generations in China, intergenerational reproduction of habitus in China is necessarily imperfect and contested: the codification and stabilisation of any particular class habitus remains a work in progress. For while Bourdieu began from the analysis of a longstanding and, in their view, ossified and ossifying post-war French class system that was and remains resilient, durable, and resistant to change – the emergent class relations and forms of distinction of the new China are, as Guo and colleagues (Chapter 2) explain, still in formation and somewhat unstable. For example, Zhao et al.'s study documents the emergent individuated habitus that has begun to blend with and, in cases, to supplant the traditional Chinese emphasis on filial duty and supersede the longstanding sublation of individual self-interest to family collective name and face.

In this case, determinism cannot be mistakenly equated with a species of resignation or fatalism; neither does it exclude degrees of freedom, even and particularly in the case of a Chinese society that still is typified by outsiders as an Althussarian iron cage of state determinism. Bourdieu explains:

> The degree to which the social world seems to us to be determined depends on the knowledge we have of it. On the other hand, the degree to which the world is really determined is not a question of opinion; as a sociologist, it's not for me to be "for determinism" or "for freedom", but to discover necessity, if it exists, in the places where it is. Because all progress in the knowledge of the laws of the social world increases the degree of perceived necessity, it is natural that social science is increasingly accused of "determinism" the further it advances. But, ... it's by raising the degree of perceived necessity and giving a better knowledge of the laws of the social world that social science gives more freedom. All progress in knowledge of necessity is a progress in possible freedom.
>
> *(Bourdieu, 1993b, pp. 24–25)*

For Bourdieu, then, the identification, naming, and understanding of both disposition and structural positioning – "knowledge of necessity", or a self-conscious understanding of one's own capital and the prevailing rules of exchange – is a precursor to any volitional position-taking in a social field. What is particularly interesting in the case studies reported by Zhao et al. and in other notable accounts of the educational aspirations and practices of the emergent middle-class (e.g., Yochim, 2016) are the degrees to which both parents and students are developing strategies not just for *gaming* the expectations and assessment systems of schooling to their advantage, but for identifying, naming, and critiquing its taken-for-granted features, practices, and characteristics. In fact, the educational scenario planning of some in the new urban middle and upper classes very deliberately involves pursuit of available alternative credentials that lead directly to university admission outside of China (Liu, 2018). For such families, opting-out of the reproductive systems of Chinese schooling may be construed alternatively as a strategic attempt to reproduce their own distinction and class position *within* China, and/or as an attempt to break out of what they construe as a restrictive (national, domestic) field of exchange and reproduction for themselves and their children. As we will argue later – it is not as if the processes of class reproduction are not occurring, especially as the emergent middle classes and a cosmopolitan, corporate elite strive to consolidate and expand their capital – but it is that the strategies and exchanges entailed in that reproduction are still emergent, variable and, compared to those of longstanding class systems in, for instance, France, in reformation.

Despite Bourdieu's defence, there has nonetheless been a persistent critique of "the often misunderstood status of the idea of determinism in Bourdieu's sociology" (Peters, 2014, p. 125). Several chapters here add new layers of complexity to this critique. Du's work (Chapter 4) examines the social trajectory of the new generation of rural teachers. These young people left rural homes to go to university and then returned to teach after graduation. Although they seem to have ended up back where they started, policy intervention through the Special Post Plan pulled them out of the rural community, augmented their capital with credentials, and channelled them to teaching, a profession affiliated in Confucian traditions with symbolic capital. Nevertheless, this newly conferred class mobility itself has thresholds and boundaries: these teachers tend to remain within the rural community. Similarly, the rural schoolteachers in Yin et al.'s study (Chapter 5), who came from relatively socio-economically advantaged backgrounds, were attracted to teach in rural schools through an alternative school teacher recruitment program. This is a counter-reproductive phenomenon because these young people did not choose to reproduce their family privilege immediately after graduation. Initially, they were seemingly indifferent to social mobility, resistant to their parents' positioning and aspirations. Many demonstrated strongly altruistic reasons for joining the

248 Guanglun Michael Mu et al.

program, only to see their idealism and commitment deterred by entrenched deficit discourses around inherited intelligence, local culture, rurality, and poverty. In these two studies, these young graduates' engagements with educational reform do not reflect or fit a seamless model of class reproduction, but an educational field that is fraught with what are transitional, historical anomalies and contradictions.

Li's study (Chapter 6) analyses rural achievers at a top university who came from the least disadvantaged strata of the most disadvantaged classes. Her study documents one of the key problematics in intergenerational studies of social reproduction, how some families are able to mobilise multiple forms of capital in the face of systemic and structural fields that have the effect of reproducing inequality and poverty. Mu (Chapter 7) continues the discussion of resilience amongst floating children and left-behind children who have long been plagued by the system deficiencies in the large-scale migration context. In the face of structural constraints, these children resist imposed social stereotypes and norms, disengage with neoliberal schooling, demonstrate indifference to the game of reproduction, and strive to define their own well-being. Their resilience *qua* resistance provides a unique opportunity to critique and reconstruct dominant worldviews, institutions, and *doxa*. Jia and Mu's study (Chapter 9) looks at the conversion of the principal's social and cultural capital into the school's organisational capital, a process whereby an individual's capital is institutionally "deemed" into symbolic value (Luke, 2018b). These studies demonstrate the difficulties of reform, and how institutional traditions and pedagogic actions remain durable and resistant even to the educational and ameliorative policies of the strong state. Taken together, this is something less than a seamless system of reproduction. Our view is that the relations of exchange in the educational field are in dynamic flux and transition, despite and because of tenacious patterns of pedagogical action, curriculum traditions, and an obsessive focus on testing and examination that militate towards classical patterns of reproduction.

Models of cultural and economic reproduction by definition entail intergenerational exchange (Luke, 2018a). There are indeed resilient and durable elements of the Chinese habitus, as we will argue in regard to the new Confucianism momentarily. But part of the anomaly facing a new Chinese sociology of education is that while there are forces of economic determinism visibly at work, especially in the shaping of the new *Homo economicus* in relation to the market economy and in the preparation of a Chinese middle and upper class for a transnational economy built around the expansion of Chinese capital, geopolitical and cultural "soft" power – this generation's parents have weathered the residual and epigenetic trauma of the Cultural Revolution and have been reshaped in the subsequent Reform and Opening-Up era. The parents in the aforementioned studies are the first generation of participants in the market economy, transnational exchange, travel, Westernised popular culture and digital media, *and* now, neoliberal educational reform. What this means is that their generational habitus, their collective unconscious, by definition cannot be reproduced with any precision in what are emergent and still fluid economic, cultural, and geopolitical contexts and relations. Further, while there remains a strong case for an economic determinism – that the market economy is informing and redefining the fields of education – even the economic field remains in its historically nascent stages, with the state almost continuously adjusting, steering, repairing, and altering its course. Economic determinism and social class reproduction are at work – but in historically unprecedented, structurally unstable, and perpetually unfinished patterns. They have relatively short and abrupt histories. This means that any attempt to describe an inter-generational reproduction that occurs as a doubling or re/production of bodily habitus, extant social and economic relations, cultural forms and ideologies is difficult and, at best, a significant empirical and interpretive challenge.

Determinism, then, is a double-edged sword, enabling a view of what are at once enabling and constraining, reproductive and counter-reproductive social conditions of choices and orientations, and of social practices. We contest a view of the new Chinese habitus as that of an over-socialised body submissive to social structures, one based on the supposition that anything less than a liberal state based on concepts of individual will and freedom will result in human subjects who respond passively to regulatory rules of control in a field such as education. At the same time, we note Bourdieu's intention to fuse habitus and freedom:

> If only to make things more difficult ... to see in the theory of habitus a form of determinism, it will suffice to point out that the habitus offers the only durable form of freedom, that given by the mastery of an art, whatever the art. And that this freedom made nature, which is acquired, paradoxically, by the obligated or elective submission to the conditionings of training and exercise (themselves made possible by a minimal distance from necessity), is indeed, as is the freedom in regard to language and the body which is called ease, a property (this is one of the senses that the Scholastics gave to the word "habitus") or, if you wish, an acquisition and inheritance predisposed by their unequal distribution to function as capital. This then raises the question of whether there can be any liberty other than that to master one's inheritance and acquisitions. Pedagogical action can thus, because of and despite the symbolic violence it entails, open the possibility of an emancipation founded on awareness and knowledge of the conditionings undergone and on the imposition of new conditionings designed durably to counter their effects.
>
> *(Bourdieu, 1999, p. 340)*

To understand this profound ambiguity of reproduction and change in the new China, we turn to the key elements in play: the historical and contemporary

250 Guanglun Michael Mu et al.

formation of social classes, of state power, residual and emergent political ideologies, and of China's complex ethnic and cultural communities and fields. These set the grounds for the current reformations of social fields and of the habitus.

On Class (Re)Structuring

Since its foundation in 1949, China has undergone fundamental social and economic changes that have redefined the social order and reshaped class structures. The Cultural Revolution was an attempt to disrupt existing social fields and subvert relations of capital value and exchange. Individuals with a family background of landlord, land-owning peasant, merchant, anti-communist, bureaucrat, and scholar/teacher had the value of their capital inverted, their forms of distinction publicly denigrated, and their economic capital destroyed or confiscated. Those with the dispositions of Communist soldier, cadre, worker, and landless peasant became the new ostensive ruling classes of then China, able to assert arbitrary power and control over longstanding social and institutional fields, where these were not entirely eliminated. Social repositioning and restructuring was accomplished through blatant physical violence, fierce class struggle, and coercive redistribution of the means of production. For all practical purposes, the economic capital of the rich, the cultural capital of the knowledgeable, the social capital of families, and the orders of symbolic violence imposed by the traditional owners of power became dysfunctional. The comparable moment in France history might be the 1793 Reign of Terror, whose scale and scope would have been much smaller.

The mechanisms of social reproduction through education were disrupted: universities and schools were reorganised, re-staffed and, in instances, sacked and destroyed. Upper and middle class habitus lost privilege that had underpinned educational success and career prosperity. Academic performance was no longer important capital required for successful entry to higher education. What trumped the field was a family background recognised and celebrated as peasant or worker or Communist. Students of working class and rural backgrounds were favoured and given the social status and educational opportunity that they had long lacked. In stark contrast, many who emerged from 1949 with reasserted cultural and social capital became second-class citizens and deprived of higher education opportunities. In practice, the aim was a proletarianised classless communist country where forms of cultural distinction were supplanted by a universal egalitarianism.

The 1978 Reform reshaped the landscape of class structure yet again – in a diametrically opposite direction. Market economy replaced the previous planned economic model, and exponentially rewarded those with an emergent entrepreneurial habitus: individual enterprise and economic risk-taking were rewarded. Individual investment in private business yielded ample financial returns, which allowed them to seize initiative in a lucrative Chinese market, even against the backdrop of continuing state ownership of major components of the means of production. They became the new *La Grande Bourgeoisie* in China. Their children inherited their social and economic capital, forming a privileged class with a habitus adapting to consumerism, transnational popular culture that is overtly sexualised, workforce competition, and digitally mediated social relations. The direct beneficiary of the economic reform, the generation has captured an increasing share of social resources, a dominant position in various institutional fields – and most importantly, engagement with and impact on the meta-fields of transnational media, consumerism, and digital cultures.

Despite what we have referred to as the imperfect and dynamic processes of social and cultural reproduction, this class has begun to assert itself as the winners of the game, with strategic investments in their children's education. This means that parents and families read and respond to new state regulatory interventions in the field, even those that attempt to reinforce meritocratic outcomes and egalitarian access. Parents with cultural, social, and economic capital as well as elite habitus required for strategic school selection knowingly choose and access school that is the best fit for their children. They have financial capacity to afford the cost of school selection and to invest in children's extracurricular activities. They have utilised their knowledge of the rules of exchange to protect their class status. In contrast, those from socio-economically disadvantaged classes and ethnic minority communities, such as the Special Post Plan teachers, are re-marginalised, unable to mobilise the requisite capital for mobility across the system.

The Cultural Revolution justified the displacement of the bourgeoisie through revolution and violence. The post proletarian revolution led to the new bourgeoisie, the class beneficiaries of the 1978 economic reform. In this last decade, this has yielded a further class of elites who have profited from the globalisation of the Chinese economy: the establishment of major transnational manufacturing corporations, the expansion and management of traditional state enterprises, powerful new digital and technological sectors, and the development and global expansion of Chinese-branded service and culture industries. With the rise of the new bourgeoisie, power is being redistributed in favour of the already privileged, pathways of social mobility of the resource-less proletariat are at further risk, and what remains a relatively new, emergent class structure is showing signs of consolidation even within its first generation of formation. In this way, contemporary Chinese society is at once an unprecedented historical anomaly and a paradox of social facticity. The success of proletarian revolution is built on the grounds of the dictatorship of the proletariat; the rise of the new bourgeoisie verifies the sublation of such a claim; yet denial of the success of proletarian revolution is a denial of Chinese success as a modern Communist state. In historical materialist terms, at the least this constitutes an ideological and economic contradiction, and may yet lead to a practical impasse and its further historical negation.

In this context, at this pivotal juncture in the history of China – the degrees and ways in which cultural, social, and economic reproduction have become a determining and structuring force, reinforcing and maintaining this new class structure, even as it remains emergent, may be a key indicator of the parameters and directions of and through that impasse. What occurs in the field of education – while not determining altogether the production of habitus, exchange, and class structure – may have become a foreshadowing indicator of the degree to which that class system is becoming reified and durable across a second generation following on from the market economy. What occurs through the combined socialisation of families and schools and its longitudinal effects in the formation of the habitus and the exchange and redistribution of capital may be both litmus test and a metaphoric "canary in the coalmine" for the sustainability of that anomalous, contradictory system of neoliberalism with Chinese characteristics, or the market with socialism described here. Again, the tension is around a school system that is simultaneously enacting processes of reproduction and counter-reproduction, within an educational field charged with expanding, attracting, and building human capital for a now globalising, Han Chinese-centred, marketised economy, while it is simultaneously expected to ameliorate the effects of the maldistribution of that capital on behalf of residual traditions of Communism and socialist egalitarianism.

On Political Capital and Statist Capital

The founding of the People's Republic of China in 1949 concluded the two-decade Chinese Civil War. The War of Liberation led by the Chinese Communist Party marked the victory of the proletarian revolution and proclaimed the establishment of the proletarian Diktatur in China. It was also the culmination of the Chinese Communist Party's drive to power after its founding in 1921. As its guiding theory, Marxism continues to provide the explicit rationale to control, oversee, and distribute power across various fields and, in the first instance, to maintain determinate legal-juridical and *de facto* control over the means of production and modes of information. The recipients of this power gain political capital, which "has the capacity to yield considerable profits and privileges, in a manner similar to economic capital in other social fields, by operating 'patrimonialisation' of collective resources ..." (Bourdieu & Wacquant, 1992, p. 119).

In Bourdieu's view, this political capital has potential to produce profits and reproduce itself in identical or/and expanded forms. It has the capacity to supersede and override the rules of meritocratic exchange:

... whatever the official meritocratic ideology may want people to believe, not all the differences in opportunities for appropriating scarce goods and services can reasonably be related to differences in possession of cultural and educational capital. It is thus necessary to hypothesise another principle of differentiation, another kind of capital, the unequal distribution of which is the source of the observable differences in patterns of consumption and life-styles. ...[T]he subspecies of social capital ... could be called political capital and ... guarantees to its holders a form of private appropriation of goods and public services.

(Bourdieu, Sapiro, & McHale, 1991, pp. 639–640)

Bourdieu cites Scandinavian social democratic elites as exemplifying the patrimonialisation of collective resources. They acquire political capital through the apparatus of the trade unions and the Labour party, and transmit their capital intergenerationally through networks of family relations, "leading to ... true political dynasties which accumulate large quantities of political, educational, and even economic capital" (p. 640). Political capital, then, is specifically a Soviet-type that can account for "distributions of powers and privileges, as well as life styles". It can be acquired through networking as a specialised form of social capital, distributed on the grounds of "not only positions in the hierarchy of political apparatuses (in the first place, that of the Communist Party itself), but also the seniority of each agent and of his lineage among the political dynasties". Where and when political capital becomes the primordial principle of distinction, "the members of the political 'Nomenklatura' have hardly any competitors in the struggle for the dominant principle of domination that takes place in the field of power" (p. 640).

Since the Reform and Opening-Up Policy began in 1978, the market economy has led both to a class restructuring and the ongoing reorganisation of political capital, in the form of party and regional hierarchies, and remaining state and military-run enterprises. By "statist capital" (Bourdieu & Wacquant, 1992, p. 114) – Bourdieu refers to a "meta-capital" that enables control and reconstitution of the fields of power, including the distribution and exchange of political capital more generally:

... the emergence of a specific capital, properly statist capital, ... allows the state to wield a power over the different fields and over the various forms of capital that circulate in them. This kind of meta-capital capable of exercising a power over other species of power, and particularly over their rate of exchange (and thereby over the balance of power between their respective holders), defines the specific power of the state. ... [T]he construction of the state goes hand in hand with the constitution of the field of power understood as the space of play in which holders of various forms of capital struggle in particular for power over the state, that is, over

254 Guanglun Michael Mu et al.

the statist capital that grants power over the different species of capital and over their reproduction via the school system in particular.

(pp. 114–115)

With the state logic of practice shifting to economic growth, the field of Chinese education has undergone the devolution of school governance and funding, the devolution of governance and funding of all but the top universities, the licensing and co-branding of degrees with foreign universities, and the emergence of a private sectors in the education market described in this volume. This should not be mistakenly construed as the state giving way to economic determinism by and for a free market. Indeed Polanyi (1944) has long reminded us of the "fictitious commodities" (p. 71) and the more "regulated", less "self-regulating" feature of the markets. This point is taken by Bourdieu to defend the collective power and conduct that construct markets "without capitulating to the imposition of a uniformly individualised economic model" (see Robbins, 2009, p. 147). If we apply Polanyi's and Bourdieu's respective views on the market to contemporary China, such a market does not and could not work without centralised or regulatory constraint of what remains an omniscient and ubiquitous strong state. Therefore, it is inaccurate to describe the emergence of the market as a correlative decline of statist power over the field of education and over the reproduction of various forms of capital via the school system. Intervention in debates on curriculum content and designation of controversial or subversive teaching and content underline the state's ideological agenda.

So while governance is not wholly dissimilar to that of the West where the neoliberal state, Ball (2009, p. 97) observes, acts "as a broker for social and economic innovations, and is very active in the focused allocation of its resources". But unlike in Western neoliberalism, the Chinese state maintains its oversight and undisputed right to steer policy making and regulate the distribution of power within and across the fields of education – for example, to regulate curriculum content, to monitor and limit the use of foreign textbooks, to roll back and re-regulate privatised schooling, to control and constrain the activities of overseas universities in China, to block and monitor access to online courses and teaching content, or to directly alter the flows of Chinese students to overseas institutions – as it sees fit, on short notice, without a process of public debate or dissent. In these ways, both political and statist capital have constituted and continue to constitute a grid of meta-power over, across, and within the logic of practice of various social fields including the marketised, privatised, and locally devolved educational institutions. It remains the prerogative of the state to intervene either ideologically or through more direct means of control including censorship, legislation, and direct enforcement of law.

Bourdieu's conceptualisation of political capital enables us to frame the continuing salience of statist power over social reproduction via education.

This has significant implications. If statist capital does grant power over the configuration and exchange of different species of capital via schooling, it also has power over the reconfiguration of capital and the recreation of a school system that clears the pathway of social mobility for currently marginalised communities and groups. The current school system, at least to a certain extent, enables some marginalised groups to achieve upward social mobility. These are multiple current efforts in policy, research, and development that target an overall ameliorative or compensatory intervention in the field enabling ethnic minorities, rural and urban poor improved access, participation, and outcomes. Questions remain, however, about those instances where ameliorative and compensatory interventions might run counter to emergent interests of the emergent elite classes and those who seek to maintain and retain political capital. While the current anti-corruption campaign offers numerous instances of the de-legitimation of arbitrary, corrupt, or illegal practices affiliated with class privilege, and the instances of the corrupt abuse of political, social, and economic capital – the campaign itself is an assertion of regulatory oversight and control of fields by the state – in effect, a reinforcement of the strong state's control over fields, rather than the relinquishing of power over those fields. It also remains to be seen how and to what degrees the self-conscious understanding of what Bourdieu termed the "necessity" of extant systems of exchange can enable the redefinition and reconfiguration of those very systems.

On Confucianism

Confucianism has proven to be a durable element of the Chinese habitus: an "embodied history, internalised as a second nature and so forgotten as history" (Bourdieu, 1990, p. 56). Anticipating current debates over epigenetic memory, Bourdieu explains that when "history turned into nature" (Bourdieu, 1977, p. 78), "the whole past" becomes "the active presence" (Bourdieu, 1990, p. 56). In other words, what historically needed to be durable and transposable through a process of continuous reproduction is now inscribed in bodies, which "is never anything other than the forgetting of history which history itself produces by realising the objective structures that it generates in the quasi-natures of habitus" (p. 56). When history is forgotten, it is naturalised, normalised, and largely taken for granted. The body, then, is a living mnemonic device, an object of both historical and everyday practices of inscription (Luke, 2018a). This is both an individual and collective phenomenon, as Durkheim comments:

> In each one of us, in differing degrees, is contained the person we were yesterday, and indeed, in the nature of things it is even true that our past

> personae predominate in us, since the present is necessarily insignificant when compared with the long period of the past because of which we have emerged in the form we have today. It is just that we don't directly feel the influence of these past selves precisely because they are so deeply rooted within us. They constitute the unconscious part of ourselves. Consequently, we have a strong tendency not to recognise their existence and to ignore their legitimate demands. By contrast, with the most recent acquisitions of civilisation we are vividly aware of them just because they are recent and consequently have not had time to be assimilated into our collective unconscious.
>
> *(Durkheim, 1977, p. 11)*

The body is "open to the world, and therefore exposed to the world, and so capable of being conditioned by the world, shaped by the material and cultural conditions of existence in which it is placed from the beginning" (Bourdieu, 2000, p. 134). Dispositions, perceptions, and beliefs are always potentially subject to modifications, rather than being passively consumed or re-inscribed. This can occur when narratives, values, and explanations generated by habitus no longer make sense; or when agents use their understanding and feel for the game as a means of furthering and improving their own standing and capital within a field, as well as adapting their dispositions.

If habitus is durable but not immutable, the renewed production of Confucian and neo-Confucian dispositions is necessarily imperfect. Children from socio-economically well-off families have begun to supplant the traditional, collective Confucian dispositions of filial piety, respect for teachers and learning, with a shift towards an individualistic habitus. Education in the new China has become an overt competitive investment, the return on which can be seen in economic gain and distinction of individual and family. In competitive institutions and the new workplace, traditional Confucian values of integrity, piety, honesty, and loyalty are readily subordinated to success and financial reward at all costs. Not surprisingly, the target of the large-scale state anti-corruption campaign has been the unethical and corrupt mobilisation of political capital and corporate power into financial reward.

After Xi came into power in 2013, he addressed the increasing threat of a moral crisis affiliated with the rise of the market economy. His response is a re-appropriation of the residual traditions of Confucianism, discarded during the Cultural Revolution. This is the state's bid to redefine and reclaim a moral order – without recourse to any overtly religious system of beliefs – in the face of unchecked forces of market capitalism and consumer-based, digitalised, popular culture. In 2013, Xi visited Qufu in Shandong province, the birthplace of Confucius, where he publicly stated his strong interest in Confucian theory and philosophy. In 2014, on the 2565th birthday of Confucius, Xi delivered a speech where he explicitly stressed the importance of Chinese traditional culture, with a specific enumeration of Confucian values. In the same year, Xi visited Beijing University and engaged in an extended public discussion of Confucianism with leading professors in philosophy. In 2016, Xi expanded "Three Confidences" – the doctrine of his precursor Hu – to "Four Confidences", namely confidence in the chosen path, confidence in the political regime, confidence in the guiding theory, and confidence in the traditional Chinese culture. Xi's doctrine of "Four Confidences" has historical roots and connotations. Confidence in the chosen path justifies the appropriateness of the socialist approach with Chinese characteristics. Confidence in the political regime reinforces the Diktatur of the Chinese Communist Party. Confidence in the guiding theory further legitimises the theoretical triad of Marxism, Leninism, and Maoism in China. Confidence in the traditional Chinese culture defines Confucianism as a foundational value system. This doctrine of "Four Confidences" is the very first time that the Party historically has advocated a neo-Confucianism as compatible with Communism.

This marks out the state's reclamation of the cultural and moral legitimacy of Confucianism. What remained as a powerful embodied residual tradition has now been re-codified in state doctrine and public discourse, reintroduced into the selective traditions of school curriculum as a new moment of "habitus realisation" (Mu & Dooley, 2015). From September 2017, the Ministry of Education has required all primary and junior high schools to use the nationally unified textbooks of literacy, history, and moral education. Comparable moves are underway to refocus elements of university study.

Confucianism has survived waves of historical attempts to wipe it out, for example, 焚书坑儒 (Burning of the books and burying of the scholars) in Qin Dynasty during the period between 213 BC and 206 BC and the Cultural Revolution. The educational and social effects of neo-Confucian selective traditions are works in progress (Liu, 2011). Does it intend to return education back to a model of classical and canonical learning elaborated in traditional versions of Confucianism (Tan, 2017)? Or is it a form of cultural obscurantism – a *doxa* – through education that helps to normalise the ruler/ruled hierarchical relations of power as Confucianism historically did? Once adopted by the state, will this mandated ideological shift serve to consolidate the emergent class structure we have described here? Or perhaps, like current mandatory university study of Marxist ideology, Neo-Confucianism will be repressively tolerated by students and families who will remain focused on competition for capital and distinction.

On Ethnicity

Bourdieu comments:

> Struggles over ethnic or regional identity – in other words, over the properties (stigmata or emblems) linked with the origin through the place

of origin and its associated durable marks, such as accent – are a particular case of the different struggles over classifications, struggles over the monopoly of the power to make people see and believe, to get them to know and recognise, to impose the legitimate definition of the divisions of the social world, and thereby, to make and unmake groups. What is at stake here is the power of imposing a vision of the social world through principles of di-vision which, when they are imposed on a whole group, establish meaning and a consensus about meaning, and in particular about the identity and unity of the group, which creates the reality of the unity and the identity of the group.

(Bourdieu, 1991, p. 221)

To understand ethnicity in the Chinese context requires the unpacking of two key prevailing "divisions of the social world". First, the simplistic, naïve view of the term "Chinese" is problematic. Chinese is an umbrella term embracing many ethnicities or *mín zú* (民族), of which Han is the most dominant, historically and politically, demographically, and socio-economically. Second, the term "China" cannot be mistakenly used as an aggregate to denote all of the states and peoples that historically have claimed political sovereignty over this land and place. The first state that claimed sovereignty of the land and established a centralised hierarchical system was called Qin (秦, 221–206 BC). Other powerful states in history include Tang (唐, 618–907), Yuan (元, 1271–1368), Qing (清, 1636–1912), just to name a few. Over history, each of these states existed side by side with many other small neighbouring states, pejoratively referred to as the Barbarian states. All these states, either central and peripheral in the field of power, never took on the self-appellation of "China". Instead, they named themselves by dynasty, for example Tang Empire in Tang dynasty, Yuan Empire in Yuan dynasty, Qing Empire in Qing dynasty. The appellation "China" emerged after the collapse of the Qing dynasty in 1912. Irrespective of claims of governance, the land has always been multicultural, resided by Han Chinese and many ethnic *Chineses*, who are now officially called ethnic minorities (*shǎo shù mín zú*, 少数民族).

Du's study (Chapter 4) was situated in ethnically diverse regions that have long been been at the socioeconomic, cultural, and educational margins. Historically, *shǎo shù mín zú* have not always been placed at disadvantage. In Yuan and Qing dynasties, the ruling ethnicities were Mongolian and Manchurian respectively, having seized sovereign power over previous dynasties ruled by Han Chinese. The two differed, however, in their ruling strategies, and hence in the duration of their rule. After the Mongolians established the Yuan dynasty, they continued to wield physical violence to consolidate their hegemony, engaging in acts of enslavement and ethnocide. The Imperial Examination System (*kē jǔ zhì dù*, 科举制度) was dismantled during the first five decades of Yuan dynasty. After its restoration, the System blatantly favoured Mongolian examinees, precluding participation and mobility of the Han.

The Qing dynasty established by the Manchurians straddled three centuries and became the most powerful state after Tang dynasty. The ruling strategy made this difference. The policies of the integration of the Man and the Han (满汉一体) seemingly celebrated the unity within diversities and the togetherness of differences. The Imperial Examination System seemed equally fair to all. Confucian culture and philosophy were respected, valued, and legitimated. Most Manchurians were bilingual. With Man-Han exogamy becoming more common, the shift to the Han Chinese language seemed inevitable. But deeply buried within the pro-Han multiculturalism and the reverse assimilation of the Manchurian was the ruling strategy of the Manchurian to rule the Han through the Han's tool. This ruling strategy, indeed, was a form of symbolic violence because "it enables relations of domination to be established and maintained through strategies which are softened and disguised, and which conceal domination beneath the veil of an enchanted relation" (Bourdieu, 1991, p. 24). Gradually, the Han bowed to the domination of the Manchurian. Compared with the overt violence employed by the Mongolians in the Yuan dynasty, the Manchurian symbolic violence became a more effective means of governance and oppression.

Historically, the Han Chinese have employed symbolic violence to reproduce the principles of domination while making these principles invisible. One of the ways has always been through language. In 221 BC, Emperor Qin (秦始皇) unified all the competing states in Central Plains (the middle and lower reaches of the Huanghe river), mandating a common language system as a means to construct national identity and cultural solidarity. Through the unified language system, laws and policies legislated centrally were promulgated and distributed locally. Many centuries before comparable moves in Europe and the Americas, linguistic hegemony was established as an instrumental tool of symbolic and statist power.

The contemporary political, social, and cultural dominance of Han Chinese and the continued educational disadvantage and marginalisation of many of China's ethnic and religious, cultural and linguistic minorities are social facts – posing what is arguably the most significant challenge to contemporary Chinese society and polity. This most explicitly applies to those Indigenous and minority cultures in Western and Northern China but as well constitutes a broader national challenge. This presents problems at every level of educational policy and practice, with established gaps and differentials in access, participation, achievement, and outcomes. Taken sociologically, the axiom offered by Basil Bernstein (1972) about British schooling in the 1960s remains insightful and relevant: that education cannot compensate for society. The empirical evidence on minority education – as well as the model minority counter-examples of Mongolian bilingual schooling and universities – underlines the embeddedness

260 Guanglun Michael Mu et al.

of any educational fields within broader cultural, economic and socio-political systems of exchange. Altering inequitable educational outcomes depends upon political economy, intercultural exchange, recognition, and local relations of power. Following Bourdieu, there is a strong case that attempts to build and enhance access to dominant forms of cultural and economic capital through education are contingent upon the cross-field availability of other forms of capital, through access to employment, housing, health care, and, indeed, civic and political engagement (Luke, 2018b). This will inevitably require that schools and universities recognise, value, and exchange vernacular knowledges, cultural practices, histories, and languages in more than token, piecemeal, and rhetorical ways. Whether and how this entails cultural inclusion and recognition, symbolic violence and geographic marginalisation, overt assimilation and policies that ignore, misrecognise, or overtly attempt to override and displace local cultural and linguistic practices and beliefs remain focal concerns. As part of a larger agenda of poverty amelioration and socialist egalitarianism, non-discriminatory equity and access may be the ultimate tests of Chinese education and educational research and policy – not the increased production of specialised technological knowledge and human capital, where it already has demonstrated efficacy.

Towards Reflexive Re-Appropriation

The export of Anglo/European canonical science and theory was a key strategy of colonialism. Where that science forms a monopoly over what will count as official language, authorised knowledge, and legitimate scholarship – its habits, practices, and habitus become universal, natural, and beyond criticism. We acknowledge Bourdieu's aspirations for a reflexive sociology, one that has a self-understanding of its own ethnological, cultural, and political economic roots in a Western academy that has founded, shaped, and generalised the Anglo/European *Homo academicus* beyond boundaries and borders – often without due regard to the consequences of its own proliferation. We also begin from a recognition not only of the radically different contexts of contemporary Chinese social life, political economy, and scholarship – but also of China's history of the selective taking and purposive use of technologies and ideas from the West.

As early as 307 BC in the Warring States Period, King Wuling (赵武灵王) adopted the costume of barbarian/foreign people and practiced mounted archery in order to strengthen the military force of the State of Zhao. In Qing Dynasty, Wei Yuan, the great thinker, proposed to learn the advanced technologies in the West in order to resist the invasion of the Western powers (师夷长技以制夷). Wei's proposal became the theoretical foundation of the Self-Strengthening Movement (洋务运动) in the mid-late Qing Dynasty. This was a period when China experienced a series of military defeats and concessions to Western powers. The pro-Western group then advocated Chinese learning as essence and Western learning for practice (西学为体中学为用). In the late Qing Dynasty (c. 1898), the Wuxu Reform Movement (戊戌变法) issued the reformative edicts to import advanced Western models to improve the cultural, political, agricultural, commercial, and educational sectors of Qing Dynasty. It is, indeed, the Maoist re-appropriation and reshaping of Marxism from 1949 and, indeed, the ongoing attempt to redefine and resituate market capitalism that set the stage for the contradictions and tensions, issues and social facts of any new sociology of education proposed here.

We understand the work in this volume as another such "taking", a deliberate critical re-appropriation of the sociological vocabularies, concepts, and frameworks placed at our disposal by Bourdieu and his contemporaries. Shi and Li's review (Chapter 3) purposefully focuses on the published Chinese literature on the use of Bourdieu, prioritising these over Western academic commentaries on or about China. Michael Singh's work with his Chinese students (Chapter 11) proposes a post-English-only approach to educational and sociological theory and research that uses Chinese analytical tools and vernacular standpoints. Mu and colleagues' analysis (Chapter 10) is a critical response to the monopoly of English language and academic registers in the globalisation of higher education.

We acknowledge that the studies in this volume just begin to skim the surface of the broad and rich field of empirical research, interpretive analysis, and new theory across China. Given the diversity and depth of this sociological work underway, given the resources, commitment, and breadth of current Chinese doctoral students' work in China and overseas – even to take our terms of reference here as a formal prolegomenon to the field would be presumptuous, especially in light of the constraints of our own standpoints and histories. Building from the energy and insights of the contributors here, our intent has been to reflect upon and to push the boundaries around issues of reproduction and capital, ideology and power that will feature in a next wave of Chinese educational research, debate, and exchange.

Everything about the new China is unprecedented and dynamic – economic, cultural, social, psychological, sociological, and educational. The emergence of new human subjects complicates and questions conventional disciplinary explanation of Anglo/European *and* Chinese theories and models alike. Post-Cultural Revolution, post-Reform and Opening-up, post-One Child Policy, the relaxation of the *Hù kǒu* System (户口), the geopolitical power of what will become the largest economy in the world, poverty amelioration and urban migration unprecedented in human history, its large-scale cultural complexity and diversity, the first generation of Chinese consumerism, media culture and digital social relations, the combination of the Communist state with market capitalism – this is the history of the Chinese present. A different axiological, ontogenetic, and phylogenetic moment is at hand. And it is at this moment, in this milieu of new social facts and fields of force that we set a course towards a critical, reflexive sociology of education in and for China.

Notes

1 Notable exceptions include work that uses Bourdieu to study language socialisation in homes and communities by Compton-Lilly (2003).
2 This habitus, in part, explains the Chinese American popular self-help literature on "tiger mothers", without rigorous sociological analysis of the intersections of gender, social class, and culture.

References

Ball, S. J. (2009). Privatising education, privatising education policy, privatising educational research: Network governance and the "competition state". *Journal of Education Policy, 24*(1), 83–99. doi:10.1080/02680930802419474

Bernstein, B. (1972). A critique of the concept of compensatory education. In C. B. Cazden, V. P. John, & D. H. Hymes (Eds.), *Functions of language in the classroom* (pp. 131–151). New York: Teachers College Press.

Bourdieu, P. (1973). Cultural reproduction and social reproduction. In R. Brown (Ed.), *Knowledge, education, and cultural change: Papers in the sociology of education* (pp. 71–112). London: Tavistock.

Bourdieu, P. (1977). *Outline of a theory of practice.* (R. Nice, Trans.). Cambridge: Cambridge University Press.

Bourdieu, P. (1990). *The logic of practice.* (R. Nice, Trans.). Cambridge: Polity Press.

Bourdieu, P. (1991). *Language and symbolic power.* (G. Raymond & M. Adamson, Trans.). Cambridge: Polity Press.

Bourdieu, P. (1993a). *The field of cultural production.* Cambridge: Polity Press.

Bourdieu, P. (1993b). *Sociology in question.* (R. Nice, Trans.). London: Sage.

Bourdieu, P. (1996). On the family as a realized category. *Theory, Culture & Society, 13*(3), 19–26. doi:10.1177/026327696013003002

Bourdieu, P. (1999). Scattered remarks. *European Journal of Social Theory, 2*(3), 334–340.

Bourdieu, P. (2000). *Pascalian meditations.* (R. Nice, Trans.). Cambridge: Polity Press.

Bourdieu, P., & Passeron, J.-C. (1990). *Reproduction in education, society and culture.* (R. NiceTrans). 2nd ed. London: Sage.

Bourdieu, P., Sapiro, G., & McHale, B. (1991). Supplement – Distinction revisited: Introduction to an East German reading. *Poetics Today, 12*(4), 639–641. doi:10.2307/1772706

Bourdieu, P., & Wacquant, L. J. D. (1992). *An invitation to reflexive sociology.* Cambridge: Polity Press.

Compton-Lilly, C. (2003). *Reading families: The literate lives of urban children.* New York: Teachers College Press.

Deng, Z. (2016). Bringing curriculum theory and didactics together: A Deweyan perspective. *Pedagogy, Culture and Society, 24*(1), 75–99. doi:10.1080/14681366.2015.1083465

Durkheim, E. (1977). *The evolution of educational thought* [L'évolution pedagogique en France. 1938]. London: Routledge & Kegan Paul.

Lingard, B., & Rawolle, S. (2004). Mediatizing educational policy: The journalistic field, science policy, and cross-field effects. *Journal of Education Policy, 19*(3), 361–380. doi:10.1080/0268093042000207665

Liu, S. (2018). Neoliberal global assemblages: The emergence of "public" international high-school curriculum programs in China. *Curriculum Inquiry, 48*(2), 203–219. doi:10.1080/03626784.2018.1435977

Liu, Y. (2011). Pedagogic discourse and transformation: A selective tradition. *Journal of Curriculum Studies*, *43*, 599–606.

Liu, Y. (2005). A pedagogy for digraphia: An analysis of the impact of Pinyin on literacy teaching in China and its implications for curricular and pedagogical innovations in a wider community. *Language and Education*, *19*(5), 400–414. doi:10.1080/09500780508668693

Luke, A. (2018a). *Critical literacy, schooling and social justice*. New York: Routledge.

Luke, A. (2018b). *Educational policy, narrative and discourse*. New York: Routledge.

Mu, G. M. (2018). *Building resilience of floating children and left-behind children in China: Power, politics, participation, and education*. London & New York: Routledge.

Mu, G. M., & Dooley, K. (2015). Coming into an inheritance: Family support and Chinese Heritage language learning. *International Journal of Bilingual Education and Bilingualism*, *18*(4), 501–515. doi:10.1080/13670050.2014.928258

Peters, G. (2014). Explanation, understanding and determinism in Pierre Bourdieu's sociology. *History of the Human Sciences*, *27*(1), 124–149. doi:10.1177/0952695113500974

Polanyi, K. (1944). *The great transformation*. New York: Rinehart.

Robbins, D. (2009). After the ball is over: Bourdieu and the crisis of peasant society. *Theory, Culture & Society*, *26*(5), 141–150.

Sriprakash, A., Proctor, H., & Hu, B. (2016). Visible pedagogic work: Parenting, private tutoring and educational advantage in Australia. *Discourse: Studies in the Cultural Politics of Education*, *37*(3), 426–441. doi:10.1080/01596306.2015.1061976

Swedberg, R. (2011). The economic sociologies of Pierre Bourdieu. *Cultural Sociology*, *5*(1), 67–82. doi:10.1177/1749975510389712

Tan, C. (2017). Confucianism and education. In G. W. Noblit (Ed.), *Oxford research encyclopedias: Education: A community of scholars*. Oxford: Oxford University Press.

Yochim, L. (2016). Navigating the aspirational city: Processes of accumulation in China's socialist market economy. In S. Guo & Y. Guo (Eds.), *Spotlight on China: Changes in education under China's market economy* (pp. 329–347). Rotterdam, the Netherlands: Sense Publishers.

NOTES ON CONTRIBUTORS

Dooley, Karen is an Associate Professor in the Faculty of Education, Queensland University of Technology. She lectures in English Curriculum, with a particular interest in language and literacy education in conditions of linguistic and cultural difference and economic disparity. She is currently researching private literacy tutoring; previous studies have investigated pedagogy for young people of refugee background, and digital and print literacies in a high-diversity, high-poverty school.

Du, Liang is Associate Professor in the Faculty of Education, Beijing Normal University. His research interests include minority education, migrant education, education and social class formation, teacher development in high-needs contexts, and globalisation and intercultural education. He is the author of *Learning to Be Chinese American: Community, Education, and Ethnic Identity*. He currently serves on the editorial board of *Teaching Education*.

Fu, Wangqian is a PhD candidate in the Faculty of Education, Beijing Normal University. Her research interests include education policy, special education, and inclusive education.

Guo, Shibao is Professor in the Werklund School of Education at the University of Calgary. He specialises in comparative and international education, internationalisation of education, citizenship and immigration, and multicultural and anti-racist education. Currently, he serves as president of the Comparative and International Education Society of Canada. He also co-edits two book series for Brill | Sense publishers: *Transnational Migration and Education* and *Spotlight on China*.

Notes on Contributors **265**

Guo, Yan is Professor of Language and Literacy in the Werklund School of Education at the University of Calgary. Her previous publications include *Spotlight on China: Changes in education under China's market economy* and *Spotlight on China: Chinese education in the globalized world.* She is currently editing *Home-school relations: International perspectives* and co-editing two book series, *Transnational Migration and Education* and *Spotlight on China.*

Hao, Dongfang is a PhD candidate in the Faculty of Education at Beijing Normal University.

Jia, Ning is a postdoctoral fellow at East China Normal University. Her research is focused on school organisational change and principal leadership.

Li, Chunying is a PhD candidate in the Faculty of Education at Beijing Normal University. She is interested in educational philosophy.

Li, He is Associate Professor of Sociology in the School of Sociology and Population, Remin University, China. Her research interests focus on educational inequality and social justice, and cultural sociology.

Liu, Liwei Livia completed her PhD in the Faculty of Education, Queensland University of Technology. Her research interests include cross-cultural studies, parental engagement, and transition to school.

Luke, Allan is Emeritus Professor, Queensland University of Technology, and author of *Critical Literacy, Schooling and Social Justice* (Routledge, 2018) and *Educational Policy, Narrative and Discourse* (2018). He is currently writing and recording music in Brisbane, Australia on https://www.reverbnation.com/artist/allanluke

Mu, Guanglun Michael is Senior Research Fellow, Queensland University of Technology. Michael's work includes negotiating Chineseness in a diasporic context; building resilience in a (im)migration context; and developing teacher professionalism in an inclusive education context. Michael has (co)authored four scholarly books. He is the Associate Editor of the *International Journal of Disability, Development, and Education.*

Qin, Yimei is a PhD candidate in the Faculty of Education at Beijing Normal University.

Selman, Robert L. is the Roy E. Larsen Professor of Education and Human Development and Professor of Psychology in the Department of Psychiatry at Harvard Medical School. Selman has been: The recipient of a Careers

Scientist Award from the National Institute of Mental Health (USA); a trustee of the Devereux Advanced Behavioural Health; a Scholar in Residence at the Russell Sage Foundation, and has received two Fulbright Fellowships to Iceland. He has been a consultant to *Highlights for Children, Sesame Street*, The Walt Disney Company, and Walden Media. With a current emphasis on the impact of new digital social media and the use of cross-media educational approaches, Selman is undertaking practice-based and translational research on the promotion of youth ethical and educational wellness and the prevention of debilitating academic, family, and cultural stress – both in the United States and China.

Shi, Zhongying is Professor in the Faculty of Education at Beijing Normal University. He chairs the Philosophy of Education Society in China. His recent research interests include values education and education reform. He is the author of 教育学的文化性格(1999), 知识转型与教育改革 (2001), 教育哲学 (2007).

Singh, Michael (Western Sydney University, Australia) undertakes teaching and research relating to localising Chinese language education through educating teachers via service learning; pedagogies for internationalising research education that explore theoretic-linguistic divergences; disruptive innovations in English-medium instruction, research, and management; and the impact of the new spirits of capitalism on the learning and earning of young adults.

Sziegat, Hongmei works as an adjunct researcher at Big Data Centre, Faculty of Education, Beijing Normal University. She is a regional representative and an expert panellist of Accreditation Agency Curacao. Her research fields include quality assurance and accreditation, technology-mediated education, fundraising in higher education, and educational management.

Wang, Xiaodong is a PhD candidate in the Faculty of Education at Beijing Normal University. His research is concerned with comparative education, with a particular focus on international education aid.

Wu, Xueqin is interested is second-language education, especially English as a second language and Mandarin as an additional language. Her other research interests include cultural diversity, learner engagement, language policy, and international education.

Yin, Melody Yue is a sociologist of education. She is interested in alternative teacher recruitment programs that channel prestigious university graduates to the teaching profession in disadvantaged schools.

Zhao, Xu is Assistant Professor at the Werklund School of Education, University of Calgary. Her research focuses on understanding youth psychosocial development and mental health issues from cultural and cross-cultural perspectives. She is the author of *Competition and Compassion in Chinese Secondary Education*.

INDEX

agency and structure 3, 5, 15, 54, 83, 101, 121–122, 126, 128–129, 137–139, 140, 144, 147, 160, 166, 170–171, 177, 189, 221–223, 230, 232

capital 5, 14–15, 21, 37, 52, 65–66, 67, 71, 72, 78, 126, 144–146, 151, 154, 177, 185, 187, 189, 199, 240, 249, 251, 252; academic capital 91–92; capital conversion/exchange 5–6, 14, 15, 16, 36, 38, 39, 83, 90, 111, 154, 161, 162, 175–176, 177, 180, 181–186, 187–188, 189, 190, 217, 224–231, 235; cultural capital 21, 34, 36, 40n4, 47, 48, 49, 50, 52–53, 58, 69, 71, 72, 73, 75, 83, 92, 100, 105, 106, 107, 108, 114, 147, 150, 154, 156, 161, 162, 164, 167, 169, 175, 180, 182–183, 188, 244, 245, 250; economic capital 11, 21, 33, 34, 69, 71, 72, 73, 75, 83, 100, 104, 154, 155, 156, 161, 162, 164, 167, 169, 180–181, 188, 250; embodied cultural capital 9, 11, 52, 53, 90, 92, 100, 104, 107, 113, 154, 181; family capital 102, 103, 107, 113, 114; human capital 14, 21, 31, 33, 34, 39, 40n4, 93, 147, 177, 252, 260; institutionalised cultural capital 52, 53, 100, 126, 154, 179, 226, 233; intercultural capital 209; linguistic capital 48, 53, 201–205, 208, 210,

215–216, 223–230, 245; objectified cultural capital 52, 53, 100, 181; organisational/school capital 175, 177, 178, 180–181, 182, 183, 185, 187, 189, 248; political capital 25, 252–255, 256; social capital x, xi, 14, 34, 36, 50, 69, 71, 72, 73, 83, 92, 100, 107–109, 147, 154, 161, 162, 164, 169, 175, 177–178, 179, 180, 183, 188, 250; statist capital 253–255; symbolic capital 5, 83–84, 92, 100, 102, 107–108, 111, 114, 161, 175, 177, 178, 181, 184, 185, 243, 245, 247

community/local ethos 75–76, 93–94, 103–104, 114

Confucian 107, 148, 153, 154, 159, 168, 205, 247, 248, 255–257, 259

Cultural Revolution 1, 57, 105, 169, 170, 171, 193, 240, 243, 248, 250, 251, 256, 257, 261

decentralisation 26, 27, 31, 32, 37, 39, 176, 178, 254

Dewey, John 3, 93

distinction 14, 33, 92, 146, 148–150, 159, 162, 167, 169–170, 175, 177, 180, 233, 240, 242, 256–247, 250, 251, 253, 256–257

doxa ix, xi, 9, 10, 12, 16, 17, 26, 38, 40n4, 94, 131–132, 139, 178, 184–189, 207, 240, 248, 257

Durkheim 7, 46, 51, 245, 255–256

elite education *see* meritocracy
Engels, Freidrich 6
equality, educational 1–2, 14, 15, 82, 120, 125–127
ethnicity xiv, 14, 68, 69, 71, 76–77, 78, 257; ethnic minority xi, xiv, 34, 35, 39, 49, 64, 67, 69, 70, 77, 78, 240, 244, 245, 251, 255, 258–259; Han 35, 64, 69, 70, 151, 240, 245, 252, 258–259

family 5, 11, 15–16, 102–109, 168, 242–243, 245, 246; education, socialisation 2, 8, 85, 130, 139, 168*; see also* habitus – formation, inculcation*; migration*
field 3, 14, 27, 30, 31, 37, 38, 47, 49, 50, 51–52, 54, 84–85, 100, 106, 107, 126, 144–147, 186, 190, 198, 202, 239, 250, 251; field analysis – "three moments" 146, 193, 197, 199–200, 207–208; field of academic competition 149–150, 215, 218–219, 232–233; field of education/ educational field 14, 21–22, 31–34, 37, 38, 52, 56, 83, 126, 169, 239, 248, 249, 252, 254; field of higher education/ higher education field 91, 101, 198, 200–201, 202, 205, 209, 210; field of mediation 81, 84, 86, 91; field of power 11, 27, 30, 37, 90–91, 146, 198, 200–201, 253, 258; field of rural education 83, 85, 90–91, 110; field of school/school field 52, 54, 55, 85, 175, 183, 186, 242, 244; field of secondary education 146, 159; fields of work 83, 91
Foucault, Michel 3–4

gāo kǎo (高考 University/College Entrance Examination) xiii, 1, 13, 17, 70, 72, 73, 74, 87, 92, 99, 103, 108, 146, 150, 152, 159, 162, 169, 200
guān xì (关系 networking) x–xii, xiii, 107, 164, 179, 183, 190n1

habitus 6, 9, 14, 15, 16, 37, 38, 39, 46, 49, 50, 53–55, 56, 58, 59, 66, 72, 78, 100–101, 102, 104, 105, 106, 109, 112, 114, 115, 144–146, 149–150, 155, 159, 161, 167, 186, 199, 205, 207, 221–223, 231, 249, 250, 251, 255–256, 262n2; cleft habitus, dual habitus, plural habitus 16, 85, 91, 114, 205–206; collective habitus 168, 170, 185, 249, 255–256; disposition 5, 15, 82, 85, 90, 128, 166,

185, 186, 199, 256; emotion 71–73, 75, 78, 114, 126, 170, 206; entrepreneurial habitus 250–251; fish in/out of water 85, 126, 207; formation, inculcation 85, 91, 131, 135; gendered classificatory schemata 74–75; habitus realisation 208–209, 257; *homo economicus* 38, 144, 243, 248, 260; individuated habitus 144, 145, 246; inertia 77, 101, 109, 244; intellectual/academic classificatory schema, source of discrimination 90–93, 127–128; linguistic habitus 206–207, 209; new Chinese habitus 144, 160, 166, 167–168, 170–171, 205, 240, 248, 249; normative 9; possessive individualism 155, 165; rational habitus 186, 208–209; resilient habitus/habitus of resilience 114, 130–131, 134–135, 139; resistance 106, 109–110, 121, 123, 128–129, 131, 134–135, 137–140, 150, 185, 247, 248; rural-urban classificatory schema 5–6, 91; rural habitus 103–104; scholastic habitus 110, 112, 224–230; trajectory effect 65, 66, 67, 72, 73, 75, 76, 78, 93; transformative habitus 101, 106, 114, 115, 178; transformational leadership 177, 181, 182, 183, 186, 187, 188, 189
Hegel, G.W.F. 7
hù kǒu (户口 household registration) 13, 24, 28, 69, 97, 98, 126, 243, 261

illusio 101, 112, 114, 125–126, 128, 136
investment 9, 11, 83–85, 87, 101, 103, 104, 112, 127–128, 136, 151, 162, 188, 190, 251

market economy 2, 6, 20, 22, 25, 27, 30, 39, 144, 165, 240, 244, 248, 249, 250, 252, 253, 256; political economy 28–31, 33, 37, 39, 149, 260
marriage 5–6
Marx, Karl: Marxism 6–7, 31, 46, 52, 55, 57, 177, 220, 240, 252, 257, 261
materialism-realism 4–9, 14, 31; cultural materialism 8–9; dialectical materialism 3; historical materialism 252; idealism-spiritualism 7
meritocracy 10, 14, 91–92, 169, 251, 252–253; key-point/high-achieving/ good school xiv, 13–14, 30, 91, 87, 111–112, 148, 162, 164; prestigious/ elite/good/985/world-class/top university 15, 47, 64, 82, 83, 84, 85, 86,

87, 91, 92, 93, 97, 98, 99, 102, 103, 114–115, 152, 155, 162, 163, 180, 194, 200, 210n1, 248
migration 24, 63; floating/migrant children 15, 24, 35–36, 39, 49, 53, 97, 99, 102, 120–121, 123–132, 176, 244, 248; left-behind children 15, 24, 39, 40n4, 98, 99, 115, 120–121, 132–135, 176, 244, 248; migrant workers/labourers 24, 63, 98, 103, 104, 106, 110, 114, 120, 153
misrecognition/misrecognise/ *méconnaissance* 90, 92, 100, 127–128, 164, 220, 228, 230, 244

neoliberalism x, xi, 3–4, 8, 10, 22, 28–31, 33–34, 40n4, 57, 83, 84, 86, 90, 91, 94, 126–128, 130, 131, 139, 140, 169, 241, 248, 252, 254; dispositions 82; educational logic of 14, 84, 86, 90, 126, 128–129, 248; educational values of 84–91

pedagogic action 2, 38, 156, 178, 242, 244, 245, 248, 249
pedagogic work 2, 245
Polanyi, Karl 6, 254
position-taking 126, 144, 147, 186, 187, 188, 189, 206, 207, 208, 247
practical logic 5

Reform and Opening-Up 1, 14, 20, 21, 25, 36, 37, 48, 57, 81, 171, 193, 200, 240, 248, 250, 253, 261
reflexive sociology 16–17, 46, 51, 59, 102, 209–210, 241, 260–261; participant objectivation 3–4, 5, 8–13, 59, 122–123, 131–132, 135–137; sociology of Chinese

education 2–3, 5, 14, 17, 37–39, 217–221, 222–223, 226–234, 241, 248, 261–261
reflexivity – everyday, spontaneous 93, 139
reproduction 5, 9, 11–12, 15, 16, 92, 123, 125–126, 130, 137, 154, 156, 163, 166, 170, 171, 178, 184, 201, 240, 241–249, 250, 251, 252
resilience 112–113, 114, 121–123, 128, 135–137, 248

school DNA 187, 189
shadow education 11, 17, 22, 33–34, 56, 176, 245; *see also* tutoring
single/one-child policy 1, 153, 171, 243, 244, 261
sociodicy 91
strategy 5, 8, 11–12, 15, 55, 65, 84, 91, 103, 122, 137, 145, 147, 149, 151, 156–158, 161–162, 164, 166, 171, 201
strong state 3, 14, 21, 22, 25, 27, 29, 30–31, 37, 38, 171, 242, 243, 244, 245, 248, 254–255
sù zhì (素质, quality) education vs examination-oriented education 82, 86, 93–94
symbolic violence, domination 5–6, 7, 9, 120, 122–123, 126, 166, 201, 214–219, 224–225, 231–235, 249, 250, 259, 260

teacher: education, training, preparation 81–82, 86–87, 93; quality 81–82; recruitment 15, 81–83, 85
tutoring 12, 33, 35, 126, 147, 161–162, 169, 246, 264; *see also* shadow education

Weber, Max 3, 7, 91